POLITICAL ELITES
IN ANGLO-AMERICAN
DEMOCRACIES

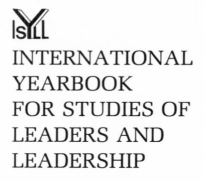

INTERNATIONAL YEARBOOK FOR STUDIES OF LEADERS AND LEADERSHIP

A Northern Illinois University Series

General Editors
Moshe M. Czudnowski
Northern Illinois University

Heinz Eulau
Stanford University

POLITICAL ELITES IN ANGLO-AMERICAN DEMOCRACIES

Changes in Stable Regimes

Edited by Harold D. Clarke
and Moshe M. Czudnowski

NORTHERN ILLINOIS UNIVERSITY PRESS

Library of Congress
Cataloging-in-Publication Data
Political elites in
Anglo-American democracies.
(International yearbook for studies
of leaders and leadership)
Bibliography: p.
Includes index.
1. Elite (Social sciences)
2. Power (Social sciences)
3. Democracy.
I. Clarke, Harold D.
II. Czudnowski, Moshe M., 1924–   .
III. Series.
JC330.P639 1987   306.2   86-21822
ISBN 0-87580-126-9

Contents

Contributors

Jean Blondel was Professor of Government at the University of Essex between 1964 and 1984 and is now Professor of Political Institutions at the European University Institute in Florence. He was educated at the Institute of Political Science in Paris and at Oxford University. He has published in the fields of British and French politics and administration, as well as in comparative politics. In the last decade he has published a number of books on national leaders. Recently, as a fellow of the Russell Sage Foundation, he worked on a study of leadership. Blondel is cofounder and ex-director of the European Consortium for Political Research and a member of its executive and research boards.

Robert G. Brookshire is Manager of Academic Computing Services at North Texas State University and holds a joint appointment as Assistant Professor of Political Science. His main research interests are political behavior, political parties, and research methodology. He is the coauthor of *Using Microcomputers in Research* and has contributed articles to *Legislative Studies Quarterly*, *The Journal of Gerontology*, and other journals.

Bruce Cain is an Associate Professor of Political Science at the California Institute of Technology. He is the author of *The Reapportionment Puzzle* and coauthor (with John Ferejohn and Morris Fiorina) of a forthcoming book on constituency service in the United States and Great Britain. He has published widely in scholarly journals on voting behavior, legislatures, and representation in the United States and Great Britain.

Colin Campbell, S.J. is University Professor in the Martin Chair of Philosophy and Politics at Georgetown University. He is author of *In Search of Executive Harmony: Carter, Reagan and the Crisis of the Presidency; Governments Under Stress: Political Executives and Key Bureaucrats in Washington, London and Ottawa; The Superbureaucrats: Structure and Behavior in Central Agencies* (with George J. Szablowski); and *The Canadian Senate: A Lobby From Within*. He coedited *The Contemporary Canadian Legislative System* and *Parliament, Policy and Representation*. He currently serves as cochairman of the International Political Science Association Study Group on the Structure and Organization of Government.

Harold D. Clarke is Professor of Political Science, Virginia Tech University. He is coauthor of *Political Choice in Canada; Representative Democracy in the Canadian Provinces;* and *Absent Mandate: The Politics of Discontent in Canada.* His articles have appeared in journals such as the *American Journal of Political Science,* the *American Political Science Review,* the *British Journal of Political Science,* and the *Journal of Politics.* He currently is doing research on the dynamics of political support in Anglo-American democracies.

Moshe M. Czudnowski received his doctoral degree from the Sorbonne, Paris. Between 1959 and 1971, he taught political science at the Hebrew University in Jerusalem and held various visiting appointments in the United States, England, and West Germany. Since 1971 he has been Professor of Political Science at Northern Illinois University. His works include books, book chapters, and journal articles on political recruitment, the social psychology of elites, and the methodology of comparative political analysis. His recent research includes the study of political elites in Taiwan and Quebec. He is cosponsor and managing editor of the International Yearbook for Studies of Leaders and Leadership.

Dean F. Duncan III is Senior Software Analyst for the Emory University Computing Center. He also is a Ph.D. candidate in the Emory University Department of Political Science. He has contributed articles to *Legislative Studies Quarterly, Public Productivity Review,* and *Popular Government.*

Brian Graetz is Lecturer in Sociology at La Trobe University, Melbourne, Australia. He is author of *Equality, Rank and Status: Images of Class in Australia* and has written on political leaders and political elites. He is currently engaged in a sociological analysis of Australian society.

Susan Webb Hammond is Professor of Political Science at American University, and coeditor of *Congress & the Presidency: A Journal of Capitol Studies.* She has written on congressional organization, change and reform, legislative staffing, and Congress and foreign policy. She is coauthor of *Congressional Staff: The Invisible Force in American Lawmaking* and is currently working on a study of informal caucuses in the United States Congress.

Dennis Kavanagh is Professor of Politics at Nottingham University. He is well known as a commentator on British politics and elections both on television and radio. His works include *Constituency Electioneering in Britain, Political Culture, British Politics Today, New Trends in British*

Politics, and *The Politics of the Labour Party.* He has been coauthor of the Nuffield election studies since 1974.

Burdett A. Loomis, Associate Professor of Political Science at the University of Kansas, teaches and writes on Congress, interest groups, and policy making in American politics. He directed the Congressional Management Project, coedited *Interest Group Politics,* and has written extensively on the development of contemporary political careers.

Ian McAllister is Professor of Politics, University College, University of New South Wales, Canberra, Australia. He is author of *The Northern Ireland Social Democratic and Labour Party* and coauthor (with Richard Rose) of *United Kingdom Facts, The Nationwide Competition for Votes,* and *Voters Begin to Choose.* He has written extensively on electoral behavior in American, British, and Australian journals.

Elizabeth M. McLeay is Senior Lecturer in the Department of Politics and Government at the City of London Polytechnic. Formerly she taught in the Department of Political Studies, University of Auckland, New Zealand. Apart from her work on the theory and practice of representation, she has published in the areas of democratic theory and public policy.

Peter Y. Medding is Associate Professor in the Departments of Political Science and Contemporary Jewry at the Hebrew University of Jerusalem. He is the author of a number of works including *Mapai in Israel: Political Organization and Government in a New Society* and *From Assimilation to Group Survival.* He has contributed numerous articles to journals such as *The Journal of Politics, Political Studies, Public Policy,* and *The Jewish Journal of Sociology.*

William L. Miller holds the Edward Caird Chair of Politics at Glasgow University, Scotland. He is author of *Electoral Dynamics in Britain since 1918; The End of British Politics?: Scots and English Political Behavior in the Seventies;* and *The Survey Method in the Social and Political Sciences: Achievements, Failures, Prospects.* He has published in *Political Studies, British Journal of Political Science, European Journal of Political Research, West European Politics, Parliamentary Affairs, Political Quarterly,* and other journals and contributed to numerous programs on BBC radio and television and on the IBA network.

Donald J. Naulls is Visiting Assistant Professor of Political Science at McMaster University in Hamilton, Ontario. His research interests include the comparative study of political chief executives and bureaucratic elites, public policy, and empirical theory and methodology. He is the coauthor of a chapter in *Social Science and Government,* edited by Martin Bulmer.

Donald D. Searing is Professor of Political Science and Research Associate in the Institute for Research in Social Science at the University of North Carolina, Chapel Hill. He writes on British politics, political elites, and political psychology and has published articles on these subjects in the *American Political Science Review*, the *British Journal of Political Science* and other major professional journals in the discipline. He currently is engaged in a long-term research project on the ideologies, roles, and socialization of Members of the British House of Commons. When in Great Britain, he is based at the University of Essex.

Editorial Advisory Committee

POLITICAL ELITES
IN ANGLO-AMERICAN
DEMOCRACIES

Introduction: An Overview and Some Theoretical Observations

Moshe M. Czudnowski and Harold D. Clarke

This third volume of Northern Illinois University's *International Yearbook for Studies of Leaders and Leadership* series focuses on elites in stable democracies. In designing this volume, we drew on ongoing research or persuaded scholars to analyze recently collected data sets on political elites from the viewpoint of political change in stable regimes. The resulting collection is perhaps less heterogeneous than other collective endeavors, including the first volumes of this series. Not surprisingly, we found that in stable regimes political change is more often measured in inches or feet than in miles and that, in order to discern significant trends, one often has to review change over fairly long periods of time. The contributions by Robert Brookshire and Dean Duncan and by Burdett Loomis exemplify this long-term approach for studies of the United States Congress, as does Elizabeth McLeay's study for the New Zealand Cabinet; and Jean Blondel's overview of elites in the British Commonwealth provides an assessment of what may be termed *the British political legacy.*

Other contributors, however, have found shorter-term changes worth reporting. This refers primarily to changes in elites and leadership in Great Britain in the past decade, a subject explored in depth in William Miller's study of the crisis in the Labour Party and the founding of the Social Democratic Party (SDP), and in Searing's analysis of the socializing effects of political involvement among members of the "attentive public," parliamentary candidates, and Members of Parliament. Both of these studies also deal with tensions between parliamentary, party, and trade union elites in the Labour Party.

Stylistic change in leadership is the theme of Dennis Kavanagh's chapter, which explores Margaret Thatcher's "mobilizing" style and contrasts this with the "reconciling" style espoused by other recent British prime ministers. Such stylistic changes reflect a new leader's personality and/or his or her judgments about the direction in which political change ought to proceed; they are also the product of a selection process in a context in which a certain political style—in this case Thatcher's mobilizing style—has a stronger appeal among groups dissatisfied with the *status quo*. Kavanagh suggests, however, that some of the ideological content of Thatcher's leadership, especially in economic matters and foreign affairs, developed fully only after she assumed office and, although she received the support of certain "right-wingers," there was no well-defined ideological mandate in her election as Tory leader. Rather, the policy positions she developed and for which she mobilized support reflected a more general and symmetrical radicalization of both the Labour and the Conservative parties, in reaction to the inability of previous governments (Labour and Tory alike) to solve the economic difficulties that had plagued Britain in the 1970s.

Another relatively recent, but increasingly frequent, phenomenon is analyzed in Susan Webb Hammond's study of recruitment of previous congressional staff aides to the U.S. House of Representatives. This is an area which deserves follow-up studies to assess the range and possible consequences of this recruitment process for both individual political careers and the composition and performance of the House. More discrete changes in political roles are the focus for both Bruce Cain's assessment of the performance of constituency service tasks by British MPs and American Congressmen and Colin Campbell and Donald Naulls' exploration of two roles assumed by senior bureaucratic officials in Canada, Great Britain, and the United States.

Finally, two chapters with a more explicit theoretical emphasis deserve separate mention: Peter Medding's "Patterns of Elite Consensus and Elite Competition," to be discussed in the context of a subsequent section of this overview, and Brian Graetz and Ian McAllister's four-country (Australia, Canada, Great Britain, the United States) comparison of public evaluations of party leaders. Using a nonrecursive causal model, the authors demonstrate the relative dominance of leader evaluations over party identification, political trust, and, with the exception of Australia, the vote itself. These findings contradict commonly offered explanations indicating the primacy of partisan affiliations in the field of attitudinal forces affecting candidate orientations and electoral choice. The similarity of the results of these analyses across four countries using data collected at approximately the same time (1979–1980) makes the evidence very impressive.

Certain differences between their respective party systems notwithstanding (in the case of the United States, differences in institutional structure as well), Australia, Britain, Canada, New Zealand,

and the United States share a variety of important political cultural characteristics. What some of the studies in this volume seem to suggest is an increasing similarity among these political cultures reflected in (but going beyond) the role of the "party leader" as a focal point of reference in public and elite perceptions. Since leaders are perceived most often in personalized terms, this could be interpreted as a tendency toward a more general personalized perception of political power and competition.

In this regard, one perhaps could view current trends in the older Commonwealth democracies as an Americanization of politics. American techniques of electoral campaigning and the impact of the electronic media on elections and political life have been evident outside the United States for some time, but there are other noteworthy tendencies as well. Cain, for example, finds that an emphasis on constituency service work—a long-standing and de facto institutionalized practice in the United States—is increasingly commonplace in Britain. He notes it is contributing to both the growing independence of the British MP and the weakening of party discipline in the House of Commons. In comparative perspective, this development has to be viewed against the background of differences in candidate selection between Britain and the United States, the decentralized American party system, and the separate power structures in the U.S. House, Senate, and "presidential" party hierarchies.

Regime Stability and Elite Career Patterns: Some Structural Considerations

The term *regime stability*, in Western democracies, usually refers to constitutional continuity and the peaceful transfer of power as a result of electoral decisions in favor of particular candidates, parties, or party coalitions. Indeed, when analyzing these political systems, we tend to consider the tolerance for political competition and the peaceful transfer of power as basic norms of their political cultures; and we recognize regime stability as evidence of a deeply entrenched democratic culture among elites and large segments of the politically alert general public. In his study of political involvement as a socializing factor in Great Britain, Searing demonstrates the importance of elite roles in the maintenance and transmission of basic regime norms.

Elite socialization explanations of the stability of democratic regimes do not rule out rational elite self-interest interpretations of this phenomenon. Of great relevance in this regard is the *elite consensus* model, recently restated by Field and Higley (1980). Essentially, what these self-interest interpretations are adding is an *explanation* of why certain patterns of elite political culture are adopted and perpetuated. In contrast, the emphasis on socialization does not provide a rationale for seeking, promoting, and accepting cultural change. Patterns of beliefs and behavior are not maintained indefinitely if they become dysfunctional for those who are conforming, or are asked to conform, to them. However, even rational self-interest theories of elite behavior are incapable of explaining why elite consensus on regime norms developed in certain historical settings but not in others. As Field and Higley (1980:32) observe: "The kind of elite that exists has been determined mainly by the occurrence or nonoccurrence of particular types of rather rare historical events. These events cannot be predicted from a knowledge of non-elite configurations, . . . that is, from the level of development attained."

Although certain elites may be more rational than others by formally or informally agreeing—in their own interest—to refrain from the use of force, one still has to explain their ability to institute and maintain nonviolent conflict resolution techniques despite the lack of agreement, and often overt conflict, over basic policy orientations among informed and active nonelites, at least some of whom aspire to elite status. The acceptance of majority rule also needs to be explained, since in order to be rational it must be based on the assumption that, in the long run, individual or group interests will be at least half the time in the winning majority, an assumption that is difficult to justify in stratified societies with little socioeconomic mobility.

Moreover, under majority rule, equilibria of preferences are infrequent and fragile. In a challenging 1980 article, Riker, a leading student of rational-choice analysis of problems arising in and from the aggregation of individual preferences, suggests that, failing equilibria in preference aggregation, we seek explanations for observed regularities in the structure of institutions. Moreover, "institutions may have systematic biases in them so that they regularly produce one kind of outcome rather than another" (1980:443). Are we, then, to shift to a structuralist emphasis to explain democratic stability? To be sure, this merely raises a question of emphasis, because the manner in which institutions function is largely the result of who inhabits them and how their rules are being manipulated by these tenants. In brief, we are driven back to observing the behavior of political elites.

The idea that institutions have built-in biases, of course, is hardly novel (e.g., Schattschneider, 1960). Even without considering the intricacies of procedures for agenda setting and decision making, it is evident that every selection and election system carries with it relative advantages for some individuals and groups and disadvantages for others, regardless of whether these were intended when the systems were adopted. Yet, regime stability does not seem to derive from structural or functional rigidities in institutional frameworks. As several decades of research on the United States Congress and legislatures in other Western democracies demonstrate, these institutions have often been sufficiently flexible to accommodate the impact of considerable, and sometimes rapid, change in social, economic and political environments (e.g., Loewenberg and Patterson, 1979:300). It is this flexibility, rather than built-in rigidities, that seems to account for the regularities we interpret as regime continuity and stability.

In "Taking the Queue: Careers and Policy in the U.S. House of Representatives," Loomis examines this flexibility and adds the observation that accommodation to the perceptions, styles, needs, and purposes of new cohorts of Congressmen has quite different meanings—and consequences—at the micro- and macro-level respectively, i.e., for individual Congressmen and for Congress. Thus, considerations of career opportunities and, collectively, the structure of intrainstitutional opportunities for members of the majority and minority parties, will tend to affect active policy-making involvement and policy outputs. This may be neither a novel nor a surprising finding (see, for example, Schlesinger, 1966), but it is important because the congressional structure of opportunities changed considerably in the 1970s, and then again, but more slowly and in an opposite direction, in the 1980s. Loomis cautions, however, that notwithstanding a "sophomore surge" in the 1970s (and especially in 1976), the impact of a political generation in the House depends on the size and the durability of a freshman cohort. He also notes that the expanded distribution of opportunities and responsibilities that occurred in the majority party during the 1970s, while providing greater incentives to individual members, contributed to a lessening of the House's collective ability to act as an effective policy maker. The margin of a majority, the size of an incoming class, the length of the queue for party leadership and committee positions, and the number of these positions are all structural parameters—with changes therein reflecting the permeability of the institution to external social and political forces.

Brookshire and Duncan, using a number of biographical and configurational variables, present an actuarial analysis of survival rates (or risks of failure) in congressional careers for the period from 1789 to 1981. While the average length of congressional careers increased from the 1896–1932 to the post-1932 period by 25 percent for those with twelve years of service and by approximately 33 percent for those with eighteen years in office, some biographical variables (other than age at first election) display larger differences in survival rates. Compared to those who lack the given characteristic, being a member of the minority party, having prior federal experience and representing a Southern state all increase the likelihood of survival; prior local or state experience—which other studies have shown to be the single most frequent political avenue of access to Congress (see Czudnowski, 1983:36)—have practically no impact at all. Although the direction of these relationships is not surprising, the magnitude of the effects is of interest. Current congressional election studies, working with disaggregated "ecological" variables, should shed additional light on the dynamics of turnover and survival in the contemporary House.

The relationship between structural parameters, career patterns, and elite behavior is further documented in McLeay's study of cabinet formation in New Zealand. The structural parameter emphasized in this study is the small size of the legislature (ninety-two members) and, consequently, the size of parliamentary parties. For New Zealand parties, the small size of their parliamentary caucuses encourages the development of strong interpersonal bonds among MPs and, therefore, of group loyalty and conformity. Moreover, the limited pool of eligible candidates for cabinet and legislative leadership positions increases the importance of seniority and thereby further strengthens party loyalty. Winning and maintaining control of the government is a collective reward. Given the size of the parliamentary parties, McLeay has no difficulty in interpreting the behavior of the New Zealand MPs in terms of Olson's principles of the logic of collective action: the smaller the group is, the larger are the stakes of each participant in collective action and, hence, the higher is the likelihood of his or her contribution to the attainment of the collective good. Crossing party lines or the formation of dissident groups becomes highly improbable and, as a result, the existing two-party system is reinforced despite the absence of ideological cleavages. McLeay adds that an apparently regrettable consequence of such party and cabinet solidarity is the absence of a tradition of individual ministerial responsibility.

Regime Stability and Elite Configurations

Searing's examination of political involvement and socialization in Great Britain and Miller's analysis of "dealignment at the top" in the British Labour Party offer opportunities for assessing and clarifying the extent to which interactions among British political elites during the 1970s and 1980s conform to the configuration referred to as "consensually unified" elites. According to the most recently developed elitist paradigm (Higley, Deacon, and Smart, 1979; Field and Higley, 1980; Higley and Moore, 1981; Field and Higley, 1985), the Anglo-American democracies constitute the most typical examples of stable regimes based on consensually unified elites. There is, however, some disagreement on the operational definitions of consensus and competition. In his paper "Patterns of Elite Consensus and Competition," Medding sharply criticizes the sometimes imprecise and misleading use of these terms in contemporary political science and proposes a redefinition of typologies based on the concepts of elite consensus and competition.

Not all of the questions raised by Medding can be addressed—let alone answered—by drawing on the analyses of British elites in the 1970s and 1980s offered by Searing and Miller. Even an attempt to deal only with the most important issues would require much more evidence than can be drawn from studies of elite interaction in one stable democracy during a limited interval, although the period considered by Searing and Miller witnessed similar challenges to established elites in several Western countries. Therefore, we will merely articulate some of the questions arising from this recent British experience that seem relevant to typologies of elite configurations and to relationships between such configurations and levels of regime stability.

Field and Higley (1980:37) define a "consensual(ly) unified elite" in broad but fairly unequivocal terms: it is a pattern in which "unity exists de facto in the failure of elite persons to organize and accentuate opposing non-elite orientations," where "rival elites . . . voluntarily moderate their quarrels" and where, consequently, "political institutions are stable and immune to the simpler and cruder forms of power seizures. . . ." So defined, the category operationalizes the concept of stability as the absence of the use of crude force to seize power, and although it assumes the existence of political conflict and "rival" elites, the definition does not stipulate the institutionalization of competition. It does emphasize, however, that consensually unified elites are compatible with representative democracy, and make "reasonably competitive and influential elections possible." It seems, therefore, that consensus focuses only on the rejection of the use of crude force.

Needless to say, the British system fits under this broad definition. Searing's study shows that there is a high degree of consensus in support for basic institutions, but considerable differences between Conservative and Labour partisans in their degree of support for "deliberative" as opposed to "representational" interpretations of the British constitution. While support for these two interpretations increases with level of involvement in the parties, higher percentages of Labour parliamentary candidates display support for the representational, i.e., nonelitist, political norms than do Labour MPs. This could be interpreted as an effect of institutional socialization; however, it is also an indication of extrainstitutional influences, which, by definition, bulk relatively larger for challengers than for incumbents. Indeed, the crisis in the Labour party, which led to the "exit" of the group of top Labour leaders who established the Social Democratic party, had been precipitated by the protracted struggle of extraparliamentary party activists for control of the Parliamentary Labour Party, a conflict couched in ideological terms. As Miller indicates, these activists were far more "left-wing" and unwilling to defer to Labour MPs than were the mass of ordinary party members and Labour voters. In the event, the activists were able to change party rules for selection of the party leader and parliamentary candidates.

The first question that emerges from a consideration of events in the Labour party is whether these ideological left-wing activists were part of the political elite. It is evident that they wanted to displace the established party leadership but did not have unequivocal support among the rank-and-file party membership. The entire set of distinctions between amateur and professional politicians comes to mind, with the former striving for ideological control of a party, even if this entails risking intraparty splits and an attendant erosion of public support. In the Labour case, a crushing electoral defeat in 1983 brought to the top a new party leadership who adopted more moderate ideological positions.

Second, does consensus on democratic "rules of the game" include acceptance of intraparty rules and procedures? Such a question should not be answered by implicit assumption (what Medding refers to as a "semantic slide"), but rather by explicit consideration of possible alternatives. In any event, if the answer is negative, presumably one would have to allow for a two-level concept of consensus in which acceptance of interparty rules may or may not include acceptance of within-party norms and procedures.

Third, how useful (for understanding regime stability) is a typology of elite configurations that does not include a longitudinal dimension of recruitment defined in terms of the transmission of "strategic positions" from one cohort of elites to the next and of the transformation, or even displacement, of elites?

Fourth, how does one operationally define membership in the elite, or the strategic positions that lend elite status to their occupants? If we include economic, cultural, and social elites who do not hold positions of political authority but do have influence in the political process (perhaps, as Medding suggests, doing so more continuously than elected governing teams), are we not blurring the lines of distinction between elites and nonelites, especially in societies where the rate of social mobility is relatively high and access to elite positions lacking formal authority is relatively open? Is not such "openness" of elites a good indicator of a regime's ability to adapt to social and economic change, a characteristic that often contributes to political stability?

Although this is largely a question of definitions, it should not be assumed that there is a clear-cut demarcation between elites and nonelites, no matter how broadly the former have been defined; instead, one should identify an intermediary stratum of informed and politically alert members of the public who are potential candidates for recruitment into elite ranks. One then must ask whether and how these potential activists and candidates for recruitment (or self-selection) into the political elite have been socialized into accepting and adhering to the norms of a *procedural* elite consensus. The crisis of the British Labour party in the 1970s is an illustration of the possibility that activists may become counterelites who will attempt to change the "rules of the intraparty game" in order to displace established leaders and force the adoption of new policies.

Finally, Medding reminds us that, in a number of Western countries (particularly in the United States and Great Britain), issue polarization and partisan disagreements have been found to be greater among elites than among the general public. He then uses the criterion of the relative amount of disagreement between elites (as opposed to nonelites) to identify systems in which there is less ideological and policy disagreement among elites than nonelites. For Medding, it is the latter which qualify as examples of elite consensus, provided there are specific agreements on major policy issues over and above those concerning rules and procedure. When there are no specific agreements on substantive policy issues, the elites are in competition, but operate within the framework of a procedural consensus. In some of these systems of elite competition there can be mutual elite accommodation without drawing upon mass support as a means of conflict resolution. Why does such elite accommodation occur in some systems but not in others? None of the models under consideration suggests an answer to this question; are we missing a critical variable?

In Medding's typology the Anglo-American democracies fall into a different category, which he defines as "multidimensional elite and mass competition." Although not included in the definition, a major characteristic of this configuration is greater disagreement between elites than there is among the general public. Medding suggests that the need for elite groups to maintain a visible distance from rival elites may be due to overlapping group memberships among nonelites and the attendant cross-pressures these generate, leading to more differentiated appeals in the efforts of elites to forestall loss of public support. This tendency is strengthened by open and pervasive channels of mass communication. It is, one should add, a configuration characteristic of modern, open, and pluralistic societies; moreover, the procedural consensus on "peaceful" competition and majority rule (with due consideration for minority rights and interests) must pervade the competing elites and large sectors of the nonelites. In attempting to fit the Australian political system into this category, Medding cites evidence comfirming the existence of a widespread "democratic political culture" among nonelites.

Though Medding draws heavily on findings from previous Australian studies by Higley and his collaborators (including the finding that issue conflict between elites is greater than among the public), he disagrees with Higley's inclusion of Australian elites in the "consensually unified" category. Medding's model of "multidimensional competition," while more detailed in its specification of variables, seems to allow for any range of values these variables can assume. It is probably also true that Higley's category of consensually unified elites needs more specific operationalizations before it can be empirically shown to denote more than the absence of the use of crude force.

Combining the Higley and Medding formulations suggests the general proposition that elite competition under elite and nonelite consensus on peaceful conflict resolution and decision-making methods explains the stability of Western democratic regimes. However, this proposition does not explain the emergence or entrenchment of such regimes.

In this respect it is important to observe that political cultures cannot be legislated or exported, and that universal suffrage and representative institutions do not guarantee the development of consensus, let alone the stability of competitive regimes. Yet, as Blondel's study of the British legacy indicates, the New Commonwealth countries, despite their manifold diversity, display certain characteristics that can be attributed to the influence of British, as opposed to French or Dutch, rule. Of these characteristics, the most significant are the existence of effective party systems, the role of parliament in processes of recruiting political leaders, the frequency of a cabinet (or "prime ministerial") form of government, the infrequency of military rule, and the longer duration of ministerial tenure of office. These characteristics are more likely to be found in the New Commonwealth countries than elsewhere in the Third World. They do not constitute indicators of elite consensus, accommodation of ethnic and cultural cleavages, or liberal democratic regimes in these countries. Still, exposure to British rule and continuing postcolonial interactions with "Old Commonwealth" countries do seem to have had an impact on the majority of New Commonwealth political systems. Will that impact last, or is it fading away as the British colonial experience recedes into the historical background? A closer examination of the dynamics of elite interaction in these countries is necessary to provide tentative answers to this question.

More generally, the paradigm of elite configurations, especially when combined with a development typology of socioeconomic parameters, is a very promising approach to the study of the performance and stability of various kinds of political regimes. Students of elites should formulate theoretical statements derived from this paradigm and thus provide departure points and incentives for empirical studies designed to test such theory-building exercises. The studies contained in this collection, as well as other recent and current works by students of elites, including those of Higley and his collaborators, should provide some guidance for the directions in which theorizing and empirical research on elites and processes of political stability and change ought to proceed.

References

Czudnowski, Moshe M. (1983) *Political Elites and Social Change.* DeKalb: NIU Press.

Field, G. Lowell, and John Higley (1980) *Elitism.* London: Routledge and Kegan Paul.

——— (1985) "National Elites and Political Stability." In *Research in Politics and Society,* Vol. 1, edited by Gwen Moore. New York: JAI Press.

Higley, John, Desley Deacon, and Don Smart (1979) *Elites in Australia.* London: Routledge and Kegan Paul.

Higley, John, and Gwen Moore (1981) "Elite Integration in the United States and Australia." *American Political Science Review* 75:581–597.

Loewenberg, Gerhard, and Samuel C. Patterson (1979) *Comparing Legislatures.* Boston: Little, Brown.

Riker, William H. (1980) "Implications From the Disequilibrium of Majority Rule for the Study of Institutions." *American Political Science Review* 74:432–446.

Schattschneider, Elmer E. (1960) *The Semisovereign People.* New York: Holt, Rinehart and Winston.

Schlesinger, Joseph (1966) *Ambition and Politics.* Chicago: Rand McNally.

PART ONE
THEORETICAL AND
COMPARATIVE STUDIES

Patterns of Elite Consensus
and Elite Competition:
A Model and a Case Study

Peter Y. Medding

The classic elite theorists, Mosca, Pareto, and Michels, sought to demonstrate that elite rule was inescapable in all political systems. In their view, even democracies that proclaimed commitment to rule by the people were governed by a more or less unified and cohesive elite. Over the years, however, the empirical experience of many contemporary democracies did not seem to support such theories of elite rule. On the other hand, neither did it validate democratic theories of active mass participation in politics and popular rule. These societies seemed to be characterized by mass publics that were less interested, active, and influential in politics and less committed to democratic rules and procedures than were political elites.

Explanations for this state of affairs were necessary from both the elitist and democratic points of view. For the elite theorist, if the elites were powerful and the mass public weak, why did the elites not rule? For the democrat, if elites were powerful and the mass public weak, why had democracy not given way to some form of nondemocratic rule, since in democratic theory the role of protecting democracy had been assigned to the people? Even more pointedly, was democracy at all compatible with the existence of elites?

Answers to these questions were found in the concepts of elite consensus and elite competition. From the elite perspective, it was argued that elite rule was seen to be maintained if the theory was amended to take account of elite consensus and elite competition. From the democratic perspective, it was suggested that, far from being incompatible with democracy, elite consensus and elite competition actually contributed to its maintenance by protecting it from tyranny and demagogic crises.

Such assumptions of elite consensus and elite competition, however, raise more problems than they solve. As just illustrated, they can be invoked to support diametrically opposed conclusions. What is more, the terms *elite rule, elite consensus,* and *elite competition* have been used interchangeably and this has inevitably led to some confusion. To increase possible misunderstandings, it is sometimes not specified whether elite consensus and elite competition are intended to describe and explain a single feature of the political system—the pattern of interaction between elites—or whether they are intended to categorize whole political systems in terms of the pattern of rule or regime type.

In what follows, these terms will be used to categorize patterns of rule and regime type, which necessarily subsumes elite interaction. The reverse, however, does not follow. In some cases, the pattern and nature of elite interaction can serve as the major defining characteristic of the pattern of rule as a whole. In others, the pattern of elite interaction, however significant, is not synonymous with regime type and may constitute only one of a number of defining characteristics that must be examined in order to categorize the pattern of rule as a whole.

This article, therefore, will seek to develop alternative models of elite consensus and elite competition, which relate to patterns of rule and regime types. It will then demonstrate how one of these models can be applied empirically to a typical western parliamentary system—Australia.

To view this approach in proper perspective, it is necessary to consider these models of elite consensus and elite competition in relation to a model of elite rule. For Mosca, "the ruling elite" was both a theory of elite interaction and a definition of the overall pattern of rule as it was a theory of "political control in the broadest sense of the term" (Mosca, 1939:329). This classic elite model and a number of more-recent approaches have been critically examined elsewhere and an alternative model proposed (Medding, 1982). Briefly stated, the alternative model specifies that elite rule is dependent upon the following conditions: (1) the elite will be a single cohesive group maintaining internal unity of purpose and action, and it will be aware of its dominance and have an interest in maintaining it (to do so it will control entry into its ranks and set the policies that are made and implemented); (2) its power will be exercised through control and domination of political institutions, organizations, and processes, which act as instruments of its rule; consequently it will be in a position to determine policies and none will be imposed upon it; and (3) the decisions made and the policies adopted will not be to its disadvantage, and it will avoid those that are.

Elite Consensus as a Democratic Mechanism

David Truman's analysis of the role and functions of elite consensus in contemporary democracies exemplifies the approach that finds it to be supportive of democracy. In his view, the main responsibility for meeting demagogic challenges to the American constitutional system rests with elites, which are broadly defined as those leaders of groups, organizations, and parties intervening between the government and citizen. Threats to the system can be repulsed if these elites ensure the validity and availability of constitutional and democratic procedures for all contestants via "mutual attachment to the requirements of the system and common concern for their protection" (Truman, 1971:59). This entails correct perception of the threat and willingness to act appropriately, particularly if the threat challenges the procedures that lie at the heart of the system. Thus, elites must develop self-consciousness about their role, awareness of their responsibility, and "consensus . . . on the nature of the challenge and the need for restraining action" (Truman, 1971:65–66).

Truman believed that it is unreasonable to expect mass resistance to such threats, not because of a distrust of or a "disbelief in the political capacities of the rank and file citizens," but because of the "axiom that a mass of people cannot act except through organization and in response to the initiatives of small numbers of leaders" (1971:57–58). Moreover, although the mass of citizens may be rational and attached to constitutional ideals under obvious threat, the division of labor in the political system neither enables them nor assigns them the responsibility to respond to disguised and subtle threats (Truman, 1971:66).

Truman's analysis of elite consensus, it should be noted, related specifically to the question of protecting democracy and was neither intended to characterize the system as a whole nor to explain its regular operation. These he found, not in elite consensus, but in the pluralistic structure and its operation and in representative democracy.

Elite Consensus as an Elitist Mechanism

Bachrach's critique of Truman laid the foundation for the analysis of the role of elite consensus in democratic societies as a mechanism of elite rule and elite control. According to Bachrach, Truman viewed the reliance on elite consensus to protect democracy as evidence that elites, not the people, are responsible for maintaining the rules of the game (1967:47–48) and therefore for the "continuing existence of the democratic process" (1967:49). This is inherently dangerous, for under these conditions "what," asks Bachrach, "would keep the self-conscious elites within constitutional bounds?" and would this not make them "capable of subverting the system?" (1967:54). Thus, although Bachrach set out to criticize Truman's analysis from the democratic perspective of seeking to broaden mass participation and political activity, paradoxically, the net result of his critique was to reinforce theories of elite power and control and to reinstate the classic elitist perspective as the appropriate framework for understanding contemporary democracies.

In recent years, the elitist thrust of Bachrach's analysis has been carried further. According to Parry, the democratic rules of the game work in such a way that elites "come to be committed to a process of decision-making in which only they participate" (1969:94). Similarly, in Prewitt and Stone's exposition, the approved players share a consensus on procedures, rules of the game, and "codes of conduct," which effectively excludes others from participation in the decision-making process (1973:151). Even though there may be sharp and public disagreements on substantive policies, they are overshadowed by the lack of disagreement about the "rules of the game and the team of players" and about the "rules and ways of rulership" (Prewitt and Stone, 1973:157).

The politics of this type of elite consensus are based upon "the principle that horizontal communication among the elite rather than vertical communication between the elite and non-elite is the primary mode of making decisions" (Prewitt and Stone, 1973:152). Nonelite participation and challenges are thus precluded.

Elite differences, disagreements, and personnel challenges, including the replacement of elite individuals and wider elite circulation, are insignificant "because the positions themselves are not stripped of the authority and force necessary to maintain law and order" (Prewitt and Stone, 1973:156). Overall, elite consensus produces a high degree of integration: "the members of the elite resemble a family. The family is not always an agreeable or unified unit. Very often it is characterized by squabbles, quarrels, and rivalries, deriving both from differences in temperament and from competing ambitions. But its cohesiveness overrides such differences" (Prewitt and Stone, 1973:156).

The elitist view of elite consensus has been elaborated theoretically and applied empirically in extensive work by Field and Higley and others. In their view, nonelites have little direct impact on elites, because nonelite orientations are only manifested in very general opinion tendencies, while the detailed treatment of political questions is largely left to elite choice (Field and Higley, 1980:19–20). Moreover, elite views on major political decisions are kept from mass publics by the shrewd use of coercive power by elites. This involves the suppression, distortion, and manipulation of issues to prevent the disastrous conflict that would arise if they were openly expressed and acted upon (Higley, Deacon, and Smart, 1979:10).

The control of conflict and the maintenance of political stability, therefore, depend upon elite unity, of which there are two main types. The first is a single, comprehensive political elite to which all elite positions are attached and which is characterized by ideological unity. The classic example is the totalitarian party (Higley, Deacon, and Smart, 1979:11). The second type is the "consensually unified elite," the existence of which enables the effective exercise of power on salient issues with only a tolerable amount of interference by non-elites or elite opponents (Higley, Deacon, and Smart, 1979:10).

The elite unity produced by consensually unified elites "exists de facto in the failure of elite persons to organize and accentuate elite and non-elite conflicts and divisions." Rival elite members voluntarily moderate their conflicts in accord "with an underlying consensus and unity." Despite clearly divergent positions on public matters, "they observe a tradition of political contest and they adhere to a set of usually unwritten rules of political conduct" that moderate conflicts. When such an elite structure exists, "political institutions are stable and immune to the simpler and cruder forms of power seizures that are characteristic of elites with a disunified structure" (Higley, Deacon, and Smart, 1979:11).

Personal interaction among members of different elite groups and circles gives them direct and unfettered access to each other and to decision makers (Higley and Moore, 1981:584). This access assures competing elite groups that they can make themselves heard effectively and gives expression to a "common interest in observing the informal rules by which the interaction system operates, and in upholding the institutions in which it is embedded" (Higley and Moore, 1981:584).

In the absence of elite unity, elites are fragmented or disunified. Such regimes are prone to violent power struggles, coups d'état, serious crises, and other manifestations of instability. This situation is to be distinguished from the opinion conflicts that exist within most western political systems. In the latter, the ideologically based and publicly expressed value and policy disagreements occur within the mutual trust and tolerance of legitimate contestants in a mutually beneficial game. "In this perspective, elite opinions are epiphenomena" (Higley, Deacon, and Smart, 1979:109).

Issue conflict among the elite thus has no impact upon elite consensus and unity because such "elite conflicts . . . are as much the symbolic and ritualistic components of a tightly set political game as they are deep convictions of those who express them" (Higley, Deacon, and Smart, 1979:144). Beneath all the opposing ideologies and opinion conflicts "there is a basic elite consensus about the worth of existing institutions" (Higley, Deacon, and Smart, 1979:144). The evidence for this is that elites are powerful persons who could easily cause substantial disruption if it suited them; nondisruption is therefore indicative of support. Similarly, elite willingness "to observe the rules of the political game and to abide by decisions is itself evidence that the policy-making process is open to individual, regular and serious elite influence" (Higley, Deacon, and Smart, 1979:179).

Elite Competition as Democracy

Schumpeter, more than anyone else, was responsible for establishing a connection between elite competition and democracy, as he defined them. He sought to reconcile democracy with the impossibility and undesirability of mass control over public policy. His solution was to turn the definition of democracy on its head. Mass control over public policy through elected leaders was removed from the center of the definition, and in its stead he placed there the choice of leaders who will decide public policy without mass control over it (Schumpeter, 1954:269).

The democratic struggle is therefore between aspirants for office, who usually operate through political parties, with the task of the electorate being to accept or reject them (Schumpeter, 1954:282–83).

According to Schumpeter, therefore, elite competition is a necessary and sufficient condition of democracy. Democracy no longer necessitates direct popular influence and control over public policy. As long as the public freely chooses which of the competing elite groups it prefers, democracy is fulfilled—for Schumpeter, elite competition as a procedure is democracy.

There have been many criticisms of Schumpeter's analysis in terms of its relation to previous democratic thought (e.g., Plamenatz, 1973:95–129) but from our perspective the major question is not whether it constitutes a "revision" of democracy, but what empirical consequences for democratic systems follow from his view of elite competition. Is it, as has been suggested, a democratizing mechanism, which gives "those outside the authority structure access to political power," and thereby "a share in effective power" (Lipset, 1962:33–34)? Or put in slightly different terms does elite competition enable the "*demos* to control and influence leaders" (Sartori, 1978:78)?

Elite Competition as a Democratic Mechanism

These questions lie at the heart of the more elaborate theory of elite competition broadly associated with pluralism,[1] which is attributed to a large and diverse group of scholars.[2] The theory connects two separate processes. In one, leading political, economic, and other societal groups, each with their own elites and specific interests and policies, compete to have their views represented in policy outcomes. This competition between elites and a wide distribution of political resources ensure that no single group is dominant, and that no single elite emerges. Different groups and elites score victories in various issue areas according to their capacity to deploy those resources in relation to the balance of contending political forces. Elites are found to be divided rather than united on substantive policy questions. Consequently, policy decisions generally reflect diverse values, policies, and interests rather than those of a single, cohesive, dominant, or ruling elite.

In the second process, competition between elites for the most significant political offices and decision-making positions is decided by the mass electorate, not by the politicians. This facilitates popular control and accountability, if only indirectly, by putting leaders on permanent probation. To be elected, political leaders must find favor with the electorate by having fulfilled its wishes, or what are anticipated to be its wishes (Sartori, 1978:72–80).

Elite Competition as an Elitist Mechanism

These formulations of the theory of elite competition have been sharply criticized on definitional grounds by those who adopt the elitist view of elite consensus. To attribute such a significant role to elite competition in contemporary democracies is, in their view, to revise and distort democratic priorities. What is more, it places the protection of democracy in the hands of elites, previously regarded by democrats as threats to democracy, while the people, formerly its guardians, now threaten it (Bachrach, 1968:8–9). Elite competition has become the fulfillment of democracy because all societal needs and interests are said to be represented in, and responded to, in the process of elite bargaining. Democratic functioning is thus reduced to elite interaction (Parry, 1969:126).

Doubts also are expressed on empirical grounds as to whether elite competition is indeed competitive. Thus it is suggested that "a pluralism among elites does not necessarily produce a competitive system among elites" (Bachrach, 1968:37), because "many of the stronger elites tend to predominate in their particular spheres of activity more or less unmolested by other elites" (Parenti, 1970:503). Elite competition, moreover, occurs within the context of an elite consensus, which severely limits and restricts it. As a result, elite competition does not facilitate popular control, lead to elite responsiveness to the electorate (even if there is formal accountability), or promote mass participation as a value in itself. To the contrary, elite competition devalues nonelite participation (Thompson, 1970:26).

Under such conditions, while competition may produce counter-elites, success in dislodging an incumbent elite has no real effect, because it simply means replacement by another elite. Similarly, apparent mass influence over the elite deriving from competition can be discounted because it can occur only as the result of elite mobilization (Prewitt and Stone, 1973:229,234). Finally, by channelling discontent and voice into the electoral format, elite competition, it is argued, protects elites rather than exposes them to disagreement and opposition (Prewitt and Stone, 1973:209–13).

Field and Higley's work epitomizes the view that elite competition does not constitute a distinctive regime type or pattern of rule. Their tripartite division of regime types—ideologically unified elites, consensually integrated elites, and disunified (fragmented) elites—makes no allowance at all for the possibility of elite competition as a separate and distinctive pattern of rule. Elite competition may simply be ignored because all issue conflicts and substantive policy differences are, in their view, epiphenomenal, symbolic, and ritualistic when viewed in the context of procedural elite consensus.

A Critique of Elite Consensus and Elite Competition As Elitist Mechanisms

The arguments that support the view of elite consensus and elite competition as elitist mechanisms are flawed by a number of fundamental theoretical weaknesses and fallacies.

1. *The Procedural Fallacy:* The elitist view of elite consensus blurs the distinction between rules and procedures for making decisions, and the substantive content of policy decisions. In doing so, it downgrades or ignores the latter and stipulates or assumes that, if elites make decisions according to the accepted rules and procedures, their substance will necessarily remain within the boundaries of accepted political and social values, which are of lesser overall importance than the rules. In this way conflicts and substantive policy differences can first be admitted and then dismissed as insignificant. Yet there is no reason to assume that making decisions according to rules and procedures either determines the substance of the decisions or is more important than them. By the same token, what the elites regard as radical, far-reaching, and undesirable decisions can be adopted only by following the same rules and procedures.

This is not to argue that the rules and procedures are, by definition, neutral. It is, however, to argue that they are operated by political actors, including elites, and the effect that their operation has on the substance of decisions is an empirical, not a definitional, question. In examining the empirical question of the effects of the rules upon the substance of decisions both the actual content of the rules and the tests applied to measure their effects must be subjected to careful scrutiny. As we shall see, the elitist view of elite consensus and competition fails on both counts.

2. *The Problem of Circularity:* The elite–mass distinction is utilized by the elitist view to permanently exclude the masses from influence and participation in decision making on the grounds that whoever participates in the making of national decisions is by definition a member of the elite. This surely is circular, and solves the problem of the possibility of mass influence by definition. Instead of

showing that elite consensus and elite competition operate in such a way as to exclude certain players and groups on the basis of shared values and understanding, the elitist view assumes that all who participate are part of the elite structures simply because they participate according to the rules.

3. *The Fallacy of the Misleading Counterfactual:* Given the common agreement among elites upon the preservation of rules and procedures, and given the greater significance of the rules as compared with the substance of decisions and as compared with policy differences and issue conflicts, the only factual situations that can falsify the theory of elite consensus are radical change of the rules, revolution, forcible seizure of power, disruption, and breakdown. Under these conditions, the existence of elite competition can never falsify the assumption of elite consensus. Conversely, so long as there are no such violent or chaotic breakthroughs, elite consensus exists. However adversarial or conflictual the relationships are between competing elites, so long as they maintain the rules and do not resort to forcible seizures of power, elite consensus remains unaffected as the distinctive defining characteristic. This view is most explicit in the works of Field and Higley and others, who admit no intervening category between consensually unified elites and disunified elites. Hence, if a situation is not that of the ideologically unified elite rule of the totalitarian party, nor that of the violence and chaos of fragmented, disunified elites, it must be one of elite consensus. The misleading counterfactual creates a range of political situations in the undivided middle so vast as to be useless in making empirical distinctions between political systems that are neither totalitarian nor disunified. To suggest that all systems between these two categories are characterized by elite consensus is to load too much onto that concept.

4. *The Content-Free Procedure Fallacy:* This consists of not inquiring into the content and substance of the rules and procedures. Thus no attempt is made to find out to what elites and nonelites are exposed by the rules. For example, the rules and procedures may expose the elite to competition and may promote and legitimize disagreement and issue conflict rather than stifle them. There is nothing inherent in the existence of rules of the game that determines their content and indicates either the promotion of opposition or the stifling of competition. This is an empirical and substantive question, rather than one to be settled by assumption or definition. One simply cannot assume that the mere existence of shared agreements and understandings about the processes of decision-making and conflict are evidence of elite consensus. The fact that opponents agree on how a conflict between them is to be conducted and settled does not eradicate the conflict or create consensus. By the same logic, two contestants in a life and death duel might be regarded as

sharing consensus by virtue of their agreement on the rules and procedures governing their conflict unto death. This is absurd.

5. *The Positional Fallacy:* This is closely connected with the procedural fallacy and consists of the argument that elite consensus is maintained wherever "the positions themselves are not stripped of the authority and force necessary to maintain law and order." This amounts to the assertion that elite consensus exists wherever there are any positions of political authority, which, of course, fits any political system!

6. *The Poverty of Sociometry:* This is most apparent in the work of Higley et al., who, as we noted, place cardinal importance upon interaction between elite members as evidence of elite consensus and integration. However, the evidence of interaction alone and plotting sociometric points of intersection and circles of interaction do not of themselves indicate the content and nature of the interaction, nor the manner in which it is conducted or the way in which issues are resolved. Indeed, relations between elite members who intersect and interact may be highly conflictual and adversarial. In such a context, to use interaction as evidence of consensus and integration is false and misleading. What is more, decisions taken on the basis of compromise between the competing parties might indicate consensus. (If they did, then all conflict resolution by some form of compromise would indicate consensus and there would be a few situations that did not reflect consensus.) But decisions may also be taken on the basis of some form of majority decision, which may involve the continued presence of policy disagreements, even if the results are accepted due to the rules of the game.

Higley and Moore claim that, to prevent violent power seizures, elites voluntarily moderate quarrels and rivalries, agree "not to push partisan interests to the point where compromise becomes impossible," "obey largely unwritten rules of conduct," and thereby "support and protect existing political processes and institutions" (Higley and Moore, 1981:583). This takes no account of other basic methods of conflict resolution, particularly majority decision. Nor is there any empirical basis to the assertion that these processes reflect the working of largely unwritten or informal rules. It seems as if the intention is to invest the rules with a conspiratorial character rather than examine the way in which they actually work.

7. *The Fallacy of Potentiality:* The strength of elite consensus as a pattern of control is said to derive from the elites' capacity to subvert the system and their power to severely disrupt it. Yet ability to subvert and disrupt a system is different from, and therefore not evidence of, ability to run or control a system. Many groups have the capacity for the former, but not the latter. To not make this distinction is to ignore the fundamental difference between potential power

and its actual exercise which was long ago pointed out by Dahl (1958:463–469). Not all of the many who seem to have the potential are capable or desirous of converting it into the actual exercise of power, in terms of the mobilization of either their own resources or of the forces that may be ranged against them.

8. *The Semantic Slide:* When used in conjunction with *consensus* and *competition elite* can mean either *intraelite* or *interelite.* The slide in meaning takes the form of using both elite consensus and elite competition in their more restrictive connotation to indicate consensus or competition *within* the elite rather than consensus or competition *between* elites. By definition, this establishes the existence of a single elite, and disposes of interelite situations. Even if we were to admit that under certain conditions consensus or competition within the elite can exist as a pattern of rule, these conditions and the arguments supporting them would not necessarily hold for consensus between elites and competition between elites, the manifestations and consequences of which may differ significantly. The slide in meaning and the misleading and false inferences that stem from it are more critical in the case of elite competition, where differences between competition within the elite and competition between elites are issues of substance.

On all these grounds the elitist views of elite consensus and elite competition must be rejected. Nor can we accept the democratic accounts as they stand. These are too narrow in scope in the case of Truman and Schumpeter, and too general in the case of the pluralist view. We therefore proceed to suggest alternative models of elite consensus and elite competition that avoid these various shortcomings.

An Alternative Model of Elite Consensus

The alternative model of elite consensus deals with consensus among a number of elites. Elites are defined as those who are influential in the operation of the political system. Included are those partisan political elites who contest elections and generally nonpartisan administrative elites, but it is not restricted to these groups, and can also include economic, military, religious, cultural, and social elites. The defining characteristic of these elites is that they influence the political decision process. This influence is not restricted either to formal decision-making processes or to those in official positions of political authority. Thus, in addition to those chosen by election, among the elites are those who are influential in the political decision process via the application of resources, and the mobilization of sources of support that stem from their societal position, activities, and interests. Because of the nature of the latter, these elite groups often enjoy greater permanence, continuity, and cohesion than those whose sources of support derive from electoral victory and formal, yet often short-term, decision-making responsibility.

Certain aspects of consensus, such as general societal agreement on the goals of the political system (which pre-exists and underlies other agreements and is generally beyond political dispute) as well as general and elite agreements on the rules and procedures, will be regarded as axiomatic because they are a prerequisite for the capacity of governments to function effectively. To deal meaningfully with consensus among elites, therefore, we must go beyond these more general forms of consensus and beyond the higher degree of agreement among elites on the rules and procedures. Consensus among elites will manifest itself in conscious awareness and explicit acceptance of the prime importance of consensus and in specific agreement on methods to achieve it. Moreover, it will include specific and articulated agreements on major policy questions and political issues.

Elite consensus will therefore be characterized by greater ideological and policy agreement between the political elites than between nonelites. For example, in a political system in which there are a number of elites and a relatively undifferentiated, less participant, less politically developed mass, elite consensus will rest upon the capacity of the different elites to reach specific policy agreements. The masses, while generally involved in the political system and sharing its general goals and accepting the rules of the game, are distinguished by their being held at a distance from policy and issue content, discussion, and output.

An important constituent element of recognition of the significance of elite consensus by elites will be agreement not to mobilize or involve the masses in the discussion and resolution of elite policy differences and issue conflicts. Such decisions will be kept internal to the elites by the adoption of various measures designed to exclude regular and effective nonelite intervention, although there may be occasional breakthroughs. Elites will regard relations with other elites and the need to reach agreement with them as being of greater significance than relations or agreement with the masses.

Elite consensus is compatible with regular elections, but these reflect changes in the internal balance of political forces among the elites, without threatening the pattern of rule, and without allowing the masses to influence elite decisions. For this to occur, the election process will need to be carefully controlled by the elites, and agreement to do so will constitute a crucial element of the elite consensus. Thus, the extent to which elite consensus promotes an internal capability to rearrange the relative importance of the various elite groups (via elections or otherwise) without its own predominance being called into question is a sure indicator of its institutional strength and capacity for self-maintenance.

An Alternative Model of Elite Competition

For elite competition to occur, we must postulate the existence of a number of elites. Competition between them is not total, but takes place within a framework of agreements. While elites share agreements (consensus) on the rules and procedures that govern the operation of the political system, competition between them occurs with regard to substantive issues and policies.

Elite competition will be characterized by policy and issue disagreements between the elites that are less sharp than those between the masses. This occurs because, to overcome the sharp ideological divisions and create a working political system, elites may consciously temper their disagreements and isolate themselves from their own masses and the impact of their intense ideological commitments. This confines the resolution of issue conflict to elite structures, while leaving ideological disagreements among the masses relatively untouched.

Consequently, the lesser degree of disagreement among elites results from elite restraints upon competition over substantive issues and policies, from specific agreements on the procedure for their resolution, and from elite control over their respective masses. Political and partisan disagreements are thus either consciously removed from political contest or resolved by competitive elite bargaining and negotiation, which leads to a general lowering in their intensity and salience. The same differences among the masses remain unresolved and salient.

This alternative model of elite competition is specifically designated as competition, despite the significant element of elite accommodation in which it results and by which it is conventionally known (for example, see Lijphart, 1975). Employing the term *competition* points to the continuing significance of the fundamental disagreements and deep conflict that characterize relations between the major segments of society. Accommodation in this context is the resolution among elites of the competition and conflict between societal blocs, rather than the substance of relations between them. Moreover, the conventional term, *elite accommodation*, is unsatisfactory because it may easily be mistaken for *elite consensus*. The usage adopted here thus avoids the trap of assuming that all conflict resolution by some kind of compromise indicates consensus. Similarly, it avoids leaving no place for *competition* between *consensus* and *chaos*.

Multidimensional Elite and Mass Competition

Elite competition may form part of a more widely based pattern of competition that develops under certain conditions, including, ideological encouragement of and institutional activity directed toward public involvement in the discussion of issues on the political agenda; public awareness and discussion of substantive policy differences; and the dependence of elites upon the mobilization of mass support in order to gain control of the major political offices involved in the resolution of issue conflicts and policy differences. This will be termed *multidimensional elite and mass competition*,[3] and is characterized by *greater policy disagreements and partisan differences among elites than among the masses*.

It also may be characterized by a degree of elite responsiveness to nonelites if this is a necessary condition for attaining major political offices. Responsiveness in this context is not intended to convey the implication that the elite does precisely and specifically what the nonelite wants, or that the elite waits to receive directions from the nonelite. It does involve, however, doing what is necessary to gain nonelite support and to increase the degree of agreement between them. This may be achieved by taking the nonelites' view into account and acting accordingly to bring the views of the elite and the nonelite closer together.

Empirical evidence indicates that issue conflicts, policy differences, and partisan disagreements among elites are greater than those among the general public in a number of western political systems, particularly the United States[4] and Great Britain.[5] This is often attributed to the greater interest of politicians in political activity, their greater access to information, and their greater sophistication in detecting even fine differences and distinctions. Often, competing elites develop a pressing need to be separated from their political rivals and to assume distinctive labels for the purpose of mobilizing support in electoral competition. Even the tendency to converge in the center so as not to alienate supporters and potential supporters does not obviate the very real need to maintain sufficient distance between rival elites.

Heightened elite responsiveness may derive from the effects of overlapping group memberships. The loyalties and the cross-pressures these generate across political and organizational boundaries expose nonelites to competitive influences. So too do open and pervasive patterns of mass communications. In both cases, recognition by elites that supporters or potential supporters are subject to considerable rival elite or peer pressure can produce responsive elite reactions aimed at preventing loss of support.

Such considerations tie in neatly with Hirschman's argument that "the *effectiveness* of the voice mechanism is strengthened by the possibility of exit" (Hirschman, 1970:83). In his view, "the best possible situation for the development of party responsiveness to the feelings of members may then be a situation of just a very few parties whose distance from each other is wide but not unbridgeable. In this situation, exit remains possible, but the decision of exit will not be taken lightheartedly. Hence voice will be a frequent reaction to discontent with the way things are going and members will fight to make their voice effective" (Hirschman, 1970:84).

Empirical evidence exists to support these basic theoretical propositions. The authors of a study of 211 organizations concluded that "if an organization must constantly bargain with other groups to realize its objectives, it will tend to involve its members more fully in the decision-making process. . . . In addition, in order to enhance their bargaining position with other elements in society, the leaders need to have the full support of their membership." The general conclusion was that "the more competitive the political system becomes, the greater the probability that organization leaders will keep in touch with the wishes of the rank and file" (Kelso, 1978:159).

Further empirical support on a much larger scale can be found in Sayre and Kaufman's study of New York City, which concluded that decisions there were the result of mutual accommodation, bargaining, and the building of temporary and lasting alliances and settlements between allies and competitors (Sayre and Kaufman, 1960:712). Bargaining took place between core groups and satellites, between various satellites, and "between one core group plus its satellites and other core groups and their satellites" (Sayre and Kaufman, 1960:713). The result was considerable activity to overcome objections and to stimulate the indifferent—the modification of plans and policies to gain or maintain support (Sayre and Kaufman, 1960:718). Within this framework every elite core and its satellite group had to continuously "acknowledge the supervisory presence of the city's electorate possessing the propensity and capacity to intervene decisively in the contest on the side of one contestant or the other" (Sayre and Kaufman, 1960:710).

More generally, whether a situation is one of elite competition or of multidimensional elite and mass competition will depend upon the interplay and relative weighting of a complex variety of factors. For example, elite competition is more likely under conditions of high nonelite dependence upon their elites, nonelite encapsulation within social frameworks from which exit is difficult, insufficient information by nonelites with regard to the issues and policy positions of elites, or inaccessibility to elites. Multidimensional elite and mass competition is more likely to occur under conditions where nonelites are not dependent on elites; nonelites possess information about issues; societal values legitimate and promote nonelite policy expression and elite responsiveness; elites are apprehensive of the consequences of nonresponsiveness; and there exist channels of access to elites, in addition to elections.

For elite consensus, elite competition, and multidimensional elite and mass competition to be more than mere constructs, it is necessary to observe them in practice and to show how these alternative models are applicable to actual systems. An example of elite consensus, as defined in this study, would be the political system of Mexico, while the consociational democracy in the Netherlands would be an example of elite competition. Australia provides an example of multidimensional elite and mass competition.

Multidimensional Elite and Mass Competition: Australia

Several recent studies by Higley et al. have examined Australian elites. Higley, Deacon, and Smart found evidence of considerable elite interaction, which they define as elite integration. They also consider whether the sharp issue divisions among leaders and the competition for public support provide evidence for the pluralist model, but they ultimately reject this because elites "exhibit much greater cohesion and integration than is compatible with the standards of representative democracy" (Higley, Deacon, and Smart, 1979:262–63). (Nowhere are the standards of cohesion and integration compatible with representative democracy specified.) Thus, they conclude that Australia is to be placed in the category of consensually unified elites.

Higley and Moore, in a later comparative study of elite networks in the United States and Australia, update and elaborate these conclusions: "the existence of a larger, densely interconnected central circle in each country fits uneasily with the pluralist image. In addition, there is extensive interaction between sectors, and inter-elite interaction is strongly centralized in core groups that are themselves so tightly integrated as to be incompatible with that model." They argue that "a more accurate description is provided by the consensually integrated elite model. . . . This model . . . portrays the structure of consensually integrated elites like the American and Australian as more comprehensively elitist in the sense of a tighter integration of more elite groups than has previously been recognized" (Higley and Moore, 1981:595).

For theoretical and methodological reasons, the claim that interaction is indicative of, or equivalent to, cohesion and integration cannot be accepted without specific empirical evidence as to the substantive nature of elite interaction. It may indicate an ongoing adversarial relationship. Without the assumption of integration and cohesion, however, the conclusion of elite unity and elite consensus does not follow. Once this assumption is removed, the evidence and data gathered by Higley and others are sufficient to invalidate the claim for elite consensus and to establish a case for multidimensional elite and mass competition. This approach is further substantiated by other survey data and by the analysis of some of the basic features of Australian politics.

The substance and style of Australian politics is the battle between the Labor and non-Labor parties. Despite the presence of three parties in the House of Representatives and at times four in the Senate, the pattern of party competition has resembled a two-party system more than anything else. This has been due, in the main, to the stability and effectiveness of coalition arrangements on the non-Labor side that have combined the parties representing urban and rural interests into one coordinated parliamentary bloc.

The Labor party was defeated in the 1949 elections after having held office for the previous eight years: for the next twenty-three years the country was governed by a Liberal-Country coalition. Labor was reelected in 1972 and governed until the turbulent constitutional crisis in 1975, when it was stripped of its right to hold office by the Governor-General in what was an extremely controversial interpretation and exercise of his constitutional authority. In the immediately ensuing election, the Liberal-Country coalition was once more returned to power, having maintained during its period in opposition the same degree of coordinated action as a single parliamentary bloc it had displayed when in office. The Liberal-Country coalition ruled until 1983, when it was beaten once more by Labor. Thus, since 1972, party competition in Australia has been based on alternating majorities, with three changes of government and six elections in just over ten years.

Australian party politics are also characterized by a high degree of cohesiveness. In part, this is because the small Australian population is socially homogeneous. The federal arrangements both reflect and reinforce this homogeneity, being best understood as structural federalism which protects and promotes states' rights where social federalism reflecting deep social, cultural, religious, and regional diversity is absent (Epstein, 1977:3–4). This is accompanied by a high degree of cross-cutting of generally low intensity social cleavage (Clarke and Kornberg, 1973:183–91).

Party cohesiveness stems also from a high degree of party discipline, particularly in the legislature, on both the Labor and non-Labor sides. Voting according to the party decision is strictly enforced, and disobeying a party whip in Parliament is extremely rare. Party discipline has been a prominent element in Labor's organizational makeup—because of both the need for unity and the fear that parliamentary leaders will act too independently and take the power of decision that rests with the party. This fear has many manifestations. The Labor prime minister does not choose his cabinet ministers; this is done by the parliamentary caucus in an exhaustive secret ballot: all that is left for the Labor prime minister to do is to allocate the portfolios. In theory, the extraparliamentary bodies are the supreme and final authority regarding party policy and can oblige Labor parliamentarians to carry out their instructions. However, this practice is rarely put to the test, as issues tend to be ironed out through a process of consultation and accommodation, rather than being brought to the point of confrontation (Medding, 1964). While not as formally stated or as blatant as in the Labor party, discipline in the other parties is still very much the rule rather than the exception, particularly with regard to MPs supporting party policy in Parliament.

The Australian Labor party adopted a socialization objective in its party platform in 1921. At the end of the 1940s, the Labor government made its most ambitious attempt to fulfill that objective by seeking to nationalize the banking industry. The issue aroused a heated political debate and was challenged in the courts, with the plan finally being declared unconstitutional by the High Court in a manner that seemed to indicate that Labor had a permanent constitutional problem with any future nationalization legislation. Nevertheless, even in the mid-1970s, Labor remained committed to the "democratic socialization of industry, production, distribution and exchange." It was in this context that the failed bank nationalization plan of 1949 was important: as long as the objective remained on the party platform, it served as a permanent reminder that Labor had made a serious attempt to implement its platform; that ideologically it was still committed to it; that it might try again in the future, however slim its chances of success were without constitutional change; and that the broader issues of government intervention and public control were very much still a part of the Australian political agenda.

Thus, in the disciplined, two-party competition of Australian politics, ideology has remained significant, particularly at the level of political discourse and political debate. According to Kemp,

> [t]here has certainly been remarkable continuity in the terminology of political debate in Australia. For seven decades the language of free enterprise, competition, individualism, achievement, initiative, incentives, freedom, national development, sound management, responsibility and loyalty to the Crown has marked the political appeals of the Liberal Party. Equality, cooperation, socialism, solidarity, the working man, nationalism, government action and anti-imperialism, meanwhile, have been equally characteristic of Labor party appeals. Moreover, there is considerable evidence that voters accurately identify the different appeals and respond either positively or negatively to the various party ideologies embodied in these appeals. (Kemp 1979a:49)

These ideological appeals and responses are maintained over time because they have been related to the particular experience of the groups to which the parties look for support and have changed slowly to accommodate changes in that experience. Thus, so long as the groups survive the ideology remains relevant. Recent research has demonstrated the strength and validity of this connection by finding a clear association between Inglehart's value tests and party identification in Australia: among the quarter of the electorate who were "materialist," 58 percent were LCP supporters and 32 percent supported ALP; among the 15 percent who were postmaterialist, 27 percent were LCP and 57 percent were ALP; and among the 60 percent who were mixed, 40 percent were LCP and 42 percent were ALP (Kemp, 1979a:54–55).

Labor came to power in 1972, led by E. G. Whitlam, on a platform encapsulated in the slogan It's Time. Labor sought not just a change in government in keeping with the democratic process, but widespread social change. After becoming party leader in 1967, Whitlam concentrated on identifying new issues, arousing new social concerns, defining and promoting policies and programs in response to these questions, and finding support for these among various sectors of society, particularly those groups newly risen to importance. Australia entered the post-industrial era. To Labor's traditional stance, he added a dimension of radicalism that had direct appeal to the middle classes and, in so doing, changed the agenda of Australian politics.

Since the end of the 1960s, quality of life, environment, poverty, ethnic minorities' situation (including both recent immigrants and aboriginals), education, improvement and extension of social security and health services, and political participation and governmental responsiveness have become key issues. It was not only these issues per se, but Labor's approach to them that came to characterize Australian political conflict in the 1970s. Government and capitalism in Australia had always been interventionist and pragmatic, looking "upon the state as a vast public utility, whose duty it is to provide the greatest happiness for the greatest number" (Hughes, 1973:140).

Whitlam pursued the issues of reform and radicalism in a highly moralizing and idealistic manner, rather than in the previously dominant pragmatic style. What is more, Labor sought reforms in Australian society that necessitated restructuring the mode of intervention of the state by a massive shifting of resources to the public sector. This was particularly evident in its plans for large-scale urban and regional development, as well as in social welfare, education, economic management, and unemployment schemes. Moreover, the schemes were ambitious and costly, an element that became painfully obvious as Australia began to encounter the worldwide economic problems of the 1970s. The country experienced rapid inflation and unemployment spirals, and a severe economic downturn occurred at the time when the Labor Government needed ever-increasing resources for its social reforms.

By 1974, the Liberals became increasingly strident in their preoccupation with tackling the economic crisis with policies that called for dismantling the structure and pattern of government intervention Labor had introduced. It was the Liberals' avowed policy to shift economic resources back to the private sector and to revert to the traditional pragmatic pattern of state intervention. Many of their policies were direct attempts to repeal Labor initiatives. Criticisms and economic realities had their effect on the electorate. Middle-class radicalism (which had been so instrumental in bringing Labor to power in 1972) began to wane as the increasing tax burdens from fiscal policies, a rapid increase in interest rates, a generally de-pressed economy, and Labor's apparent incapacity to cope with these problems lessened enthusiasm for policies of social reform.

One clearly documented result of these conflicts was that by 1974 the electorate had become more divided and that into the high level of partisan identification there had been injected a strong strain of partisan polarization. A survey in that year indicated that 62 percent of Liberal identifiers thought that the Labor government "certainly" or "probably would seriously endanger Australia's well-being." Partisan polarization increased with the strength of identification: 88 percent of very strong Liberal identifiers thought that Labor was a danger. During 1975, this pattern of partisan polarization was found to have continued and even intensified (Kemp, 1979b:6–7).

In 1975, during this atmosphere of high partisan polarization, Australia was cast into its most severe constitutional crisis when the Liberal-Country Opposition in the Senate blocked Supply, and the governor-general dismissed Whitlam as prime minister and installed in his place Malcolm Fraser, the Opposition leader. This challenged the long-established principle that the government was responsible to the lower house, the House of Representatives, and that it had the right to govern as long as it maintained its majority there. On both political and constitutional grounds, opinions were sharply divided on the question of whether the Senate had the right to refuse Supply and whether the governor-general had the authority to dismiss a popularly elected government.

Beyond these important procedural issues, the critical political element in the whole episode was that Labor leaders and partisans saw it as an establishment conspiracy designed to frustrate a left-wing government in its mission of reform. Thus, the crisis had the effect of intensifying an already high level of partisan polarization and placed at the center of political debate the rights of a popularly elected majority to undertake social reform and the issue of the ex-tent and limits of government activity and intervention. The new Liberal-Country Government consciously sought to increase the strength of the private sector, to undo many of Labor's reforms, to let others lapse and generally to decrease the degree of government involvement and intervention.

Viewed in this light, the conflict over political office between the

two major political parties under conditions of high partisan polarization cannot meaningfully be described in terms of elite consensus or
consensually unified elites. To the contrary, relations between the
party elites were highly competitive and epitomized the adversary
relationship. Thus, on being dismissed, Whitlam called on his colleagues, followers, and supporters to "maintain their rage" and during the election campaign went on to charge that his Liberal-Country
opponents had "shown with brutal clarity . . . that they will obstruct
and disrupt, will defy the Constitution, break its conventions, set
aside the will of the Australian people to get their way." He referred to
their "contempt for the law of the land" and suggested that their
actions would "destroy Australia's good name as a stable Parliamentary democracy." Fraser, the Liberal leader, described Whitlam as a
man "who tried to rule without Parliament, who defied a fundamental principle of our constitution, and who finally forced the Governor-
General to dismiss him; the man who took Australia the first significant step on the road to dictatorship" (Kemp, 1979b:1).

Despite the intensity of conflict between these competing and partisan political elites, they shared a common commitment to, and
consensus upon, the rules of the game. Nothing can be more striking
in this regard than the response of Labor in 1975 when it did nothing
to challenge either the rules used to dismiss them from office or the
ensuing election. Whitlam subsequently wrote that it did not occur
to him to contest the decision (Kemp, 1979b:1). Further strong con-
firmation of our contention that under conditions of multidimensional elite and mass competition, even intense and partisan elite
conflict and competition will take place within a context of consensus on procedures and rules of the game, which may therefore be
taken as axiomatic, is provided in the survey of Australian political
leaders conducted at this time by Higley et al.

Despite their conclusions, which, in keeping with their theoretical
assumptions, find that the data indicate elite unity, their documenta-
tion of the sharp diversities of opinion among the various elites and
their identification of clearly divergent ideologies is, indeed, most
impressive. Their analysis of elite responses on a wide variety of
issues and questions found that elites were situated in a trichoto-
mous pattern of ideological cleavage corresponding to left, center,
and right. The core of the left were the ALP leaders and top union
officials; the core of the right were Liberal party leaders and top
business managers; while the center consisted of senior members of
the Commonwealth Public Service, church leaders, voluntary association leaders, top mass media executives, and senior academics
(Higley, Deacon, and Smart, 1979:110–26).

Further examination of this pattern of cleavage reveals that there
were considerable variations in opinion and disunity even among
like-minded elites. This meant that although conflict between left

and right on the various issue sets was high, it was not fully polarized. In other words, high conflict between the left and right was never coupled with high consensus within both, although it was often coupled with high internal consensus on the right. Thus, the overall result was that high left-right conflict was moderated by respondents who either took intermediate positions or identified with the other side (Higley and Cushing, 1977:54–57).

When the pattern of conflict between left and right was examined more closely, it revealed particularly striking differences between the ALP and LCP leaders, who were generally the most left and right respectively on almost all issues surveyed. The average left-right difference in percentage points was 54: ranging from 19 at the lowest end of the scale to 84 at its height. Higley et al. concluded that "partisan alignments are strong and comparatively comprehensive . . . widespread agreement among leaders appears to be a very occasional thing. . . . In these respects, elite cleavage appears to be highly durable" (1979:137).

These findings accord with Kemp's argument that partisan polarization and the adversarial nature of elite relations in Australia stem from the association of major parties with elites in the industrial system: the LCP with business elites and the ALP with trade union elites. Adversarial relationships are a permanent feature of interactions among industrial elites in Australia, and the strong feelings among the population, both positive and negative, toward these elites carry over into the political system via the political parties (Kemp, 1979b:17–19).

Partisan conflict and cleavage among Australian elites are moderated by the effect of crosscutting ideological cleavages, as might be expected from our model of multidimensional elite and mass competition. Once more, evidence can be found in the work of Higley et al. In analyzing responses of the center, they found that its opinions did not line up consistently with those of either the left or the right bloc; and, except for three issues, the center lacked high consensus. In essence, center opinions were generally similar to those of the left on social issues and foreign and defense policy, but, on questions of institutional structure and economic and industrial relations, they were more similar to those of the right. Because the center was truly "centrist" on nearly all issue sets, it was in a position to act as a buffer between left and right (Higley and Cushing, 1977:55).

Higley and Cushing are puzzled as to how such moderation might be effected, "considering that no major political party represents the centrist position," and they suggest that "the media seem to be the only vehicle available" (1977:56). The important effect of this centrism is to put pressure on the political parties to moderate their positions in order to gain the support of those sections of the electorate who do not share the views of either left or right. What is more, given the nature of the center elites, their critical role in opinion formation, and their direct association with the media, there is every reason to assume that this may affect a large section of the electorate, including those with a clear sense of party identification. For the major political elites to take account of these centrist opinions, one need not look for a center party: one need only recognize that the existence of the center position puts both left and right party leaders under the pressure of elite competition and obliges them to take action to maintain or win the support of the target groups.

In accordance with our model, partisan conflict and polarization among elites in Australia is much more intense than among the mass public. We have already noted some evidence for this in the finding that stronger Liberal identifiers were much more likely to believe that Labor would endanger the country. Further direct evidence of a comparative nature is provided by Higley, Deacon, and Smart. In comparing responses to questions put to the elite sample with those for similar questions from mass public opinion polls taken at about the same time, they conclude "that on half of the issues for which comparisons could be made at all, there was considerably greater issue conflict between elites than among the public, and that on only two of the ten issues was there greater conflict among the public than among the elites" (Higley, Deacon, and Smart, 1979:143). They also point out that the overall amount of issue conflict among the public had been overstated, because between 10 to 20 percent of those polled were undecided.

Multidimensional elite and mass competition in Australia was accompanied by responsiveness to the views of supporters and potential supporters. We have already noted that during 1974 and 1975, relations between the Labor government and business and employers worsened considerably as a result of the economic crisis. Moreover, many members of the middle classes who previously had been attracted to Labor's policies of social change were now negatively affected by them: they were alienated by what they regarded as evidence of economic mismanagement and irresponsibility on the part of the Labor government, and apprehensive of the consequences of a further exacerbation of conflict between it and the business sectors.

Labor's 1975 budget was in many ways a direct response to these concerns, and the economic approach they adopted reflected the shift in the mood of the electorate. Similarly, it may be said that by the 1980s, Labor and the electorate had learned the lessons of the 1970s. When Labor swept into power under Hawke, the former president of the Australian Council of Trade Unions, it did so on a platform of solving the nation's continuing economic problems via policies that depended upon maximum cooperation between various groups. Once more Labor was returned to office through the votes of the middle classes.

Responsiveness to the public figured prominently among the views of the various elites surveyed by Higley et al. Thus, 49 percent of all elite members regarded the government as an obstacle in pursuing their policies, while 44 percent viewed it as a source of support. Not surprisingly, this was a direct reflection of their partisan affiliations. The public was thought to be an obstacle by 25 percent of the elite, but 39 percent saw it as a source of support. When the two responses were compared, there was, significantly, an inverse relationship between them, indicating distinctive patterns of political mobilization by the competing elites: those who regarded the government as an obstacle looked to the public for support and vice versa (Higley, Deacon, and Smart, 1979: 186–88).

These elites were somewhat ambivalent in their views about public opinion on political issues, with 19 percent finding it favorable, 23 percent open to change, 37 percent indifferent or uninformed, 10 percent divided or inconsistent, and 11 percent unfavorable. All in all, then, just over a third had an unequivocally negative view of the nature of public opinion, while two thirds regarded it as a factor to be reckoned with and taken into account. Predictably, very few regarded the public as a valuable source of information. Yet despite these reservations, all elites acknowledged that they made considerable and consistent efforts to communicate with the public on important issues, and most significantly, the widest and most concerted effort was made by the politicians (Higley, Deacon, and Smart, 1979:199–209).

A high degree of popular support for political competition that involved the public was found in Kemp's 1974 survey: 82 percent thought that although political parties had their faults, they were necessary if democracy was to work properly, while 78 percent agreed that election campaigns were needed so that the public could judge candidates and issues. Winning elections was not sufficient, however: 77 percent of the sample believed the victorious party was still expected to take the views of the opposition into account, while 65 percent believed that winning an election did not necessarily give a party the right to put all its policies into effect. The necessity of leadership was recognized and accepted, but at the same time, 83 percent thought that governments should not go ahead with any major policy until there had been thorough public discussion with as many people as possible taking part. The electorate was somewhat skeptical of political leaders and their motives, with 51 percent believing that most politicians were looking out for themselves above all else. In keeping with this pattern of opinion, the most important leadership quality sought was honesty, while those qualities associated with the capacity to reach the public and respond to the needs of the electorate were rated the next most important, all being more frequently cited than education or experience (Kemp, 1979b:Table 2).

Popular demands for involvement and responsiveness were reinforced by dissatisfaction with the existing situation. Thus, 76 percent thought that people should have more say in government decisions that affect them, and about half the sample thought that voters did not have enough power in Australia today, while 55 percent agreed that politicians should rely less on experts and listen to the people for a change (Kemp, 1979b:Table 9). These attitudes, indicating public awareness and a degree of vigilance, suggest that while multidimensional elite and mass competition is deeply rooted in the Australian political system, it is still subject to the quest for improvement.

Notes

1. The usage of *pluralism* here accords with Pluralism$_2$ as defined by Polsby (1980:154).

2. According to one account, this group consists of Robert Dahl, David Truman, Wallace Sayre, Herbert Kaufman, Edward Banfield, Charles Lindblom, and William Kornhauser (see Kelso, 1978:13).

3. I have adapted the term *multidimensional elite and mass competition* from the analysis of McFarland (1969:176–219). According to McFarland, conflict takes place between many actors at different levels: "At any point, political elites are engaged in n-party, multilateral conflicts among various groups of voters, party activists and elites, both within a particular political party, within the other party and outside both parties (e.g. interest group leaders)" (p. 188). This clearly indicates conflict involving both elites and masses. Additionally, he argues that such conflict also occurs over a number of issue dimensions and that it does not entail the complete opposition of actors to each other: they may agree on some questions while disagreeing on others, i.e., they have "both compatible and incompatible goals" (p. 188). Thus, while McFarland's full definition of such situations is that of "multilateral, multidimensional and mixed motive" political conflict, I have adopted the term *multidimensional elite and mass competition* as more convenient.

4. See the discussion of various empirical studies in the United States and elsewhere confirming this finding in Putnam (1976:87–93, 115–18).

5. Budge (1970). A recent study in Britain has suggested that these party and ideological differences also shaped politicians' attitudes to the rules of the game and their interpretations of the constitution, thereby questioning previously accepted theories of elite consensus in such matters (see Searing, 1982:239–59).

References

Bachrach, Peter (1967) *The Theory of Democratic Elitism: A Critique.* Boston: Little, Brown.

Budge, Ian (1970) *Agreement and the Stability of Democracy.* Chicago: Markham.

Clarke, Harold D., and Allan Kornberg (1973) "Social Cleavages and Democratic Performance." In *Australian Politics: A Third Reader*, edited by Henry Mayer and Helen Nelson. Melbourne: Cheshire.

Dahl, Robert A. (1958) "A Critique of the Ruling Elite Model." *American Political Science Review* 52:463–69.

Epstein, Leon D. (1977) "A Comparative Study of Australian Parties." *British Journal of Political Science* 7:1–21.

Field, G. Lowell, and John Higley (1980) *Elitism*. London: Routledge and Kegan Paul.

Higley, John, and Robert J. Cushing (1977) "Consensus and Conflict Among Australia's Leaders." *Politics* 12:38–58.

Higley, John; Desley Deacon; and Don Smart (1979) *Elites in Australia*. London: Routledge and Kegan Paul.

Higley, John, and Gwen Moore (1981) "Elite Integration in the United States and Australia." *American Political Science Review* 75:581–97.

Hirschman, Albert O. (1970) *Exit, Voice and Loyalty: Responses to Decline in Firms, Organizations and States*. Cambridge, MA: Harvard University Press.

Hughes, Colin A. (1973) "Political Culture." In *Australian Politics: A Third Reader*, edited by Henry Mayer and Helen Nelson. Melbourne: Cheshire.

Kelso, William Alton (1978) *American Democratic Theory: Pluralism and Its Critics*. Westport, Conn: Greenwood Press.

Kemp, David A. (1979a) "The Australian Electorate." In *The Australian National Elections of 1977*, edited by Howard Penniman. Canberra: American Enterprise Institute and Australian National University Press.

——— (1979b) "The Stability of Australian Polyarchy: Aspects of Political Crisis." Paper prepared for XI IPSA World Congress, Moscow.

Lijphart, Arend (1975) *The Politics of Accommodation: Pluralism and Democracy in the Netherlands*. 2nd ed. Berkeley: University of California Press.

Lipset, Seymour Martin (1962) "Introduction." In *Political Parties*, edited by Roberto Michels. New York: The Free Press.

McFarland, Andrew S. (1969) *Power and Leadership in Pluralist Societies*. Stanford: Stanford University Press.

Medding, Peter Y. (1964) "Cabinet Government and Decision Making in the Australian and British Labour Parties." *Public Policy* 13:271–301.

Medding, Peter Y. (1982) "Ruling Elite Models: A Critique and an Alternative." *Political Studies* 33:393–412.

Mosca, Gaetano (1939) *The Ruling Class*. Edited and revised by Arthur Livingston. Translated by Hannah D. Kahn. New York: McGraw-Hill.

Parenti, Michael (1970) "Power and Pluralism: A View From the Bottom." *Journal of Politics* 32:501–30.

Parry, Geraint (1969) *Political Elites*. London: Allen and Unwin.

Plamenatz, John (1973) *Democracy and Illusion*. London: Longman.

Polsby, Nelson W. (1980) *Community Power and Political Theory*. 2nd ed. New Haven: Yale University Press.

Prewitt, Kenneth, and Alan Stone (1973) *The Ruling Elites: Elite Theory, Power and American Democracy*. New York: Harper and Row.

Putnam, Robert D. (1976) *The Comparative Study of Political Elites*. Englewood Cliffs: Prentice-Hall.

Sartori, Giovanni (1978) "Anti-elitism Revisited." *Government and Opposition* 13:58–80.

Sayre, Wallace S., and Herbert Kaufman (1960) *Governing New York City.* New York: Russel Sage Foundation.

Schumpeter, Joseph A. (1954) *Capitalism, Socialism and Democracy.* London: Routledge and Kegan Paul.

Searing, Donald D. (1982) "Rules of the Game in Britain: Can the Politicians Be Trusted?" *American Political Science Review* 76:239–59.

Thompson, Dennis F. (1970) *The Democratic Citizen: Social Science and Democratic Theory in the 20th Century.* Cambridge: Cambridge University Press.

Truman, David B. (1971) "The American System in Crisis." In *Political Elites in a Democracy,* edited by Peter Bachrach. New York: Atherton Press.

Popular Evaluations of Party Leaders in the Anglo-American Democracies

Brian Graetz and Ian McAllister

There is a growing tendency in modern industrial society to personalize political power in party leaders, most notably in the Americanization of "elections" in Europe and Australia into "presidential" contests between two competing political personalities. Three reasons have been adduced to account for this: the electoral significance of class has been weakening since the 1960s, with the result that party leaders and political issues have an enhanced role in determining electoral outcomes; the growth of the electronic media has meant that the public more easily associates power and authority with a readily identifiable political personality rather than an abstract institution or political ideal; and the weakening of party loyalties in many countries in the last two decades has brought politicians, rather than the parties to which they belong, into sharper relief.[1]

How the electorate views a leader has crucial implications for the political system. For example, a leader who exercises a high level of charisma and who enjoys widespread mass support will have more opportunity to downplay controversial issues and implement radical or unpopular plans. Conversely, a less popular, noncharismatic leader may be reluctant to implement certain policies for fear of jeopardizing his or her popular support and may be more vulnerable to controversial, short-term political issues. Moreover, the identification of a political personality with the political system means that affective orientations toward the party leader may be transferred, to some degree, to the system itself.

Despite the theoretical significance of popular evaluations of party leaders in democratic societies, relatively little is known about the processes that shape these evaluations. It has been shown, for example, that their roots lie in the socialization undergone by adolescents before they join the active electorate (Green-

stein, 1965, 1975; Sigel, 1968). It is also known that these evaluations are anchored in partisan feelings, but that partisanship alone
does not account for all the effect (Rusk and Weisberg, 1972). Finally, it is evident that popular evaluations of leaders have important consequences for the political system and the governmental
system in particular—indirectly, through judgments of how effectively the system operates, and directly, through voting behavior
(Converse and Dupeux, 1966).

Apart from studies of political socialization, little attempt has
been made to disentangle various influences on popular evaluations
of party leaders, or to estimate their significance for the political
system. Most important of all, few studies have placed their results
in a comparative context that would provide an estimate of their
general applicability across a range of societies. It is only through
comparison of a range of countries that conclusions can be reached
about the general nature of the social processes at work. In this
paper, we seek to redress these shortcomings by analyzing factors
influencing popular evaluations of party leaders as well as their
political consequences. The analysis compares Australia, Britain,
Canada, and the United States[2] using similar multivariate techniques
and a similar range of variables. The data come from large, representative sample surveys, carried out in 1979 in Australia, Britain, and
Canada[3] and in 1980 in the United States.

The Anglo-American democracies are particularly appropriate for
a comparative case study of this kind. Despite differing political
institutions, all four share a common set of underlying political values that emphasize liberalism, individualism, and a willingness to
compromise (Alford, 1967:71). Three of the four have political systems based on a major socioeconomic cleavage, and the imprint of
that cleavage is found in their party systems, which generally divide
on left–right lines. The exception is Canada, where the socioeconomic cleavage, in so far as it is reflected in voting behavior, is
particularly weak (Alford, 1963; Clarke, Jenson, LeDuc, and Pammett, 1979). Instead, the major Canadian cleavages revolve around
regional ethnic and linguistic factors, which tend to crosscut the
socioeconomic cleavage.

In addition, the governmental and electoral systems in each
country generally encourage the persistence of a two-party system
at the national level, despite frequent electoral interventions from
minor and third parties, such as the Democrats in Australia, the
Liberals in Britain (and more recently the Social Democratic Party),
and the New Democratic Party in Canada.[4] Finally, the style of
political leadership tends to be pragmatic, compromise-seeking,
and nonideological. Although there is a major difference between
the presidential leadership of the United States, where party loyalties are less strong, and the prime ministerial leadership of

Australia, Britain, and Canada, leadership is used as a resource to overcome disunity and fragmentation in each of these societies (Hargrove, 1967).

The two-party systems in the four countries enable us to focus on the leaders of these parties, since these are the personalities who are in the public eye. Moreover, the different characters of these leaders, plus their varying periods in the public's purview, provide the basis for useful comparisons. In each case, the leader of the governing party was an established political personality at the time the survey used here was carried out.

In Australia, Malcolm Fraser had become leader of the Liberal Party in March 1975. He won power in the December 1975 federal election, and remained as prime minister until his defeat in 1983. Fraser's opponent, Bill Hayden, was also an established political figure. He had been treasurer and a senior minister in the former Whitlam government, and became leader of the Labor party in 1977, a position he held until just prior to the 1983 federal election. In Britain, Margaret Thatcher had been leader of the opposition for four years by 1979, while her opponent in the 1979 general election, James Callaghan, had succeeded Harold Wilson as prime minister after the latter's resignation in 1978.

In Canada, the Liberal leader Pierre Trudeau had been prime minister for eleven years when the Canadian survey was undertaken in 1979. His opponent, the Conservative party leader Joe Clark, defeated Trudeau in that election, but lost office nine months later following the breakdown of his minority government, which had been dependent on the votes of a handful of Social Credit MPs. In the ensuing 1980 election, Trudeau was once again returned as prime minister. In the United States, Jimmy Carter had been president since 1976, when he gained the Democratic nomination and defeated Gerald Ford. The Republican candidate in 1980, Ronald Reagan, had been a controversial governor of California and only narrowly missed the Republican nomination in 1976. He was therefore well known to electors at the time of his presidential victory over Carter.[5]

It is on the sources of the support these leaders attract, and on the consequences of their leadership for the political system in general, that this study concentrates. The first part discusses evaluations voters make of their leaders in the four countries, and examines the variety of ways in which these evaluations can be measured. The second section analyzes the correlates of those evaluations, while the third examines their political consequences, both for the political system as a whole and for the electoral fortunes of the parties. The final section discusses implications of the analysis.

Evaluating Political Leaders

Research conducted over the past two decades consistently has shown that electorates tend to view party leaders in predominantly personal terms. Voters are significantly more likely to refer to the leader's personal image, rather than to policy stances or leadership qualities (Aitkin, 1977:247–55; Clarke et al., 1979:ch. 7; Greenstein, 1965; Nimmo and Savage, 1976:ch. 3). Moreover, there is a consistent tendency for voters to reify the personal characteristics of the winning candidate in an election. It also has been shown that the proportion of personal references to a leader remains stable over time. In the United States, Nie, Verba, and Petrocik (1976:169) found that evaluations of candidates' personal attributes remained "strong and relatively constant in each presidential election from 1952 to 1972." By contrast, evaluations using party terms declined significantly and evaluations in terms of issues steadily increased during the same period. Butler and Stokes (1976:357–62) have reported a similar level of stability in personal evaluations of party leaders in Britain.

Two separate methods have been used to elicit respondents' evaluations of leaders. Starting with the American voting studies of the 1950s, respondents have been asked via open-ended questions to mention their likes and dislikes of candidates. This produces a broad range of responses highlighting particular characteristics of leaders, but it does not provide an overall assessment of the candidate: voters give their likes and dislikes separately, so there is no definitive measure of their net preference (cf. Repass, 1971). For example, a voter may actually dislike a certain candidate, but still find something positive to say; the net judgment against the candidate would not necessarily show up in weighing the responses. The second method used is to ask respondents to rate candidates on a scale running between 0 and 10 or 0 and 100. Such thermometer measures produce a clear net judgement of the leaders concerned, but inevitably lose detailed information about specific likes and dislikes that contribute to this summary evaluation.[6]

The Canadian and the U.S. surveys used here employ both evaluative measures, while the British survey includes only the thermometer measure, and the Australian includes only the open-ended questions. Table 1 shows the means and the standard deviations for these measures. The results for the open-ended questions have been converted into metric scales by calculating the number of mentions of likes and dislikes. In Canada and the United States, where comparisons of the open-ended and thermometer measures are possible, little variation emerges between the two methods. In both countries, respective differences between candidates are preserved. In Canada,

TABLE 1.

Evaluating Party Leaders using the Open-Ended and Thermometer Questions[a]

| | Evaluations (scaled 0 to 10) | | | | | |
| | Open-ended | | Thermometer | | Correlation between measures |
	Mean	Std dev	Mean	Std dev	
Australia					
Fraser (Incumbent)	4.4	1.7	n.a.	n.a.	n.a.
Hayden (Challenger)	5.1	1.3	n.a.	n.a.	n.a.
(Incumbent−Challenger)	(−0.7)		n.a.		
Britain					
Callaghan (Incumbent)	n.a.	n.a.	6.7	2.3	n.a.
Thatcher (Challenger)	n.a.	n.a.	6.2	3.0	n.a.
(Incumbent−Challenger)	n.a.		(+0.5)		
Canada					
Trudeau (Incumbent)	5.5	1.4	5.7	3.0	.63
Clark (Challenger)	5.0	1.4	5.0	2.4	.57
(Incumbent−Challenger)	(+0.5)		(+0.7)		
United States					
Carter (Incumbent)	4.6	2.1	5.7	2.7	.70
Reagan (Challenger)	4.8	1.9	5.6	2.5	.64
(Incumbent−Challenger)	(−0.2)		(+0.1)		

[a]For a description of how these questions were scaled, see the Appendix.

Sources: 1979 Australian National Political Attitudes Survey (N=2,016);
   1979 British Election Study (N=1,893);
   1979 Canadian National Election Study (N=2,762);
   1980 US Presidential Election Study (N=1,614).

Trudeau leads his opponent, Clark, by about half a point on both measures, while in the United States there is little difference between candidates on both measures. The two measures are also highly correlated for each candidate, ranging from .57 for Joe Clark in Canada to .70 for Jimmy Carter in the United States.

Given their greater public prominence, it might be expected that incumbent candidates would score better than challengers. In Britain and Canada this is certainly the case, even though both incumbents lost office. The advantage is approximately half a point on the 0 to 10 scale. In the United States, there is little separating the two candidates. The exception here is Australia, where the challenger in the 1980 federal election, Bill Hayden, led the incumbent Malcolm Fraser by one half of one point, presumably reflecting the poor media image of the prime minister at that time.

Open-ended responses from the Australian, Canadian, and U.S. surveys reaffirm the findings of previous research: personal characteristics of leaders are most likely to be mentioned by voters, as opposed to policies or other leadership qualities. In Australia and Canada, the large majority of evaluative responses—both positive and negative—concern personal qualities. In the United States, personal qualities are less often mentioned. They represent 50 percent of all positive Carter evaluations and a surprisingly low 35 percent of Ronald Reagan's: of Carter's negative evaluations, only 31 percent referred to personal qualities. In their place, policy matters are mentioned much more frequently than in Australia or Canada, perhaps because the separation of powers in the United States identifies policies more directly with the chief executive than in other political systems.

Clear patterns emerge in the type and range of these personal mentions. In Australia, some thought Fraser was "strong, decisive and courageous" (13 percent) while others felt he went too far and was arrogant and conceited (21 percent). Some (23 percent) considered him honest and sincere while others (14 percent) considered him to be dishonest and insincere. For Hayden, by contrast, 23 percent considered him honest and sincere, and relatively few thought otherwise. However, many (30 percent) regarded Hayden either as weak and indecisive or as a "nonentity" who lacked charisma. Canadian voters also expressed clear views about their leader Trudeau: he was considered "intelligent and smart" as well as "too arrogant" and possessing an unpleasant "manner and attitude" (20 percent each). Like the opposition leader in Australia, the Canadian opposition leader Joe Clark was variously labelled "honest and sincere" (11 percent) as well as "too young and inexperienced" (13 percent). Finally, in the United States, Carter's record and experience proved his best personal quality: this was mentioned by one in five of the respondents, followed by his "honesty and sincerity" (11 percent).

Like Carter, Reagan's strongest quality was thought to be his record and experience (13 percent), but Reagan's age proved to be the main reason for people's misgivings about his leadership potential (10 percent).

Among the nonpersonal evaluations, the Australian and Canadian respondents mentioned a variety of factors. However, foreign or domestic policies, as well as party responses, attracted relatively few mentions. In the United States, by contrast, policies were a substantially more important reason for liking or disliking the presidential candidates. Among positive evaluations for Reagan, domestic (23 percent) and foreign policies (13 percent) were most frequently mentioned. These two aspects of Carter's policies proved to be his greatest drawback, with more than half of the respondents mentioning one or the other as a reason for disliking him, compared to less than one-third for Reagan.

Overall, these aggregate results suggest two patterns: personal qualities are the most salient in the public's view, although this is much more prominent in Australia and Canada than in the United States;[7] and relatedly, policy factors are significantly more salient in the United States than elsewhere. These patterns undoubtedly can be attributed, in part, to the limited extent to which the public is directly involved or, indeed, interested in matters of policy, with the result that the electorate's evaluation of a leader draws upon the more visible aspects of leadership embodied in personality. Another part of the reason is that leaders themselves will "avoid issues of a divisive sort, and place (as nearly as possible) no emphasis on them" (Page, 1976:749).[8] However, U.S. voters appear more likely than their Australian or Canadian counterparts to take their political cues from leaders, rather than parties. The next section seeks to isolate the factors underlying these evaluations.

Sources of Leadership Evaluations

Most people do not form spontaneous evaluations of political leaders; on the contrary, their views represent a complex interaction of influences. As Graber (1972:50–51) argues, people "combine current political data supplied by the mass media with existing knowledge and attitudes and then weave these strands into a plausible and pleasing gestalt." In order to test a series of possible hypotheses, a range of independent variables was chosen on the basis of their proven or potential importance in studies of comparative electoral behavior. We might expect a person's ascribed characteristics (such as age, race, or gender) to influence their view of a party leader in various ways. For example, women might more positively evaluate a woman leader, such as Margaret Thatcher, while older voters might be more inclined to endorse an older candidate, such as Ronald Reagan. Socioeconomic status could affect views of leadership through economic self-interest—persons in higher status occupations would be more likely to endorse a candidate prepared to protect their status—or through affinity, with persons endorsing a candidate from a similar socioeconomic background. Partisanship is an obvious influence, and "merely associating the party symbol with [the candidate's] name encourages those identifying with the party to develop a more favorable image of his record and experience, his abilities, and his other personal attributes" (Campbell, Converse, Miller, and Stokes, 1960:128). There also is evidence that if a candidate is unknown to the voters then partisanship will be used to make an evaluation (Rusk and Weisberg, 1972).

The sources of political information a person has are potentially among the most important influences. A major source is the extent of talk about politics with friends: one might expect that such conversations would frequently center on the performance, ability, and personal characteristics of political leaders.[9] Another major source of political information is media exposure, either through newspapers or electronic media. Although it is generally accepted that people who use newspapers rather than television or radio for their political information are seeking a wider range of knowledge (Bogart, 1968; Clarke and Ruggels, 1979), research has indicated that media influence during a political campaign is relatively negligible, provided people hold partisan loyalties (DeVries and Torrance, 1972).

To estimate the effect of these variables on evaluations of party leaders, ordinary least squares regression methods are used. Table 2 shows the partial regression coefficients for eight equations predicting evaluations of incumbent and opposition leaders in the four countries. Since the evaluations all are scored from a low of 0 to a high of 10, the partial coefficients represent a unit change on this 0 to 10 scale induced by a unit change in the independent variable.

In Australia, the predominant direct influence on the evaluation of a leader is, as one might expect, partisanship. However, the effect is substantially greater in evaluating Malcolm Fraser (1.7 points on a 10 point scale) than Bill Hayden (only .73 of a point), suggesting that, for the electorate, Fraser represented a stronger partisan figure. Among other significant factors, church attenders and people of Mediterranean birth rank Fraser more highly, the latter reflecting his attempt to capture the ethnic vote in the late 1970s (Lajovic and Theophanous, 1984). Surprisingly, given Fraser's wealth and political conservatism, those with lower incomes are more likely to support him. By contrast, Hayden gains higher evaluations from trade union members (.23 of a point on the 0 to 10 scale) and white collar workers (.18 of a point).

In Britain, partisanship is again the strongest influence, clearly

TABLE 2.

Determinants of Evaluations of Party Leaders (Partial Regression Coefficients)[a]

	Australia		Britain		Canada		United States	
	Fraser	Hayden	Callaghan	Thatcher	Trudeau	Clark	Carter	Reagan
Ascribed characteristics								
Age	.00	.00	.01*	.02**	-.01**	.01**	.00	.01
Gender	.03	.09	.43**	-.18	-.06	.02	.05	.20
Race/ethnicity	.43*	-.03	.59	.19	.36**	-.21*	.46*	-.29
Socioeconomic status								
Education	-.02	-.02	-.01	-.05	-.01	-.01	.01	-.02
Head of household white collar worker	-.08	.18*	-.05	.03	.24*	.02	.05	-.02
Family income	-.09*	-.07	.02	-.04	.03	.02	-.34**	.06
Union member	-.14	.23*	-.04	.19	-.01	-.11	.15	-.15
Religion								
Church attendance	.36**	.09	.37	.17	.12	.26*	.53*	.34*
Partisanship								
Supports left party	-1.7**	.73**	2.4**	-3.7**	1.2**	-.77**	2.1**	-1.8**
Political information								
Talks politics with friends	-.12	-.10	.07	-.36*	-.18	-.21	-.01	.07
Follows politics in media	-.04	.06	.30	-.01	.03	.04	.09	.31
Follows politics in newspapers	.18*	-.04	-.21	.19	.20	.01	-.54*	.07
R-squared	.25	.08	.26	.35	.21	.11	.25	.19
Constant	6.0	5.3	4.7	7.9	4.6	4.7	6.5	5.1

[a]Partial regression coefficients predicting evaluations of party leaders (scored from 0 to 10).

*$p<.05$, **$p<.01$

dominating the evaluations made of both political leaders to the exclusion of almost all other influences. In 1979, Conservative partisans were likely to give Margaret Thatcher an extra 3.7 points, while James Callaghan gained 2.4 points from Labour partisans. The only additional contributions to positive evaluations of Thatcher are derived from older persons and from those who did not discuss politics with their friends. Contrary to a widely held belief, women voters were neither more nor less likely than men to think well of Thatcher, supporting the view that in the 1979 general election "the prospective Prime Minister's sex was not one of the important issues" (Sarlvik and Crewe, 1983:133). As with Thatcher, positive evaluations of Callaghan also were more likely to be made by older persons, indicating that younger voters were not enamored of either party leader. Callaghan gained additional support from men rather than women—almost half a point, other things being equal.

The results for Canada reveal more diverse influences. As in Australia and Britain, party has a strong effect on evaluations of the incumbent leader. Liberal partisans rated Trudeau 1.2 points higher on a 0 to 10 scale than non-Liberals, net of other influences. He also gained support from French-speaking Canadians (just over a third of a point) and from younger electors. For Clark, the challenger, the effect of partisanship is somewhat less (.77 of a point), but still the strongest of a larger set of influences. Older people and church attenders were more likely to positively evaluate him, while French speakers were less enthusiastic (see also Clarke et al. 1979:ch. 7).

In the United States the sources of leader evaluations are the most diverse. For Reagan, the successful presidential challenger, partisanship was again the most important source of positive evaluations, with Republican supporters evaluating Reagan 1.8 points higher than did non-Republicans. Church attenders also were more likely to regard him favorably. The contribution of partisanship to evaluations of Carter is slightly more than that for Reagan (2.1 points). Like Reagan, Carter also attracted support from church attenders and blacks, but, unlike Reagan, gained additional support from low income earners. However, Carter's public image was not particularly favorable among those who followed politics in newspapers—they rated him about half a point less than did other voters.

In summary, the primary source of leadership evaluations in Australia, Britain, Canada, and the United States is undoubtedly partisanship. In Australia, Canada, and the United States, ascribed characteristics (age, ethnicity) and affiliations such as church attendance also play some part, while in Australia and the United States, status characteristics (family income) are of some importance.

Given the increasing emphasis placed upon the political information available to electors during political campaigns, it is perhaps surprising that this factor does not weigh more heavily in determining popular evaluations of party leaders. Whether or not the respondent discusses politics with friends has a significant effect only in Britain, and then only for evaluations of Thatcher. Following politics on the electronic media appears to have no influence on leader evaluations in any of the four countries, and following politics in newspapers (which identifies those seeking detailed political information) has a modest impact in Australia and the United States. Clearly, political information has only a limited net impact on leader evaluations.

The Political Consequences of Evaluating Leaders

The preceding analysis has given a broad outline of how voters perceive political leaders, and the sources of those views. One would expect these views to have important consequences for the general attitudes people hold toward the political system and, ultimately, for their decision on how to vote. For example, the close identification of leaders and their parties with government and the political system means that the strong views of a leader (either positive or negative) will have indirect consequences for evaluations of the political system as a whole. Thus a strong and popular leader could enhance the standing of politics and political activity and improve the popularity of his or her own party; an unpopular leader could produce equally strong deleterious effects.

Attitudes toward the political system involve, in their most basic form, general orientations of persons toward the institutions of authority and basic political laws, but they also involve attitudes toward fundamental social and political issues (see, for example, Almond and Verba, 1963:11–26; 1980:1–27). Two measures are used here: *trust*, the sense of how far people regard the government as honest and trustworthy; and *efficacy*, the sense of to what extent people believe their views are taken into account by government, the civil service, and politicians. In each country, except Britain, these attitudinal components were identified from a factor analysis of a large pool of items. The measures of trust and efficacy were constructed from multiple items and scored on a 0 to 10 scale. In Britain, only one item was available to represent each attitude. Since the scale for each country is composed of different items, the results are not directly comparable across countries. Even so, the measures tap broadly similar attitude structures within the respective electorates.

Most analyses assessing the effects of these variables have examined only recursive (that is, one-way) relationships. However, recent research has shown that estimating nonrecursive (that is, two-way) relationships significantly improves understanding of the processes at work. For example, Page and Jones (1979:1087; see also Jackson, 1975; Markus and Converse, 1979; Weatherford, 1983) show that recursive voting models of U.S. electoral behavior in 1972 and 1976 "fail to reproduce faithfully the underlying complexity of the electoral decision process." The present analysis follows the Page and Jones approach by estimating a nonrecursive model for party identification, evaluations of party leaders, attitudes toward the political system, and their consequences for vote. To do this, two-stage least squares analysis is used—this being the most appropriate technique when a model is over-identified (Asher, 1983:56–72; Hanushek and Jackson, 1977:258–269).

We have already estimated the effect of party identification on how voters evaluate party leaders, i.e., if a person identifies with a particular party, he or she will rate the leader of that party more highly (see Table 2). But it is also highly plausible that the person's perception of a leader will influence his or her party identification, i.e., there is a reciprocal interaction between these two variables. Similarly, one may argue that the evaluation of a leader not only will influence attitudes toward the political system, but also will be influenced by these attitudes. Finally, one may estimate the effect of leader evaluations and political attitudes on the voting decision. The various other variables in the model are exogenous factors that theory and past empirical research suggest are linked to the variables of interest. This yields five equations:

$$\text{EvalLd} = a + b1\text{Party} + b2\text{Trust} + b3\text{Efficacy} + b4\text{Union} + b5\text{Race} + b6\text{Occup} + b7\text{Age}$$

$$\text{Party} = a + b1\text{EvalLd} + b2\text{Union} + b3\text{Race} + b4\text{Occup} + b5\text{Education} + b6\text{Income}$$

$$\text{Trust} = a + b1\text{EvalLd} + b2\text{TalkPols} + b3\text{FolMed} + b4\text{ChAtt}$$

$$\text{Efficacy} = a + b1\text{EvalLd} + b2\text{Age} + b3\text{Education} + b4\text{FolPapers}$$

$$\text{Vote} = a + b1\text{EvalLd} + b2\text{Trust} + b3\text{Efficacy} + b4\text{Union} + b5\text{Occup} + b6\text{Age} + b7\text{ChAtt}$$

The results of this analysis are presented in Figure 1. First, it is evident that there is a mutual interaction between party identification and evaluations of political leaders (measured as the score for the incumbent leader minus the score for his opposition counterpart). *In all four countries, leader evaluations are a considerably stronger influence on party identification than vice versa.* In Australia, Britain, and the United States, party identification is about half as important in determining views of leaders as the latter is in determining party identification. In Canada, party identification has almost no effect in shaping popular views of party leaders.

Second, evaluations of party leaders have an important influence on attitudes toward the political system in general. In Australia and Canada, favorable leader evaluations enhance both trust in the po-

Australia

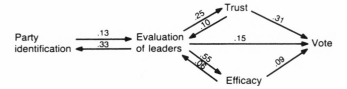

Britain

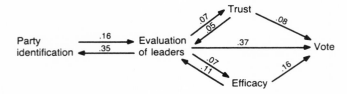

Canada

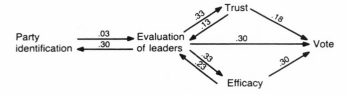

United States

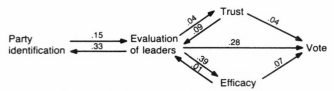

FIGURE 1. Multivariate Nonrecursive Model of Party Identification, Evaluations of Leaders, Attitudes toward the Political System, and Vote, Showing Standardized (2SLS) Regression Coefficients

litical system and feelings of political efficacy; the effect of these attitudes in determining leader evaluations is, however, substantially less. In Britain, trust and efficacy have little effect on leader evaluations or vice versa, though one should note here that the actual items measuring these attitudes are not as reliable as those for the other three countries. In the United States, there is little or no relationship between trust and evaluations of leaders (in either direction), but leader evaluations do have a substantial impact on efficacy.

In terms of the vote, evaluations of party leaders are the most influential effect in Britain and the United States, while attitudes toward the political system are of lesser significance. In Canada, evaluations of leaders are equal in importance of feelings of efficacy, and nearly twice as important as trust. However, in Australia, trust is more than twice as important as leaders, and more than three times as important as efficacy.

Overall, the estimation of the reciprocal paths between these variables indicates that a recursive model greatly understates the complexity of relationships between how voters view party leaders and party identification, vote, and attitudes toward the political system. Specifically, the greater significance of leaders in determining party identification, rather than the reverse, suggests a fundamental revision of voting theories stipulating the exogenous status of partisanship.

Conclusion

Party leaders are key actors on the political stage in modern, democratic societies. With the advent of the electronic media, leaders have become the focus of party competition, and the topic of most news items that deal with parties. During election campaigns in particular, the personality, character, and competence of party leaders become a constant preoccupation of the media. The parties have responded to this trend by making great efforts to present their leader in the most favorable light, by employing mass-marketing consultants to advise not only on the content of the leader's speeches, but on his or her speaking ability, dress, and general demeanor. Together with the use of sophisticated opinion poll techniques, party strategists can gauge in a matter of days, if not hours, how their leader's image is being received by the electorate.

Despite the undoubted importance of party leaders in contemporary democracies, few studies have attempted to disentangle the factors that contribute to the images voters construct of these political figures. This analysis has attempted to shed light on this question by looking at the social structural correlates of leader evaluations and the impact of these evaluations on voting behavior and orientations toward the political system as a whole.

Voters in Australia and Canada see their leaders in predominantly personal terms and, although no comparable recent figures are available for Britain, previous research has shown that this is also the case there (Butler and Stokes, 1976:358–59). The main exception is the United States, where voters are equally likely to mention either issues or personal characteristics when discussing party leaders. At least part of the explanation for this lies in the nature of U.S. politics, notably the separation of powers and the weaker party system, all of which encourage a greater policy emphasis from presidential candidates.

In terms of social structural sources of leader evaluations, ascribed characteristics such as age and ethnicity are important, as are church attendance and trade union membership. Perhaps surprisingly, given the intense media coverage of party leaders, sources of political information were relatively unimportant in determining what evaluations voters made of party leaders: if respondents used television and radio as the major source of political information or discussed politics with their friends, this was not likely to influence their views of particular leaders. There is a modest effect in shaping leader evaluations in Australia and the United States for persons who use newspapers as their major source of political information, but not in Britain or Canada.

The major determinant of evaluations of party leaders has little to do with social structure or political information, but is bound up with the feeling of attachment a voter has to one of the major parties. Since its original formulation (Campbell et al., 1954, 1960), party identification has been a key variable in explanations of the political stability of many Western democracies. It has been argued that an enduring sociopsychological attachment to one party induces diffuse support for the party system, and thereby enhances the legitimacy of the political system itself (Budge, Crewe, and Fairlie, 1976:3). The results presented here indicate that leadership and partisanship are strongly linked—a nonrecursive model suggesting, for every country except Canada, that evaluations of party leaders are the dominant influence on partisanship, rather than the converse.

The relationship between party identification and evaluations of party leaders permits us to draw several inferences about trends in partisanship in Western democracies. First, party identification in Britain and the United States has declined consistently since the early 1960s (e.g., Crewe, Sarlvik, and Alt, 1977:148–49; Nie, Verba, and Petrocik, 1976:47–53). Since it has been shown that leader evaluations are more likely to affect partisanship in these two countries than vice versa, it could be argued that the decline of party identification is a consequence of weakening confidence in British and American political leaders. In Australia, partisanship has remained constant (Aitkin, 1982:287), and there has been no significant diminution of confidence in political leadership. In Canada, party identification has been volatile for many years (Clarke et al., 1979:135ff; LeDuc, 1981), and the declining confidence in political leaders there may exacerbate the situation since leader evaluations have much stronger effects on party identification than vice versa.

Finally, it is apparent that party leaders exert a substantial influence on attitudes toward the political system itself. Specifically, party leaders may encourage (or discourage) trust in politics, as well as a sense of individual efficacy: these in turn may enhance evaluations of leaders. At the same time, party leaders exert a pronounced influence on voting behavior. In all four countries, this influence is direct, while, in Australia and the United States in particular and Canada and Britain to a lesser extent, additional indirect effects on voting are evident through attitudes toward the political system. Undoubtedly, parties and the polity as a whole have much to gain by choosing leaders carefully; their policies, but especially their personal qualities and styles of leadership, are vital components of the political process.

Appendix

Data

The data are taken from four large, nationally representative sample surveys. These are the 1979 Australian Political Attitudes Survey (N=2016), the 1979 British Election Study (N=1893), the 1979 Canadian National Election Study (N=2762), and the 1980 American National Election Study (N=1614). Because some of the items central to the present analysis were not included in the 1980 Canadian survey, we confine our attention to the 1979 election.

The 1979 Australian Political Attitudes Survey was originally collected by Don Aitkin and made available by the Social Science Data Archive at the Australian National University. The 1979 British Election Study was originally collected by Ivor Crewe, Bo Sarlvik, and James Alt and made available by the British SSRC Survey Archive at the University of Essex. The 1979 Canadian Election Study was originally collected by Harold Clarke, Jane Jenson, Lawrence LeDuc, and Jon Pammett. The 1980 U.S. Presidential Election Study was originally collected by Warren E. Miller and associates and made available by the ICPSR at the University of Michigan. Neither the original collectors of these data nor the disseminating agencies bear any responsibility for the analyses or interpretations presented here.

Methods

The analyses are based on ordinary least squares (OLS) and two-stage regression methods (Hanushek and Jackson, 1977) which assume that relations between the variables are, to a reasonable approximation, linear and additive. Although there are reservations about using this technique with a dichotomous dependent variable (as is the case with vote), there are no practical consequences unless the marginals are highly skewed and the sample size is small, which is not the case here (Kmenta, 1971). Missing data were handled by the pairwise deletion procedure, which is statistically preferable to the usual alternatives (Hertel, 1976).

Measurement

The full set of variables used for the analyses and how they were used and their mean scores in each country are available from the authors upon request. All variables are single item measures unless otherwise indicated. For political trust and efficacy, composite scores are used, except in Britain where single items only were available. In Australia, Canada, and the United States, principal components factor analysis with varimax rotation was used to identify suitable scale items (Kim and Mueller, 1978). The items chosen have factor loadings in excess of .50. Scales were constructed by assigning missing data for each component item to the mean, dividing each by its standard deviation and summing them. Scales were adjusted as necessary for sign, and standardized to 0–10 metric to provide comparability between countries and a more intuitive interpretation of the results. As the latter is a linear transformation, it does not alter the underlying results. The single item measures of trust and efficacy used for Britain are not identical to these scales, but are the best measures available.

For Canada, questions on discussing politics and media usage were asked only of a random half sample. A comparison of results for this half sample alone with the results for the sample as a whole, with missing data excluded by the pairwise deletion procedure, revealed broadly similar results. Accordingly, the full sample has been retained for the analyses reported here, even though missing data on these variables are substantial, on the grounds that using a larger sample will yield more reliable results overall.

The measurement of leadership evaluations varies between countries. In Britain, respondents were asked to evaluate politicians by giving them "marks out of ten." In Canada and the United States, "feeling thermometer" assessments were made on a scale of 0 to 100. These ratings were subsequently divided by 10 to provide a metric comparable with the British evaluations. These two different measures provide essentially similar results and interpretations. In Australia, neither of these summary ratings was available, so the evaluation measure for each politician is calculated as the number of likes mentioned minus the number of dislikes (cf. Butler and Stokes, 1974:363–64). This, too, was transformed to a 0–10 metric to provide a broadly comparable measure. In principle, the net result is similar to, though not the same as, the evaluation measures used in Britain, Canada, and the United States.

For Canada and the United States, where it was possible to compare both measures directly, the results obtained were broadly similar, and any differences were essentially of degree rather than kind. The results shown for these two countries use the feeling thermometer rating in preference to mentions of likes and dislikes, as this provides a better net evaluation of leadership.

Notes

1. There is a substantial literature examining the decline of class and party loyalties in the Anglo-American democracies: on Australia, see Aitkin (1982:ch. 21) and Kemp (1978); on Britain, see Kelley, McAllister, and Mughan (1985), Rose (1982), and Sarlvik and Crewe (1983:82–91); on Canada, see Clarke et al. (1979:107–19); and on the United States, see Nie, Verba, and Petrocik (1976).

2. Although New Zealand is traditionally considered to be one of the Anglo-American democracies, the lack of suitable nation-wide survey data has forced its exclusion from this analysis.

3. Although data for the 1980 Canadian election are available, this wave does not update some of the important variables used for the present analysis, so the 1979 survey is used instead.

4. Once again, Canada is a possible exception here, in so far as there are normally more than two parties operating at the federal level. However, as Sartori (1976:188–89) points out, the NDP and Social Credit intervention simply means that either of the two major parties rule as minority governments and "this pattern attests, more than anything else, to the force of the inner, systematic logic of twopartism." In Britain, the first-past-the-post electoral system has always ensured that the frequently substantial Liberal vote (in 1983, the vote for the Liberal-SDP Alliance) fails to be transformed into parliamentary seats (McAllister and Rose, 1984).

5. The 1980 American National Election Study shows, for example, that 95 percent of electors both had heard of Ronald Reagan and felt they knew something about him by the time of the 1980 election. The corresponding figure for the defeated President Carter was only marginally higher at 97 percent.

6. There is, of course, a respondent interaction caused by their ability to conceptualize thermometer scores. In countries where metric systems are used, the idea of rating a leader on a metric scale will be more readily comprehended. In Britain, for example, there is a discernible increase in the *overall* 0 to 10 rating of parties and leaders between 1974 and 1979, which is probably less the result of increasing confidence in these institutions than the increasing use of metric scales in Britain during those years (see McAllister and Graetz, 1986).

7. Although the open-ended question was not asked in the 1979 British Election survey used here, it was asked in the 1964 to 1970 Butler and Stokes surveys. Their findings accord with the results presented here for Australia and Canada: "the vast majority of the positive and negative themes spontaneously associated with the Conservative and Labour leaders were personal rather than ones whose content was supplied by the goals which

the leaders were seen as the instrument for achieving" (Butler and Stokes, 1974:357).

8. However, in the 1974 Canadian federal election, Robert Stanfield, the Progressive Conservative Leader, espoused the particularly divisive issues of wage and price controls.

9. Discussing politics face-to-face with friends and relatives is also strongly associated with political interest—those having higher interest being more likely to engage in such discussions.

References

Aitkin, Don A. (1977; 1982) *Stability and Change in Australian Politics.* Canberra: Australian National University Press.

Alford, Robert R. (1963) *Party and Society.* Chicago: Rand McNally.

—— (1967) "Class Voting in the Anglo-American Political Systems." In *Party Systems and Voter Alignments,* edited by Stein Rokkan and Seymour Martin Lipset. New York: Free Press.

Almond, Gabriel, and Sidney Verba (1963) *The Civic Culture.* Cambridge: Cambridge University Press.

Almond, Gabriel, and Sidney Verba, eds. (1980) *The Civic Culture Revisited.* Boston: Little Brown.

Asher, Herbert B. (1983) *Causal Modelling.* London: Sage Quantitative Applications in the Social Sciences No. 07-003.

Bogart, L. (1968) "Changing News Interest and the News Media." *Public Opinion Quarterly* 32:560–74.

Budge, Ian, Ivor Crewe, and Dennis Fairlie (1976) *Party Identification and Beyond.* New York: Wiley.

Butler, David, and Donald Stokes (1974) *Political Change in Britain.* 2nd ed. London: Macmillan.

Campbell, Angus, Philip Converse, Warren E. Miller, and Donald Stokes (1960) *The American Voter.* New York: Wiley.

Campbell, Angus, Gerald Gurin, and Warren E. Miller. (1954) *The Voter Decides.* Evanston, Ill.: Row, Peterson.

Clarke, Harold D., Jane Jenson, Lawrence LeDuc, and Jon H. Pammett (1979) *Political Choice in Canada.* Toronto: McGraw-Hill Ryerson.

Clarke, P., and L. Ruggels (1970) "Preferences Among News Media for Coverage of Public Affairs." *Journalism Quarterly* 47: 464–71.

Converse, Philip E., and George Dupeux (1966) "DeGaulle and Eisenhower: The Public Image of the Victorious General." In *Elections and the Political Order,* edited by Angus Campbell et al. New York: Wiley.

Crewe, Ivor, Bo Sarlvik, and James Alt (1977) "Partisan Dealignment in Britain, 1964–1974." *British Journal of Political Science* 7:129–90.

DeVries, Walter, and V. Lance Torrance (1972) *The Ticket Splitter.* Grand Rapids, Mich.: Eerdmans.

Franklin, Mark F. (1983) "The Rise of Issue Voting in British Elections." Glasgow: Strathclyde Papers on Government and Politics No. 3.

Graber, Doris A. (1971) "The Press as an Opinion Resource During the 1968 Presidential Election Campaign." *Public Opinion Quarterly* 35:168–82.

—— (1972) "Personal Qualities in Presidential Images: The Contribution of the Press." *Midwest Journal of Political Science* 16:46–76.

Greenstein, Fred I. (1965) *Children and Politics.* New Haven: Yale University Press.

——— (1966) "Popular Images of the President." *American Journal of Psychiatry* 122:523–29.

——— (1975) "The Benevolent Leader Revisited: Children's Images of Political Leaders in Three Democracies." *American Political Science Review* 69:1371–98.

Hanushek, E. A., and John A. Jackson (1977) *Statistical Methods for Social Scientists.* New York: Academic Press.

Hargrove, Erwin C. (1967) "Popular Leadership in the Anglo-American Democracies." In *Political Leadership in Industrialized Societies,* edited by Lewis J. Edinger. New York: Wiley.

Hershey, Majorie Randon, and David B. Hill (1975) "Watergate and Pre-Adult's Attitudes Toward the President." *American Journal of Political Science* 19:703–26.

Hertel, Bradley R. (1976) "Minimizing Error Variance Introduced by Missing Data Routines in Survey Analysis." *Sociological Methods and Research* 4:459–475.

Jackson, John E. (1975) "Issues, Party Choices, and Presidential Voters." *American Journal of Political Science* 19:161–185.

Kelley, Jonathan, Ian McAllister, and Anthony Mughan (1985) "The Decline of Class Revisited: England, 1964–79." *American Political Science Review* 79:400–415.

Kemp, David (1978) *Society and Electoral Behavior in Australia.* Brisbane: Queensland University Press.

Kim, Jae-On, and Charles W. Meuller (1978) *Factor Analysis: Statistical Methods and Practical Issues.* Beverly Hills: Sage Quantitative Applications in the Social Sciences No. 07-014.

Kmenta, Jan (1971) *Elements of Econometrics.* New York: Macmillan.

Lajovic, Misha, and Andrew Theophanous (1984) "The Major Political Parties and Ethnic Affairs." In *Ethnic Politics in Australia,* edited by James Jupp. Sydney: Allen and Unwin.

LeDuc, Lawrence (1981) "The Dynamic Properties of Party Identification: A Four-Nation Comparison." *European Journal of Political Research* 9:257–68.

Markus, Gregory B. (1982) "Political Attitudes During an Election Year: A Report on the 1980 NES Panel Study." *American Political Science Review* 76:538–60.

Markus, Gregory B., and Philip E. Converse (1979) "A Dynamic Simultaneous Equation Model of Electoral Choice." *American Political Science Review* 73:1055–70.

McAllister, Ian, and Brian Graetz (1986) "Party Leaders and Electoral Outcomes in Britain, 1974–79." *Comparative Political Studies* (forthcoming).

McAllister, Ian, and Richard Rose (1984) *The Nationwide Competition for Votes.* London: Frances Pinter.

Neuman, W. Russell (1981) "Differentiation and Integration: Two Dimensions of Political Thinking." *American Journal of Sociology* 86:1236–68.

Nie, Norman H., Sidney Verba, and John R. Petrocik (1976) *The Changing American Voter.* Cambridge, Mass.: Harvard University Press.

Nimmo, Dan, and Robert L. Savage (1976) *Candidates and Their Images.* Pacific Palisades, CA.: Goodyear.

Page, Benjamin I. (1976) "The Theory of Political Ambiguity." *American Political Science Review* 70:742–52.

Page, Benjamin I., and Calvin C. Jones (1979) "Reciprocal Effects of Policy Preferences, Party Loyalties, and the Vote." *American Political Science Review* 73:1071–89.

Repass, David E. (1971) "Issue Salience and Party Choice." *American Political Science Review* 65:389–400.

Rose, Richard (1982) "From Simple Determinism to Interactive Models of Voting: Britain as an Example." *Comparative Political Studies* 15:145–69.

Rusk, Jerrold G., and Herbert F. Weisberg (1972) "Perceptions of Presidential Candidates: Implications for Electoral Change." *Midwest Journal of Political Science* 16:388–410.

Sarlvik, Bo, and Ivor Crewe (1983) *Decade of Dealignment.* Cambridge: Cambridge University Press.

Sartori, Giovanni (1976) *Parties and Party Systems.* Cambridge: Cambridge University Press.

Sigel, Roberta (1968) "Image of the President: Some Insights into the Political Views of School Children." *American Political Science Review* 62:216–26.

Sullivan, John L. (1978) "Ideological Constraint in the Mass Public: A Methodological Critique and Some New Findings." *American Journal of Political Science* 22:233–49.

Weatherford, M. Stephen (1983) "Reciprocal Causation in a Model of the Vote: Replication and Extension." *Political Behavior* 5:191–208.

Weisberg, Herbert F., and Jerrold G. Rusk (1970) "Dimensions of Candidate Evaluation." *American Political Science Review* 64:1167–85.

Constituency Service and Member Independence: An Anglo-American Comparison

Bruce E. Cain

There is growing evidence that representatives from a variety of political systems take their constituency service chores very seriously (Cain, Ferejohn, and Fiorina, 1983, 1984; Clarke, 1978; Clarke and Price, 1980, 1981; Maheshwasi, 1976; Heyden and Leys, 1972). The range of services that modern representatives offer to their constituents is impressive: at various times, they are called upon to act as ombudsmen, lobbyists, personal advisors, arbitrators, and publicists. That this behavior is common in countries with different institutions and political cultures is curious per se, but is it more than this? Does constituency service bear any relation to broader representational issues or to a country's political institutions?

One important strain of the constituency service literature maintains that there is no such relation—that constituency service is largely an expression of personal style (Fenno, 1978). This line of argument is particularly prevalent in the British literature about the constituency activities of MPs (King, 1974). Representatives, according to this view, consciously or unconsciously find ways of "presenting" themselves that are compatible with their personalities and the people they represent. While this "presentation of self" can be strategic, it is also personal—as much as a representative's accent, sense of humor, or mode of dress.

By contrast, there is little in the "constituency service as personal style" thesis that ties representation to political incentives as a whole, suggests whether or why there might be aggregate changes in homestyles over time, or speculates about connections between homestyle and housestyle (i.e., behavior in the legislative body). For the purposes of this essay, that representatives engage in a significant amount of constituency service is taken as established. The relevant question is whether it matters: does it have broader significance for political systems?

The focus of this study is on the activities of British MPs and U.S. Congressmen.[1] This contrast was chosen because it highlights the connections between institutional and behavioral variations. The two systems share common electoral features that should strengthen the incentive to do constituency service—e.g., geographically based single-member districts. At the same time, the functioning of the British parliamentary rules should work to deny individual members the incentive to attempt to establish a personal vote since swings in Britain have been highly nationalized and uniform during the postwar years. Mayhew, for this reason, chose the British system as his foil in *Congress: The Electoral Connection*. Thus, while there is a fundamental similarity in the electoral rules of these two countries, there is a fundamental dissimilarity in the legislative rules (e.g., staff allowances, the ability to claim credit in committees, etc.). The question is how these variations influence the way that MPs and MCs distribute their time and resources. Since the credit-claiming incentives of the American electoral and legislative rules reinforce one another, we should expect higher levels of constituency activity in the United States. In Britain, the institutional incentives are mixed, and this should create some tensions and contradictory expectations.

Some of the effects that will be discussed are easily specified and measured. Others are harder to uncover and more speculative in nature. My point is not to deny that personal style is important, but only to argue that homestyles may be systematically related to electoral outcomes and ultimately to the form of national institutions.

Electoral Mandates and Constituency Service

One potentially important effect that constituency service might have is electoral. The way that members behave can determine, in part, how they are evaluated by voters. Hence, the level of constituency service will be reflected in the degree of personal support individual members receive from the voters in their districts. The key concept is that of personal support. What is it? What value does it have in parliamentary systems like the British? What meaning should be ascribed to variations in the level of personal support across political systems?

Assuming that the various determinants of a voter's decision could be measured, Stokes has argued that the forces affecting the vote can be divided into several components (Stokes, 1967). One would be a national component—i.e., the effect that national forces, issues, and images have on a voter's decision. Thus, whether a representative belongs to a particular party, is a member of the government, or has regularly supported the programs of the president or prime minister can be highly important pieces of information. The degree to which the voter's decision is influenced by such factors determines the size of the vote's national component. A crucial characteristic of the national component is that it cannot be controlled by most members (the exceptions are the most powerful members of Congress or the Cabinet). A member who wishes to tailor his party's or chief executive's positions in order to maximize his electoral chances must build a coalition with other members, many of whom might have different interests. In the language of structural models, the national component is largely exogenous for most members.

The second component is the state (United States) or regional (United States, United Kingdom) one. Examples of regional differences are the pronounced North–South variations in both Britain (Curtice and Steed, 1980) and the United States (Nie, Verba, and Petrocik, 1976). State influences can matter also as Rosenstone (1983) has shown in his study of U.S. national election forecasts. This second component can result from the identification with the state/regional party label, from the impact that national policies have on specific states/regions or from the member's association with state/regional interests. Since the state/regional arena is smaller than the national one, the ability to control electoral forces at this level is somewhat greater. Even so, the management of the state/regional environment in order to maximize a member's electoral chances is still an unwieldy collective action problem, one that will be almost indistinguishable in nature from the national collective action problem when the regions/states are large.

That leaves the local component, or personal vote (Williams, 1967; Crewe, 1979; Cain, 1983; Curtice and Steed, 1980; Fiorina, 1977; Ferejohn, 1977; Cover, 1977). The personal vote is that part of the variance in a member's vote attributable to constituency factors. Clearly, name recognition, the member's reputation, his or her record on issues affecting the district, and the like will be critical at this level if at all. The distinguishing feature of the personal vote is that there is a less considerable collective action problem in attempting to control local reputations than there is in attempting to control the national and state/regional components. While there are collective action problems at the local level—e.g., members have to work with local officials (Cain and Ritchie, 1981) whose cooperation is not assured—it is easier for members to take effective independent action at the local level than it is for them to do so at the state, regional, or national levels. A distinguishing characteristic of the personal vote is that it is the most manageable component of the member's environment. A positive personal vote can serve as a valuable buffer against adverse national electoral tides. Though individual members cannot prevent adverse national electoral tides from occurring, they can at least minimize the impact of national adversity by activities at the local level.

How does one establish a personal vote? One needs to find relatively riskless activities that are valued by voters: *riskless* because members will want to know with some degree of certainty whether their efforts will be positively received, and *valued by voters* because they must offset or reinforce the strength of regional/state forces. Constituency services appear to fit both these criteria. In the era of the large welfare state, the role of ombudsman and district lobbyist is much appreciated by constituents; and constituency services are by and large riskless. The only danger entailed in offering to help people with their problems is the possibility of frustration and negative reaction if the intervention is unsuccessful. However, the majority of the MPs interviewed seemed to feel that unsuccessfully resolved cases did not constitute much of a risk because the member's effort is appreciated even when constituents fail to get what they want.

The goal then is to establish personal support by undertaking riskless but valued local activities. The connection between the final aim (electoral support) and the immediate means (constituency services) is the development of high name recognition, a good reputation for protecting constituent and constituency interests, and, as a consequence, a high personal evaluation among voters. We will not consider these steps in the process in any detail here. Rather, we shall proceed to the bottom line: have Members of Parliament and Congress been successful in establishing a personal vote?

Evidence for this can be found in a two-stage model displayed in Table 1. The first equation establishes the link between constituency activities and member reputations, and the second between member reputations and the vote. Consider the first equation.[2] The dependent variable is the response to the following survey question (sometimes referred to as the "expectation of helpfulness" item): "If you had a problem that Representative (your MP) (name) could do something about, do you think that he/she would be very helpful, somewhat helpful, or not very helpful to you?"

The explanatory variables fall into several categories. The first is the nature of contact the member has had with the constituent—i.e., personal, via the media (such as newspaper, radio, or TV), and by word of mouth ("secondhand contact"). The purpose of these variables is to test the idea that constituents who have been contacted are more likely to evaluate their representatives positively. The second category of variables encompasses direct or indirect knowledge of the members' constituency services. The casework variables include whether constituents were satisfied with the member's efforts on their behalf (i.e., casework) or on the behalf of someone they knew (i.e., secondhand casework). District service measures whether

TABLE 1.

Expectation of Access Equations: United States and Great Britain

	United States (N = 811)	Great Britain (N = 821)
Contact		
Personal	.36**	.56**
Media	.39**	.23**
Secondhand	.24*	− .02
Casework		
Very Satisfied	1.07**	.92**
Somewhat Satisfied	.17**	− .60*
Not Satisfied	−1.22**	−1.39**
Secondhand Casework		
Satisfied	.66**	—
Somewhat Satisfied	.02	.57**
Not Satisfied	− .67*	—
District Service	.38**	.55**
Party Identification		
Independent	.02	—
Minor	—	− .44*
None	—	.24*
Same	.19*	.41**
Recall Incumbent	.16	.05
Recall Challenger	− .05	− .02
Year Elected	− .01*	.01
Constant	1.25**	.14
$\hat{R}^2$	.36	.29

*p < .05

**p < .01

the respondent could recall anything the representative had done for the district as a whole. The remaining variables control for factors that one might expect to be related to the member's reputation for helpfulness: controls for partisan bias, the level of the incumbent's name recognition and the member's seniority (since reputations may follow a cumulative pattern).

The second equation then relates the member's expectation for helpfulness to the vote, controlling for other variables. The latter includes party identification once again, the rating of the president/prime minister, name recall (suggesting that name recall might have an effect on the vote over and beyond its influence on the expectation of helpfulness) and a challenger contact item (for the United States only). In essence then, the second equation measures the relative effect of national (i.e., party and executive ratings) as opposed to local (i.e., expectation of helpfulness) forces on the constituent's vote.

TABLE 2.

Incumbent Vote Equations, United States and Great Britain

	United States (N = 644)	Great Britain (N = 1,111)
Incumbent Name Recall	.44**	.46**
Challenger Name Recall	− .77**	− .35**
Challenger Contact	− .57**	—
Expectation of Helpfulness		
Very	1.76**	.35*
Somewhat	.82**	.07
Don't Know	.43*	− .22
Depends	—	− .02
Party Identification		
Independent	.57**	—
None	—	.99**
Other	—	.99**
Same	1.19**	2.43**
Executive Job Rating		
Out-Party Incumbent		
Approve	.23	.01
Fair/DK	− .47	.34*
Disapprove	− .29	.50*
In-Party Incumbent		
Fair/DK	− .76	− .20
Disapprove	− .13	− .60**
Constant	− .71**	−1.65**
$\hat{R}^2$	.51	.64
Correctly Predicted	80%	86%

*p < .05
**p < .01

The estimations in Table 1 show that contacts, casework, and district service are indeed statistically related to the member's reputation for helpfulness, which is in turn associated with the vote. This statement applies to Great Britain as well as the United States. Indeed, the coefficients for personal contact and recollection of district service suggest that the effects of these variables are greater in Britain than in America.[3] Partisan biases do matter, as one might suspect: people are more likely to think the incumbent helpful when he or she belongs to their party. This is true in both countries, as is the corollary that independents and minor party identifiers are less likely to think the incumbent helpful.

The first equation demonstrates that what representatives do affects their constituency service reputations. The second equation shows that their constituency service reputations affect the vote. Incumbents who are thought to be very helpful with constituent problems have a higher probability of receiving a constituent's vote. High name visibility also contributes to the incumbent's vote in both countries, but the rating of the president's performance does not in the United States. So, in this sense, the effect of the national component does appear to be greater in Great Britain than the United States.

What does this all mean: in what sense does the electoral impact of constituency service matter? I maintain that the development of the personal vote weakens the national mandate of elections and causes a separation of individual and collective responsibility. Both of these effects are more evident in the United States where the personal vote is larger than in the United Kingdom. The dampening of the president's coattails in Congressional elections is one manifestation, one that was very much evident in Reagan's 1984 election. The consequence is that presidents have less control over the legislature and more difficulty turning their personal mandate into implementable programs.

Another, perhaps even more important, manifestation is Fenno's puzzle: that voters can like their individual representatives but dislike their legislatures. This can occur when representatives run against the legislature (i.e., disavowing responsibility for the consequences for the action of the legislature as a whole) while acting as parochial representatives in the legislature (voting for local interests without regard for the collective consequences). The United States is the best example of this. The decentralized committee structure of the House of Representatives seems to give freer rein to parochial representation (pork barreling and the like) than does the House of Commons.

Still, there are nascent indications in Britain that electoral independence and policy independence may be correlated. Dissent from the party whip in the House of Commons has been increasing over the past fifteen years, precisely the same period of time that casework demands have also increased (Norton, 1980; Schwartz, 1980). This suggests that the two trends may be related. A way to test this proposition cross-sectionally is to correlate an index of constituency activity with the propensity to dissent from the party whip. This can be done for votes in the 1974–79 period using the sample of MPs from the CFF study.[4] The result is a strong (and statistically significant) correlation (i.e., .50) between the level of a Labour MP's constituency service activities and his/her propensity to dissent from the party whip, but not for Conservative MPs.

A closer inspection of the data suggests some reasons for the asymmetry of the pattern: namely, that the Labour MPs were part of a governing party that was putting forward unpopular economic (spending cuts, EEC) and political (devolution) programs while the Conservative front bench, as leaders of the opposition party, were abstaining from critical votes and allowing members to vote as they pleased. In addition, members of the governing party have more need for policy independence since, as the voting literature and common sense suggest, voters are more inclined to blame the governing party for unfavorable conditions than the opposition, however irresponsible the latter's statements may be (Bloom and Price, 1975).

Thus, the separation of legislative and national executive mandates is much further along in the United States than the United Kingdom, but there are nonetheless signs that local considerations influence the voting choices of British voters (Table 1), and that the policy and constituency activities of MPs are correlated. Is this a temporary phenomenon in Britain, or will the trend toward separation of mandates increase to more significant levels? This is, of course, impossible to predict with certainty, but there are a couple of reasons to think that it will increase.

To begin with, recent changes in the procedure for nominating Labour candidates will likely increase the importance of local considerations. Most importantly, the end of automatic selection has made the preferences of party activists more crucial than ever. Apart from their much publicized ideological extremity, party activists tend to place a high premium on local considerations in the selection process. This is evident in the various studies on parliamentary candidate selection and in the testimony of members themselves (Rush, 1969; Ranney, 1965). In one case study, a local Conservative party actually dropped a candidate it initially selected in favor of another because it felt a "local" man was necessary to defeat the incumbent (Cain and Ritchie, 1982).

The other reason to suspect that the personal vote in Britain might continue to increase in importance is that there seems to be a natural unraveling tendency to these processes. The electoral rules create a strong incentive to establish a personal vote. Various parliamentary institutions conspire to minimize the personal vote—e.g., interpreting defeat on a critical vote as a motion of no confidence. As these institutions weaken, MPs have more opportunities to distinguish themselves from the national party. As the voters respond more to the individualistic appeals of their members, the members will demand more resources and opportunities to distinguish themselves. This was certainly the pattern followed by the U.S. Congress since the early sixties, and it provides a plausible explanation for the observation that British backbenchers have in recent years aggressively demanded greater resources (e.g., larger staff), more committee powers, and greater freedom on votes in the House. Thus, while the effect of the personal vote is more pronounced in the United States, its emergence as an important factor in future British elections should not be lightly dismissed.

The Process of the Personal Vote

The existence of the personal vote has important implications, as we have seen. At the same time, the quest for a personal vote per se can have significant consequences. In particular, it can cause members to shift the balance of their activities toward those that create local visibility and reputation. In this way, the personal vote can play a determining role in what members do with their time and resources and in fashioning the type of representation that Britain and American constituents receive. These changes can occur without anyone— voters or members—really controlling or understanding them. We will examine this argument in discrete steps: How much time and resources are consumed in the quest for the personal vote? Is this aspect of the Anglo-American representative's job increasing or not? Is the quest for the personal vote causing this change, if it exists? How can we characterize the process by which these changes are occurring?

Up to this point, we have treated the statement that members of Parliament and Congress devote much effort and resources to constituency service as an established fact. While this is not the appropriate forum for an extensive description of member activities, it would be useful to highlight some of the more significant findings. Any comparison of American Congressmen and British MPs must begin with the contrast between the bureaucratic approach of the former and the more personal orientation of the latter. In the United States, the representation that constituents receive from their Congressmen consists of the total bundle of services provided by the Congressional office. Therefore, in asking the question How has Congressional representation changed as a result of the quest for the personal vote?, the U.S. focus must be on the size and nature of staff activities.

When the question is looked at in this way, it is immediately evident that there has been a dramatic growth in staff generally and district staff in particular. The allowance for Congressional staff has increased from 8 in 1959 to 18 in 1975: the number of staff actually employed on the clerk hire during this period rose from a mean of 5.3 to 13.9. This trend has been fairly steady since an initial takeoff in 1963. District staff have grown even more rapidly. The average number of district staff was less than .8 in 1959, but had risen to 5.5 by 1979.

How many of these staff are involved in constituency matters? The CFF sample found that Congressmen kept an average of between four and five full-time caseworkers—i.e., staff who worked exclusively on constituency service problems (Cain, Ferejohn, and Fiorina, forthcoming). While most Congressmen place their caseworkers in their district offices, Washington staff are also involved in casework in various ways. In about a quarter of the sample, the Washington office directly supervises district office activities. In most cases, there is much coordination between the district and Washington offices, especially when the cases or projects involve Federal agencies. The distribution of casework chores varies across the Washington and district offices widely, but not randomly. Washington staff more frequently handle written requests, while district staff more often get requests by phone or personal visit.

As measured by resources, the Congressman's commitment to constituency activities is large: as measured by commitment of time, it is far less so. Only 9 percent of the CFF sample of Congressional offices indicated that their Congressmen spent more than 10 percent of his/her personal time on constituency services per se. If time devoted to district meetings, effort spent on bills affecting the district, and other related activities could also be accurately measured, the total time committed to constituency matters would no doubt be even greater. This, however, does not detract from the central point that staff commitment lies at the heart of constituency activity in the United States.

By comparison, the personal time devoted by the MP is the crucial consideration in Great Britain. Thirty-seven percent of the MPs said that they spent between 50 and 60 percent of their time on constituency service, and another 10 percent gave no specific estimate but said "most" or "a good deal" of their time. Only 5 percent of those sampled said that they spent 10 percent or less of their time on constituent affairs. Most MPs have a part-time secretary to help them with their casework, although many only use their secretaries to handle their correspondence and phone calls, reserving the actual negotiations with local officials for themselves. When asked about the amount of autonomy their secretaries had in dealing with cases, about half of the MPs stated that they directly supervised each case themselves and that their secretaries had no autonomy in such matters.

Aside from secretarial support, members can also be assisted by the party agent, if their constituency is fortunate enough to have one. Although the agent's primary tasks are to maintain the local party organization and assist in the conduct of the campaign, some also take on the responsibility of screening cases for their MP during the week and arranging appointments for the weekend surgeries (i.e., the designated time when members meet with their constituents to talk about their problems). However, the extent of the agent's personal involvement depends on the nature of his relationship with the MP, since it is not a formal duty. Only half of the agents surveyed said they had any casework responsibility.

Having established that casework can be costly, the question is whether casework demands have increased over time. This is difficult to answer since there are only a few previous studies on the subject to draw upon, and there is little uniformity in the wording or intent of the questions posed then and in the CFF study. Still, interviews with MPs who had served in Parliament for many years suggested that the constituency demands placed upon members had increased over the years. One retiring MP stated that the expansion of the welfare state "had increased the number of areas where intervention by the MP was necessary." At the same time, he told us that the present surge in constituency activities was induced "in great part by electoral considerations."

Are there any signs of this surge aside from the informal testimony of members? One piece of evidence is a comparison of the frequency of surgeries over time. R. E. Dowse's 1963 study of surgery frequency can be compared with the relevant CFF numbers. The reader should bear in mind, however, that any comparisons must be tempered by some sensitivity to the differences in the sampling design of the two studies. The CFF data come from personally administered questionnaires of members whose districts were sampled in the Gallup poll of voters surveyed immediately following the 1979 election. The Dowse data come from a mail-back survey. As Dowse acknowledges, it is quite possible that there is some selection bias in the 1963 response rate—in particular, one cannot rule out the possibility that Members who were most enthusiastic about constituency work were more inclined to report their activities. If this were so, then the 1963 data would overestimate the frequency of surgeries conducted by all Members. This caveat, however, only supports the trend of the data further, i.e., that the frequency of surgeries has increased between 1963 and 1979. In 1963, 37 percent reported that they either held no surgeries whatsoever or that they only held them on an ad hoc basis. By 1979, that number had dropped to 7 percent, and the number who held surgeries at least twice per week had increased from 32 to 58 percent.

There are other strands of evidence that suggest an increasing commitment of time to constituency matters. For instance, Barker and Rush, in their 1967 study on MPs and their sources of information, asked about the hours members spent per day reading constituency mail. We asked members to do the same. The result was that whereas 15 percent of the members surveyed by Barker and Rush spent less than one hour per day on their mail, only 2 percent were found to do so in 1979; and there was a 15 percent increase in those who spent between one and two hours per day in 1979.

Apparently, then, the commitment to constituency matters in both Great Britain and the United States is not only substantial, but has increased over time. But, has this shift been fueled by the quest for the personal vote? Certainly, the CFF study found a lot of informal testimony that confirmed that it had (Cain, Ferejohn, and Fiorina, forthcoming). We typically heard such comments on both sides of the Atlantic as "Oh, I would have thought so. I only suffered a 3.1 percent swing against a regional swing of 8 percent"; or "My God, that's why we're here. We're the only office on the Hill with twenty-four-hour turnaround. [The opponent] was defeated because of a six-month turnaround"; or "People don't know about legislative performance, but they do know if the sewers work."

While the personal testimony of members is illuminating, it is legitimate to wonder whether there is more systematic evidence on this point. The electoral incentive can take several forms, but one that is obvious is that members in marginal seats should feel a stronger need to establish a personal vote and should therefore work harder at constituency service. A test of whether the electoral incentive is at work is to see if there is any relation between the marginality of the member's seat and the level of constituency effort. Table 3 presents the results of such a test.

The dependent variable is an additive index of constituency activities undertaken by the incumbent. Those included in the U.S. measure are whether the Congressman's office solicits cases from constituents, whether it publicizes successful cases, whether it handles state or local cases, and whether it has a large number of caseworkers (defined as being in the top third of the distribution). The British index consists of whether the member solicits additional casework from his constituents, whether he publicizes successful cases, whether he handles local cases, and whether he holds surgeries more frequently than twice per week. The explanatory variables are previous margin (i.e., the electoral incentive), party (coded 1 if Labour/Democrat), and the year the member was elected (last two digits). If the electoral incentive matters, then the sign of the coefficient on marginality should be negative (i.e., the smaller the margin the higher the level of effort) and statistically significant. As the table clearly shows, this is precisely the result obtained, suggesting that the level of constituency effort is in fact related to the safety of the member's seat in both countries.

While it is important to realize that the electoral impact of constituency service is greatest among those in marginal seats, it would be a mistake to think that the electoral impact is limited to those who need the votes the most. Electoral considerations have much broader and subtler effects. British and American constituents have very high expectations of constituency service.

In response to the question Which of these activities of the mC/MP is the most important?, the American respondents ranked these activities in the following order: keeping in touch (30 percent), policymaking (19 percent), protecting the district (15 percent), oversight (15 percent), and helping people (11 percent). The British respondents ranked them in this order: protecting the district (26 percent), keeping in touch (24 percent), helping people (19 percent), and policy (11

TABLE 3.

A Model of Constituency Effort in Great Britain and the United States

	United States	Great Britain
Previous Margin	$-.022^*$	$-.023^*$
	(.088)	(.009)
Party	.350	$.410^*$
	(.240)	(.225)
Year Elected	$.036^*$	$.023^*$
	(.017)	(.010)
Constant	.465	.181
X^2	15	17
R^2	.16	.15
N	102	101

Procedure: Probit

$^*p < .05$

percent). In other words, policy-making was not considered the most important activity of representatives in either country. Rather, constituency-related functions—keeping in touch (United States) and protecting the district (United Kingdom)—ranked first. This is particularly surprising in the United Kingdom since the power of the backbencher to protect local interests is severely circumscribed by civil service traditions and the absence of powerful oversight committees. At the same time, this result corresponds with the personal testimony of the members themselves who mentioned many specific things they had done for their districts such as leading a campaign to prevent the closing of a hospital, urging the government to have a road constructed, helping raise funds for the local football team, and organizing a job fair in areas of high unemployment.

How did these expectations get formed? Members are certainly not formally required by law in either country to do casework, protect the district, and maintain close contacts with constituents. Our conversations in Britain were particularly illuminating on this question. There appear to be several routes by which expectations of constituency service have grown. One of these can be termed the *demonstration effect.* Several of those interviewed suggested that they had been pressured into a higher level of constituency service by the actions of neighboring members. Consider the following example. An enterprising member seeks to secure his electoral base upon election by undertaking a high level of constituency service in a region of the country/state where there had been little such activity before. Constituents from neighboring districts hear about the services being offered by this member and bring their cases/complaints to him. If their cases are resolved successfully, they come to appreciate the service more and wonder why their representative does not offer the same service. This shift in expectations is articulated to the neighboring members by party activists or by constituents. The desire to please these activists and constituents forces the surrounding members to copy the behavior of their enterprising neighbor.

A second way that expectations about constituency service grow out of the electoral incentive is from the threat of competitors for the local party's nomination. This was a major factor in the retirement decision of one of the members we interviewed. He had noticed "increasing pressure in the rural constituencies like my own from ambitious young officials in the farmer's unions and the like for seats in Parliament." This caused "an excessive local orientation on the part of the new members." "In the later years," he complained, "these pressures were getting unpleasant." He speculated that the demise of automatic selection would exacerbate these pressures. The incumbent is thus constrained by the behavior of local politicians and political aspirants. If local city/state legislators in the United States or local councillors in Great Britain maintain active casework and district operations, then they pose a serious potential nomination challenge. In the days before automatic selection in Britain, this took the form of pressure by local party members upon the MP not to run again. In the United States, it can mean that the incumbent receives a primary challenger who is able to raise money and get credible endorsements.

A third example of how the electoral incentive can form general constituent expectations can be termed *the legacy effect*. An enterprising Member who works hard to establish himself in the district raises constituent expectations, and this becomes the baseline for judging potential successors. The successor must at the very least match those expectations to get the nomination or to maintain local support: if he or she hopes to gain even higher support, this will cause a further escalation in the level of constituency service. A given level of work at an early point might be sufficient to win a good constituency service reputation. However, as more representatives (and their competitors) also adopt that level of service, it becomes necessary to undertake an even higher level of constituency activity to win the same reputation. This causes a ratchet effect for vote-winning nonpartisan activities, escalating the level of constituency activity over time.

An important aspect of this escalation is that members can feel as though they have no choice over how to allocate their time. They may believe that they have to act in this way just to meet expectations or to establish themselves, and that to do otherwise would be political suicide. This can be called the negative electoral incentive:

i.e., the votes or support members can lose by not meeting expectations that have been built up over time. In a sense, this problem resembles a prisoner's dilemma. Each representative might prefer to see constituency expectations lowered so that they can devote more time to other, more glamorous responsibilities. But if any one member does not match the expectations that have been created by the actions of other members, then that member faces the prospect of losing support as a result of invidious comparisons. The safest strategy is to at least meet average expectations.

How a member spends his/her time or resources is therefore not an isolated individual decision over which the member has total control. What others do affects the expectations of each member's constituents, and all must meet those expectations or suffer the consequences. If those in the marginal seats set the pace, it can have general implications for the behavior of all members. A good example of this is the way the original grassroots strategy of the Liberal party in the 1960s forced Conservative and Labour members to alter their strategies and to emphasize local issues and constituency service more (Kavanagh, 1970; King, 1974). In this view, it is a mistake to think that only marginal members are affected by the electoral incentive or that role expectations are totally divorced from electoral considerations.

Conclusion

There is a strong incentive for representatives in Anglo-American democracies to create a buffer for themselves against adverse electoral tides. This leads them to try to establish a personal vote based on nonpartisan, noncontroversial activities such as casework and district service. If this strategy is successful, then it can produce a discrepancy between national and local results. The national vote might swing heavily against a given party, but the party's individual representatives will be unaffected by these changes if voters base their decisions on local considerations. I have shown that the national swing in the 1979 British election was influenced by the personal vote (Cain, 1984). To be sure, the national swing in Britain has become nonuniform in many other ways, but the personal vote has contributed to the variation (Curtice and Steed, 1980).

The evolution of member electoral independence can affect policy-making. Those who win on the basis of their local efforts will be less inclined to follow the national party leadership, leading to less cooperation between the President and Congress (United States) or to higher incidences of cross-voting (United Kingdom). It can also affect the manner of interest-group bargaining in a political system. When members have a high degree of electoral independence, then interest groups will have many points of entry into the legislative arena. Members will want to take up the causes of various interests because they can be rewarded for it. At the same time, since members have the electoral base to act independently, interest groups will be more inclined to think that it is worthwhile to lobby individual members. In this way, the structure of interest-group bargaining (i.e., centralized or decentralized) is associated with the degree of member independence.

In addition to policy-making effects, the process of trying to win a personal vote can have important consequences for the role of the member. The electoral incentive is strongest for those who represent marginal districts, but it is by no means restricted to them. Most importantly, the activities undertaken by marginal members can become the baseline by which others are evaluated. The positive electoral incentive (i.e., the desire to win over new supporters) for one group of members can become the negative electoral incentive (i.e., the desire to avoid losing supporters) for another. Constituency service expectations in both Great Britain and the United States are very high. In both countries, members in marginal seats who wanted to establish themselves and third party candidates (i.e., the Liberals) who wanted to challenge major party candidates developed the initial casework strategy. As they became successful, it affected the demand for these services in neighboring areas. In order to satisfy selection committees and key supporters/activists, it became necessary to match the high levels of constituency service the marginal members had introduced. Thus, the job of the Anglo-American representative has been changed by the escalation of constituency expectations.

The incremental, unplanned manner in which the role of the Anglo-American representative has been defined raises broad questions for democratic theory. Is it desirable that representatives should allocate as much time and resources to constituency affairs as they do? The nature of the member's role certainly affects the type and quality of individuals who run for the legislature. It also affects the public's evaluations of the legislature, and ultimately support for the government as a whole (Mezey, 1979; Clarke, Kornberg, and Stewart, 1984). One can only marvel at the irony of systems that carefully circumscribe the actions of bureaucrats, but leave those of elected officials to self-interest and chance. This may be desirable, but political scientists interested in the question of institutional design might want to consider whether the role of the Anglo-American member has evolved in the best direction.

Notes

1. This study is a cross-sectional analysis of both mass voting and MP/MC behavior in the United States and Great Britain. In each country, we

attempted to procure an elite interview for each constituency in the sampling frame of the mass survey. In the United States, we completed interviews for 102 of 108 districts in the 1978 CPS Congressional election survey sample. One target was the congressional administrative assistant who, our preliminary research suggested, would be the best source of information on office organization and activities. In Great Britain, we completed interviews with MPs or party agents or both for the 133 constituencies included in the 1979 Gallup postelection survey sample. When reporting the data, of course, we include only one interview for each of the 101 constituencies in the sampling frame, or in some cases, only for the 69 constituencies in which we interviewed the incumbent MP. The questions we wrote into the Gallup postelection survey were designed to duplicate, or at least parallel, those in the 1978 CPS Congressional study.

2. All equations discussed in this paper are estimated by a probit procedure. The reason for this is that the dependent variables are in all instances discrete; therefore analysis by normal OLS procedures will lead to inconsistent estimates of the coefficients. A readable discussion of this can be found in *Statistical Methods for Social Sciences* by Hanushek and Jackson (1977).

3. Since these are not standard linear OLS models, the effects themselves are not linear. Hence, a simple comparison of the magnitudes of the coefficients does not provide an accurate interpretation of the relative effect of the variables. Rather, we must stick to hypothesis testing about the significance of relationships, or simulate the marginal effects of a variable by assuming values of the other ones.

4. There is good reason to expect that the pressures of the whip will vary according to whether a party is in office or opposition. For this reason, it made sense to divide the sample by party and examine the relationships in this manner.

References

Baker, A., and M. Rush (1970) *The Member of Parliament and His Information.* London: Allen and Unwin.

Bloom, H. S., and H. D. Price (1975) "Voter Response to Short-Run Economic Conditions: The Asymmetric Effect of Prosperity and Recession." *American Political Science Review* 69:1240–54.

Cain, Bruce E. (1980) "Blessed Be the Tie That Unbinds: Constituency Work and the Vote Swing in Great Britain." *Political Studies* 31:103–11.

Cain, Bruce E., John Ferejohn, and Morris Fiorina (1983) "The Constituency Component: A Comparison of Service in Great Britain and The United States." *Comparative Political Studies* 16:67–91.

—— (1984) "The Constituency Service Basis of The Personal Vote For U.S. Representatives and British MPs." *American Political Science Review* 78:110–25.

—— (1986) *A House Is Not A Home.* Forthcoming.

Cain, Bruce E., and David Ritchie (1982) "Assessing Constituency Involvement: The Hemel Hempstead Experience." *Parliamentary Affairs* 1:73–83.

Clarke, Harold D. (1978) "Determinants of Provincial Constituency Service

Behavior: A Multivariate Analysis." *Legislative Studies Quarterly* 3:601–28.

Clarke, Harold D., Allan Kornberg, and Marianne C. Stewart (1984) "Parliament and Political Support in Canada." *American Political Science Review* 78:452–69.

Clarke, Harold D., and Richard G. Price (1980) "Freshman MP's Job Images: The Effects of Incumbency, Ambition and Position." *Canadian Journal of Political Science* 13:583–606.

—— (1981) "Parliamentary Experience and Representational Role Orientations in Canada." *Legislative Studies Quarterly* 6:374–89.

Cover, A. D. (1977) "One Good Term Deserves Another: The Advantage of Incumbency in Congressional Elections." *American Political Science Review* 71:523–542.

Crewe, Ivor (1979) "The Voting Surveyed." In *Times Guide To The House of Commons*. London: Time Books Limited.

Curtice, John, and Michael Steed (1980) "Appendix 2: An Analysis of The Voting." In *The British General Election of 1979*, edited by D. Butler and D. Kavanagh. London: Macmillan.

Dowse, Robert E. (1963) "The MP and His Surgery." *Political Studies* 2:333–41.

Fenno, Richard (1978) *Home Style: House Members in Their Districts*. Boston: Little, Brown.

Ferejohn, John A. (1977) "On The Decline of Competition in Congressional Elections." *American Political Science Review* 71:166–76.

Fiorina, Morris P. (1977) *Congress—Keystone of The Washington Establishment*. New Haven, Conn.: Yale University Press.

Hanushek, Eric, and John Jackson (1977) *Statistical Methods for Social Scientists*. New York: Academic Press.

Heyden, G., and C. Leys (1972) "Elections and Politics in a Single Party System: The Case of Kenya and Tanzania." *British Journal of Political Science* 2:389–420.

Kavanagh, Dennis (1970) *Constituency Electioneering in Britain*. London: Longmans.

King, Anthony (1974) *British Members of Parliament: A Self-Portrait*. London: Macmillan.

Maheshwasi, S. R. (1976) "Constituency Linkage of National Legislators in India." *Legislative Studies Quarterly* 1:331–54.

Mezey, Michael (1979) *Comparative Legislatures*. Durham, N.C.: Duke University Press.

Nie, N., S. Verba, and J. R. Petrocik (1976) *The Changing American Voter*. Cambridge: Harvard University Press.

Norton, Philip (1980) "The Changing Face of The British House of Commons in the 1970s." *Legislative Studies Quarterly* 5:333–58.

Ranney, Austin (1965) *Pathways to Parliament: Candidate Selection in Britain*. Madison: University of Wisconsin.

Rosenstone, Steven J. (1983) *Forecasting Presidential Elections*. New Haven: Yale University Press.

Rush, Michael (1969) *The Selection of Parliamentary Candidates*. London: Nelson.

Schwartz, John E. (1980) "Exploring a New Role in Policy Making: The

British House of Commons in the 1970's." *American Political Science Review* 74:23–37.

Stokes, Donald (1967) "Parties and the Nationalization of Electoral Forces." In *The American Party Systems*, edited by W. N. Chambers and W. D. Burnham. New York: Oxford University Press.

Williams, P. M. (1966–67) "The M. P.'s Personal Vote." *Parliamentary Affairs*, 24–30.

Policy Makers and Facilitators: The Boundaries Between Two Bureaucratic Roles

Colin Campbell, S.J. and Donald Naulls

The boundary between legislators and bureaucrats is not clearly drawn. In parliamentary systems, many legislators are involved in administration as departmental ministers. Virtually all legislators spend some time as caseworkers for constituents. Public servants are involved in development and implementation of legislation as drafters of policies and bills, and as aides to members of Cabinet. Legislators frequently use officials to further their plans and priorities; public servants often depend on legislators for escalated and brilliant careers. They are both engaged in the business of government, and, in this sense, their paths must cross—even double-cross.

The emergence of complex bureaucratic systems in this century sparked concerns about the power of officials in relation to legislators. Early commentators held that bureaucracy was becoming the main source of policy initiatives (e.g., Galloway, 1946:150). Some dwelt at length on whether senior civil servants' independence in the policy process posed a menace to constitutionalism (e.g., Long, 1952:810). Such analyses posited a gradual process whereby the supremacy of legislatures has eroded in the face of relentless politicization of bureaucracy.

Much of the influence of senior civil servants derives from their ability to achieve autonomy through the exercise of a largely unequalled command of information. Legislation increasingly requires technical knowledge. Civil servants' access to and control over the flow of information contributes greatly to their ability to influence the views of other participants in the policy arena. However, the erosion of and, in some cases, the destruction of legislative supremacy by bureaucracy stems from more than the technical expertise of officials. Two other factors—political culture and structure—exacerbate concern over the power position of bureaucrats vis-a-vis legislators (Brodie and Macnaughton, 1980:243).

Findings about the effects of political culture emerge from recent research indicating an underlying value consensus among legislators and civil servants (Aberbach and Rockman, 1977:43; Sigelman and Vanderbok, 1977:616–23). Such results do much to lay to rest the optimistic arguments of observers who held that large bureaucracies were more representative of the general population than legislatures and, therefore, more responsive to the will of the general public (e.g., Long, 1952:810). As Presthus (1974:57) notes, while conflicts between legislators and administrators frequently arise, they often occur on a narrow range of secondary issues rather than on questions concerning fundamental goals. Dye and Ziegler (1975: 4) take the same view: "[E]litism implies that competition takes place within a very narrow range of issues and that elites agree on more matters than they disagree on. Disagreement usually occurs over means rather than ends."

Even if bureaucrats brought backgrounds and attitudes to their careers that are notably different from those of legislators, structural factors influencing executive-bureaucratic politics in contemporary polities tend to make top officials adept at obtaining and exerting power. Also, such officials tend to adopt views that correspond with those of the institutional structures within which they work regardless of their backgrounds (Brodie and Macnaughton, 1980:244).

Students of such structural factors take two views of how they actually work (Campbell and Clarke, 1980:308–11; Peters, 1978: 137–38). A sort of textbook orthodoxy has officials relying on *objective* accountability to the legal, or formal, locus of authority. Here public servants take a passive approach to the determination of the public interest. They keep uppermost in their minds accountability to those who possess constitutional authority to govern, that is, members of Cabinet. When making and recommending decisions, officials maintaining objective accountability anticipate and reflect the desires of their political and public-service superiors. They do not seek the views of other actors in the policy arena unless fulfilling explicit directions to do so. They prefer that their superiors resolve value dilemmas and ascertain the broad contours of the public interest.

Bureaucratic power revisionism, on the other hand, provides a striking contrast to textbook orthodoxy. The revisionist view holds that all officials exercise at least some *subjective* accountability. To a degree, they act as independent agents who decide courses of action after considering diverse prescriptions as indicated by personal conscience, individual and societal values, career goals, pressures from clients, democratic sensibilities, preservation of bureaucratic programs, units and communities of interest, and responsibilities toward political authorities in legislative and executive posts.

We adopt in this paper the bureaucratic power revisionism perspective. In doing so, we add two caveats. First, the norms of a system might seriously inhibit or obscure officials' actual subjective accountability. The popular British television series "Yes Minister" derives from this point. It satirizes the incongruity of Whitehall's continued obeisance to ministers coupled with its officials' exceptional cunning at the art of getting what they want from their "political masters." Second, that subjective accountability enables officials to weigh conflicting prescriptions does not suggest that they will see the merits of each in the same light. With respect to our present topic, public servants can take very different views of both the legitimacy and value of policy-making roles.

We will focus our attention on officials who work in governmental organizations permitting involvement in the highest levels of policy decisions. These institutions (called central agencies) assume functions within the bureaucratic community that transcend narrow departmental lines and involve special reporting relations to chief executives and/or cabinets and their committees (Campbell and Szablowski, 1979:2). Broadly speaking, the responsibilities of central agencies fall into three major categories: mapping administration/ government strategies and assuring that key substantive positions and initiatives taken by operational departments adhere to them; developing and integrating economic and fiscal policies; and allocating and managing physical and human resources. Central agents thus provide a pool of officials both schooled in and experienced with the highest levels of executive-bureaucratic gamesmanship.

Data available through the central agency project[1] enable us to examine senior central agents' views of their involvement in policy decisions in three countries: the United States, the United Kingdom, and Canada. We chose these countries because of their relatively similar politico-cultural and institutional legacies. As well, all three nations have developed exceptionally advanced central-agency systems. In the United States, interviews were conducted with 132 senior officials in the White House Office and the Executive Office of the President—including an especially large complement in the Office of Management and Budget, the Department of the Treasury, and the Office of Personnel Management. In the United Kingdom, the project involved forty-one respondents from No. 10 Downing St., the Cabinet Office, the Central Policy Review Staff, HM Treasury, and the Civil Service Department; in Canada, it included ninety-two public servants in the Prime Minister's Office, the Privy Council Office, the Federal-Provincial Relations Office, the Department of Finance, the Treasury Board Secretariat, and the Office of the Comptroller General.

As the interviews were conducted in Canada in 1976, in the United Kingdom in 1978, and in the United States in 1979, readers will want to keep in mind that some structural changes have altered central agencies in each country. Most important here is the addition of two new coordinative departments in Canada—the ministries of state for Economic and Regional Development and Social Development—and the abolition in the United Kingdom of the Central Policy Review Staff along with the changing of the Civil Service Department's name to the Management and Personnel Office and the transfer of many of its former functions back to HM Treasury.

Although data limitations confine us to a study of central agents in the United States, United Kingdom, and Canada, systemic differences in the three bureaucratic milieus make these constraints almost propitious. Most obviously, the British and Canadian cases provide opportunities for comparison of officials operating under a cabinet-parliamentary system of government with those working within the United States's presidential-congressional format. In the former two countries, that career officials rise much higher in departments and agencies combines with the strong ethos of *ministerial responsibility* to obscure their involvement in policy decision making.

In theory, United Kingdom and Canadian ministers remain the sole accounting agents to Parliament: *individually* (as political head of departments) and *collectively* (as members of the government). Their responsibility is comprehensive in that it covers all the acts and omissions of officials who serve a minister or, more generally, Cabinet and its committees. The most serious lapses can and often do result in ministers' resignations or the fall of governments. Ministers and Cabinets derive from this cloistering of career officials the image of harmony in the executive branch and the aura of competent administration. These traits, in turn, help maintain the confidence of the House of Commons and support among the electorate. Officials' retiring folkways redound to their benefit in relative personal immunity from bad publicity and punitive job action should "the government" founder.

Even United Kingdom–Canadian comparisons offer numerous avenues in which to contrast central agents' views of their involvement in policy decisions. For example, the highly institutionalized nature of Canada's Cabinet committee system has so overloaded ministers that senior officials must share the burden of attending meetings (Campbell, 1983:277–80). Even when ministers personally represent their department at committee sessions, career officials usually accompany them and often feel free to participate as full discussants. Thus, the Canadian case represents one of the most extreme instances available to students of executive-bureaucratic behavior in which the work worlds of political authorities and career civil servants have merged all but completely.

A Matter of Discretion

In the lay world, *discretion* means caution about what one says or does—prudence. In the world of political power, it connotes the freedom to make individual or collective interpretative decisions or choices in circumstances not explicitly anticipated. The debate surrounding the degree to which senior officials involve themselves in policy decisions centers most clearly on whether they avail themselves substantially of interpretative discretion. However, discretion plays a part here as well. Executive-bureaucratic systems such as Britain's and Canada's place a very high premium on governmental secrecy. Thus, they provide frameworks in which officials may invoke principles of prudence while concealing the ways in which their discretionary interpretations have amounted to the use, even abuse, of political power.

It was not until the third quarter of this century that scholars began to question seriously the applicability of the administration-policy dichotomy to actual executive-bureaucratic dynamics. For instance, Simon (1957:57–58) wanted to modify the distinction to state simply that, while both politicians and bureaucrats make policy decisions, the latter should stick to the "factual" elements behind choices. Shubert (1960) gave further expression to this ideal by arguing that the tenants of public service require that officials base their decisions on professional and informed assessments of issues. Yet, by the 1960s and 1970s many researchers began to register grave doubts even about watered-down formulations of the dichotomy. In the early 1960s, Martin Landau (1962:10) offered the unequivocal assertion that bureaucrats make policy. A few years later, Matthew Holden (1966:944) pointed up ways in which officials might seek personal goals contrary to the wishes of their elected masters while Herbert Kaufman (1969:4–5) noted how civil servants might, consciously or not, obfuscate politicians' efforts to achieve governmental reforms.

In their classic study of Whitehall, Hugh Heclo and Aaron Wildavsky (1974:3) devised the term *political administrator* to express how senior civil servants and cabinet ministers in the United Kingdom share a collegial bond based on the primacy of two common tasks: integration of political and administrative goals; and maintenance of the formal and informal mechanisms whereby coordination of the two elements might be achieved. Two years earlier a Canadian scholar serving a stint in the bureaucracy inverted Woodrow Wilson's (1941:493) classic policy—administrative dichotomy—by asserting that politicians rely upon public servants' analyses of the political consequences of policies, including how various alternatives might affect their chances for reelection (Hartle, 1972:2–18).

Recently, Aberbach, Putnam, and Rockman (1981:ch. 1) have postulated four images of the relationship between bureaucrats and politicians. The first is the traditional dichotomy between policy and administration. It has proven inadequate because it "assumes a degree of hierarchy of authority, of simplicity of decision, and of effective political supremacy" that overlooks the pervasiveness of bureaucratic discretionary power. The second image corresponds to Simon's and Shubert's theses. Although both bureaucrats and politicians participate in policy decisions, the former bring facts and knowledge to bear on issues while the latter introduce value sensitivity to the reconciliation of diverse interests. This characterization, the authors maintain, fails to acknowledge the educational training and professional expertise that many politicians bring to their work. It overlooks as well the overwhelming evidence in empirical studies that bureaucrats involve themselves heavily in mobilizing and mediating sectoral interests.

Having rejected images I and II, Aberbach, Putnam, and Rockman turn to two additional types more suited to analyses of the interplay of politicians and bureaucrats in the modern state. Image III asserts that both politicians and bureaucrats engage in policy making—indeed, politics. However, public servants tend to mediate narrow concerns expressed by formalized groups rather than express the broad-based representations of the unorganized. As well, officials eschew passionate, partisan, idealistic, or ideological approaches to issues.

Image IV disputes III's modest level of differentiation between the folkways of the two groups. The authors here adduce evidence, based on studies of "harbingers," of a more complete merging of roles of public servants and politicians. The early signs of transformation include the introduction of "outsiders" and "irregulars" as advisers in previously career-dominated bureaucracies in countries such as the United Kingdom and West Germany. They also note that, although central coordinative departments such as the U.K. Cabinet Office and Canada's Privy Council Office are staffed entirely by career officials, these organizations increasingly assume integrative tasks that call upon the highest order of gamesmanship within the executive-bureaucratic arena. In reporting the findings of Campbell and Szablowski's (1979) study of Canadian central agents, Aberbach, Putnam, and Rockman (1981:18) explain how the image IV bureaucrat has outstripped his image III counterpart: "the staff members of these central agencies differ from more traditional civil servants in the broader, more flexible authority they enjoy; in their greater social representativeness and substantive innovativeness; and in their recognition of the legitimacy of politics—not merely in the sense of responsiveness to clientele interests, but in the broader sense that Image III ascribes to politicians alone."

Policy Makers v. Facilitators

A series of questions in the central agency project interview schedule sought to ascertain whether and to what degree respondents
involve themselves in facilitator and policy-maker roles.[2] The former
functions correspond with Aberbach, Putnam, and Rockman's Image
III approach to bureaucracy. Insofar as they view themselves as facilitators, top officials will emphasize ways in which—notwithstanding their very heavy involvement in the policy *process*—they
mainly attempt to simplify and expedite decisions. In describing this
role, facilitators will tend to focus on specific policy questions and
style themselves as process managers, communicators between various segments of the policy arena and monitors of implementation. In
contrast, respondents reporting policy-maker roles will volunteer
that they engage their ideas and values in efforts to achieve political
objectives. Here officials' agendas could amount simply to the
machinations and timing necessary to get one's way in the executive-
bureaucratic maze. For appointees in our three countries, however,
political goals usually entail broader commitments based on explicit
reference to partisan mandates. In any case, officials articulating
policy-maker roles stress in some way their concern with the overall
direction of a government/administration. Thus, they style themselves as active advocates and energizers within the policy arena.

Table 1 summarizes the responses of central agents in the three
countries to questions about their roles. Since multiple responses
were coded, the total number of answers under each broad category
exceeds considerably the size of each country group. The results
listed under "responsibilities" suggest that officials lean toward the
facilitator role in providing us a view of the sector of central-agency
activity in which they involve themselves. In no country do more
than 14 percent of responses highlight development of strategic
plans for the government/administration. Interestingly, the 6 percent
of U.S. answers citing such roles trails considerably behind the comparable figure in the Canadian and British groups. Similarly modest
proportions—between 7 and 11 percent—prevail in accounts of
work relating to central review of expenditure budgets. More robust
figures appear in respondents' reporting of efforts to establish priorities among various substantive policy issues. In fact, 22 percent of
both U.S. and U.K. accounts suggest engagement in such activities.
In sharp contrast, between 59 and 62 percent of responses in each
country focus on central-agency responsibilities covering specific
policies, process management tasks, and administrative programs.

The figures under *style* and *mandate* indicate two very strong
national effects. The 26 percent of Canadian responses in which
officials characterize the style of their work activities as that of a
policy maker exceeds by far comparable figures for both the

TABLE 1.

Responses to Role Orientation Variables

Variables	U.S.	Canada	U.K.
Sector of Central-Agency Activity (% of responses):			
Strategic Plans	6.3	14.1	11.1
Priorities Among Substantive Policy Areas	22.3	15.0	22.2
Expenditure Budgeting	11.5	8.5	7.8
Specific Policy and/or Administrative Activities	59.9	62.4	58.9
Total Number of Responses	(269)	(234)	(90)
Respondents' Work Styles (% of responses):			
Policy Maker	5.6	26.4	6.2
Facilitator	19.9	14.5	28.4
Adviser	36.8	26.4	45.7
Manager, Implementor, Communicator	37.6	32.8	19.8
Total Number of Responses	(266)	(235)	(81)
Respondents' Compass of Activities (% of responses):			
Less than Entire Mandate	96.3	94.4	74.0
Entire Agency Mandate	3.7	5.6	26.0
Total Number of Responses	(191)	(161)	(50)

United States and United Kingdom. We have already noted that the Canadian cabinet committee system accords senior officials near-colleague status with ministers by virtue of their relatively full entree to the give-and-take of meetings. The exceptional Canadian result, thus, appears to reflect a strong tendency among many central agents in that country to see themselves as co-participants in policy decisions. Short of clear association with policy-making roles, other interesting national differences emerge under the style categories. The British yield by far the highest percentages of responses describing facilitative and advisory policy roles. These findings might reflect the formal distance between elected political leaders and bureaucrats in the United Kingdom. For instance, top officials in that country usually imbibe the rarefied atmosphere of cabinet-level committees only as secretaries of meetings. While the functions connected with running proceedings call upon considerable diplomatic and coordinative skills, Whitehall folkways dictate that officials avoid overt manifestations of executive-bureaucratic gamesmanship.

With respect to the amount of their agency's mandate with which respondents identified, the British took much wider compasses than did the others. Twenty-six percent of responses indicated that British officials felt a strong responsibility toward the entire mandate of their agency, whereas only 4 and 6 percent of, respectively, U.S. and Canadian responses articulated such inclusive foci. We should remember here that civil servants in Whitehall tend to belong to the same department throughout their careers. If they work for a few years in another agency, they consider themselves simply to be on secondment. Even within their departments, officials tend to have served in various sectors of each agency's activities rather than in one specialized area. Thus, it is not all that surprising that U.K. respondents proved relatively loath to describe themselves as policy makers yet delineate more sharply than the others a sense of responsibility toward the mandate of their agency. In the words of one Cabinet Office respondent reflecting upon stances taken by HM Treasury, departmental lines take shape quite independently of the government-of-the-day's coloration:

> The Treasury. . .is more or less the classical Whitehall department where advice is embodied in folklore. That is, the Treasury actually has its own line on different subjects independent of its ministers, almost, however constitutional that might be. . . . Advice, in the first instance at least, will almost 80–90 per cent consist of folklore: "Our line on flexible exchange rates is this and here it is. . . ." (Campbell, 1983: 57)

Influences on Facilitator and Policy-Maker Roles

A growing body of research has traced the relationship between bureaucrats' views of their roles and various factors that help explain the emphasis they place on any given function.[3] This section will discuss four categories of influences: officials' positional circumstances and activities, their career orientations, their career routes, and their sociodemographic backgrounds.

Nine variables index the positional factors behind respondents' views of their roles. Consideration of these elements takes a major leaf from Aberbach, Putnam, and Rockman. They found that significant proportions of their officials were involved in a "policy net" in which they did business continuously with offices serving the chief executive, cabinet members, top civil servants in other departments and party leaders (1981: 203). These respondents registered the strongest associations with policy-making roles.

The first of the positional variables reflects whether our respondents believed they interacted on a regular basis with the chief executive, political heads, and officials three tiers lower in the hierarchies of their own and other departments. Respondents who styled their contacts as regular with all levels received the maximum of nine points. United States respondents tend more than the others to characterize their interaction at various levels as regular. They also outstrip their U.K. and Canadian opposite numbers in their calculations of the annual frequency of interactions with the chief executive and cabinet secretaries. Further, U.S. respondents much more than those in the United Kingdom and Canada describe their interactions at different points in the nine levels as concerning policy matters. Our fourth variable gauges the frequency of officials' interactions with the top three in departmental hierarchies short of the agency heads. Here again the Americans prove to be somewhat more active than do the Britons and the Canadians.

Clearly, participation in committees comprises a major component of officials' links with policy-oriented networks. Campbell speaks to this issue in explaining the consequences of Canadian central agents' exceptional access to cabinet-level meetings:

> [in comparison to U.S. and U.K. respondents] they provide the largest proportions who say they use them for keeping informed about others' positions on major issues. . . , influencing the way in which ministers study a problem, especially by lending the perspective of expertise and experience. . . , getting their point of view across so as to actually influence policy decisions. . . , learning the ropes by watching how various ministers perform and how things get done . . . , and simply fulfilling a specific part of secretarial functions by taking notes and recording decisions. . . . (1983:279–80)

In this regard, the Canadians report much more regular participation in cabinet-level committees than do American and British respondents. Americans appear more reliant than the others upon interdepartmental bodies short of cabinet-level groups, as indicated by their membership, on average, to over three such committees. In subcabinet settings, the British and Canadians tend more than Americans to consider themselves active participants in discussions.

Americans' reports of the frequency of contact with legislators fall short of Canadians'. This result probably owes to the degree to which U.S. legislative staff serve as surrogates for congressmen and senators in contacts with bureaucracy. Canadian legislators for the most part do not have policy-oriented aides. The decidedly low figure for Britons' interaction with legislators appears to reflect Whitehall norms discouraging such direct relations. While U.K. officials prove to be less expansive than the Americans, they appear more inclusive than Canadians in the sources they consider to be among the best for gathering advice and information on the issues they face.

A second series of variables probed respondents' career orientations. The questions upon which these variables are based assessed, first, why officials took on their public service career and, second, what they consider the most important things they have accomplished during their time in government. All of the variables are additive-multiple response—the first three relating to career entry and the second three tapping career satisfaction. With regard to the former, the British reveal the greatest idealism in their reasons for entering public service. Both Americans and British cite considerably more than do Canadians elements of their formal education and/or work experience that contributed to their career choices. Canadians give, more than the others, explanations recounting the desire to be "where the action is" or to achieve specific policy or partisan objectives.

Concerning the principal motives that have maintained their careers, three variables combine responses to two questions—one concerning what officials believed they had accomplished during their careers and the other asking what they would miss if they left government. Here the Americans and, somewhat less, the Canadians surpassed the British in noting specific issue sectors in which they cherish a contribution to certain policy goals. Roughly equal proportions of respondents in all three groups take satisfaction from helping to keep the governmental process running smoothly. In descending order, the British, Canadians, and Americans gave responses stressing the self-fulfillment they derived from the challenges, excitement, and calibre of work found in the higher levels of public service.

Several variables examined the career routes of our respondents. Both Robert Putnam (1973:268, 279) and Ezra Suleiman (1974:117) found that, respectively, Italian and French civil servants follow sharply defined career routes harking to the Weberian era in which public service was a vocation. In such systems, officials will adhere more than in others to the traditional view whereby administration is for public servants and policy is for their elected masters. Britain continues to follow a highly stratified routing of individuals into and through civil service careers. Indeed, the British respondents have, on average, spent more of their working lives in government than the Americans and Canadians. By a large majority, they have traded on university education that did not go beyond the bachelor's degree. Hence, British central agents rarely brought to their careers professional certification and/or specialized scholarly training—they are mostly masters of no trade besides bureaucracy.

The results concerning the point at which our respondents say they decided to enter government place the British well ahead of Canadians in reporting that they embraced their preference while in university or before. However, the Americans do not fall far behind the British in "early vocations." The Canadians' hesitancy fits well with data gathered as early as 1953 that indicate top officials in

Canada normally have worked in the private sector before entering government (Porter, 1965:436–37; Chartrand and Pond, 1970:48–49). Almost half of our U.S. respondents are political appointees. Thus, the large proportion of the U.S. group saying they decided to enter government before leaving university appears to support one of Hugh Heclo's (1977) contentions. He has asserted that two public service career tracks operate parallel to one another in the United States—one for those whose partisan commitments have led to career-long availability for government service whenever called upon and another for permanent officials who enter once and for all at a relatively early age.

Finally, some sociodemographic characteristics might relate to respondents' views of their roles as either facilitators or policy makers: type of secondary school, gender, father's occupational background, and religious preference. While it is difficult to predict exactly how these factors might relate to officials' role perceptions, they do comprise a group of background characteristics upon which respondents in the three countries differ considerably.

The British tend much more than the others to have received their secondary education at private schools. Canadian central agencies have lagged behind their U.S. and U.K. counterparts in the admission of women to their ranks. Both the United Kingdom and Canada recruit somewhat more disproportionately from their central-core regions—respectively, South England, and Ontario and Quebec—than does the United States from the industrial North East. The American and Canadian central agents come in greater proportions than do the British from homes in which the father belongs to a professional occupational group. On the other hand, British respondents reported much more than the others that their fathers had worked in managerial positions. American officials came from homes described as "blue collar" more than did the British or the Canadians. With regard to religious identification, the Canadian group provides the highest proportion of Catholic respondents. The British, in contrast, include by far the smallest percentages of Catholics and persons without a religious affiliation.

Multivariate Analyses

Regression analysis is employed to determine how facilitator and policy-maker role emphases are related to the different possible influences discussed in the previous section. The analysis begins by assessing the effects of blocks of variables grouped under the headings "positional circumstances and activities," "career orientations," "career routes," and "sociodemographic backgrounds" (see Tables 2 and 3 for details).

Looking first at influences on officials' reports of policy-making

TABLE 2.

Regression Analyses for "Policy Maker"

Independent Variable	U.S.	Canada	U.K.
Positional Circumstances and Activities			
Contact, all categories	.115	−.065	−.348*
Agency-head level	.053	.462**	.198
Sub-Agency-head level	−.031	.152*	.521**
Legislators	−.022	−.359**	.689**
Contacts Concern Policy	.195**	.018	−.125
Interdepartmental Meeting Attendance	−.074	.074	.531**
Active in Interdepartmental Meetings	.012	−.215	.477**
Attends Cabinet-Level Meetings Regularly	.019	−.133*	.010
Consults Groups	.039	−.287**	.198
Career Orientations			
Idealism	.125*	−.007	.238
Training	−.188**	−.054	−.065
Action	−.171**	−.043	.256**
Impact	.049	−.142*	.191
Process	.046	−.248	.401*
Personal Satisfaction	−.175**	.016	−.152
Career Routes			
Decided to Enter before Leaving			
University (reversed for Canadians)	.000	−.092	−.656*
Years in Government	−.236*	.043	−.884*
Number of Positions Held	−.152**	−.019	.089
No Education Beyond Bachelor's			
(reversed for U.K.)	.204**	−.117*	.027
Political Appointee	.016	.480**	.755*
Sociodemographic variables			
Independent Secondary Education	−.037	.001	.410**
Age	−.075	.151*	−.912**
Male	−.043	−.119*	.811**
Peripheral Region (reversed for U.S.)	.108*	−.138	.095
Professional	reference	−.089	−.567**
Managerial	.278**	reference	reference
White Collar	−.122*	−.295**	.277
Blue Collar	−.114	−.079	−.213
Farmer	−.081	.218**	none
Catholic	−.052	−.045	−.530*
Jewish	−.056	.206**	none
Nonbelievers	.010	.107	.508*

*significant at .05
**significant at .01

roles, we find the lowest amount of variance (3.3 percent) explained occurs among the Americans (versus 5.2 percent for the United Kingdom, and 6.4 percent for Canada). In the U.S. case, in addition, it proves difficult to ascertain which of the blocks has the greatest effects. The Canadian data contrast sharply in this regard. Positional

TABLE 3.

Regression Analyses for "Facilitator"

Independent Variable	U.S.	Canada	U.K.
Positional Circumstances and Activities			
Contact, all categories	−.275**	.082	−.064
Agency-head level	−.305**	−.325**	−.061
Sub-Agency-head level	.292**	−.109	−.481
Legislators	−.062	.043	−.046
Contacts Concern Policy	.073	.210**	.093
Interdepartmental Meeting Attendance	.048	−.092	−.308
Active in Interdepartmental Meetings	−.136*	.077	−.010
Attends Cabinet-Level Meetings Regularly	−.018	−.039	.239
Consults Groups	.095	.161*	−.040
Career Orientations			
Idealism	.038	.105*	−.186
Training	.131	−.155*	.152
Action	.098	.031	−.332
Impact	.047	.335**	.082
Process	.035	.041	−.149
Personal Satisfaction	.218**	−.005	−.083
Career Routes			
Decided to Enter Before Leaving			
University (reversed for Canadians)	.127	−.030	−.018
Years in Government	.199	.005	.498
Number of Positions Held	.169**	.057	.291
No Education Beyond Bachelor's			
(reversed for U.K.)	.152*	−.113*	.239
Political Appointee	.031	−.225*	−.143
Sociodemographic Variables			
Independent Secondary Education	−.049	.246**	−.210
Age	−.161	.104	−.285
Male	−.050	−.244**	−.485
Peripheral Region (reversed for U.S.)	−.027	.193**	−.139
Professional	reference	.089	.142
Managerial	.242**	reference	reference
White Collar	.039	.118*	.133
Blue Collar	.126*	.006	.384
Farmer	−.051	−.172**	none
Catholic	−.066	.285**	−.335
Jewish	−.037	−.051	none
Nonbelievers	−.129	.056	−.297

*significant at .05

**significant at .01

circumstances and activities play a clear part in officials' self-ascriptions of policy-maker roles. While an analysis of zero-order effects suggests that both career routes and sociodemographic factors have secondary influences, a consideration of unique effects indicates that the latter pull harder than the former. Roughly the same patterns occur with U.K. respondents. However, the positional-circum-stances-and-activities variables retain virtually all of their weight when the others are held constant. The sociodemographic block op-erates as the secondary cluster of influences on adoption of policy-maker roles.

As for the facilitator role, the American regressions again yield the weakest relations (2.4 percent variance explained, versus 7.5 percent for the United Kingdom and 6.3 percent for Canada). However, U.S. respondents' positional circumstances and activi-ties take more than twice the part they did in the policy-maker regression. The Canadian regression occasioned once again rela-tively robust figures—especially with regard to the effects of posi-tional circumstances and activities and sociodemographic factors. The British analyses turn out as the most successful in explaining variance in assumption of facilitator roles. However, neither the U.K. zero order nor unique effect regressions delineate an espe-cially dominant block.

Tables 2 and 3 present variable-by-variable breakdowns of the separate regressions of the two role types. Standardized coefficients depict the relative weight of each variable within the equations. Beginning with the U.S. findings, we see that whether respondents' contacts with others in the executive-bureaucratic arena mainly con-cern policy issues has a strong effect on their reporting policy-maker roles. The relations between policy making and the career orienta-tions of U.S. officials indicate that idealism and the attractiveness of public service had a fairly strong positive influence. On the other hand, motives originating in education and previous employment, the desire to be where the action is, and the experience of deriving personal satisfaction from the calibre of government work all appear to manifest negative effects on assumption of policy-maker roles.

Regarding career routes, a very strong generational motif emerges in the U.S. group, i.e., the longer officials have served in government and the more positions they have held the less they describe them-selves as policy makers. A generalist theme reveals itself here as well. Those who pursued no education beyond a bachelor's degree tend more to embrace policy-maker roles. These relations might sug-gest that political appointees disproportionately assume policy-maker roles. However, whether respondents are appointees or career officials appears to have little influence in our U.S. group.

The regression of policy maker on the sociodemographic variables produced three significant results. Respondents from the northeast United States tend somewhat to prefer the role. With respect to father's occupation, respondents whose fathers worked in manage-rial positions appear to opt more frequently than do those whose fathers were professionals ("professional" is the reference category for the occupation variables). In contrast, those with fathers in white-collar occupations seem less inclined than those whose father held a professional position to adopt a policy-maker role.

Within the Canadian group, the regression of policy maker on the positional-circumstances-and-activities variables points up a paradox. Those respondents who interact very frequently with the prime minister and other members of Cabinet take exceedingly well to policy making. The same relationship, although less dramatic, applies to officials with very frequent contacts extending right down to the assistant deputy ministers of agencies. However, the negative relation between regular cabinet committee attendance and policy makers argues for the conclusion that we have tapped here a stratum of officialdom operating slightly above the fray. Canadian policy makers evidently do not rely entirely upon the entree provided by cabinet-level bodies while maneuvering in the executive-bureaucratic community.

Interestingly, we find in these Canadian results corroboration of Aberbach, Putnam, and Rockman's observations about the movers and shakers. These officials best fit the image IV mold by virtue of their connection to the most vital segments of policy networks. As the authors noted regarding contacts:

> The strongest and most consistent correlations involve contacts with the cabinet office and party leaders. Bureaucrats who are favorable to politics appear to be well-connected to the centers of political power in their systems. On the other hand, politicalness . . . is only mildly related to contacts with parliamentary politicians, virtually unrelated to contacts with clientele groups, and even inversely related to contacts with ordinary citizens. (Aberbach, Putnam, and Rockman, 1981:221–22)

The results of the Canadian analysis indicate, indeed, that assumption of policy-maker roles relates negatively both to interaction with legislators and consultation of extragovernmental groups. Canadian movers and shakers enjoy precisely the ethereal political life anticipated by Aberbach, Putnam, and Rockman for bureaucrats functioning according to image IV.

As judged by the relatively low coefficients, career orientations do not appear to wield much of an effect on the policy-maker role. However, one career-route variable, whether a respondent is an appointee or a permanent civil servant, weighs in quite considerably. Canadian appointees demonstrate a very strong preference for policy making.

Some fairly strong relations suggest themselves in the sociodemographic block. However, a thematic pattern proves elusive. Older respondents, those whose fathers were farmers (the reference occupation in the Canadian group is "managerial") and those of the Jewish faith show the greatest inclination to rate themselves as policy makers. Officials who tend less to style themselves as pursuing the role include males and those from white-collar homes.

Regarding policy-maker roles among the British respondents, we should note at the outset that the coefficients suggest strong associations with political appointments and youth. The readings for the positional circumstances and activities appear to bifurcate. On the one hand, we find a strong coefficient between interaction with legislators and assumption of policy-making roles. This probably argues for an interpretation assigning most of the responsibility for the strong relation to political appointees in No. 10. Such officials represent the group most likely to have especially strong links with legislators. Yet, policy makers tend with great frequency to interact with departments' top civil servants, to attend interdepartmental committees, and to participate fully in such meetings. All of these activities conjure up images of career civil servants', rather than appointees', networks.

In a modest way, the variables in the career-orientation block support a bimodal interpretation of the above findings. British policy makers disproportionately attribute their entry to government to a desire for being where the action is or having an impact in a policy area—the types of orientations we might expect from appointees. In contrast, policy makers tend to esteem what they have accomplished by way of keeping the process of government on an even keel—more as we might expect from career civil servants.

The findings for the career-route block clearly support the appointee thesis. Yet, generational career-service influences might operate in the strong coefficient between policy-maker roles and delayed decisions to enter government and a relatively short period of service. The first three sociodemographic variables lend further credence to the view that elements in addition to political appointments dispose officials to policy-maker roles. Young respondents overwhelmingly style themselves as policy makers as do men. More important, graduates of private (i.e., "public") schools favor the role. Our Labour government appointees mostly did not avail themselves of such private secondary schools. Finally, nonbelievers—presumably more numerous in the younger generation—assume the role.

The regressions of the facilitator role on the various blocks provide almost classic results in the United States (Table 3). The American officials preferring facilitator roles claim less than others regular contact at the different strata of the executive-bureaucratic complex. To quite a significant degree, they tend not to report high frequencies of contact with the president and/or cabinet secretaries. Even in interdepartmental meetings involving subcabinet officials, they avoid describing themselves as active and full participants.

Facilitators in the United States stand out in attributing their career enjoyment to the personal satisfaction of being involved in processes of a scale that only government provides. Three variables connected with the length and diversity of respondents' public service careers—early rather than delayed decisions to enter government, the number of years, and the positions held since entrance— relate positively to assumption of the facilitator role. However, only a third of these variables achieves significance. Also with respect to career routes, a disproportionately large number of respondents who received no education beyond a bachelor's degree chose the facilitator role. The sociodemographic variables generated two coefficients relating strongly to the role. The sons and daughters of managers and blue-collar workers frequently describe themselves as facilitators.

Although less sharply defined, similar patterns emerge with the Canadian group. Here facilitators interact relatively infrequently with the prime minister and ministers. As well, many downplay their participation in interdepartmental committees—saying that it is more passive than active. However, facilitators do claim more than others that their interactions at various levels concern policy matters. Regarding career orientations, facilitators tend to cite idealistic reasons for entering government. They do not generally believe that their education or precareer occupations contributed greatly to their decision to become public servants. As they look back on their careers, they derive the greatest satisfaction from the belief that they have had an impact in some specific policy areas.

Canadian facilitators' career routes suggest that they mostly pursued university work beyond a bachelor's degree and came up through the permanent civil service. Collectively, sociodemographic factors have the greatest impact on facilitator roles in Canada. A closer look reveals that those who receive their secondary education in private schools, those from the periphery rather than Ontario or Quebec, those whose fathers were white-collar workers, and Roman Catholics all favor the role to a significant degree. On the other hand, females and those whose fathers were farmers reported involvement in the role less frequently than others.

The small size of the British group presents problems in our regressions of the facilitator index on the various blocks. None of the resulting coefficients reached statistical significance. However, some comparisons with stronger results under the policy-maker regressions shade in interesting contrasts. Whereas policy makers interact quite frequently at subcabinet levels, facilitators do not. Roughly the same situation prevails with regard to members of the two groups' participation in interdepartmental meetings. While policy makers often pointed to the importance of the scale of government and the challenges it provides as a motivating force behind their careers, facilitators seem cool toward such considerations. Unlike policy makers, who were in very large numbers political appointees, facilitators tend to be career officials. This probably helps account for their relatively long service in government and the comparatively numerous positions they have held. Further divergence emerges when facilitators' sociodemographic backgrounds are contrasted with policy makers'. The former tend to come from state-supported rather than private schools, to be female rather than male, to claim blue-collar origins and to espouse a religious belief rather than claim none. Gender aside, such relations indicate that the facilitators are more "middle-British" than their policy-maker colleagues.

Conclusion

The analyses in this paper draw upon a very specialized data set—the only existing comparative study of members of central, coordinating departments. Although limited to respondents in these bureaucratic agencies in the United States, Great Britain, and Canada, the data provided an opportunity to probe issues relating to senior government officials' involvement in policy-making roles in contemporary Anglo-American countries. In the vernacular of public administration studies, they enabled us to examine the degree to which our central agents have set aside the traditional dichotomy between administration and politics. Under the old rubrics, officials allegedly sought simply to execute on a managerial level the will of their elected political masters who, in turn, relied upon legislative authority.

Numerous scholars have put the sharp delineation of administration and politics to the test and found it wanting. Principal among these are Aberbach, Putnam, and Rockman whose recent book posits two types of bureaucrats who break the stylized molds put forth in the traditional literature. Here facilitators embrace explicitly political roles: yet, they explain that they simply want to advance vital governmental processes. On the other hand, policy makers take the step beyond, i.e., they acknowledge that vested bureaucratic interests and even partisan motives operate at the root of their executive-bureaucratic gamesmanship. The central agency data from our three countries prove especially germane as Aberbach, Putnam, and Rockman view such departments as the institutional contexts in which their two advanced images most likely have taken hold.

Our examination suggests that facilitators and policy makers find happy homes in all three of our central agency systems. Tendencies toward adopting these two roles fell pretty much within the same ranges in each country, and in each our respondents appear more strongly oriented toward the former than the latter. Even before assessing various individual-level factors related to whether or not an official adopts one of these roles, certain systemic influences suggested themselves simply in the types of activities that respondents stressed while reporting their roles. Most obvious here were the Canadians' relatively spontaneous descriptions of their work styles as those of policy makers and the British officials' strong identification with the entire breadth of their agencies' mandates. We noted that the high level of integration of the work worlds of Cabinet members and top bureaucrats in Canada, especially through joint participation in the most senior committees of the government, must contribute strongly to the former finding. The British result must partially stem from the relatively high association of permanent civil servants' careers with specific departments and the policy approaches these champion over relatively extended periods.

The factors that conceivably influence association with the roles included positional circumstances and activities, career orientations, career routes, and sociodemographic backgrounds. However, a series of multivariate analyses pointed once again to cross-national commonalities existing alongside many individual-level relationships. In a global sense, officials well-connected to the innermost circles of their respective systems register the greatest propensity for the policy-maker role. Thus, we lend full support to Aberbach, Putnam, and Rockman's conclusions to the same effect. Canadian central agents—the clearest beneficiaries of insertion into policy networks—walk along the most sharply delineated policy-maker path. They tend to eschew interactions with those in the policy arena who are not seen as movers and shakers. Conversely, analyses of the facilitator role in all three countries suggest that less well-connected officials register the strongest associations with this role. Even more fundamentally, facilitators in all three countries appear to have pursued relatively traditional career aspirations and routes. Some evidence suggests as well that they claim comparatively modest sociodemographic backgrounds.

In addition to hammering another nail in the coffin of the politics-administration dichotomy, our findings pose two serious problems for students of legislative leadership. First, it suggests that observers of the dynamics of representative democracy miss the point if they emphasize vagaries of legislative scrutiny of the executive. With the exception of the U.S. Congress, even the strongest legislators only nibble along the periphery of the apparatus of state as it churns out policies and regulations. Too close attention to the atmospherics of legislatures, such as better support staff for members and improved investigative latitude for committees, amounts to advanced forms of X ray rather than exploratory surgery.

More compelling, the study of executive-legislative relations increasingly operates one step removed from the real issue in the policy arenas of advanced liberal democracies. The rise of central agencies attached to the chief executive and/or cabinet-level committees has spawned a suprabureaucratic culture. Using the most advanced instruments of decisional technology and exerting authority derived from proximity to (even intimacy with) the political executive, central agents operate within a milieu significantly closed to the people in the civil service chained to day-to-day responsibility for actual government programs. In theory, the new bureaucratic culture gives political authorities a greater capacity for coordination and control. But, this can be and has been bad news for many politicians. Cabinet ministers in charge of operational departments find themselves open to shortcircuiting by well-placed advisers at the very center of the executive-bureaucratic community. Legislators trying to monitor departments' programs become exposed to the dysfunctions and frustrations of doing business with Cabinet secretaries and officials who must refer everything to silent, but politically influential, partners in central agencies.

Notes

1. This project was supported by several generous grants from the Social Sciences and Humanities Research Council of Canada.

2. Detailed discussions of the methodological aspects of this study may be found in Campbell and Szablowski (1979:Appendix I) and Campbell (1983:Appendix I).

3. To assist analysis of factors influencing officials' responses along the facilitator and policy-maker dimensions, we devised two additive variables registering the degree to which our central agents identify with each role. The first, facilitator, assigns one point to respondents for any association with each of the following: specific policies, process management tasks and/or administrative programs; facilitating; advising; managing; implementing and/or communication; and relatively narrow aspects of an agency's mandate. The maximum number of points an official could obtain under the multiple response format would be 16. The second, policy maker, allots one point for any mention of each of the following: setting strategic plans for the government/administration; establishing priorities among substantive policy objectives; central coordination of expenditure budgeting; express policy-making activities; and the entire compass of an agency's mandate. The maximum number of points a respondent could receive for this additive variable would be 5. Empirically, none of the central agent contingents exceeds an average of two responses corresponding to the policy-maker role. On the other hand, U.S. and U.K. officials, on average, volunteered nearly four responses connected with the facilitator role. The Canadians made just short of five mentions of activities related to the function.

References

Aberbach, Joel D., and Bert A. Rockman (1977) "The Overlapping Worlds of American Federal Executives and Congressmen." *British Journal of Political Science* 7:23–47.

Aberbach, Joel D., Robert D. Putnam, and Bert A. Rockman (1981) *Bureaucrats and Politicians in Western Democracies.* Cambridge: Harvard University Press.

Brodie, M. Janine, and Bruce D. Macnaughton (1980) "Legislators versus Bureaucrats: The Norms of Governing in Canada." In *Parliament, Policy and Representation*, edited by Harold D. Clarke et al. Toronto: Methuen.

Campbell, Colin (1983) *Governments Under Stress: Political Executives and Key Bureaucrats in Washington, London and Ottawa*. Toronto: University of Toronto Press.

Campbell, Colin, and George J. Szablowski (1979) *The Superbureaucrats: Structure and Behavior in Central Agencies*. Toronto: Macmillan.

Campbell, Colin, and Harold D. Clarke (1980) "Conspectus: Some Thoughts on Parliamentary Reform." In *Parliament, Policy and Representation*, edited by Harold D. Clarke et al. Toronto: Methuen.

Chartrand, P. J., and K. L. Pond (1970) *A Study of Executive Career Paths in the Public Service of Canada*. Chicago: Public Personnel Association.

Dye, Thomas R., and L. Ziegler Harmon (1975) *The Irony of Democracy*. Belmont, CA: Duxbury.

Galloway, George B. (1946) *Congress at the Crossroads*. New York: Crowell.

Hartle, Douglas G. (1972) *The Objective of Government Objectives*. Ottawa: Treasury Board Secretariat.

Heclo, Hugh (1977) *A Government of Strangers: Executive Politics in Washington*. Washington: The Brookings Institution.

Heclo, Hugh, and Aaron Wildavsky (1974) *The Private Government of Public Money: Community and Policy Inside British Politics*. Berkeley: University of California Press.

Holden, Matthew (1966) " 'Imperialism' in Bureaucracy." *American Political Science Review* 60:943–51.

Kaufman, Herbert (1969) "Administrative Decentralization and Political Power." *Public Administration Review* 29:3–15.

Landau, Martin (1962) "The Concept of Decision-Making in the Field of Public Administration." In *Concepts and Issues in Administrative Behavior*, edited by Sidney Mailick and Edward H. Van Ness. Englewood Cliffs, N.J.: Prentice-Hall.

Long, Norton C. (1952) "Bureaucracy and Constitutionalism." *American Political Science Review* 46:808–818.

Peters, B. Guy (1978) *The Politics of Bureaucracy*. New York: Longmans.

Porter, John (1965) *The Vertical Mosaic: An Analysis of Social Class and Power in Canada*. Toronto: University of Toronto Press.

Presthus, Robert V. (1974) *Elites in the Policy Process*. London: Cambridge University Press.

Putnam, Robert D. (1973) "The Political Attitudes of Senior Civil Servants in Western Europe: A Preliminary Report." *British Journal of Political Science* 3:257–90.

Shubert, Glendon (1960) *The Public Interest*. Glencoe, Ill.: The Free Press.

Sigelman, Lee, and William G. Vanderbok (1977) "Legislators, Bureaucrats, and Canadian Democracy: The Long and Short of It." *Canadian Journal of Political Science* 10:615–23.

Simon, Herbert A. (1957) *Administrative Behavior*. New York: Macmillan.

Suleiman, Ezra N. (1974) *Politics, Power and Bureaucracy in France: The Administrative Elite*. Princeton: Princeton University Press.

Wilson, Woodrow (1941 reprint) "The Study of Administration." *Political Science Quarterly* 16:481–506.

PART TWO
GREAT BRITAIN

Political Involvement and Socialization in Great Britain

Donald D. Searing

This paper develops and assesses a theory about relationships between involvement in political life and *beliefs* about political institutions. The theory claims that political involvement embodies socialization experiences that build support for procedural rules of the game and thereby safeguard political institutions. From this perspective, the socialization of politicians has been characterized as the shield of constitutions and the scourge of political change. Yet very little is known about the subject, for the field of socialization research has studied mainly members of the general public, illustrating thereby Berrington's (1974:347) rule: "The amount of intellectual energy devoted to understanding the behavior of political participants varies inversely with their importance." Hence, it is necessary to begin at the beginning and clarify the key concepts and assumptions involved.

Concepts and Assumptions

Although the terms *political learning* and *political socialization* are used synonymously, there is an important distinction between them. Political learning refers to the acquisition, usually casual, of any beliefs related to any political activity. This concept fits best the limited political experience of the public. Since it is usually the public that has been investigated in socialization research by political scientists, political learning has been identified with the entire field.[1] By contrast, other social science disciplines have defined the concept "socialization" more along the lines suggested in the *Oxford English Dictionary*: "to render social, to make fit for living in society." "To render social" refers to processes that integrate individuals into a collectivity by teaching them its established ethos and skills (Lovell, 1980:88; Hyman, 1969:vii; Clausen, 1968:3–5). In the political world, such teaching is primarily encountered by those who participate in organizations such as political parties, local councils, and national parliaments. Here, the term *political socialization* will refer to both political learning and political socialization unless the theory requires specificity.

Political learning and political socialization occur throughout the life cycle (Kavanagh, 1983; Dawson, Prewitt, and Dawson, 1977:75–81); but differences between adult and preadult experiences are not sufficiently appreciated. Since the political involvement variable in our model concerns mainly adult experience, such differences require emphasis. One approach in preadult research is that which interprets socialization as a process of molding political character and producing a "political self." This is unsuitable for adult studies because the minds of adults are not blank tablets; nor are most adult characters very malleable. Adult socialization is more accurately described as a process that modifies minds and has more in common with studies of communication and attitude change than with child development. When the focus is on communications that help groom people for responsibilities in collectivities, the important point is that the people involved already have many views: adult socialization works with the products of preadult experience. Of course it also teaches new beliefs, but it is primarily concerned with elaborating, modifying, and reintegrating existing attitudes, with lessons learned during recruitment and training for roles in collectivities (Lovell, 1980:88–89; Clausen, 1968:13–14).[2]

Role acquisition is a prominent feature in the socialization of political activists. As adults, all citizens undergo some political learning. Yet those who become increasingly involved in politics encounter experiences of a more encompassing kind, i.e., socialization in political roles that reshape values, norms, skills, and ideologies. The most efficacious socialization occurs in adapting to collectivities such as party organizations or committees—being rendered "fit" for institutions like the House of Commons. Fenno (1962), for example, showed how the power of the U.S. House Committee on Appropriations was sustained by teaching established outlooks to newcomers and reinforcing them among veterans. In the same vein, Gertzog (1970) has described socialization in the House of Representatives as a process that promotes continuity by teaching norms and skills that are essential for performing congressional work. Socialization, then, is a conservative process that cultivates the continuity most collectivities require to function smoothly. It was no accident that Talcott Parsons and David Easton made stability the focus for political socialization research. Socialization generates support for existing institutions and arrangements that distribute power, income, and status; it tends to legitimize the status quo and the positions of those who run it and benefit from it (Kavanagh, 1983; Tapper, 1976; Brimm, 1966). That institutions are usually durable and policy innovations incremental rather than fundamental has been attributed to socialization's encouragement of institutional defenders and retraining of insurgents. As one Labour MP, a former rebel, put it: "I think instead of me turning this place inside out, they turned me inside out a little."[3]

If the socialization of political actors must be counted a conservative force, it is essential to acknowledge the ability of exogenous variables to undermine socialization's protective efforts and drive political institutions away from the status quo. Political parties and parliaments are particularly sensitive to such factors, because they are less well-insulated than most collectivities that serve as models in organization theory. Parties and parliaments are open to outside pressures on their recruitment and procedures; indeed, such openness is essential to their effectiveness as democratic institutions. This must be taken into account in conceptual and theoretical work on socialization.

It is difficult to chart the exogenous variables convincingly because so many can achieve significance. Nevertheless, the overall framework seems fairly clear. On one side are *selection* factors that may offer their own explanation for results attributed to socialization. If political activists, for instance, support a norm more strongly than do members of the attentive public from which they were selected, the explanation might be due to biased selection procedures as well as to socialization. On the other side, *ideological interventions* may be undertaken by radicals who aim to short-circuit socialization's conservative consequences. The radicalization of the British Labour party during the 1970s provides a dramatic example of such forces at work. Both types of variables will be examined in this paper, but first we shall construct our theory and test it with British data on general publics, attentive publics, parliamentary candidates, and MPs.

Theory and Methodology

The theory addresses relationships between involvement in political life and support for procedural rules of the game. It is driven by socialization processes that shape the attitudes of individuals whose actions affect the conduct of political systems. Socialization theories that consider the systemic implications of socialization have been labeled "political theories of political socialization" (Dawson, Prewitt, and Dawson, 1977:16). Their central theme is that socialization into political roles builds support for established patterns of power (Tapper, 1976:78). The political theory of political socialization developed here consists of three simple, interrelated propositions from which others can be derived to suit specific conditions. The first is the most general and, like the others, is rooted in the observation that political change proceeds slowly in modern societies. Political involvement helps preserve existing routines by instilling beliefs that moderate political conflict and deter new governments from dismantling institutions or sweeping away their predecessors' programs. Thus,

> the greater the involvement in a political collectivity, the greater the support for the central views of that collectivity.
> (P1)

This proposition should be interpreted as probabilistic and should not be overdone. Important innovations certainly do occur; and some leading politicians are iconoclasts. Normally, however, the resistance of the status quo to forces of transformation and change is shielded by socialization. Moreover, P1 points to relative political positions rather than to specific commitments or ideologies. As the political spectrum tilts to the right or to the left, those who are most involved in political life may become more or less supportive of the status quo. What the proposition suggests is only that they will, in any case, be relatively more supportive than those who are less involved.

Thus P1 simply claims that collectivities tend to protect their procedures and outlooks by teaching them to those who become involved in their affairs—the greater the involvement, the more effective the teaching. Degrees of involvement can be measured in many different ways; but P1 is designed to apply mainly to the following groups, which can be ranked easily by political involvement from lowest to highest: general public, attentive public, activists, candidates, Members of Parliament. The attentive public is distinguished from the general public by the greater interest it takes in political affairs. It forms the bottom of the stratum of party activists, the top of which, the candidates, is working to join those most deeply involved in established political activity, Members of Parliament (Cf. May, 1973:135–36). The proposition predicts a pattern of consequences distributed across these groups involved in the following collectivities: political systems for citizens, extraparliamentary parties and local councils for activists, and parliaments and parliamentary parties for MPs.

Although diffuse political learning characterizes the experience of general and attentive publics, it is socialization in organizations such as parties and parliaments that is believed to have the greatest impact upon an individual's belief system. A party organization's informal induction processes, for instance, may deflate and disorient new members and make them susceptible, even in middle age, to substantial attitude modification. This is why in numerous elite studies occupational role variables have been found to be related to political outlooks, and why role socialization is regarded as the place to look for process explanations. The general proposition (P1) can be applied to different types of attitudes and collectivities. In particular, it can be applied to building support for procedural rules of the game.

Institutional Support

Procedural rules of the game are the types of attitudes, the central views, of primary interest in research on institutional support. Political scientists, mainly Americans, who have developed this research believe that adult role socialization is heavily involved (Searing, 1982; Budge, 1970; Key, 1967; Almond and Verba, 1963; Dahl, 1961). Some of the more obvious procedural rules, such as freedom of speech, may be encountered during childhood or adolescence. Many more norms apparently are learned only in political roles, for survey research has found that they are not well recognized by the general public (Sullivan, Pierson, and Marcus, 1979; McClosky, 1964; Stouffer, 1963; Prothro and Grigg, 1960). At the same time, it is argued that support for these principles is essential to the stability of representative government and that this support is generated by a socialization process that, according to a senior Member of Parliament, "makes a politician conscious of the fact that there's more to be done than winning one round of the battle, that there's a permanence of the fabric that can be damaged if one doesn't honour the sort of unwritten principles."

Differences in types of collectivities are not stressed in institutional support accounts, partly because the focus is on consequences rather than processes of socialization, but primarily because all relevant collectivities are believed to teach much the same constitutional message, i.e., support for procedural rules of the game, the main difference being that some are believed to teach the message more fully and effectively than others. Hence,

> the greater the political involvement, the greater the support
> for political rules of the game.   (P2)

This proposition predicts a monotonic relationship between degree of political involvement and support for constitutional positions (see Figure 1). Explanations of the relationship usually emphasize formal education and political interest and exposure during adult life. McClosky and Brill (1983:420) argue, for example, that formal education has a direct impact upon learning rules of the game because some of these rules are taught explicitly in school. Education also has an important indirect effect because those who gradu-

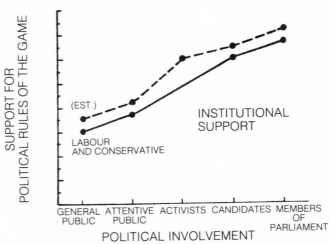

FIGURE 1. Political Involvement and Institutional Support

ate from universities are most likely to expose themselves as adults to political information and activity. Such adult exposure, again according to McClosky and Brill (1983:28–31), is the key process at work, since many norms will only be encountered in political environments. That is why Figure 1 predicts a sharp rise from the attentive public to the activists and candidates: individuals involved in political organizations are far more likely than the members of the public to discover something like the full range of norms and to discover which norms are considered most inviolable. The broken line in Figure 1 represents an estimate because it includes an estimate for activists, a group for which we do not have data for our tests. The solid line represents the prediction that will be examined empirically.

Procedure and Policy

It was Balfour who said, "Our whole political machinery presupposes a people so fundamentally at one that they can safely afford to bicker." Yet politicians may bicker all too cautiously, for their consensus may flow too freely between procedural questions and policy agendas. The third proposition suggests that attachment to political rules of the game can strengthen support for existing economic and social arrangements, and vice versa.[4] In other words, socialization's shield may protect more than the institutions of representative government.

> There is a direct, positive, and reciprocal relationship be-
> tween support for political rules of the game and support for
> the economic and social status quo.   (P3)

Commitment to procedural rules is not inevitably intertwined with loyalty to existing economic and social arrangements. Logically, political rules of the game need not tether the status quo; nor need commitment to central economic and social policies necessarily safeguard procedural rules. Nevertheless, historically one seems to lead to the other via socialization, particularly among national politicians who guide the policies and guard the rules. Political procedure is said to canalize policy thinking by setting institutional constraints within which politicians' socialization takes place. When the Parliamentary Labour party, for instance, has been Her Majesty's Loyal Opposition, it has adhered to the principle of accepting given frameworks; its opposition has been "opposition up to a point" (Punnett, 1973:13). The party's record in government is consistent with the Left's claims about the lack of determination among Labour MPs to introduce radical economic and social change.

Mastery of procedural rules is much admired both for its technical elegance and strategic utility. What is less often appreciated is that many rules of the game have important consequences for what is and what is not accomplished; they can fix boundaries upon behavior and confine political change to reformist rather than revolutionary directions. The norm of functional representation, for example, structures the composition of politicians' reference groups by necessitating regular meetings between ministers and elites outside Whitehall. Likewise, norms of collective responsibility and confidentiality give politicians incentives to covet their own institutional power and to respect that of other elite groups. But when political actors are portrayed as agents of a ruling class, this often misrepresents the nature of their situation and unfairly implies that they are factotums of privileged cabals. Following P3, the status quo may be secured more effectively by the invisible hands of "biased procedures" than by plots of "power elites."[5]

From the other end of the proposition, political moderates rarely attack procedural rules, because, unlike radical colleagues, they find few such norms inconvenient. Since their policy aims usually can be accomplished within existing procedural frameworks, it is easier for them to accept socialization cues and endorse the rules of the game (Searing, 1982:250; Whiteley, 1981:170). Moreover, they are sympathetic to tacit agreements to keep proposals for sweeping departures in policy off the agenda. They have little interest themselves in such potentially divisive proposals; and they value procedures that help maintain existing arrangements while facilitating the pursuit of modest reform. Socialization is certainly not the only instrument by which routines and programs are preserved, but it is a principal one. Politicians learn values, norms, and assumptions that make certain types of procedural departures and policy alternatives seem inappropriate or even preposterous.

To investigate the theory's fit with the data, a great deal of data are required. This paper examines survey responses collected during 1972 and 1973 from British Members of Parliament, candidates, attentive publics, and general publics. Members of Parliament (N=521) were interviewed by means of tape-recorded discussions. They also filled in printed forms and returned a mail-back questionnaire. A response rate of 83 percent applies to backbenchers, members of the Government and Opposition spokesmen alike. At the same time, a sample of candidates was drawn from the activist stratum's topmost layers. It is composed of 107 individuals (response rate 90 percent) who stood and came closest to winning in the 1970 General Election, but who had never been MPs. The attitudes of attentive publics and general publics are drawn from an opinion survey, also administered at the same time, with a probability sample of 2,500 British adults. The attentive publics are those respondents (16 percent) who scored highest on a Likert-type item about interest in politics.[6] The general publics include all the rest who, responding to a standard party identification question, indicated that they regarded themselves as Labour or Conservative.

These four groups are located at different steps on the scale of political involvement. Attitudes toward rules of the game are then assessed by Likert-type scales offering four responses: agree without reservations; agree with reservations; disagree, but with reservations; and disagree without reservation. The institutional support proposition will be examined first. Then we shall consider the proposition that posits a relationship between procedure and policy. An analysis of the impact of exogenous variables will conclude the investigation by introducing forces that potentially contradict socialization's claims and undermine its results.

An Analysis of Institutional Support

Institutional support accounts claim that consensus about procedural conventions is essential for democracy's survival; political institutions rest on underlying habits and ideas concerning the proper conduct of government. Socialization theory enters the further claim that there is no reason to expect people to support the institutions of representative government unless they have learned to believe in them. But which people?

The assumption that support from general publics is a prerequisite to successful democracy was undermined when survey research found that many rules of the game were not endorsed by the American public (Sullivan, Pierson, and Marcus, 1979; McClosky, 1964; Prothro and Grigg, 1960; Stouffer, 1963). The search for democracy's effective defenders then turned to political activists who might be more likely to endorse the appropriate principles and might be better positioned to practice what they preached (Budge, 1970; Liphart, 1968). According to Key (1967) and Truman (1951), socialization in political environments produces guardians of representative government's health and strength. Surely the survey evidence pointed in this direction: education and political involvement were consistently related to learning constitutional norms. It did not seem unreasonable to extrapolate and posit the existence of a highly educated and involved stratum of political actors who had absorbed the principles by which the political game is played.

Since institutional support theories were formulated largely through empirical work in the United States, they need to be probed further through investigations in other systems. American research, moreover, has investigated mainly the attitudes of the public and, to a lesser extent, political activists, but not the attitudes of national politicians (in whose hands representative government is said primarily to rest). Perhaps it is the absence of such data that has permitted unrealistic characterizations of politicians as a democratic praetorian guard, despite their socialization being based on existing rules of the game that may be democratic depending upon the character of the collectivity in question. Our political theory of political socialization does not comment on the quality of the democratic credentials of political actors. All that its general proposition (P1) predicts is that the greater the involvement in a political collectivity, the greater the support for whatever may be that collectivity's central views. All that its institutional support proposition (P2) does is apply this general notion to procedural rules of the game.

Rules of the Game

In most countries, the concept "rules of the game" is broader than that of "constitutional norms" (Matthews, 1968). However, the British experience brings these two concepts together, since British constitutional norms cover so much more ground than do the constitutions of other nations (Johnson, 1977:29–32; Phillips, 1970:1–2). They encompass the sort of principles that Americans draw from the Declaration of Independence, judicial decisions, congressional folkways, and the Federalist Papers. In Britain, such norms are derived from three sources: laws, both statute and common; conventions, which embody many of the central principles; and usages, guides for proper political behavior, derived from law and convention (Marshall and Moodie, 1967; Phillips, 1970). Whatever the source, they are all norms because they are standards recognized by "those actively concerned with the government of Britain" (Mackintosh, 1968:13).[7] Procedural rules of the game are whatever "persons of authority" accept as appropriate (Jennings, 1969:1–12).

All constitutional norms are rules of the game, but not all rules of the game are constitutional norms. To count as constitutional norms, procedural rules must satisfy two criteria. One is recognition by political actors that they are obligatory, a criterion often illustrated by parliamentary supremacy, representation, and ministerial accountability. These topics are addressed by our data and represent three of the four most fundamental doctrines of the Constitution's Liberal interpretation (the other is the rule of law), which was developed during the latter half of the nineteenth century and still prevails today (Birch, 1964:65–66). The other criterion is that a norm must promote one or more of the Constitution's basic features: democracy, parliamentary supremacy, monarchy, and cabinet government (Jennings, 1959:13). This covers the remaining subjects in our analysis: political opposition, freedom, functional representation, and political compromise and trust (Searing, 1982). Taken together, these topics address many of the most important constitutional doctrines. They also encompass many rules of the game of the type considered by those institutional support theorists who claim that the public is not a reliable bulwark of representative government and that a substantial part of the explanation for "how democratic regimes manage to function. . . is to be found in the motives that actuate the leadership echelon. . ." (Key, 1967:537).

Two Interpretations

The items used to examine these rules of the game are presented in the Appendix. To aid the analysis, these data were reduced by building composite indices from multiple indicators for doctrines tapped by more than one attitude item. The aim was to create a single summary measure for each of the topics. All items first were classified under the British Constitution's established principles. A correlation matrix was then created that supplied justification for most original item assignments, since the strongest relationships were concentrated among items within the designated sets. Next, negative items were recoded in a positive direction so that high scores on all items would consistently signify support for rules of the game. Each set's internal reliability was then examined with an adaptation of the Spearman-Brown formula. The final step was to add item values within sets, thereby constructing a new variable for each norm measured by more than one survey item.

To map the structure of attitudes toward the rules of the game that exist in the minds of the political authorities, each norm was crosstabulated with all others to produce a new matrix, which revealed two striking patterns (Searing, 1982): one was that the relationships between many norms were extremely weak; the other was that many of the correlations were negative. The six norms with the highest mean correlations with all other items in the matrix then were partitioned into two distinct sets that were compatible internally but incompatible with one another. The first includes "parliamentarism," "flexible tactics," and "adaption: accept limitations." The other joins "role of the electorate," "individual responsibility," and "vigorous and critical opposition." Within each set, all correlations are positive and among the strongest in the original matrix. Between sets, by contrast, eight out of nine correlations are negative, again including the most robust offered. To each set of core norms, three cluster norms were added, as they were the only other norms in the data that were correlated positively with these core doctrines: "concession: give opponents their due," "trust in politicians," and "supremacy of Parliament" to the first set; and, "freedom," "functional representation" and "trust in citizens" to the second. This resolves the attitude structure into two views of the British Constitution that are quite incompatible—every significant correlation between core norms in one and either core or cluster norms in the other is negative. The two configurations can be characterized as *deliberative* and *representational* interpretations of the British Constitution. It long has been recognized that the Constitution embodies two conflicting principles, direction and responsiveness, that correspond to these interpretations (Johnson, 1977:205). However, the opposition between the principles has been underestimated: together they create an axis that splits the Constitution into alternative renditions. Indeed, the first principal component produced by a factor analysis of these data is plainly a deliberation-representation dimension (Searing, 1982).[8]

The deliberative interpretation brings together parliamentarism and all of the attitudes in this study that focus on compromise. Its advocates tend to reject the notion that policy should be determined by electoral mandates, and they would rather pursue the common interest through consultation among leaders: "I get people who write to me and say, 'You've no right to speak on my behalf on so-and-so.' And I just write back and tell them I was elected to speak on their behalf whether they like it or not, and this is what I intend to do." By contrast, the representational interpretation substitutes themes of responsiveness for these patrician images. This second outlook rejects the deliberative interpretation's implicit equation between public opinion and irresponsible policy. The core theme of the representational interpretation is that of "giving people a chance to decide for themselves: taking people's preferences seriously." Adherents of this view are likely to believe that ordinary citizens should be active in politics and to regard with suspicion traditions of governmental strength, autonomy, and privacy which shut them out.

The split between these two interpretations of rules of the game has much to do with partisanship. In supporting these norms, Conservative and Labour politicians are separated by 10 percent or more, often much more, on three-quarters of them. Their disagreements are sharpest over core norms such as parliamentarism and the role of the electorate. One way to summarize the party positions is to compare, for each interpretation set, proportions of respondents that support not one or another norm, but nearly all at the same time. Approximately two-thirds of the Conservatives consistently approve at least five out of six norms from the deliberative interpretation, and a similar proportion of Labour politicians likewise supports representational norms. But the Conservatives are joined by only 38 percent of Labour politicians, and merely 16 percent from their own ranks cross over to endorse the full-blown representational viewpoint.[9] Since socialization teaches mainly norms that are dominant in a collectivity, it is desirable to examine these two interpretations of rules of the game separately by the party within which they are most likely to be regarded as the orthodoxy. Thus, we shall investigate the relationship between political involvement and support for procedural rules of the game first for Conservatives on the deliberative interpretation, and then for Labour on the representational.

Deliberative Rules of the Game

At the core of the deliberative interpretation are "parliamentarism," "flexible tactics," and "adaption: accept limitations." Parliamentarism is a norm derived from Whig and Idealist theories of politics that portray Parliament as a deliberative assembly for discussing and reconciling conflicting opinions to discover the common interest (Birch, 1964). Consistency and prudent policy are expected to prevail even when elite deliberation uncovers common interests that prove unpopular. Flexible tactics denotes a very general and very English approach to compromise, which commends it as a constructive process for fitting together different approaches rather than turning everything upside down. From the viewpoint of adaption, it is regarded as desirable to seek accommodations and to realize that compromise is an appropriate and prudent political strategy. The phrase *art of the possible* is widely used in British politics to reflect awareness of limits upon political action imposed by a complex society and a system based upon consent.[10]

In Figure 2, Conservative endorsements for parliamentarism, flexible tactics, and adaptation are plotted against degrees of political involvement. The pattern is nearly exactly as predicted by P2: the greater the political involvement, the greater the support for political rules of the game. Consistent with the considerable gap the theory posits between public and politicians, the sharpest rise in support

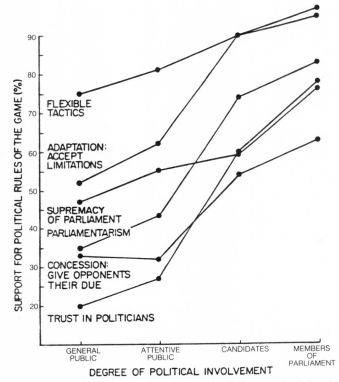

FIGURE 2. Conservative Support for Core and Cluster Principles of the Deliberative Interpretation of the Constitution, by Degree of Political Involvement

for the rules is between the attentive public and the candidates. Formal education during childhood and adolescence may teach some aspects of these rules, but it is clear that the general public is not firmly committed to the flagship doctrine of parliamentarism, most likely because its meaning and significance are not well understood. Further formal education may succeed in teaching the principles, but formal education cannot explain the rise between candidates and MPs, for the latter are not noticeably better educated than the former. These subpatterns in the data are quite consistent with the thesis that political involvement is an important feature of socialization to political rules of the game.

The secondary or cluster norms associated with deliberative outlooks are "concession," "trust in politicians," and "supremacy of Parliament." Concession is more difficult than flexible tactics, for it involves giving political opponents concrete political deals and adjustments. It involves recognition that if one wishes to get one's way in a representative political system, one must grant the same opportunity to political enemies (Griffith, Plamenatz, and Pennock, 1956:125). To function effectively, representative systems require compromise. And compromise requires mutual trust to unclog communication channels and thereby permit civilized debate among opponents. It does this by stressing the sincerity and honesty of those with whom one disagrees: "We are a group of people with the same interest—different ideas on how it should be done, but we're all here for the same purpose."[11] The last secondary norm, parliamentary supremacy, completes the deliberative configuration by protecting Parliament, and particularly the Government's decisions, from outside interference. It is a doctrine that means exactly what it says. No authority can legitimately challenge or override any law passed by Parliament.[12] At the same time, Parliament is politically dependent upon the public: its claim to supremacy is accepted primarily because Parliament represents the people; and its supremacy thereby guarantees the majority's political sovereignty (Jennings, 1959:13).

It can be seen clearly in Figure 2 that Conservative support for these three secondary or cluster norms is distributed in the same pattern as the others. With the exception of concession (i.e., give opponents their due) between the general and attentive publics, endorsements never decline across the steps of political involvement, but rather increase dramatically. The gap between publics and political actors is highlighted by the response to supremacy of Parliament, the norm regarded as the Constitution's keystone. It is perhaps remarkable that more politicians do not endorse it, which suggests that their constitutional bona fides have been exaggerated (Searing, 1982). More remarkable still is the finding that less than 50 percent of the general public endorse this principle.

Constituency political parties provide the most obvious settings where those who become active in politics may begin to absorb the system's norms. Thus, DiPalma (1977:77–79) argues that merely a few years' exposure to organized party politics is sufficient to acquire many key attitudes. The same point has been made by studies in Canada and Britain: the more the individual is exposed to extraparliamentary political life, the more he or she is likely to learn about its rules of the game (Price, Clarke, and Krause, 1975; Putnam, 1976:89–90). By being attentive to politics, citizens are exposed to political learning that is missed by the general public. However, by being active, they are also exposed to political socialization regarding central norms of the collectivities in which they participate or towards which they aspire.

Local government is thus the obvious setting for absorbing rules of the game. Contracts and experiences in council roles, for instance, teach norms as well as the skills required for effective service. Gertzog's (1970) interviews with freshmen U.S. Congressmen show that those with prior service in state legislatures had the greatest familiarity with parliamentary organization and procedure. In the same vein, candidate experience must not be overlooked as an apprenticeship, for success is frequently preceded by several unsuccessful campaigns over several years. The time between selection and entrance may involve visits to the House of Commons, talks with MPs, and reading literature about Parliament, experiences that surely familiarize candidates with the etiquette of the order. Once inside Westminster there are socialization processes that shake newcomers loose from previous perspectives and encourage working within the system rather than against it.

Representational Rules of the Game

"Role of the electorate," "vigorous opposition," and "individual responsibility" constitute core norms of the representational interpretation favored by Labour. That the public's views should be "heard up here" and have a significant impact upon public policy is a basic principle of the contemporary constitution (Mackintosh, 1968:14). Although the electorate's role in the political system has never been precisely defined, representation of individuals' opinions has been an important obligation since the Reform Act of 1832.[13] Vigorous opposition promotes the desired ambience. It provides, as one backbencher put it, "an opportunity for MPs, representing ordinary people, to get up and say that they think such and such an idea is lousy and ought to be changed, and to try to stop it." This is a check against corruption and incompetent administration, but it is also the system's principal engine for protecting minority rights and expressing the electorate's discontent.[14] In Britain, opposition assumes an adversary style, which is valued because it punctures complacency and guards against Bonapartism in relationships between government and citizen (Johnson, 1977:61–62).

These representational themes are armed with the weapons of individual responsibility, the doctrine that states that ministers are answerable to the House of Commons for their department's work and can be compelled by the House to resign for serious errors (Marshall and Moodie, 1967:67–71). This norm, which was not included in the public opinion survey, is intended to insure ministerial attentiveness to the electorate's representatives (Birch, 1964:139–49).[15] It retains vitality because it maintains a responsibility function over and above redress of grievances, albeit the doctrine still serves redress in every Parliament. Individual responsibility's principal function has become exploring and testing the competence of ministers and their Governments. It puts ministers on the spot to defend their department's activities and provides useful opportunities to attack administrative incompetence and to animate civil servants (King, 1974:87).

With regard to Labour endorsements of the representational interpretation, Figure 3 depicts steep increases in support for these rules of the game among the general public, attentive public, and candidates who participate in extraparliamentary party organizations and look towards Westminster. But the next step, career involvement as an MP at Westminster, reverses the trend: support for role of the electorate and individual responsibility actually declines at this step on the political involvement scale. Support from Labour MPs may be stronger than that from Labour's electorate, but it is weaker than that from Labour candidates. Why?

The answer, it may be argued, is that representational themes are more unambiguously established in Labour's extraparliamentary party collectivities where candidates are socialized, than they are in the House of Commons where Labour MPs are "fitted in." In other words, each group of political actors is behaving as our theory's general proposition anticipates: each is learning the prevailing norms of his or her collectivity. The difficulty is that representational doctrines are newer and more radical than deliberative doctrines, and their writ does not run as strongly at Westminster as it does in the party outside. Moreover, since representational doctrines are the most democratic in the constitution, this situation hammers home the point that socialization attaches politicians to the *prevailing* norms of their collectivities however democratic, imperfectly democratic, or even undemocratic these norms may be.

Labour MPs also are less keen than Labour candidates about representational rules of the game because they are more keen than these candidates about the contrary deliberative interpretation. The deliberative interpretation of the constitution is the most ancient of the two views and the most deeply entrenched at Westminster. It is therefore difficult to dismiss, especially for members of a parliamentary party whose constitutional credentials are questioned from time to time and who, in response, deem it necessary to announce that they uphold the constitution and propose to work within existing rules of the game (Punnett, 1973:13–15). Yet the deliberative interpretation is less compatible than the representational with the party's traditions and practices. In particular, it does not sit easily with Labour's tradition of mandates and rigorous majority rule (Kavanagh, 1982:203–4; Brand, 1976). Hence, as Labour MPs at Westminster are drawn towards the deliberative interpretation, it should not be surprising if they become correspondingly more reserved than candidates about representational rules of the game.

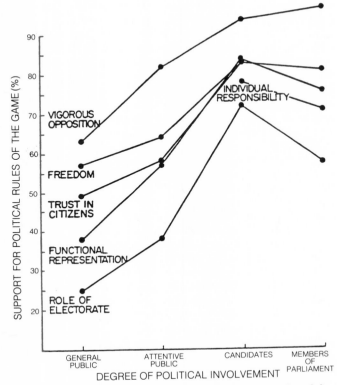

FIGURE 3. Labour Support for Core and Cluster Principles of the Representational Interpretation of the Constitution, by Degree of Political Involvement

The secondary or cluster norms of the representational interpretation include "freedom," "functional representation," and "trust in citizens." Freedom of speech is a constitutional norm because the constitution's democratic and parliamentary characteristics would make little sense without it. Free elections presuppose free speech, which is essential for informed public opinion, meaningful deliberation, and political participation.[16] Since 1700, it has been accepted that the government should not seek to control the expression of opinion, and that the state's only duty is to punish libels when these occur (Dicey, 1959:253). Functional representation is a constitutional usage that suggests that representation should not be restricted to the House of Commons: it should also be developed through contacts between the civil service and organizations like trade unions, industrial associations, and professional organizations. Such groups are said to have a right to be consulted about the formulation of policies that affect their interests. It is not surprising that the representational interpretation replaces trust in politicians with trust in citizens. This cluster norm has importance for representative government because citizens are unlikely to join in political activity with associates they suspect are untrustworthy.

The pattern for these three secondary norms is the same as for role of the electorate and individual responsibility: a steady increase in endorsement from Labour's general public to candidates, broken by a decline in support with the next level of political involvement, the Labour MPs (Figure 3). Again, although this development is not incompatible with the spirit of P2, it is certainly inconsistent with the prediction. What matters is the orthodoxies in particular collectivities, orthodoxies that can lead to departures from monotonicity. With the exception of the step between candidates and MPs, however, the pattern of Labour's support for representational rules is much the same as Conservative support for the deliberative interpretation. Labour's slopes between the attentive public and the candidates, and between the general public and the attentive public also are somewhat steeper, on average, than are those for the Conservatives. This may reflect a partisanship that boosts support for doctrines that best fit party ideology. The responses of Labour's general public reflect lack of information and, beneath that, possibly disinterest. On norms such as freedom and vigorous opposition, which are both ancient and well-projected through the media, the general public's support does rise above 55 percent. On the other rules of the game, however, its views seem undeveloped: correlations in the general public's matrix are statistically significant in less than one-fourth of the cases. By contrast, the attentive public is a partisan public, and the structure of its thinking about rules of the game is more highly constrained: correlations among its attitudes reveal no more weak relationships than do those for the politicians.[17]

Overall, the data on deliberative and representational rules of the game provide powerful backing for the institutional support proposition (P2). Moreover, the wide gap between the public on one side of the involvement spectrum and the politicians on the other is consistent with the elite culture concept that underlies previous accounts (e.g., Budge, 1970). At the same time, politicians' commitments to these rules should not be exaggerated. Their attitudes are pushed and pulled about by political values and partisan advantage far more than is implied by some versions of institutional support theory (Searing, 1982). Nor should it be assumed that political learning and role socialization are the only factors that shape attitude formation and change. Other variables are certainly involved, and we shall consider them after examining the Balfour proposition.

An Analysis of Procedure and Policy

Left to its own devices, role socialization normally weaves consensus around existing institutional arrangements. When the rules of the game are desirable, this consensus-building effect is desirable, because it helps hold politicians in check and thereby helps maintain valued procedural frameworks. The consequences of consensus in central economic and social policies can be desirable too, for if there is nothing on which political opponents agree, they are unlikely to be able to manage a political system that is capable of addressing serious problems. But policy consensus is also suspect. Indeed, the socialization of politicians is more likely to be condemned than praised by commentators whose policy preferences are well to the left or right of center. Moreover, unless politicians divide over important policies, elections can become purely ritual occasions, and representative government can lose its essential characteristic of popular control (Friedrich, 1950:ch. 5). The ideal formula, following Balfour, is that consensus on political rules of the game should unite protagonists who remain divided over significant matters of economic and social policy.

In contemporary Britain, politicians are not divided sufficiently to satisfy intense partisans on either side. The reason they are not so divided returns us to the theory's third and final proposition (P3), which submits that there is a direct, positive and reciprocal relationship between support for rules of the game and support for the economic and social status quo. This proposition applies primarily, of course, to socialization in parliaments, for it is mainly in these collectivities that both types of support are likely to be established as central views and presented to political actors via role socialization. Moreover, the projected positive relationship is not simply an artifact of each variable being promoted by socialization into the parliamentary and party collectivities. There are direct, independent connections between these two sets of beliefs, and the flow of influence is reciprocal. Attachment to political rules of the game is said to contribute to accepting the economic and social status quo because established rules frequently favor existing policies and arrangements (Tapper, 1976:92). Working within the rules of the game thereby leads politicians to reformist rather than radical programs. Thus, radical parties often face demands to validate their constitutional credentials by demonstrating good intentions towards existing economic and social institutions.[18] Conversely, attachment to the economic and social status quo promotes accepting political rules of the game because moderation and incrementalism are best achieved by working within the system. Given the reciprocal nature of this relationship, it cannot be analyzed conclusively. Nevertheless, it does suggest a consequence worth investigating: that the strongest commitment to rules of the game should be found in political groups with the strongest commitment to the economic and social status quo.

The most valuable support for procedural rules of the game is support for the types of rules that are most favored by one's political opponents. In our data, this would be Labour support for the deliberative norms and Conservative support for the representational. Table 1 reports this information for ideological groups within each parliamentary party. The groups have been ranked from high to low by their general approaches to defending the mixed economy and welfare state. The "high" ranking is assigned to the moderate Social Democrats on the Labour side and to members of Pressure for Economic and Social Toryism (P.E.S.T.) on the Conservative. The Fabian Society and the Bow Group hold the "intermediate" rank. The "low" support level for existing economic and social arrangements is represented by the Tribune Group and the Monday Club.[19]

For each group within each party there are two entries. The first reports the percentage of the group's members who approve all three core norms of the constitutional interpretation favored by their political opponents. The second entry is the percentage who approve at least five of the interpretation's six core plus cluster norms. These data plainly show that the strongest endorsements for procedural rules of the game are indeed found in groups that have the strongest commitment to the economic and social status quo. The only exception is in Labour's column for core and cluster norms, but even here approval for rules of the game most favored by political opponents is four times as strong among both the high and intermediate supporters of the status quo as among the low group.

The flow of influence is reciprocal: support for the economic and social status quo can help boost support for constitutional norms too. Indeed, the data just as easily might be interpreted from this perspective as from the other. Politicians near the center of the political spectrum find it easier to accept the legitimacy of inconvenient rules than do their more politically radical colleagues (Searing, 1982:250; Whiteley, 1981:170). Those who stand to lose more by following rules of the game find it more difficult to endorse such norms and, as the political struggle intensifies, lose taste for rules that hinder their efforts. It is not at all surprising, therefore, that the decade of the 1970s, which raised the temperature of conflict over the mixed economy and welfare state, was also a decade of constitutional improprieties. By 1980, the Master of the Rolls complained publicly that matters had gone so far as to require introducing judicial review; and others proposed a written constitution (Searing, 1982; Norton, 1981). Likewise, the constitutional struggle within the Labour Party between 1979 and 1982 was a conflict between opponents who were seeking to structure the rules of the game to further

TABLE 1.

Support for Economic and Social Status Quo, By Support for Political Rules of the Game

Support for Economic and Social Status Quo**	Support for Rules of the Game Favored by Opponents*			
	Labour		Conservative	
	Core Norms	Core and Cluster Norms	Core Norms	Core and Cluster Norms
High	71	48	19	29
Intermediate	53	49	7	14
Low	20	12	0	10

*For Labour this is the deliberative interpretation, for Conservatives the representational. Entries for both Labour and Conservative represent the percentage of those who endorse all three Core Norms and those who endorse at least five of the six Core and Cluster Norms.

**High = Social Democrat (Labour, N=50), P.E.S.T. (Conservative, N=42). Intermediate = Fabian Society (Labour, N=103), Bow Group (Conservative, N=40). Low = Tribune Group (Labour, N=49), Monday Club (Conservative, N=25).

their ideological goals (Kavanagh, 1982:219; Kogan and Kogan, 1982:13). These uses and abuses of constitutional principles are a tribute to the strength of forces that can counteract the conservative consequences of political socialization, and a reminder that the theory we have constructed in an empty cell actually operates in a very full and complicated world.

Exogenous Factors

Our theory integrates the results of many empirical studies and commentaries and enjoys a plausibility derived from these sources. We have found that it has a reasonable fit with a large British data set encompassing most of the key points on its political involvement scale. Nevertheless, we must distrust this socialization theory, because in seeking clarity and parsimony it has excluded variables that may contradict its thesis or confound its results. Since each group, beginning with the attentive public, is drawn from the previous group, selection or recruitment effects are the most obvious missing variables that might work in the same direction as socialization to produce the patterns for procedural rules of the game reported in Figures 2 and 3. And, since political collectivities are comparatively permeable, ideological interventions are the most obvious missing variables that can check socialization's hypothesized tendency to protect the economic and social status quo (and which have recently radicalized the Parliamentary Labour party in Britain).

Recruitment Effects

Pure selection models are impossible and implausible. They are impossible because they cannot exclude socialization—beliefs must, after all, be learned somewhere. They are implausible because they stuff all learning into the earliest stages and disallow it thereafter. A more convincing approach to studying the undoubted importance of recruitment effects assumes that either selection or socialization variables, or both, may be affecting distributions of attitudes towards procedural rules of the game at each step on the scale of political involvement. The problem, then, is to estimate at each step how much of the observed differences can be attributed to one set of variables and how much to the other.

A method for estimating the relative influence of recruitment and socialization factors is illustrated in Figure 4. The first step on the scale of political involvement is from the general public to the attentive public. If selection variables are dominant here, members of the attentive public would have learned most of their present attitudes when they were members of a distinctive subgroup within the general public. By contrast, to the extent that socialization variables are driving the process, the attentive public would have learned its distinctive attitudes after emerging from the general public and increasing its exposure to new political information.

To estimate the mix, the postulated distinctive subgroup within the general public is reconstructed by looking for characteristics that match the attentive public. To retain full information, this is accomplished by weighting the general public according to the attentive public's distributions for age and level of education. There are now three groups—general public, matched general public, and attentive public—represented by rectangles in the top row of Figure 4. The matched group is the key. *Correspondence between the views of the matched group and those of the attentive public suggests selection whereas correspondence between its views and those of the general public suggests socialization.*

In the same way, candidates' distributions on age and education were used to create from the attentive public a matched attentive public, matched to the candidates' background profile. These three groups are represented in the second row of Figure 4. The rectangles in the third row carry the analysis from the extraparliamentary party into Westminster. They are likewise arranged to facilitate estimating the mix between recruitment and socialization factors, but the matched subgroup here has been constructed differently. It consists

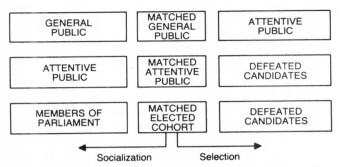

FIGURE 4. Illustration of Methodology for Comparing Relative Influence of Socialization and Selection Factors

of the subset of Labour and Conservative MPs first elected in 1970. This matched elected cohort suits the test well since none of them had ever before been MPs and, until the general election, they were, like the candidates (who by margin of victory came closest to winning in 1970), "serious candidates." When interviewed, this matched elected cohort only had been in the House of Commons for two or three years, probably not long enough for extensive socialization but certainly long enough to display signs of socialization effects if any are present.

We shall use means to compare attitude distributions among groups. Means are calculated for each group and for the matched general public that stands between them. If the matched general public's mean resembles that of the attentive public, this is evidence for selection, since the attentive public apparently did not go on to acquire new views of its own. If, conversely, the matched general public's mean is closer to that of the general public, as is the case in our example, this is evidence for socialization, since the attentive public has apparently undergone postrecruitment attitude change. Table 2 reports means by party for attitudes towards political rules of the game. At each step on the political involvement scale, the estimate of the mix of socialization and selection factors is indicated by the distance of the matched groups' means from the means of groups on either side.

Overall, socialization proves more important than selection, but selection is prominent and occasionally predominant for particular stages and political parties. The first row, which reports means for the first step on the political involvement scale, shows little evidence of recruitment effects upon political rules of the game. Although the point spread between the general and attentive publics here is too small to justify much confidence in the result, the means of the matched general publics are very close to those of the general

TABLE 2.

Socialization and Selection Compared: $\overline{X}$s for Groups Matched by Age and Education

Political Rules of the Game					
Conservative			Labour		
General Public	Matched General Public	Attentive Public	General Public	Matched General Public	Attentive Public
43.7	43.2	50.0	46.2	47.8	59.8
Attentive Public	Matched Attentive Public	Defeated Candidates	Attentive Public	Matched Attentive Public	Defeated Candidates
50.0	62.3	71.2	59.8	63.2	98.8
Other MPs	Matched Elected Cohort	Defeated Candidates	Other MPs	Matched Elected Cohort	Defeated Candidates
78.8	79.0	66.0	76.0	81.5	82.3

publics. This pattern indicates that many procedural rules of the game are rarely seen clearly outside political environments. Freedom of speech is the most conspicuous exception to this generalization: and freedom of speech is the only individual rule of the game that displays clear selection effects. Information about constitutional norms is conveyed implicitly through partisan propaganda, political news, and television narratives, sources more likely to be encountered by attentive rather than by general publics. Such exposure is, according to McClosky and Brill (1983:28–31), the key to the character of the attentive public's outlook.

The picture changes at the next step on the scale of political involvement, i.e., from attentive publics to candidates (Table 2, row 2). Here recruitment effects and socialization effects are evenly balanced in the Conservative case, while socialization predominates for Labour.[20] Thus, Conservative members of the attentive public who make the leap from interest to involvement are sometimes better informed about rules of the game than those they leave behind. They have, for example, already learned a good deal about "parliamentarism." Once inside, however, they learn more

(DiPalma, 1977:77–79; Price, Clarke, and Krause, 1975). It is in the extraparliamentary party organizations and in local government that Conservatives absorb other procedural norms including less palatable ones like "concession."

The relative significance of selection effects increases at the next highest level of political involvement, the step from candidates to Members of Parliament (Table 2, row 3). Again, the results differ by party, this time dramatically. Conservatives show no selection effects whatsoever for rules of the game. By contrast, selection dominates for Labour, albeit the point spread, and hence confidence, is smaller here. This may be further evidence of a strong ideological valence for representational norms in Labour's extraparliamentary constituency parties, which are in charge of recruitment. In any event, the patterns are compatible with stereotypes of the decade: Conservatives selecting by "character," Labour by "principles."

In sum, socialization factors predominate in the table, but recruitment effects are important as well. Selection's significance grows with increases in political involvement; and it attains its strongest position on the Labour side.

Ideological Interventions

Ideological interventions press in the opposite direction. Even as the interviews for the present study were being conducted, these countervailing forces were working to confound the conservative consequences for public policy that are attributed to role socialization. It is often argued, in particular, that members of parliaments tend to become increasingly supportive of the economic and social status quo and thereby more moderate than their parties' activists (Coates, 1975; Miliband, 1973; May, 1973; Hindess, 1971; Parkin, 1971). Yet, during the 1970s, ideological interventions were hard at work checking this slide towards the center. Such forces equally challenge commitments to procedural rules, because, according to P3, the two sets of commitments are intertwined. Thus, the decade offers a showcase for variables that can neutralize and even override socialization's usual effects.

To pursue their representative duties, members of Parliament must maintain constant communication and contact with various outside groups and individuals. This hampers fitting newcomers to Parliament's central views, for they will continue to be open to influence and pressure from many external sources. Yet the exogenous sources of attitude change are so many and so subject to temporary fluctuations in strength that it would be extremely difficult to construct a general theory covering the entire field of socialization and countervailing forces. Case studies of recent events in the Labour party, however, can help identify some of the most common forces involved and suggest what some of the dynamics might be.

Three primary variables are changes in events, reactions to these events, and actions that may affect politicians' outlooks. Events include changes in polity, economy, and society. People who react to these changes may be members of external organizations, members of internal party factions, or politicians in top leadership positions. The configuration of reactions can also involve period or generational effects. Period effects spread across most groups concerned and lead most of their members to similar conclusions. Generational effects, by contrast, structure the reactions of a particular age cohort and give it distinctive and long-lasting views. The last step in the process occurs when the people who are reacting to events act themselves to try to change the attitudes of MPs. They may do so by concentrating on recruitment, on selecting new members whose views will gradually transform the existing parliamentary orthodoxy. They may also simply seek to deselect or retire from Parliament as quickly as possible those whose outlooks differ most from their own. Or, they may look to existing members and seek to alter their views by a combination of reasoned arguments and rewards and sanctions. This last enterprise is not at all as naive as it may seem, for it addresses adult socialization, which can involve quite conscious and rational decisions: politicians do test their ideological and career goals against what seems efficacious in their environment.

The key events began when the Wilson Governments of 1964–1970 glossed over awkward Conference decisions and did not make Britain more equal. This led to widespread disillusionment among activists and to the suspicion that after six years of Labour Governments, capitalism was actually stronger than it was before. From the viewpoint of the Left, Labour had failed to control the economy satisfactorily. It had overestimated the power of the state and underestimated the power of private enterprise. When the party returned to government in 1974–1979, it proved again to be cautious, pragmatic, and Crosland-like, and continued to follow the trails of revisionism (Whiteley, 1981; Arblaster, 1977:425–27; Mackintosh, 1978:259). The new prime minister, James Callaghan, continued to turn a deaf ear to militant rank-and-file opinion. He subsequently was accused at the 1979 Conference of having lost the election by having failed to accept Conference decisions on pay policy thereby producing the discontent that helped Margaret Thatcher win. Perhaps it was because of the radical soul-searching between the 1964–1970 and 1974–1979 Labour Governments that the Left was even more disappointed with what it regarded as the "mixed and dismal" record of Labour's latest period in power. Once again, it accused members of the parliamentary party of backsliding on socialist convictions (Coates, 1980:258).

The critical reaction to these events came from young, middle-class activists who would achieve in a short time remarkable changes in the Labour party's constitutional structure and policy directions. During the late 1960s and early 1970s, these middle-class graduates ousted many working-class party members from leadership positions in the constituency associations. The party became increasingly acrimonious because the former regarded themselves as every bit as educated and informed as Labour MPs and were in no mood to defer to superior knowledge at Westminster. As the influence of the activists extended over organization and opinion in the extraparliamentary party, MPs soon found themselves facing critical management committees of their constituency associations that wanted to know why they were not doing more to advance socialist goals (Bradley, 1981:49–51). The young Turks were not simple-minded and doctrinaire but rather "articulate, principled and suspicious of those who advocate a devaluation of socialist principles in pursuit of power" (Whiteley, 1981:162–63).

They were led by a new group of party activists who called themselves the "Outside Left" to claim a position outside the traditional power structure and different from that of the traditional Left (the Inside Left) in Parliament and the Tribune Group. The key unit was the CLPD, the Campaign for Labour Party Democracy, which was organized in 1973 to deliver power to the activists by changing the Labour party's constitution. Eventually, the Militant Tendency joined with the other Outside Left groups in the Rank and File Mobilizing Committee (RFMC), an umbrella organization led by the CLPD and devoted to insuring that the "betrayals" of recent Labour Governments would not be repeated (Kogan and Kogan, 1982:15–19).

The Campaign for Labour Party Democracy (CLPD) quickly turned to the trade unions, because Labour is dependent on the unions that support it financially and control 90 percent of the votes at its Annual Conference. Nothing could be achieved without union support; but, throughout most of the party's history, the unions had backed the parliamentary leadership against left-wing activists. Nevertheless, sufficient union support was won because just as new left-wing, middle-class radicals had entered the extraparliamentary party during the late sixties and early seventies, so new left-wing union leaders had risen to the top of some of the larger unions. And, like the activists, they were discontented with the performance of recent Labour Governments.[21] These trade union leaders did not direct the movement for radicalization, but their support enabled the activists to achieve the left-wing gains of the 1970s (Kogan and Kogan, 1982:45–58; Crouch, 1982). The activists and their trade union allies aimed to change the attitudes of the Parliamentary Labour party so that when it next formed a government it would be less reluctant to transform existing institutional arrangements. Their strategy was to intervene in recruitment and retirement in order to replace revisionist MPs with radical ones and counteract the conservative consequences of socialization at Westminster.

These tactics concentrated on securing several key changes in Labour's constitution. Because they had achieved substantial influence in many Labour constituency associations, and because they expected this influence to grow rather than diminish, they sought changes that would devolve power to these extraparliamentary collectivities. They were already able to insure that many selection conferences preferred left-wing candidates. In 1979, they won the battle for mandatory reselection of MPs. This meant that, during each parliament, each sitting Labour MP would be evaluated by his or her constituency association against other possible candidates— which gave the activists an opportunity to get rid of sitting revisionists and others who might move in this direction. At the 1980 Party Conference and the Wembley Conference of 1981, they also took away from MPs the right to elect the Leader of the party and turned it over to an electoral college dominated by the unions and the activists. These ideological interventions had implications for existing members too. By constantly hounding the revisionist leadership (the Leader and Deputy Leader were shouted down at the 1976 Party Conference at Blackpool), and by increasing the powers of constituency associations, they hoped to retard the tendency of socialization in the House of Commons to dampen the zeal of left-wing MPs (Berrington, 1982:70).

What were the results? By the middle of the decade, observers began to note that Labour selection conferences seemed to be preferring more left-wing candidates. By the end of the decade, it was quite clear that this recruitment pattern had been effective in counterbalancing some of socialization's conservative consequences and shifting the Parliamentary Labour party to the left (Berrington, 1982). Up till the mid-1960s, constituency associations selected their candidates more by personal or sectional considerations than by ideological criteria. A major change took place from 1974 onward, as the Left penetrated comfortable and safe seats. Even when Labour was defeated in 1970 and 1979, the Left managed to inch forward as older right-wing MPs were replaced by younger left-wing Members (Berrington, 1982:70). Through the electoral college arrangement, the Left was also able to block right-wing candidates for the Leadership. And these signs of the times began to modify the definitions of orthodoxy in terms of which sitting MPs are socialized in the parliamentary party. There was a rush to join the Tribune Group, and formerly moderate MPs began to take unilateralism and further nationalization more seriously than they had before. By the end of the decade, the Left had achieved some of the major changes in party policy towards which it had been working.[22]

This movement to overcome the effects of role socialization in the Parliamentary Labour party was unusual in that some of its leaders had been trained in the social sciences, knew what "role socialization" meant, and explained, in a theoretical way, what they proposed to do about it. They would attack it head-on by trying to change orthodoxies at Westminster, but their principal strategy was, shrewdly, to bypass its operations. Through reselection, they would eliminate MPs who had most succumbed to its blandishments. Through selection, they would bring in a new generation of committed, middle-class socialists who would be resistant to prevailing role socialization tendencies and who could be kept up to the mark by reselection.

Conclusion

Political involvement presents a field of situations covering both political learning and political socialization. Individuals pass through these situations and adapt to them. As they receive political news and partisan propaganda, participate in political clubs, canvass in campaigns, serve apprenticeships in local government, stand in general elections, enter the House or take up ministerial responsibilities, they encounter situations with unfamiliar attributes. Because socialization continues throughout the life cycle, there is a continuous flow of new experiences, information, and expectations that invite adaptation. Individuals may absorb the lessons without much deliberation or evaluate them and consider how they fit with goals and viewpoints already held. In either case, they tend to adjust to new situations by modifying their beliefs and behavior. The magnitude of these modifications differs for different people: few reshape their characters, but some conform more readily and thoroughly than others. No one except the psychotic or incompetent is immune from making minimal accommodations and learning through experience.

Socialization's accommodations have consequences for the system as well as for the individual. The first and most general proposition (P1) in the socialization theory offered here suggests that the greater an individual's involvement in a political collectivity, the greater his or her support for the central views of that collectivity. This suggestion has been applied to the particular case of support for procedural rules of the game. Thus, P2, the institutional support proposition, predicts that the relationship between political involvement and support for rules of the game is monotonic. Data on attitudes towards deliberative and representational norms are for the most part consistent with the prediction. The only departure was found at the step between Labour candidates and MPs, a departure that underscored the importance of considering carefully the collectivities involved and the central views of each.

The step on the spectrum between interest and involvement, between attentive publics and candidates, proved to be a very important one. This is the step from political learning to political socialization in collectivities where even part-time activity can produce dramatic results in teaching new norms and reinforcing and elaborating those already held. In countries like Britain, such socialization processes also help preserve representative government, since those who are involved in politics (especially full-time politicians) are the people who run the system. More generally, however, what tends to be preserved is not necessarily democratic ideals, but rather whatever procedural rules are embedded in the political present.

It is normal for political involvement, through political socialization, to promote political stability. It does so by fostering commitments to established views of existing institutional arrangements. Proposition three (P3) suggests that this protection may extend beyond procedural rules of the game to cover central aspects of public policy. It suggests that there is a direct, positive, and reciprocal relationship between support for political rules of the game and support for the economic and social status quo. This prediction was found to be consistent with the data from an indirect test that assessed support for the status quo by ranking ideological groups according to their general orientations towards the mixed economy and welfare state.

Still, something was obviously missing from this analysis, for socialization cannot be the only factor at work on the attitudes of politicians: it is a conservative force; yet as the interviews for the present study were being conducted, both parties were pulling away from the social democratic consensus of the previous two decades. Socialization's usual performance cannot explain institutional change and innovation in policy.

This led to an analysis of key exogenous factors: recruitment effects, which were investigated by creating matched groups and comparing means; and ideological interventions, which were explored through a case study of efforts to radicalize the Parliamentary Labour party during the 1970s. Both types of variables were shown capable of having substantial results—results that press in the same direction as socialization as well as results that work to neutralize socialization's effects. Parsimonious socialization theories of the sort developed in this paper are not, then, likely candidates for universal laws of human behavior. Because the field of forces behind the formation of attitudes is extremely complex, socialization has been examined as though it exists in isolation, which is certainly not true, as the analysis of selection effects and ideological interventions makes clear. There will, therefore, be times and places where our socialization theory articulated above fits less well than it does in the present case considered, and times and places where it does not fit at all.

Moreover, this theory, like most current socialization theories, is concerned with consequences, i.e., the outcomes of political involvement, rather than the processes by which such outcomes are produced. The next step is to investigate systematically these socialization engines of the explanation.

Appendix

Political Rules of the Game

Agree/Disagree labels indicate the direction of response interpreted as support for rules of the game.

PARLIAMENTARISM

Policy should be determined more by deliberation and consultation among MPs than by instructions or mandates from the electorate.   Agree

The electorate ought to have the opportunity to vote in a referendum on crucial matters affecting the nation's vital interests.   Disagree

ADAPTATION: ACCEPT LIMITATIONS

Politics is best understood as "the art of the possible."   Agree

Confidential cooperation between the Government and Opposition is essential for the effective management of parliamentary business.   Agree

CONCESSION: GIVE OPPONENTS THEIR DUE

To compromise with political adversaries is dangerous because it normally leads to the betrayal of one's own side.   Disagree

Control of the Government should pass from one party to another every so often, rather than one party having control for a long time.   Agree

SUPREMACY OF PARLIAMENT

There should be no limitations on Parliament's power to make or unmake any law whatsoever.   Agree

FLEXIBLE TACTICS

A constructive approach requires flexible tactics.   Agree

TRUST IN POLITICIANS

Often those who enter politics think more about their own welfare or that of their party than about the welfare of citizens.   Disagree

ROLE OF THE ELECTORATE

In a world as complicated as the modern one, it doesn't make sense to speak of increased control by ordinary citizens over governmental affairs. Disagree

The strength and efficiency of a Government are more important than its specific policies.   Disagree

It is not dangerous, but essential that the Government reach its policy decisions in private.   Disagree

INDIVIDUAL RESPONSIBILITY

There should be greater opportunities for Members to question Ministers publicly on the affairs of their Department.   Agree

Ministers should be prepared to reveal to Parliament virtually all information on their Department's affairs.   Agree

The concentration of power in the hands of the Prime Minister has gone too far.   Agree

VIGOROUS AND CRITICAL OPPOSITION

By constantly criticizing the Government, the Opposition is performing a constructive public duty.   Agree

The Opposition should have better resources for factual briefing and information.   Agree

FUNCTIONAL REPRESENTATION

Relations of close collaboration between a ministry and the groups and sectors most affected by its activities are improper and unnecessary. Disagree

Business organizations do not have an automatic right to be consulted about the making of policies which affect their interests.   Disagree

Trade union organizations do not have an automatic right to be consulted about the making of policies which affect their interests.   Disagree

FREEDOM

No matter how despicable his views, any man ought to have the freedom to publish his opinions and present them in public speeches.   Agree

The Government ought to prohibit the sale of adult magazines which are obscene.   Disagree

TRUST IN CITIZENS

It is true that people are basically trustworthy.   Agree

It is safest to assume that all people have a vicious streak and it will come out when given a chance.   Disagree

Hobbes was right when he said that all men are basically selfish.   Disagree

Notes

This research was supported by a grant from the National Science Foundation (SOC 71-3575 A03).

1. Kavanagh (1983:34), for instance, defines political socialization as "the process by which individuals learn about politics."

2. Role acquisition is the most important aspect of adult socialization, particularly for the political socialization of politicians. Still, it is only one aspect, for even politicians learn many beliefs that are politically significant but not essential components of their roles.

3. Because socialization investigates sources of stability, it has been criticized as a biased avenue of inquiry. This is a peculiar criticism, since radicals have just as much interest as conservatives in understanding the

impediments to political change. Nor are the subjects of such studies necessarily "conservative"—socialization perspectives can be applied to studying the Italian Communist Party as well as to the Vatican. Furthermore, the existence of ideological prejudices of whatever kind among investigators does not necessarily result in error-laden research (Searing, 1970). It is true that when systematic errors appear in socialization research, they often involve overestimating consensus among members of a collectivity. Socialization research, however, need not necessarily overlook diversity.

4. In this vein, Putnam (1976:97–98) has argued that socialization to parliamentary norms is likely to undermine radical predispositions; and Fenno (1962) has claimed that socialization processes within the U.S. House of Representatives tend to retard innovation.

5. Parry and Morris (1974:321) suggest that biased political outcomes produced by procedural routines might be interpreted as a special type of power—consequential power. But however the situation is characterized, what matters is that "government routinely works within the prevailing mode of economic production and exchange."

6. **Q.** "How much interest do you generally have in what's going on in politics—a good deal, some, or not much?"

7. The laws have both legal and constitutional status, the conventions have constitutional status alone, and usages have status only as mores, for they have yet to receive constitutional sanction. In terms of consequences, these distinctions are quite unimportant. What counts from the perspective of institutional support is success in guiding behavior. None of the three is patently more successful, or even easier to change, than the others. All three—laws, conventions, and usages—rest on affirmation and can be described as rules of the game and norms.

8. This factor, which has an eigenvalue of 2.45 and explains 19 percent of the variance, represents the best single summary of the data's linear relationships. Deliberation-representation is the main factor structuring politicians' thinking about these rules of the game. Since the rules of the game are, in effect, what the politicians say they are in Britain, this is the main factor that structures the rules. Moreover, deliberation norms define the factor's negative pole, while representational norms define the positive, thus showing again the opposition between these two views.

9. The Conservatives have a particular attachment to the deliberative set; during the nineteenth century their party helped formulate and institutionalize the Constitution's Liberal interpretation, which closely resembles our deliberative rules of the game. When Labour appeared on the scene, these doctrines were making room for popular sovereignty, a principle and a perspective for constitutional interpretation to which the new movement's goals and strategies would become closely attached.

10. This encompasses three closely related interpretations (Johnson, 1978). The first and most common advises that half a loaf is better than none. The second advises sensitivity to prevailing climates of opinion. The third takes the long view and notes that achieving part of one's goals may entail accepting minor evils. Thus, according to Lord Butler (1971:29), Parliament's business is managed best when protagonists understand that accepting half a loaf does not constitute political betrayal: "In no instance did I attempt to push politics beyond the limits of the possible—to repeal some

latter-day Corn Laws, so to speak, at the risk of splitting my party irreparably or sending it for years into the wilderness."

11. Moreover, compromise presupposes that agreements will be honored, that almost everyone will follow reciprocity norms and play according to conventional standards, and that opponents will accept with grace decisions that might adversely affect their interests (Griffith, Plamenatz, and Pennock, 1956:132).

12. Parliament can pass any law whatsoever. It can legislate on any subject matter and for any persons or places. Constitutionally, each Parliament is a legal sovereign. It has the right to enact laws on any subject. It is not legally bound by acts of its predecessors. Nor is it legally dependent upon the electorate, for Parliament has the right to prolong its own existence.

13. The difficulty is that political authorities differ over what this obligation entails, over the ends and means of citizen control. Should the public join in by voting only, by expressing opinion between elections, or by active participation? The usual response is to opt for communications with constituents between elections and for traditional forms of participation in political parties, youth groups, and local government.

14. The Opposition's duty, which is to oppose and to oppose in Sir Toby's preferred style ("So soon as ever thou seest him, draw; and as thou drawest, swear horrible"), subtends the Government's duty to govern (Jennings, 1959:499).

15. It requires ministers to provide necessary information, "keeps the Government of the day on its toes," and forces it to respond to attacks.

16. "So much of the history of freedom is part of the history of parliament that freedom and parliamentary government are often considered to be the same thing" (Jennings, 1969:526). Freedom of speech is not enshrined in any constitutional document, for custom and convention have long been considered more reliable safeguards.

17. Moreover, the core norms here, those with the greatest number of relationships to other rules (supremacy of parliament and role of the electorate) are appropriately repelled rather than attracted to one another and provide hubs for two constitutional interpretations that clearly resemble the politicians' views.

18. Furthermore, working within the system often requires securing the cooperation of powerful interest groups. This establishes boundaries to policy innovation because there will be limits to what can and cannot be accomplished without alienating such bodies. This is why many left-wing commentators have seen politicians' socialization as the handmaiden of inequality. For example, Aneurin Bevan described it as the "social shock absorber placed between privilege and the pressure of popular discontent" (1961).

19. This classification is based on the assumption, widely accepted in Britain, that the economic status quo is the mixed economy and the social status quo is the welfare state. Moderation involves resisting pressures for radical change, supporting the mixed economy and welfare state, and insisting on gradual reform as the proper approach to policy making.

20. The selection effects are less pronounced when the matched attentive public is constructed by criteria that, compared to those used to produce the data in Table 2, are less precise in one respect and more precise in another.

Because the candidates are so much higher than the attentive publics in level of education, and considerably higher in age, many cells used to weight the attentive public included either very few cases or none at all. The remedy is to collapse the nine-cell matrix for education and age to a four-cell matrix, which is less precise. The outcome is at the same time more precise in that it eliminates a number of peculiarly deviant scores and yields smoother means. The smoother mean for the Conservative matched attentive public produces a comparatively closer fit with the mean of the attentive publics to its left and, hence, somewhat less evidence of pronounced selection effects.

21. The trade union leaders had, in the past, a "formula" with the parliamentary party whereby they supported the party's leadership in return for respect for free collective bargaining. It was the interventions of Labour governments into industrial relations that most raised their ire. They regarded these interventions as hostile meddling, and though there was an effort to patch up affairs under the "social contract," this proved temporary only. They also blamed the incomes policy of the Labour government for the winter of discontent (Kogan and Kogan, 1982).

22. These were won at party conferences held between 1979 and 1982 that rejected previous party policies and demanded radical transformation, including withdrawal from Europe, the alternative economic strategy, and unilateral nuclear disarmament (Kogan and Kogan, 1982:14). Whether the Left's grip on recruitment and its jiggling of rewards and sanctions in parliamentary socialization will produce radical institutional change when Labour returns to government remains a question for the future.

References

Almond, Gabriel A., and Sidney Verba (1963) *The Civic Culture.* Princeton: Princeton University Press.

Amery, L. S. (1953) *Thoughts on the Constitution.* 2d ed. London: Oxford University Press.

Arblaster, Anthony (1977) "Anthony Crosland: Labour's Last 'Revisionist'?" *Political Quarterly* 48:416–28.

Berrington, Hugh (1974) "The Fiery Chariot: British Prime Ministers and the Search for Love." *British Journal of Political Science* 4:345–70.

—— (1982) "The Labour Left in Parliament: Maintenance, Erosion and Renewal." In *The Politics of the Labour Party,* edited by Dennis Kavanagh. London: Allen and Unwin.

Bevan, Aneurin (1961) *In Place of Fear.* London: MacGibbon and Key.

Birch, A. H. (1964) *Representative and Responsible Government.* London: Unwin.

Bradley, Ian (1981) *Breaking the Mould?* Oxford: Martin Robertson.

Brand, Jack (1976) "Support for Democratic Procedures in Scottish Cities." *Political Studies* 24:296–305.

Brim, Orville G., Jr. (1966) "Socialization Through the Life Cycle." In *Socialization After Childhood,* edited by Orville G. Brim, Jr. and Stanton Wheeler. New York: Wiley.

Budge, Ian (1970) *Agreement and the Stability of Democracy.* Chicago: Markham.

Butler, Lord (1971) *The Art of the Possible.* London: Hamish Hamilton.
Clausen, John A., ed. (1968) *Socialization and Society.* Boston: Little Brown.
Coates, David (1975) *The Labour Party and the Struggle for Socialism.* London: Cambridge University Press.
——— (1980) *Labour in Power.* London: Longmans.
Crouch, Colin (1982) "The Peculiar Relationship: The Party and the Unions." In *The Politics of the Labour Party,* edited by Dennis Kavanagh. London: Allen and Unwin.
Dahl, Robert A. (1961) *Who Governs?* New Haven: Yale University Press.
Dawson, Richard E., Kenneth Prewitt, and Karen S. Dawson (1977) *Political Socialization.* Boston: Little Brown.
Dicey, A. V. (1959) *An Introduction to the Study of the Law of the Constitution.* 10th ed. London: Macmillan.
DiPalma, Guiseppe (1977) *Surviving Without Governing.* Berkeley: University of California Press.
Fenno, Richard F., Jr. (1962) "The House Appropriations Committee as a Political System: The Problem of Integration." *American Political Science Review* 56: 310–24.
Friedrich, Carl J. (1950) *The New Image of the Common Man.* Boston: Beacon Press.
Gertzog, Irwin N. (1970) "The Socialization of Freshmen Congressmen: Some Agents of Organizational Continuity." Paper presented at the 1970 Annual Meeting of the American Political Science Association.
Greenstein, Fred I. (1965) *Children and Politics.* New Haven: Yale University Press.
Griffith, Ernest S., John Plamenatz, and J. Roland Pennock (1956) "Cultural Prerequisites to a Successfully Functioning Democracy: A Symposium." *American Political Science Review* 50:101–37.
Hindess, Barry (1971) *The Decline of Working Class Politics.* London: MacGibbon and Kee.
Hyman, Herbert H. (1969) *Political Socialization.* New York: Free Press.
Jennings, Sir Ivor (1959) *Cabinet Government.* 3d ed. Cambridge: Cambridge University Press.
——— (1969) *Parliament.* 2d ed. Cambridge: Cambridge University Press.
Jennings, M. Kent, and Richard G. Niemi (1974) *The Political Character of Adolescence.* Princeton: Princeton University Press.
Johnson, Nevil (1977) *In Search of the Constitution.* Oxford: Pergamon Press.
Kavanagh, Dennis (1972) *Political Culture.* London: Macmillan.
——— (1982) "Representation in the Labour Party." In *The Politics of the Labour Party,* edited by Dennis Kavanagh. London: Allen and Unwin.
——— (1983) *Political Science and Political Behaviour.* London: Allen and Unwin.
Key, V. O. (1967) *Public Opinion and American Democracy.* New York: Knopf.
King, Anthony (1974) *British Members of Parliament: A Self Portrait.* London: Macmillan.
Kogan, David, and Maurice Kogan (1982) *The Battle for the Labour Party.* London: Kogan Page.

Lijphart, Arend (1968) "Typologies of Democratic Systems." *Comparative Political Studies* 1:3–44.

Lovell, R. Bernard (1980) *Adult Learning*. London: Croom Helm.

McClosky, Herbert (1964) "Consensus and Ideology in American Politics." *American Political Science Review* 58:361–82.

McClosky, Herbert, and Alida Brill (1983) *Dimensions of Tolerance*. New York: Sage.

Mackintosh, John P. (1968) *The British Cabinet*. 2d ed. London: Stevens and Sons.

———— (1978) "Has Social Democracy Failed in Britain?" *Political Quarterly* 49:259–70.

Marshall, Geoffrey, and Graeme C. Moodie (1967) *Some Problems of the Constitution*. London: Hutchinson University Library.

Matthews, Donald R. (1968) "Rules of the Game." In *International Encyclopedia of the Social Sciences*, Vol. 13, edited by David L. Sills. New York: Macmillan and Free Press.

May, John D. (1973) "Opinion Structure of Political Parties: The Special Law of Curvilinear Disparity." *Political Studies* 21:135–51.

Miliband, Ralph (1973) *Parliamentary Socialism*. 2d ed. London: Merlin Press.

Norton, Philip (1981) "The House of Commons and the Constitution: The Challenges of the 1970s." *Parliamentary Affairs* 34:253–71.

Parkin, Frank (1971) *Class Inequality and Political Order*. New York: Praeger.

Parry, Geraint, and Peter Morriss (1974) "When Is a Decision Not a Decision?" In *Elites in Western Democracy: The British Political Sociology Yearbook*, Vol. 1, edited by Ivor Crewe. London: Croom Helm.

Phillips, O. Hood (1970) *Reform of the Constitution*. London: Chatto and Windus.

Prewitt, Kenneth, Heinz Eulau, and Betty H. Zisk (1966–1967) "Political Socialization and Political Roles." *Public Opinion Quarterly* 30:569–82.

Price, Richard G., Harold D. Clarke, and Robert M. Krause (1976) "The Role Socialization of Freshman Legislators: The Case of Canadian MPs." In *Foundations of Political Culture: Political Socialization in the Canadian Context*, edited by Jon Pammett and Michael S. Whittington. Toronto: Macmillan.

Prothro, James W., and Charles M. Grigg (1960) "Fundamental Principles of Democracy: Bases of Agreement and Disagreement." *Journal of Politics* 22:276–94.

Pulzer, Peter (1972) *Political Representation and Elections in Britain*. Revised ed. London: Allen and Unwin.

Punnett, R. M. (1973) *Front Bench Opposition*. London: Heinemann.

Putnam, Robert D. (1976) *The Comparative Study of Political Elites*. Englewood Cliffs, N.J.: Prentice-Hall.

Rose, Richard (1974) *Politics in England*. 2d ed. Boston: Little, Brown.

Searing, Donald D. (1970) "Values in Empirical Research: A Behavioralist Response." *American Journal of Political Science* 14:71–104.

———— (1982) "Rules of the Game in Britain: Can the Politicians Be Trusted?" *American Political Science Review* 76:239–58.

Sears, David O. (1975) "Political Socialization." In *Handbook of Political*

Science, Vol. 2, edited by Fred I. Greenstein and Nelson W. Polsby. Reading, Massachusetts: Addison-Wesley.

Stouffer, Samuel A. (1963) *Communism, Conformity and Civil Liberties.* Gloucester, Massachusetts: Peter Smith.

Sullivan, John, James Pierson, and George Marcus (1979) "An Alternative Conceptualization of Political Tolerance: Illusory Increases 1950s–1970s." *American Political Science Review* 73:781–94.

Tapper, Ted (1976) *Political Education and Stability.* London: Wiley.

Truman, David B. (1951) *The Governmental Process.* New York: Alfred A. Knopf.

Whiteley, Paul (1981) "Who Are the Labour Activists?" *Political Quarterly* 52:160–70.

Dealignment at the Top:
The Nature, Origins, and
Consequences of Labour's Crisis

William L. Miller

And this is law I will maintain
Until my dying day, sir!
That whatsoever King shall reign
I'll still be the Vicar of Bray, sir!

One simple model of elite—mass interaction portrays the composition and structure of the political elite as dependent upon social conditions, social cleavages, or the patterns of mass attitudes. Changes at the elite level are viewed as the result of changes at the mass level. While elites can generate policy outcomes that change social conditions or social attitudes, it is only in this indirect way that elites influence mass alignments. By contrast, mass alignments affect the elite immediately and directly. For example, the poor electoral performance of the Labour party in recent years can be explained by changes in occupational structures that have increased the size of the middle class and reduced the size of the traditional working class. Or Labour's decline can be attributed to a swing of public opinion against socialism, the welfare state, and big government. Such changes in social structure and public opinion threatened to end the Labour/Conservative duopoly that has dominated British politics since the 1930s.

This model, however, does not fit the course of British political history. In particular, it does not explain the major realignments of 1885–86 and 1918–31. The last two party alignments in Britain were created by elite initiative, at least in the negative sense, in that they reflected a party split at the highest level. Chamberlain's split with Gladstone over the issue of Irish Home Rule produced the Unionist versus Liberal party system of 1886–1915. Similarly, Lloyd George's split with Asquith over the conduct of the war provided the opening for a previously unambitious and electorally unsuccessful Labour party. On both occasions the dangers inherent in a Liberal party split were exacerbated by an extension of the franchise and the inclusion of large numbers of new voters with weak party attachments. Weak party identification at the mass level helped make realignment possible, but it was intraparty divisions among leaders and activists that provided the driving force for a reconstruction of the party system.

In the early 1980s, the British party system appeared on the brink of another upheaval. Even more than in the past, the cause appeared to be intraparty quarrels. Social and attitudinal change had not had a major impact on changes in the party system. In England at least, there had been no new issues equivalent to Irish Home Rule or the First World War to stir the passions of the mass electorate. (In Scotland, Wales, and Northern Ireland new issues were apparent, but collectively these areas held less than a fifth of the seats in Parliament.) Although the minimum voting age was lowered in 1970, increasing the electorate by about 10 percent, this was not equivalent to the change brought about by the franchise extension of 1918, which tripled the prewar electorate and dramatically changed its social profile.

In the 1980s the role of the mass electorate was essentially passive and responsive. The springs of causation in the alignment crisis lay within the parties themselves at activist and leadership levels. The 1980s electorate resembled those of 1886 and 1918 only in the respect that levels of party attachment were low and the potential for voter volatility correspondingly high.

In 1886 and 1918, political elites structured the options open to voters and largely determined both the political agenda and the cleavage structure within the electorate. In the 1980s this happened once again. If one wishes to understand the possibilities for political realignment in the 1980s one must focus not so much on British voters' disenchantment with governments of both parties as on party activists' disenchantment with the leaders of their own party.

Over the last two decades, British politics have been characterized by a decline in deference towards leadership and a growing sense of individualism. Trade unionists, especially union activists, have become less willing to follow the advice of their leaders; party activists have become less deferential to MPs and party leaders; and MPs have been asserting their independence of their leaders in Parliament.

The central feature of Labour's recent troubles has been that the intraparty struggle was not about policy but about deference, i.e., the power and tenure of its parliamentary representatives. Right-wing Labour MPs feared they would lose their rights to choose their leader, control policy, and enjoy security of tenure. They would be reduced to the same position as the Vicar of Bray—able to retain their livings only by suppressing their political opinions. MPs who had so recently asserted their independence of the whips in Parliament were hardly likely to react kindly to new controls imposed by activists outside Parliament.

This attack on the powers and tenure of Labour MPs added an

unprecedented degree of personal bitterness to intraparty debates. Without control of policy or security of tenure and with no prospect of regaining either, some MPs' commitment to the party was shaken. Some left the party to form or join the new Social Democratic party. Others remained within the Labour party but did not shrink from sabotaging its election campaigns. If dealignment at the bottom provided the potential for voter volatility, dealignment at the top provided the impetus for reconstruction of the party system.

Nature

Electoral Dealignment

Since the mid-1960s it has been apparent that British voters have become significantly less constrained by party loyalties. Until the 1980s there was little indication of realignment, but plenty of evidence of dealignment. During the 1950s the swing between Labour and Conservatives at general elections averaged 1.6 percent, but in the 1960s it averaged 3.5 percent. At the same time the swings at by-elections increased sharply. This was, in part, the result of public disappointment with economic trends under the 1966–70 Labour government and merely foreshadowed the 4.7 percent swing against it in 1970. It also reflected sheer unconstrained volatility. The variation in party support within each year's set of Gallup polls also increased sharply during the 1960s (Butler and Stokes, 1976:207); and if the government lost more support than usual in the parliamentary midterm, it also regained support faster than usual in the run up to the next general election (Miller and Mackie, 1973).

Conservative/Labour swings were low at both elections in 1974, but the electorate demonstrated its volatility by discovering a sudden affection for minor parties in the autumn of 1972. At by-elections between October 1972 and November 1973, five Liberals, one Scottish Nationalist and one Democratic Labour (Dick Taverne) took seats from Labour or the Conservatives, although no seats changed hands between the major parties (Craig, 1976:63–64). In the 1974 general elections, the Liberal Party won 20 percent of the vote— almost three times its 1970 share.

In 1979 the Liberal vote collapsed, but the Conservative/Labour swing, at 5.3 percent, was the highest since 1945. Even more remarkable, polls showed that between November 1978 and February 1979 a Labour lead of 6 percent had been turned into a Conservative lead of 23 percent (Butler and Sloman, 1980:241). After their victory in the 1979 general election, the Conservatives' lead in the opinion polls disappeared within three months after the election: the traditional postelection honeymoon of popular support had been wiped out by a new restlessness in the electorate (Worcester, 1983: 4).

A series of election surveys (by Butler and Stokes, and Sarlvik and Crewe) charted the decline in the electorate's sense of identification with the parties. In surveys conducted between 1964 and 1970, 40 percent of the respondents claimed they identified "*very strongly*" with either the Labour or Conservative parties. In contrast, only 27 percent, 23 percent, and 19 percent were very strong party identifiers in February 1974, October 1974, and October 1979 respectively (Sarlvik and Crewe, 1983:335–336). Despite the decline of Liberal and Nationalist voting in the latter year and the resurgence of Conservative/Labour votes, the sense of strong *commitment* to the major parties did not return to earlier levels, but rather continued to decline. The data also show that the degree of "very strong" identification with the Liberal party declined in the 1970s. It was less in 1974 when Liberal votes peaked than it had been in the mid-1960s. The surveys revealed dealignment, not realignment.

These findings on strength of party identification need careful interpretation. Although they suggest that partisan dealignment occurred suddenly, in 1974, other surveys by Butler and Stokes show that the strength of party identification was weak in the nonelection years of 1963 and 1969—which fits the evidence from by-elections and monthly Gallup polls (Butler and Stokes, 1976:470). In addition, the sharp rise in strength of identification in 1963–64 and 1969–70 cautions against the argument that the strength of partisanship is immutable (the direction is likely to be much more resistant to change than strength). Further, the declining numbers with "very strong" identification were partially offset by increasing numbers with "fairly strong" identifications, so we must not overstate the amount of psychological change.

Nonetheless, the weight of evidence suggests that by the start of the 1980s partisanship in Britain was no longer a severe constraint on voting choice. Perhaps of equal or greater significance, the concept of dealignment gained widespread publicity during the 1970s, and influenced the political elites' view of their constraints. On at least one important occasion Ivor Crewe attended a meeting in Shirley William's flat with Labour politicians pondering their chances of success should they form a new party. His analyses informed and encouraged their decision to leave the Labour party (Bradley, 1981:86).

The Absence of an Electoral Imperative for Realignment

Partisan dealignment among the voters may have created an opportunity for politicians anxious to try their luck with a new party, but it did not constitute a demand for a new party. The parties that did well because of dealignment—Liberals and Nationalists—suffered from even lower levels of commitment than the major parties. Indeed, the level of very strong partisanship among Liberal identifiers in the 1970s was less than half what it had been in the 1960s: 35 percent of Liberals had "very strong" identification in 1966, but only 12 percent in 1974 (Sarlvik and Crewe, 1983:337).

No new issue arose (in England) to detach voters from the Labour and Conservative parties and link them to the Liberals, or to provide a coherent issue basis for a new party, or even to switch a sizable block of voters between the major parties (as happened in the Roosevelt realignment in the United States during the 1930s). Lemieux (1977) shows that the Liberal vote in 1974 was characterized by policy contradiction and confusion.

Crewe (1982) points to the difference between Labour party policies and the views of its supporters in 1979. Almost every survey ever done in Britain has found that Labour voters were not socialists in any ideological sense (see Miller, 1983:144–45). Crewe suggests that the discrepancy between the party and its supporters' views was especially significant after 1979 for two reasons. First, the discrepancy was getting larger: between 1964 and 1979 there was "a spectacular decline in support for the collectivist trinity of public ownership, trade union power, and social welfare." Second, Labour's electoral support traditionally had rested upon its image as the party of the average man in the street—the working class or working people and their families. However, social change was shrinking the size of the manual working class, and class differences were declining. Labour's traditionally strong link to a large working class was becoming a weaker link to a smaller class. Therefore, Crewe argues, Labour's disadvantage on issues and ideology assumed a new importance. Always a handicap, Labour's ideology was no longer outweighed by its class image (Crewe, 1982:37).

These arguments have some validity, but they do not constitute clear proof that Labour's time was past and that a new party was necessary to satisfy electoral demand. At most they suggest the normal balance of political forces had turned in favor of the Conservatives rather than Labour. Even that conclusion cannot be accepted without reservation, however.

Support for more public ownership, trade union power, and social welfare declined over the period 1964–79, during which all three were greatly extended. Polls show as much opposition to cutting welfare in the 1980s as support for extending it in the 1960s. There was no popular demand for a return to the pre-1964 situation (see *Economist*, 1983:65). As for the trade unions, which had fought bitter battles against Labour governments in 1969 and 1979, it is not at all obvious that everyone who thought they had too much power was automatically debarred from voting Labour. Labour governments, perhaps against their will, had made the case against trade union power.

On some issues the climate of public opinion in the 1980s was clearly unfavorable towards Labour; on some (like public ownership) it was so far removed from voters' priority concerns as to be irrelevant; on others it was favorable. On many issues opinions were clearly volatile, lightly held, and greatly influenced by partisan attachments. Indeed, the Labour party did itself some damage by assuming the stability of popular attitudes on issues like Britain's membership in the EEC or the Thatcher government's handling of unemployment. Labour enjoyed a substantial advantage on these issues in early 1980s; but, instead of these issues moving voters toward Labour, voters moved their issue attitudes toward the Conservatives as the 1983 election approached.

Similar remarks might be made about the thesis of social change. The manual working class was certainly shrinking; and, other things being equal, that was likely to damage Labour. But other social changes were very much in the party's interest. The percentage of male employees in trade unions rose from 53 percent in 1961 to 66 percent in 1979, and trade unionism amongst women employees rose from 24 percent in 1961 to 39 percent in 1979. (The total number of trade unionists decreased in the early 1980s only because the number of people employed decreased.) The percentage of public employees rose from 24 percent in 1961 to 31 percent in 1981 (Social Trends, 1983:55). Sarlvik and Crewe's 1979 survey showed that over 41 percent of the middle class earned their living in the public sector; and that, within classes, public or private sector employment greatly influenced voting choice. The 1979–83 Conservative government presided over a return to unemployment levels that had not been experienced since the depression of the 1930s. Lastly, since the mid-1970s, the share of income (both before and after tax and welfare redistributions) going to the bottom 60 percent of households has been declining while the share going to the top 40 percent has increased (Social Trends, 1983:76). None of this constitutes an argument for a great political switch to the left, but it does mean that important social changes were not uniformly biased against Labour and that there was no social reason for a dramatic political collapse on the left.

If patterns of issue attitudes were insufficient to indicate the end of the Labour party, they were the weakest of foundations for a new party. When the Social Democratic party (SDP) was founded in 1981, it based its appeal on images rather than issues. The SDP-Liberal Alliance's share of support in monthly opinion polls rapidly rose to 45 percent, putting it well ahead of both Labour and Conservative; but, at the same time, polls showed that few electors had much idea about its policies. Questioned about his policies by a bystander on one occasion, David Owen cheerfully replied (for the benefit of the media as much as the woman herself), "Look dear, if you want a manifesto, try one of the other parties."

A MORI poll taken shortly after the founding of the SDP showed that, of those SDP supporters offering an opinion, 23 percent favored more nationalization, 33 percent favored unilateral disarmament, and 59 percent wanted Britain out of the EEC. Such policy positions were the very opposite of those held by the parliamentary elite that founded the SDP. In particular, the SDP's founders were linked together most of all by an almost fanatical devotion to the EEC (Bradley, 1981:168). The clearest antecedent of the SDP defection was the parliamentary vote on EEC entry on 28 October 1971 when Roy Jenkins (then Deputy Leader of the PLP) led 69 Labour MPs in defying a three-line whip and voting for entry. Early in 1972 Jenkins wrote to Wilson criticizing his "constant shifting of ground" on EEC. Shortly afterwards, Jenkins, Lever, Taverne, and Owen resigned their official positions in the party, and Taverne resigned his seat to fight a by-election. Yet in 1981, a majority of those who flocked to the SDP banner wanted Britain out of the EEC!

Indeed the growth of support for the Liberal/SDP alliance to such absurdly high levels as 45 percent was only possible because its support was not based upon issues. No issue existed to motivate so many people so fast. For its new supporters, it was very much a "wish-fulfillment party" that they could support precisely because it did not have any policies or because they had no knowledge of what its policies were. If the SDP did not articulate the specific policy positions of its supporters and merely expressed a diffuse wish for something new in style but not new in policy, then one must conclude that the electoral push for a new party system was weak or absent. Voters were simply up for grabs. The active threat to the existing party system came from those political leaders who tried to convert dealignment into realignment.

Leadership and Realignment

The threat of realignment in the 1980s took two forms: a catastrophic decline in Labour votes and a surge of support for the Liberal/SDP alliance. The two were connected in many ways, not least by the massive switch to the Alliance by about a quarter of former Labour voters. Nonetheless, for every three voters who left Labour for the Alliance, two switched from Labour to Conservative or abstained (Crewe, 1983). Leadership behavior played a major part in stimulating both kinds of voter defection.

On 25 January 1981 the so-called Gang of Four issued their *Limehouse Declaration* and formed the Council for Social Democracy (CSD). The four were all former Labour cabinet ministers: Bill

Rodgers, Shirley Williams, David Owen, and Roy Jenkins. Owen had been foreign secretary, Jenkins had been chancellor of the exchequer, home secretary and, for two years, deputy leader of the Labour party. Nine other Labour MPs joined the CSD the next day. A large advertisement in the *Guardian* paid for by 100 well-wishers netted 80,000 pounds in further donations—big money in British politics—and the Social Democratic party was launched in a blaze of publicity on 26 March 1981. Jenkins and Williams had already been in close touch with David Steel, the Liberal leader, before they launched the SDP, and the new party moved quickly into an alliance with the Liberals.

Until the Gang of Four issued their *Limehouse Declaration*, Liberal support in MORI's monthly opinion polls had stayed between 10 and 14 percent ever since the 1979 general election. By March 1981, when the SDP was formally launched, support for a Liberal/SDP alliance had reached the midthirties, and by the end of 1981 it had peaked in the midforties. Labour was the main loser. In the year between October 1980 and November 1981, Labour's share in the MORI poll dropped from 50 percent to 27 percent, and its lead over the Conservatives plunged from 16 percent to zero (Miller, 1984).

Altogether, the SDP recruited a total of 29 sitting Labour MPs and one Conservative, in addition to Jenkins and Williams who were not sitting MPs in 1981. It also won over many other Labour politicians, including George Brown, who had been deputy leader of the Labour party from 1960 to 1970, deputy prime minister and foreign secretary. These defectors alleged that their former party had fallen into the hands of extremists, that it was "not the Labour Party they had joined" in their youth. Their charges gained credibility because of their seniority in previous Labour governments and because they were willing to risk their political futures by leaving the Labour party in such circumstances that they could never return. Moreover, they defended the record and personnel of the Wilson and Callaghan governments, which many current Labour activists attacked.

The SDP succeeded moderately well in their attempt to label Labour as extremist. However, although they were joined by many second rank Labour figures, or political has-beens like George Brown, they failed to win over anyone with quite the stature of the original Gang of Four. If, as they hoped, Dennis Healey had been defeated in the 1981 contest for deputy leader and had then switched to the SDP, he would have been followed by a sizable group of Labour MPs and would have given the SDP a real chance to claim that it was the true descendant of the party of Attlee, Gaitskell, Wilson, and Callaghan. As it was, the SDP's success was largely negative. Enough weighty Labour politicians joined it to make its allegations about Labour convincing, but not enough to let it inherit the Labour tradition itself.

Elite action, therefore, created the SDP and led it into alliance with the Liberals. The celebrity of the SDP leadership guaranteed enormous publicity for the new party and the new Alliance. That publicity boosted the Liberal (or Alliance) share of the polls from 15 percent to 45 percent. In return for this media-inspired boost, the Liberal party effectively offered the fledgling SDP a local campaign organization in the half of the constituencies allocated to the SDP under the Alliance agreement. The strengths of the SDP and the Liberals were complementary (in the short term): the SDP was strong at the top, the Liberals at the bottom.

Equally significant, in terms of its effect on the 1983 election, was the behavior of those leaders who stayed on in the Labour party. While the SDP succeeded, up to a point, in labelling Labour as extremist, those leaders who stayed labelled the party as disunited.

Throughout 1981, Wedgewood Benn battled to replace Dennis Healey as Labour's deputy leader. Michael Foot, a left-winger, was unopposed as Leader. The point at issue was whether Labour should continue to have a balanced left/right pair at the top, or a left/far-left pair. Like a primary campaign in the United States the Healey/Benn contest lasted the best part of a year; it was punctuated by a series of intermediate votes (at trade union conferences); and it was accompanied by a great deal of personal abuse and media speculation. It ended with a televised conference vote that Benn lost by a margin of less than 1 percent amid well-founded charges that he had, in some sense, been cheated—some right-wing Labour MPs delayed their defection to the SDP just long enough to cast a vote against Benn, while thirty-five left-wing Labour MPs voted for another left-wing candidate on the first conference ballot and then abstained instead of voting for Benn in the run-off ballot. Even without the SDP defectors, Labour had a multiplicity of highly publicized leadership problems throughout 1981.

That kind of behavior is familiar in the United States where it occurs at least every four years. Being familiar, it has a less dramatic effect upon public opinion. It was, however, a novel way for a major British party to select a leader or deputy leader and it contributed to the popular view that Labour was now unfit to govern.

Disunity amongst the remaining Labour leaders was seldom out of the news after 1981, but was particularly evident in the 1983 election campaign. During the first fortnight of the campaign, a large number of polls showed Labour steady at 32 percent, the Alliance at 18 percent. Alliance support had been on the wane since it peaked at the end of 1981 and had been squeezed further by the coming of a general election. Then at the half-way point in the four week campaign Healey (the deputy leader), Foot (the leader), and Callaghan (Foot's predecessor) had a public disagreement about defense policy. All three stressed the critical importance of the issue and each defined a policy that was clearly incompatible with the other two. Since Labour was so far behind the Conservatives in the polls that there was no hope of it winning the election, none of the three had any reason to fear they would find themselves in office with commitments they could not support. They chose the press and TV during the closing two weeks of an election campaign as the place and time for an internal party debate. Within two weeks, Labour's 15 percent margin over the Alliance was reduced to zero before recovering to a mere 2 percent in the vote itself (Miller, 1984).

Gallup's election-day poll for the BBC showed that almost half of the (many) Labour identifiers who voted for the Conservative or Alliance parties quoted Labour extremism or disunity as a reason for their voting choice: 14 percent mentioned disunity, 20 percent mentioned extremism, 10 percent mentioned both. All of these defectors were overwhelmingly in favor of retaining the British nuclear deterrent, but were also overwhelmingly opposed to tax cuts if that meant a cut in public services.

Superficially, it is possible to explain the 1983 election result in terms of issues: voters declared that they had voted for the party that had the best policies, and they rated the Conservatives best on most of the issues (Crewe, 1983). But that neglects the question of why they thought the Conservatives were good and Labour bad on the issues, and it neglects the very low issue rating they gave the Alliance.

Over the year prior to the 1983 election the most important issue in the polls remained unemployment, but Labour's initial advantage on that issue declined so much that, by election week, at least two polls showed the Conservatives were the party most trusted (Harris) or preferred (NOP) on that issue, despite the tripling of unemployment during the Tories' term of office. On the EEC, a large majority in favor of withdrawal (Labour's policy) at the end of 1982 turned into a large majority in favor of Britain remaining a member (the Conservative policy) by election day. Labour retained a large lead as the party with the best policies towards the very popular National Health Service, but failed to make the NHS a salient election issue. On defence, Labour's opposition to the deployment of Cruise and Trident weapons (a popular position according to the polls) did not become a major issue, while alleged Labour plans to give up Polaris (an unpopular position) became *the* defense issue. In many people's minds, giving up Polaris came to mean the same thing as leaving NATO and "going neutral"— although Labour's policy was explicitly to remain a full member of NATO while making a conventional rather than nuclear contribution to the western alliance.

It is difficult to avoid the conclusion that Labour's poor standing on the issues was a by-product of its image as a disunited party falling under the control of extremists. Labour failed to retain its initial advantage on some major issues and allowed its policy on other issues to be misrepresented. In short, a crisis in leadership contributed to Labour's inability to "manage" the presentation of issues.

At the same time, a disunited leadership offered no alternate reason for voting Labour to those who found its policies unconvincing. Of those Labour identifiers who voted Labour, only 58 percent could bring themselves to say their party had the "best team of leaders"; among those Labour identifiers who voted for other parties a mere 3 percent said it had the best leaders. Last, but not least, the example of disloyalty at the top gave no incentive to Labour identifiers to swallow their doubts about policy and leadership and vote their party identification.

Disunity among Labour's past and present leaders—the founders of the SDP, the right-wingers clustered round Healey and Callaghan, the far left who worked with Benn, and the "inside left" who supported Foot—damaged Labour's electoral performance in several ways: it labelled Labour as extremist; it destroyed Labour's ability to manage the issues; it prevented Labour from offering a team of leaders that could act as an alternative government; it weakened morale among Labour identifiers; and it encouraged them to show as little party loyalty as they observed among the leadership.

Origins

McKenzie's classic study of power in the Labour party (and British parties generally) was based upon Michels' model of power in the prewar German Social Democratic party:

> Now if we leave out of consideration the tendency of the leaders to organize themselves and to consolidate their interests, and if we leave also out of consideration the gratitude of the led towards their leaders, and the general immobility and passivity of the masses, we are led to conclude that the principal cause of oligarchy in the democratic (i.e., socialist) parties is to be found in the technical indispensability of leadership. . . who says organization, says oligarchy. (Michels, 1968:364–65)

Michels' incipient fascism is evident in the tone of this quotation from his final chapter. Oligarchy was primarily the result of the "incurable incompetence" (1968:367) of the masses. Elsewhere he gives considerable weight to the other influences towards oligarchy—particularly defensive action by the leadership. Michels' study reveals something less than an iron law of oligarchy, but McKenzie was able to conclude that "there is ample evidence of the working of what Michels calls the technical and psychological factors which tend to ensure the emergence of, and retention of power by a small group of leaders in each party" (McKenzie, 1964:15).

Unlike the Conservative, Liberal, and SDP parties, Labour was not created by a pre-existing parliamentary caucus, but like them it was created from the top (see Leys, 1983:ch. 10 for a brief history). It began in 1900 as a committee of the powerful Trades Union Congress and had no members at all until after the First World War. By the 1980s the unions still provided in excess of 80 percent of Labour's finance and controlled the election of twenty of the twenty-nine members of the party's National Executive Committee. The unions also controlled 89 percent of the Labour Conference vote on organizational and policy resolutions—a share that had increased since the 1950s as constituency membership declined while union membership rose (see Minkin, 1978a; 1978b).

Formally, the Labour party's annual conference had the power to "lay down the policy of the party and issue instructions which must be carried out by the NEC, the affiliated organizations and its representatives in parliament and on the local authorities. . . the Labour Conference is in fact a parliament of the movement" (Attlee, 1937:93). But that was always a polite illusion; the reality was established from the start by Kier Hardie and Ramsay MacDonald: the parliamentary representatives (the PLP) would elect *their* leaders—who would be the party leaders who would rule through an "understanding" with half a dozen trade union leaders who controlled well over half the votes at Conference. The Labour party could be run from a very small smoke-filled room, and most people in that room would be drawn from the moderate center and right wing of the party. All of them would have a "leadership perspective," all would head large organizations. When Professor Harold Laski, as chairman of the Labour party in 1945 tried to remind Attlee of the supreme authority of Conference, Attlee issued one of the most celebrated one-liners in British political history: "a period of silence on your part would be welcome."

McKenzie subsequently reaffirmed Michels' law of oligarchy as a normative rather than empirical theory: "in the case of political parties oligarchical control by the party leaders of their party organization is *indispensable* for the well-being of a democratic polity" (McKenzie, 1982:195). The tendencies Michels recognized and deplored were recognized and praised by McKenzie.

Still the illusion persisted. No one truly believed Conference was a parliament of the Labour movement but all leading Labour politicians went through the ritual of reaffirming this claim. It was a proud claim, something that distinguished the democratic Labour party from the feudal Conservative party. Eventually the illusion caught up with reality.

The PLP Loses Control of Conference

Because the Labour party was based upon a Committee of the TUC, it was slow to develop any individual membership, and it never developed a truly mass membership (Crouch, 1982:175). Such membership as it had peaked in the early 1950s and declined thereafter. Accurate figures are unobtainable since, until 1963, each constituency party had to pay the minimum affiliation fee for 1000 members, though many had less members than that. On the basis of a sample survey, Whiteley estimates that, in 1978, the party had 250,000 members (and only 55,000 activists) (1983:115). That was probably a substantial decline since the early 1950s, though not perhaps so very different from the party's pre-1945 level of membership.

Until 1973 the party maintained a list of proscribed organizations whose membership was incompatible with membership of the Labour party. Its purpose was to prevent infiltration from the Left. After 1973 the abolition of this list, coupled with such a small total as 55,000 activists, made the constituency parties easy prey to organized entry from the Left. At the same time many established members of the party were unhappy at the opportunism of the 1966–70 Labour government and supported more radical policies (Whiteley, 1983:48).

Loss of the constituency activists' support would have been a flea bite if the PLP leadership had been able to rely upon union leaders to continue their *praetorian guard* role (McKenzie's term for their habit of rubber stamping PLP decisions by using their block votes to impose PLP decisions on Conference). There had been an "understanding" between TU and PLP leaders that the latter needed freedom of maneuver and that the former would stay out of politics while PLP leaders stayed out of TU affairs. But several factors ended the unions' role as protector of the PLP leadership. First, union control of Conference was extremely "lumpy" and became more so. In 1975 the six largest unions controlled 53 percent of the votes at Conference: by 1977 the six largest unions controlled 58 percent, and the four largest unions alone had effective control with 48 percent. Union delegations became less deferential in the 1970s than the 1950s, but it was still generally true that less than half a dozen men had Conference in their pocket if they chose to act together. If those men retired, the whole power structure of Conference could change dramatically—not just because new leaders might impose their anti-PLP views on their conference delegations, but because they might no longer exert themselves (like Lord Carron of the engineers) to restrain the anti-PLP elements in their union delegations to party Conference.

In 1955, the right-wing president of the largest union (the TGWU), Arthur Deakin, retired, having arranged that his successor would be another right winger. That successor died prematurely and left winger Frank Cousins took over. More generally, in the years 1967–69, new left-wing leaders took over four of the five largest unions (Minkin, 1978b:470). In addition some left-wing unions like the Supervisory Staffs and the Public Employees were rapidly gaining members because of the changing industrial structure, increasing their affiliation fees to the Labour Party, and thus getting a larger share of the Conference vote.

In the mid– to late-1960s, other factors also drove a wedge between the union and PLP leaderships. Though British unions were centralized politically, they were highly decentralized in terms of industrial power. They had a strong shop-floor movement. When the 1964–1970 Labour government disappointed expectations of increased economic growth and rising wages, shop-floor pressure (exerted through local "unofficial" strikes) caused something of a wage explosion. Union leaders were unable to control it, and the Labour government produced the White Paper *In Place of Strife*, which proposed legal penalties to crush this wave of unofficial strikes (Crouch, 1979).

In Place of Strife was proposed by Barbara Castle and backed by Harold Wilson. Both Castle and Wilson had been associated with the left of the Labour party in their younger days, but they believed socialist planning meant labor discipline (as it does throughout Eastern Europe). The unions, though led by other supposed left-wingers, reacted like true capitalist interest groups and opposed the legislation. Left-wing constituency activists made common cause with self-interested union shop-stewards to oppose a Labour government which, in their eyes, had failed to deliver either ideological or economic benefits. In response, those members of the PLP who believed in strong government publicly attacked trade unions as special interest groups. That broke the "understanding" whereby union leaders left politics to the PLP while the PLP left the unions unfettered by law: in a word, it *politicized* the union leadership and encouraged it to take action on *all* aspects of politics—not just on the issue of industrial relations.

This new antagonism between a Labour government and the unions, coupled with the election of more left-wing leaders in several key unions, meant that the PLP leadership could no longer rely upon union leaders to control Conference for them. Wilson's Government was defeated on at least a dozen major issues at party conferences in the late 1960s. While it was true that the PLP had never really submitted to Conference control in the past, it had always been able to avoid a constitutional crisis by itself controlling Conference. Now, in addition to all his governmental problems, Wilson faced a new crisis of intraparty democracy.

Five Alternatives for the PLP Leadership

How could the PLP respond? What were the options? Three possibilities are encapsulated in Hirschman's title: *Exit, Voice and Loyalty*. In reverse order, the PLP Leadership could submit to Conference direction; or they could try to mobilize support within the party and reverse Conference decisions; or they could exit—give up and go away. Hirschman uses the term *exit* to describe customers who stop buying a faulty product instead of complaining to the management, or voters who give up voting for an unsatisfactory party. *Exit* in that sense was a very much higher cost strategy for PLP leaders than for ordinary voters, though it was the course eventually adopted by those who founded the SDP.

Michels quoted straight exit as a standard procedure for socialist MPs to exert their power over the party members. He said that MPs threaten to resign if their party criticizes them, and "if necessary, they go still further, and actually resign their seats, appealing to the electors as the only authority competent to decide the question in dispute. In such cases they are nearly always re-elected and thus attain to an incontestable position of power" (Michels, 1968:83).

Alas, although that strategy may have worked on the continent, the history of British socialism has usually shown that those who cut themselves off from the Labour party seldom survive in the long-run. For example Dick Taverne, a very articulate lawyer, kicked off the run of third-party victories in 1972–73 by resigning his seat at Lincoln and standing as a Democratic Labour candidate in the subsequent by-election. He won the by-election, but lost his seat in the February 1974 general election.

Exit could also take more subtle and less risky forms. One form was to remain in the party, but assert personal independence and "teach the party a lesson" by withholding personal influence during an election campaign or showing by decisive intervention that one could wreck the party's prospects. Consciously or unconsciously, that strategy was followed by Healey and Callaghan in the 1983 election campaign. We might call this "psychological exit."

In the 1960s Wilson followed yet another classic Michels exit strategy, i.e., "appeal to the electorate as the body which has conferred a political mandate" (Michels, 1968:185–86). Wilson neither obeyed nor overturned Conference decisions that went against him. He relied upon his *electoral* mandate, rather than his *party* mandate, and ignored the party Conference. In happier times, Wilson had asserted the supremacy of Conference. Explaining his 1960 contest with Gaitskell for the PLP leadership, Wilson declared: "If Hugh Gaitskell is returned unopposed this will be taken as a mandate for his parliamentary colleagues to defy Conference, ignore the NEC and plunge the movement into still worse conflict" (Stewart, 1974:93). But in the late 1960s he chose what we might call the "parliamentary exit" option. Gaitskell did not ignore Conference—he fought back and overturned the original votes against him. It was Wilson who chose to ignore Conference. Under Wilson, the PLP leaders who had lost control of unions, Conference, and party were now reduced to attacking the legitimacy of the institutions within their own movement.

Intraparty Democracy: Whatever Happened to the Iron Law of Oligarchy?

Where did that leave the activists and militants who had won what turned out to be such hollow victories at the party conferences of the late 1960s and early 1970s? They too faced the options of exit, voice, and loyalty. In a more deferential age, they might have chosen loyalty as Michels suggests. If the history of left-wing splinter groups had been a little less daunting, they might have chosen exit. Whiteley (1983:63) suggests that the ideologically disappointed, middle-class Labour activists were too committed to socialism and too realistic about the chances of small leftist parties either to exit into apathy or exit into other left-wing parties. But the working-class Labour activists who were less ideological yet equally disappointed in the 1966–70 Labour government's economic performance were much more likely to exit into apathy, leaving the left-wing middle-class ideologues in control of the constituency parties.

Certainly, there was little point in fighting more battles over policy when they could win Conference votes yet simply be ignored by the PLP and its leaders. Their dilemma became more acute in the early 1970s when the party approved a major policy statement, *Labour's Programme 1973*, but Wilson promptly disassociated himself from it (Kogan and Kogan, 1983:26).

The only real alternative to loyalty or exit was to turn the old illusion into reality by asserting the power of Conference over the PLP. In 1974 the index to the *Times* introduced a new, quite apt subheading: "Labour Party—Power Clash." The struggle in the Labour party during the 1970s was not primarily about policy but about power. And power clearly meant tenure. The only way to prevent members of the PLP from ignoring Conference was to replace them with members who would obey Conference and then make their continued tenure conditional upon good behavior.

That strategy was pursued in two ways. First, the one unchallenged right of the local activists was to select the party's parliamentary candidate in a constituency where a vacancy occurred through the retirement or electoral defeat of a sitting member. Sitting Labour MPs had security of tenure. Nonetheless turnover was high. Although there were 255 Labour MPs in 1961 and 289 in 1972, only 100 of the original 255 remained in Parliament ten years later (Berrington, 1982). Using a variety of statistical procedures to classify Labour MPs as left-wing or right-wing, Berrington found that there was little evidence of Labour candidates being selected for their ideology before the 1970s, but thereafter constituency activists were consistently biased toward selecting left-wing candidates. Bochel and Denver's (1983) survey-based study of Labour selection committees confirms Berrington's inference. Selection committees took many things into account, but ideology was one important factor in their choice in the 1970s. Moreover, left-wing activists placed more emphasis on candidate ideology than did right-wingers. So, a right-wing ideology could lose a potential candidate the votes of left-wingers on the selection panel without gaining the votes of right-wingers. Right-wing activists looked for vote-getting ability rather than ideological compatibility (Bochel and Denver, 1983:68).

Partly through the accidents of which candidates were in winnable marginal seats in 1964 and 1966, and which MPs were defeated in 1970, but also through the deliberate action of local selection committees, the PLP in the 1970s included a larger left-wing minority than in earlier years—so much so that Berrington described the right's majority as "precarious" (1982:91).

The second part of the left-wing activists' reaction to Wilson's high-handed disregard of Conference was to press for constitutional change. Initially they wanted some rather meaningless declaration of Conference supremacy. Later they focused on three more mechanical reforms, all of which they achieved by the early 1980s:

1. The PLP's right to elect the party leader should end, and leaders chosen by the party outside Parliament should assume leadership of the PLP. (Separate party and PLP leaders on the German model were not acceptable.)
2. All members of the PLP should appear before local selection committees at least once during each Parliament for reselection or deselection; this procedure was misleadingly titled *mandatory reselection*.
3. The Manifesto should be drawn up by the NEC; in the past it had been drawn up by the PLP leadership and the NEC at a special joint committee—the "clause 5" meeting. (At least that had been the theory. The reality had been that the PLP leader alone decided the tone and content of the Manifesto.)

The right-wing in the PLP found these proposals difficult to resist. They were, in a sense, ideologically neutral proposals concerned with the relationship between the leaders and those led, rather than left and right. Labour or trade union activists who were not extreme left-wingers could support them, and the general public combined an antipathy towards Labour's "left-wing extremists" with considerable support for the main reform proposals being advanced by those extremists. On the other side, the 1970 general election defeat damaged the internal authority of Wilson's leadership, and the increasing assertiveness of Conference delegates was matched by a pathetic defensiveness on the part of ex-ministers that John Grant MP described as "almost obsessional acts of contrition" (Minkin, 1978a:335).

The only way to oppose these reforms without appearing unacceptably elitist in an era of populist participation was to assert that they did not go far enough. While the activists were left-wing and unwilling to defer to MPs, the mass of ordinary party members and trade unionists were likely to be both right-wing and relatively deferential. Figures from the deputy leadership election of 1983 provide firm evidence for this: those constituency parties whose executive committee decided their Conference vote backed Meacher (the left-winger) against Hattersley (the right-winger) by a margin of 2 to 1; those that held branch meetings to decide their Conference vote backed Hattersley by 3 to 2; while those that balloted their membership backed Hattersley by 9 to 1 (Times, 5 October 1983). However, the right was slow to reach the conclusion that the only defense against populism was more populism. By the time right-wingers like David Owen began to press for one-man-one-vote elections within the party it looked like what it was—a desperate diversionary tactic.

So with encouragement from obscure left-wing groups like the CLPD (Campaign for Labour Party Democracy) the Labour Conference changed the rules by accepting mandatory reselection in 1979. In 1980 it accepted the principle of an electoral college for the election of the party leader and deputy leader, though it was not until the special Conference in January 1981 that the details were settled: trade unions would have 40 percent of electoral college votes, constituency activists 30 percent, and the PLP 30 percent. Conference did not give the NEC power to write the manifesto until after the 1983 election; but in 1983 the party leader, Michael Foot, agreed to adopt a long NEC policy document as his party manifesto.

The Consequences of Demands for Democratization

The demand for democratization may actually have had greater consequences than democratization itself. From the mid-1970s onward, the struggle within Labour was about the powers and tenure of the PLP, not about policy as such. Michels noted that this combination of "rebellion on one side, and usurpation on the other" means that "in all modern popular parties a spirit of genuine fraternity is conspicuously lacking" (Michels, 1968:176). The key words used by numerous observers and participants at the 1979 Conference were "malevolence," "hysteria," "venom," and "intimidation." Kogan and Kogan note that "not only deference but some of the ordinary conventions of public debate have gone" (Kogan and Kogan, 1983:69).

As soon as mandatory reselection had been accepted the CLPD published a pamphlet, *How to Select or Reselect your MP*, which rated each Labour MP on a ten-point "index of moral fervor" (Kogan and Kogan's term) according to their parliamentary voting record. The *Almanac of American Politics* regularly publishes several such indices of Congressmen's behavior, and they are accepted as a normal, legitimate part of the American political process. Not so in Britain where any external controls on the behavior of MPs conflict with unarticulated notions of parliamentary supremacy. That pamphlet alienated even left-wing members of the PLP. From a parliamentarian's point of view it was "intimidation." Joe Ashton MP predicted a "night of the long knives" (Criddle, 1983:1).

Similar levels of bitterness and hysteria characterized later conferences. In 1981 Hattersley went on BBC-TV to complain that leaflets handed out by left-wing activists were "typically intimidatory" and Kinnock was treated to cries of "Judas" because he refused to vote for Benn in the run-off ballot for the deputy leadership (Kogan and Kogan, 1983:126–27).

Aware that selection committees in the 1970s had begun to emphasize ideological criteria more than in the past, MPs feared that mandatory reselection would mean a wholesale purge of the right-wing in the PLP. Reforms that removed their right to elect their own leader and to determine the manifesto were an insult to the status and integrity of MPs. Mandatory reselection was a threat to their careers. Nothing could be less fraternal or more personal. Nothing was more likely to reduce MPs' sense of loyalty and commitment to their party. If the "key to party cohesion is control over patronage" (Ware, 1979:83), the effect of patronage had now gone negative: the MP's hope that the PLP leader would reward loyalty with government office was now replaced by the fear of deselection when the member faced his or her local activists.

Voice and Exit Once Again

In the 1980s, as in the late 1960s, those who could not accept the dictates of left-wing activists had four options—voice, exit, psychological exit, and parliamentary exit. In the interval, however, the left had grown stronger within the PLP; PLP leaders no longer had the authority that comes from being the government of the day, and they had tried to defuse demands for an electoral college by electing the left-winger Michael Foot as PLP leader. Moreover, the power of Conference to determine the party constitution was more widely accepted than its power to determine immediate political policy. So one option, *parliamentary exit,* was closed.

If circumstances had not been so uniformly unfavorable, the PLP could have ignored Conference on the leadership question as it had earlier done on policy. It could not have prevented Conference electing a party leader, but it could have asserted its independence by electing its own PLP leader—a Schmidt/Brandt solution. Moreover the PLP could have endorsed any sitting MP who was deselected by his local activists—as it had done in the early years of the century. In addition, the PLP leader could have issued a personal manifesto, as Conservative leaders have done until quite recently. Without question, the press and the media would have focused on the PLP leader, and PLP-endorsed candidates would have fared better than activist-endorsed candidates in general elections. However, with Foot as leader, that scenario was just not an option.

All three of the remaining options were adopted, however, by different groups within the PLP. Owen, Rodgers, Williams, Jenkins and twenty-seven other Labour MPs chose *straight exit* and formed the SDP. They regarded the party's constitutional reforms as final and took a pessimistic view about how the party would operate under its new constitution. They were encouraged to defect by the return of Roy Jenkins from his period as president of the EEC Commission; by the willingness of David Steel to offer Liberal support for realignment; by opinion polls that showed great popular enthusiasm for a new center party coalition; and by academic studies that suggested voter loyalty to the old parties was weak and that well-known leaders and good media coverage could substitute for the lack of a grass-roots party organization.

They ignored or discounted the possibility that Labour activists would use their new powers with discretion; they discounted the fact that opinion polls frequently indicated great popular enthusiasm for a center party coalition without presaging a major realignment; they discounted the evidence that Labour and Conservative loyalties in the mass electorate, though weakening, were much stronger than any other political loyalties; they discounted the crucial significance in a constituency-based electoral system of the spatial distribution of party support whether based upon local organization or some kind of collective party identification; and they discounted evidence from the press reaction to the SNP (Scottish National party), which showed that a new center party would enjoy a torrent of favorable publicity, quickly followed by unfavorable publicity, and then bored reticence. It would be wrong to pretend the SDP's leaders were unaware of these difficulties, but they were so alienated by activist attacks on the PLP that they were willing to gamble their political futures. Some of their followers, however, had nothing to gamble—they quit the

Labour party to avoid the threat of deselection (which was not always the result of their *ideological* failings). Among the "Gang of Four," neither Jenkins nor Williams was an MP when they founded the SDP; so they, too, had little to lose.

Dennis Healey's position was important. If he had left the Labour party the SDP gamble might just have worked. Conversely, if the PLP had been less compromising (or cowardly) in 1980 and elected Healey instead of Foot as PLP leader, then the SDP gamble would not have been so attractive. David Owen declared after the 1983 election that he would never have left the Labour party if Healey had been leader. In the event, Healey was elected deputy leader by the PLP in 1980 and narrowly overcame Benn's challenge in the 1981 electoral college election.

Right-wing defections to the SDP reduced the right's strength in the PLP, but the remaining right-wingers pursued both the *voice* and *psychological exit* options with considerable success. They tried to mobilize a counterrevolution within the party—sometimes in alliance with those PLP left-wingers who had no wish to become mere puppets of the constituency activists or who recognized the futility of concentrating on ideological purity to the neglect of electoral performance. At the same time, some of the right-wingers, notably Healey and Callaghan, but not Hattersley, reserved the right to state and restate their political positions at any given time. Thus, while Foot and Conference supported unilateral nuclear disarmament, Healey insisted that the 1983 NEC policy document, which later served as a manifesto, must reflect his views as well as theirs. As a result, the Manifesto contained one unconditional unilateralist sentence and one clear multilateralist sentence in the same paragraph. It is not surprising that two weeks before the election Foot and Healey had a public disagreement about whether the party's manifesto meant unconditional rejection of the existing Polaris weapon system. Callaghan simply disagreed with it and publicly supported the deployment of the new Cruise nuclear weapon system.

Consequences

The past two decades have witnessed traumatic upheavals within the British Labour party. Based on the results of similar intraparty "democratizing" experiences in other countries (see e.g., Tsurutani, 1982), one might expect dramatic consequences for Labour's future. Democratizing the party certainly had a disastrous effect upon its electoral performance in 1983. But Labour activists noticed that disaster as much as anyone else and the ultimate consequences could be slight. In Britain, as in the United States, the ultimate *Consequences of Party Reform* (Polsby's title) may be more in keeping with Michels' skepticism than Polsby's fears.

A Failed Realignment

Historically, exits from the Labour party have always ended in failure. That does not mean they always will, but the odds have been against the SDP from the start. The SDP defection, along with other evidence of Labour disunity certainly did enormous short-term damage to Labour's electoral performance. But, in 1983 at least, it did not restructure voting patterns; it had little effect upon party identification; and it had little effect on representation in Parliament.

The surge of support for the Liberal/SDP Alliance during the 1979–83 parliament looked suspiciously like earlier surges of support for the Liberals alone, although on this occasion it peaked about 5 percent higher than before, and the Alliance won about that much more in the 1983 election. Alliance supporters showed little coherence in policy preferences or social background, they were especially likely to describe their vote in negative terms (i.e., as motivated by disliking the other parties rather than liking the Alliance), and they expressed a very low sense of commitment to the Alliance or its component parties. As time passed, they tended to claim identification with the Liberals rather than the SDP.

On election day 1983, the voters cast 43 percent of their votes for the Conservatives, 28 for Labour, and 26 for the Alliance. But that same day 43 percent expressed psychological identification with the Conservatives, 38 percent with Labour, and only 16 percent with the Alliance. Over a third of Labour and Conservative voters claimed a *very strong* identification with those parties, but only one tenth of Alliance voters claimed a *very strong* identification with the Alliance—indeed many did not identify with it at all (Miller, 1984).

The unstructured nature of Alliance votes meant that they were spread evenly in all kinds of constituencies and seldom added up to a local plurality. Thus the Alliance vote produced a Conservative landslide in Parliament. Only seventeen Liberals and six SDP members were elected. That electoral outcome can be traced back to the SDP's issueless exit from the Labour party, its quick alliance with the Liberals, and the decision by the most senior Labour right-wingers to remain within the party and fight. A "Mark II" Labour party would have found it much less easy to soar in the opinion polls but might have built up a more structured vote, received a better return in terms of MPs elected, and had a genuinely realigning effect on the voters. Even the Liberals were scared of the genuinely realigning effect of such a party (Beith, 1983:115). Instead, the SDP served as another vehicle for short-term protest.

The Alliance could not take over the role of principal opponent to the Conservative government with only twenty-three MPs when Labour had almost ten times that number. It was also in a weak position to press for proportional representation when so few of its voters identified with it. Indeed, in the aftermath of the election, its standing in the polls declined and removed what force the demand for PR might have had.

Realignment, however, need not mean success for the Alliance—it could mean a permanent collapse of Labour support. Conservative hegemony would be very different from a Conservative/Labour two-party system. However, after the 1983 catastrophe, the Labour party showed signs of mending its ways and presenting a more credible alternative to the Conservatives.

Restoration of What?—Moderation, Fraternity, or Oligarchy

For well over a decade prior to 1983, Labour politics were character-ized by extremism, disunity, and what Samuel Beer calls the "col-lapse of deference" towards leadership (Beer, 1982:107–220). But after the strife that led up to 1983, the whole style and atmosphere of Labour politics changed sharply. There was some kind of restora-tion. But what was restored—Did policy moderation replace policy extremism? Did fraternity replace division, disunity, and personal bitterness? Or did the forces of oligarchy reassert themselves after a period of anarchy and mob rule?

At the time of writing, Conference has not abandoned its generally left-wing policy positions. Neil Kinnock, the new leader, like Wilson before him, began on the left and gradually moved to the right as he moved up. Kinnock has a strong nerve guided by a strong ambition for government office. He distanced himself from the extreme left by voting against Healey on the first ballot in the 1981 deputy leader-ship election, but then abstaining in the run-off ballot between Healey and Benn. On the NEC, Kinnock cast his vote for the reintro-duction of a proscribed list and exemplary expulsions. Along with Foot, Evans, and Kitson, Kinnock was one of the four NEC members the Times categorized in 1982 as neither left nor right. Kinnock's moderation has been expressed more in terms of fraternity than pol-icy. He protected moderate and right-wing MPs while acting against the militants infiltrating from the left.

It would be wrong to stress the policy changes after 1983. What-ever happened to restore Labour's image and electoral fortunes, it was not a massive switch from left-wing policy extremism to moder-ate or right-wing policies. Since policy was not the essence of La-bour's problem before 1983, it should not be surprising that policy was not a factor in its revival after 1983. So, policy moderation was not restored.

Contrary to Michels' assertion, the Labour party clearly has enor-mous reserves of fraternity. History has taught Labour a sharp lesson. In the 1983 electoral college elections caused by Foot and Healey's resignations after the general election, many union delegations, activists, and MPs voted for the so-called dream ticket of Kinnock and Hattersley—a combination of a (now) moderate leftist and a (now) moderate rightist. Perhaps most significant was the report that the TGWU delegates voted 27 to 18 to overturn the recommendation of their union executive and vote for Hattersley in the deputy leadership election. Their executive had advised them to vote for Hattersley's left-wing opponent. Moss Evans, their general secretary, explained his delegates' decision by stating the need for Labour to remain a "broad church." A vote for a broad church was a vote for party unity and tolerance for both wings of the PLP.

Tolerance did not extend to the far left associated with the *Militant* newspaper. The 1982 Conference voted by over three to one to reintroduce the system of proscribed organizations, and the NEC carried out some exemplary expulsions of extreme left-wingers associated with the *Militant*. The 1983 Conference approved those expulsions, again by more than three to one.

The whole tone of the 1983 Conference contrasted sharply with the tone of the 1979 Conference. Paraphrasing Kogan and Kogan, we could say that not only the ordinary conventions of public debate but deference towards leadership returned in 1983. Events had demonstrated the need for unity on the platform and deference from the floor. So, yes, fraternity among long established members of the Labour party was restored—at least to a normal level.

Which brings us to the question "what has happened to Michels' Iron Law of Oligarchy?" Certainly the operation of that law was suspended in the 1970s, but it was not repealed. In the 1950s the PLP leadership ran the party through the union leaders' control of the block vote. Despite the democratization of the 1970s, it seemed that in the 1980s the PLP leadership still ran the party the same old way.

As noted earlier, the constitutional changes in the Labour party were ideologically neutral, though few thought so at the time. The CLPD and its associates saw them as a mechanism for imposing left-wing policies and leaders on the PLP. So did the PLP. But Conference itself was not reformed. So the Electoral College and NEC control of the manifesto took power away from the PLP and gave it to the union leaders, not to the constituency activists. Some of the left-wing union leaders elected in the late 1960s retired in the late 1970s, others were appalled by the shambles in the party and its electoral consequences. Right-winger Terry Duffy replaced Hugh Scanlon as leader of the engineers, for example. But even before that, Jones and Scanlon had become only symbolic left-wingers. They still moved in left-wing circles, but they had been deradicalized by their close links with Labour governments and had developed a very leadership-oriented view of politics (Minkin, 1978b:480–81).

In 1981, the electoral college system was introduced, and Benn came within a whisker of beating Healey. But in the NEC elections at that same conference, union votes threw six left-wingers off the twenty-nine-member NEC and replaced them by right-wingers. In 1982 the *Times* categorized the NEC as comprising nine left-wingers, including Benn; four centrists, including Foot; and sixteen center-right members, headed by Healey. The 1983 Conference confirmed that broad pattern. So, while Benn may have come close to winning the deputy leadership, what actually did happen was that he lost the chairmanship of the NEC's important Home Policy Committee. Unless there are further changes in the NEC's composition, it is likely to give the party leader the manifesto he wants.

The electoral college made surprisingly little difference to the 1983 leadership and deputy leadership elections. Kinnock won 73 percent of the union votes, 91 percent of the constituency votes, and 49 percent of the PLP vote—which, in a four-candidate contest, made him the overwhelming winner in all sections of the college. In the deputy leadership election, Roy Hattersley won 88 percent of the union votes, 51 percent of the constituency votes, and 56 percent of the PLP votes. So the Kinnock/Hattersley combination (*team* would be too strong a word for them) chosen by the electoral college was the PLP's own choice anyway. And if we think of oligarchy in terms of succession, the new leader (Kinnock) was the known favorite of the outgoing leader (Foot).

Mandatory reselection did not lead to a massive purge of the PLP's right-wing. Only a handful of MPs were deselected (not all of them for ideological reasons), though half a dozen may have retired and others modified their behavior in anticipation of reselection difficulties. Certainly the PLP has shifted somewhat to the left as the NEC has shifted to the right. Of sixty-four Healey MPs with Bennite constituency parties in 1981, thirteen retired, nine defected to the SDP, and four were deselected (Criddle, 1983). But if MPs are frightened to disagree with their local activists, their voting in the 1983 Electoral College elections does not show it. Of 209 MPs who voted, 142 voted differently from their local constituency party. They are unlikely to suffer for their independence. While selectors did take account of candidate's ideology, Bochel and Denver's survey showed that only 13 percent of selectors (whether left or right themselves) made ideology their primary criterion. Many more, on all wings of the party, put greatest emphasis on electability. When faced with a sitting MP, ideology is unlikely to be the sole consideration. One decision of the 1983 Conference actually strengthened the tenure of MPs. By a three-to-one majority, Conference defeated a motion to have internal PLP votes recorded and published. Members of the PLP will not have to account to their local activists for their votes within the parliamentary caucus.

For electoral reasons, and for reasons of genuine fraternity, the activists were reluctant to use their new constitutional power to purge right-wing MPs, and both unions and constituency parties backed the PLP's choice of leader and deputy leader.

It is not altogether fanciful to imagine that a convention may become established whereby it would seem a disruptive act of disloyalty for the electoral college to overrule the PLP's known choice for leader, or install an incompatible NEC, or inflict upon the leader a manifesto he or she could not in conscience present to the electorate. Indeed, it is quite likely that increased formal powers for activists and Conference will impose new restraints upon them.

If Kinnock as prime minister were to face a Conference in circumstances similar to the late 1960s, Conference would have the awesome power to dismiss the prime minister from leadership of the party. If it chose to use that power, it would have no guarantee that he would go quietly—he might remain as prime minister, or he might resign and request a dissolution. When Wilson's job as prime minister lay in the gift of the PLP, the PLP could not dismiss him for fear of the electoral consequences. Now that Conference has that power, it will have the same fear. Labour leaders enjoyed better security of tenure when their job depended upon the PLP than Conservative leaders enjoyed even when there was no formal mechanism for dismissing them. Thatcher is the first Conservative leader to depend upon annual reelection, but she has lasted longer than Heath, Home, Macmillan, or Eden.

Now, if the Labour Conference has the power to dismiss the leader but chooses not to do so, then its criticism of his or her policy and judgment will be muted. The leader will be able to demand (or infer) a vote of confidence from Conference that will delegitimize any of its more specific criticisms.

After Labour's third postwar electoral defeat, observers asked the question: *Must Labour Lose?* (Abrams, Rose, and Hinden, 1960). They argued that social change, growing affluence, and a lack of popular support for socialism gravely handicapped a socialist party that spoke for the working class and the poor. The force of that argument was somewhat reduced when the party went on to win four of the next five elections. But those victories raised another, more fundamental question: Must Labour fail? Is the Labour party allergic to government? Must it either alienate the electorate or alienate its own members? Must its commitment to planning force its governments into confrontation with the unions and turn its chief supporters into its chief enemies?

Labour's new constitutional arrangement may have the opposite effect to their authors' intentions. New mechanisms of formal democracy could turn into new instruments of oligarchic control. Instead of making Labour leaders more responsible to the party activists, they are likely to make the Labour party more responsible for

Labour governments, and thereby help to reduce Labour's allergic reaction to being in power.

"Back me or sack me" is the choice Labour leaders used to put to their followers in the PLP. Now they must put it to the Electoral College.

When incumbent leaders retired, resigned, or defected, PLP leadership elections gave ordinary MPs some choice of leader, though they were usually heavily influenced, as in 1983, by the outgoing leader's own choice for his successor. But there are very few examples of PLP elections being used to dismiss an incumbent Labour leader. No incumbent has been refused reelection since 1922 when Macdonald defeated Clynes. Indeed there are only a handful of occasions when the leader even had to undergo the indignity of an opposed reelection.

Much more frequently, incumbent leaders have used the implicit threat of disruption contained in "Back me or sack me" to enlarge their own freedom of action, constrain their followers, and devalue any criticisms coming from below—for Labour leadership elections have been primarily a device for top-down discipline, not bottom-up control. By extending the electorate from the PLP to the Electoral College, the scope for top-down discipline has been widened.

At a lower level, Labour MPs must now tell their local constituency activists to "Back me or sack me." And just as Labour leaders can imply disaster for the party if they are sacked so, on a more limited scale, can local MPs.

The significance of 1983 for leader–follower or MP–activist relationships is that it made the threats in "Back me or sack me" credible. Incumbent MPs who defected to the SDP or simply chose to stand as Independent Labour candidates showed that, while they could not guarantee their own reelection to Parliament, they could severely damage the chances of any candidate who replaced them. With mandatory reselection, the local activists can threaten an MP with the loss of his job, but he can threaten them with the loss of representation in Parliament. If the activists shrink from the consequences of deselecting their MP, if they do not "sack him," they cannot avoid having "backed him" by voting for his reselection.

Michels claimed that all too often in socialist parties, election to a specific office for a specific time turned into a leadership role for life. It will take a lot more than the current constitutional reforms in the Labour party to change that. Oligarchy in Labour would only be ended if formal elections were treated as opportunities for choice rather than occasions for demonstrating party loyalty and fraternity. The right to dismiss the leader and deselect an MP will simply not be a credible threat, nor an important source of leverage, unless it is exercised with some frequency and without producing disastrous consequences for the party.

That seems a most unlikely scenario. The Labour party, its Conference, and its electoral college are controlled by the unions, and it is a
principle of British trade unionism that elections are not to be used
for dismissing incumbent trade union leaders. Truly competitive
elections for top union leaders only occur when there is a vacancy.
So, regular deselection of MPs and defeat of party leaders would not
only contradict the instincts of most people in the labor movement,
it would set an example that could endanger the tenure of union
leaders. It is neither in the character nor the interests of the union
leaders to use their power to throw out incumbent party leaders
except in the most exceptional circumstances (see Edelstein and
Warner, 1979:96–97).

Ever since the 1960s, observers have criticized Michels' theories as
no longer applicable to Labour politics. Power seemed to be slipping
away from the leadership and toward the local activists. Now it
looks as if Michels was right all along, and the events leading up to
1983 were just part of the mechanism for reemphasizing the need for
oligarchy.

Michels' claim that "who says organization, says oligarchy" does
not carry any logical force—there are alternatives to oligarchy that
do not imply disorganization. But the experience of the last few
years suggests that the Labour party has not been able to find them.
For Labour, the effective choice seems to be between chaos and
oligarchy. It has tried chaos and is now reverting to oligarchy.

References

Abrams, M., R. Rose, and R. Hinden (1960) Must Labour Lose? Harmonds-
    worth: Penguin.
Alt, J. (1979) The Politics of Economic Decline. Cambridge: Cambridge Uni-
    versity Press.
Attlee, C. (1937) The Labour Party in Perspective. London: Odhams.
Beer, S. (1982) Britain Against Itself. London: Faber.
Beith, A. (1983) The Case for the Liberal Party and the Alliance. London:
    Longman.
Berrington, H. (1982) "The Labour Left in Parliament: Maintenance, Erosion
    and Renewal." In The Politics of the Labour Party, edited by D. Kavanagh.
    London: Allen and Unwin.
Bochel, J., and D. Denver (1983) "Candidate Selection in the Labour Party:
    What the Selectors Seek." British Journal of Political Science 13:45–69.
Bradley, I. (1981) Breaking the Mould? The Birth and Prospects of the Social
    Democratic Party. Oxford: Martin Robertson.
Butler, D., and A. Sloman (1980) British Political Facts 1900–1979. London:
    Macmillan.
Butler, D., and D. Stokes (1976) Political Change in Britain. London:
    Macmillan.
Craig, F. W. S. (1976) British Electoral Facts 1885–1975. London: Macmillan.

Crewe, I. (1982) "The Labour Party and the Electorate." In *The Politics of the Labour Party*, edited by D. Kavanagh. London: Allen and Unwin.

———— (1983) "Why ~~Conservatives Won~~ Labour Lost the British Elections." *Public Opinion* 6 (June/July):7–9, 56–60.

Criddle, B.J. (1983) "Candidate Selection 1980–83." Paper presented at the Political Studies Association Annual Conference, Newcastle.

Crouch, C. (1979) *The Politics of Industrial Relations*. Manchester: University of Manchester Press.

———— (1982) "The Peculiar Relationship: The Party and the Unions." In *The Politics of the Labour Party*, edited by D. Kavanagh. London: Allen and Unwin.

Economist 3 December 1983:65.

Edelstein, J. D., and M. Warner (1979) *Comparative Union Democracy: Organization and Opposition in British and American Unions*. New Brunswick, N.J.: Transaction Books.

Hirschman, A. O. (1970) *Exit, Voice and Loyalty: Responses to Decline in Firms, Organizations and States*. Cambridge: Harvard University Press.

Kavanagh, D., ed. (1982) *The Politics of the Labour Party*. London: Allen and Unwin.

Kogan, D., and M. Kogan (1983) *The Battle for the Labour Party*. London: Kogan Page.

Lemieux, P. H. (1977) "Political Issues and Liberal Support in the February 1974 British General Election." *Political Studies* 25:323–42.

Leys, C. (1983) *Politics in Britain*. Toronto: University of Toronto Press.

McKenzie, R. T. (1964) *British Political Parties: The Distribution of Power within the Conservative and Labour Parties*. New York: Praeger.

———— (1982) "Power in the Labour Party: The Issue of Intra-Party Democracy." In *The Politics of the Labour Party*, edited by D. Kavanagh. London: Allen and Unwin.

Michels, R. (1915, 1968) *Political Parties: A Sociological Study of the Oligarchical Tendencies of Modern Democracy*. New York: The Free Press.

Miller, W. L. (1983) *The Survey Method in the Social and Political Sciences: Achievements, Failures, Prospects*. New York: St. Martins Press.

———— (1984) "There Was No Alternative: The British General Election of 1983." Glasgow: Strathclyde Papers on Government and Politics, No. 19.

Miller, W. L., and M. Mackie (1973) "The Electoral Cycle and the Asymmetry of Government and Opposition Popularity." *Political Studies* 21:263–79.

Minkin, L. (1978a) *The Labour Party Conference: A Study in the Politics of Intra-Party Democracy*. London: Allen Lane.

———— (1978b) "The Party Connection: Divergence and Convergence in the British Labour Movement." *Government and Opposition* 13:458–84.

Polsby, N. (1983) *The Consequences of Party Reform*. New York: Oxford University Press.

Sarlvik, B., and I. Crewe (1983) *Decade of Dealignment*. Cambridge: Cambridge University Press.

Social Trends (1983) London: HMSO.

Stewart, M. (1974) *Protest or Power? A Study of the Labour Party*. London: Allen and Unwin.

Tsurutani, T. (1982) "The Japanese Political System." In *Politics and Gov-*

ernment, edited by A. N. Dragnich, J. T. Dorsey, and T. Tsurutani. Chatham, N.J.: Chatham House.

Ware, A. (1979) *The Logic of Party Democracy*. London: Macmillan.

Whiteley, P. (1982) "The Decline of Labour's Local Party Membership and Electoral Base." In *The Politics of the Labour Party*, edited by D. Kavanagh. London: Allen and Unwin.

―――― (1983) *The Labour Party in Crisis*. London: Methuen.

Worcester, R. M. (1983) *British Public Opinion Newsletter: April 1983*. London: MORI.

Margaret Thatcher: The Mobilizing Style of Prime Minister

Dennis Kavanagh

Margaret Thatcher has been prime minister for a sufficient period to test a number of propositions about prime ministerial leadership in Britain. If she survives until June 1988, when the next general election has to be held, she will have been in office for nine years, the longest uninterrupted spell in the twentieth century. She has already established a number of landmarks in political history and psephology, as the first woman prime minister in any major western industrial state, the first Conservative prime minister to have been reelected after a full term since Lord Salisbury in 1900, and the only one in this century to have been reelected with an increased majority after such a term. Alone of twentieth century prime ministers, she has had her name given to a supposed political doctrine and undoubted political style. She is the first British prime minister to mount a sustained challenge to postwar consensus politics. And, more than any other postwar prime minister, she is often regarded as a figure apart from her Cabinet.

This paper argues that Thatcher provides a particular style of political leadership in Britain. This is termed *mobilizing leadership* and, in some respects, resembles the wartime style of Lloyd George (1916–22) and Winston Churchill (1940–45). Her bold personal style of leadership distinguishes her, as it distinguished Lloyd George and Churchill, from other prime ministers. But, unlike them, she did not come to office during a wartime emergency and head a coalition government. This paper describes and analyzes Thatcher's leadership. It is also a theoretical case study insofar as it presents an argument about leadership style in Britain.

The political style of British political leaders varies broadly between the mobilizing and the reconciling. The mobilizer emphasizes decision, task performance, and changing the status quo, whereas the reconciler maintains consensus and group cohesion. The former is mainly concerned with the achievement of goals, not overly concerned about opposition and the costs of disturbance; the latter tries to represent and respond to diverse interests and is willing to arrive at compromises by sacrificing policy goals if necessary (Kavanagh, 1980).

Political Leadership

There seems to be an inverse relation between personal leadership and political institutionalization. Political institutionalization refers to the existence of established structures for political participation and decision making. In the British case, the structures obviously include political parties, Parliament, Cabinet, and the civil service. Personal leadership refers to the opportunity (a product of circumstances and the institutions) and capacity (which varies with the individual office holder's skills, personal drives, and ambitions) to take action. The distinction borrows from Weber's typology of charismatic authority (which approximates personal leadership) and bureaucratic authority (which approximates institutionalization).

Britain is widely regarded as a political system that scores high on institutionalization and low on personal leadership. Disciplined political parties and a system of parliamentary and cabinet government have been conducive to a restrained, impersonal style of political leadership. This style has been reinforced by the values of partisanship and collective leadership of the Cabinet. Unlike those of France or the United States, the political head of state in Britain is not the focus of regime loyalty. Personal leadership is less appropriate for a British prime minister who is a servant of the Crown. Lloyd George and Winston Churchill were exceptions, but exceptions that proved the rule. Both were in some respects political outsiders who came to power during a breakdown of "normal" party politics and exercised personal leadership at a time of national crisis (Kavanagh, 1974).

By contrast, many third world states have low levels of institutionalization and have been prone to bouts of Caesarism. France also has veered between cycles of routine and heroic leadership (Hoffman, 1967)—between consuls and compromisers (Avril, 1969). The two traditions have been embedded in contending political values and political institutions. In the United States, the constitutional separation of powers, popular suspicions of executive power and strong government, and weak political parties have both depressed the scope for presidential leadership and made it necessary at a time of crisis.

British political science has little or no literature on political leadership. In Britain, one refers to the office of prime minister and his or her performance rather than national leadership or leaders. The academic literature on the prime minister has given rise to one of the few serious debates in British political science: the thesis of prime ministerial government versus the thesis of cabinet government. The first view is associated with the late John Mackintosh and Richard Crossman and is regarded as being a constant, regardless of incumbent. According to Mackintosh, "the country is governed by a Prime Minister, his colleagues, junior ministers and civil servants, with the Cabinet acting as a clearing house and court of appeal" (1977:541). For Crossman, the postwar period has seen the transformation "of Cabinet government into Prime Ministerial government" (1963:51). This view is reinforced by the mass media's tendency to personalize politics (e.g., "Mrs. Thatcher's Government").

A different interpretation points to the limitations placed on any prime minister—constraints of time; the greater departmental resources available to other cabinet ministers; and the prime minister's need to keep the Cabinet together, conciliate rivals, and manage the political party in Parliament (Brown, 1968; Jones, 1965). In addition, the prime minister must contend with inevitable pressures from the outside world, difficulties with the British economy, and various lobbies. Limits on British government are, in effect, limits on the prime minister. In this debate on prime ministerial as opposed to cabinet government, Thatcher's rise to power and her political beliefs and leadership are of inevitable interest.

The Rise of Margaret Thatcher

In explaining how and why Thatcher came to the leadership of the Conservative party, one has to take account of certain problems in both British politics and the Conservative party in the mid-1970s. In 1970, the Conservative Edward Heath became prime minister, armed with a set of policies designed to reverse Britain's economic decline. There was nothing new about that. All prime ministers since 1964 have made the reversal of national economic decline their goal. In 1970, however, Heath's policies appeared to mark a clear break with the past. These policies encompassed trade union reform, reduction of state intervention in the economy, avoidance of a formal price and income policy, cuts in public expenditure and direct taxes, and greater selectivity in welfare. Joining the E.E.C. also marked a break with the Atlanticist-Commonwealth legacy that was so strong in both parties (but particularly among Conservatives). The economic policies were regarded at the time as a neoliberal challenge to the postwar collectivist consensus and a step towards the adoption of more free market policies. Within two years, however, Heath's government had to perform two spectacular U-turns, adopting an elaborate statutory price and income policy and intervening to rescue troubled firms. The coal miners challenged the income policy in the winter of 1973 and caused widespread industrial disruption. Under pressure, Heath called a general election in February 1974 to defend his government's statutory income policy, and lost. Another general election in October 1974, fought on a national unity and coalition platform, resulted in an even greater defeat for the Conservatives.

Between 1929 and 1964 the Conservatives had lost power only twice (1945 and 1964). By 1974, however, the sense that the Conservative party was the natural party of government had been severely shaken. Labour won four of five general elections held between 1964 and 1974 and was in office for all but three-and-a-half of the ten years. In addition, the political agenda placed the Tories at a disadvantage. For a number of years, governments of both parties had pursued income policies and sought the goodwill of the unions in the battle against inflation. These interventionist and collectivist policies and the bargaining power of the unions were more in tune with Labour than Conservative interests, and the latter party seemed to have lost its sense of direction. There was therefore considerable pressure on a chastened Heath to stand down or offer himself for reelection as Conservative leader in the new Parliament.

Yet in 1974 the party had no formal procedure for removing a leader. Only after the resignation of Sir Alec Douglas Home in 1965 had the election principle for the leadership been introduced, and Heath was the first leader of the party to be so chosen. Previously, a group of older party statesmen had taken soundings from backbenchers and made a recommendation to the monarch if, as was often the case, the party was in office. The system, informally called the "magic circle," usually produced a candidate against whom there were the fewest strongest objections within the party. But until 1975, when new rules were introduced to allow Conservative MPs to elect the leader annually, there was no procedure by which the leader could be forced to stand for reelection. The problem of the leadership of the party could be resolved by either confirming Heath or by ousting him and choosing a successor.

In the early stages, one name rarely suggested as a likely candidate was that of Margaret Thatcher. She had been Secretary of State for Education in the 1970–74 government, but not closely involved in the strategic decisions of the Conservative government, and certainly not part of Heath's inner circle. In opposition, she took a prominent part in the October 1974 general election campaign with her party's promise to reduce the mortgage rate on houses to 9½ percent or less and abolish property taxes. She also impressed her colleagues when leading the parliamentary opposition to the Finance Bill in the winter of 1974. At the time, she was a supporter of the leadership claims of Sir Keith Joseph. During 1974, Sir Keith, who had served as a cabinet minister under Heath, was rethinking Conservative principles, and he soon emerged as the most prominent free-market spokesman among those who disowned Heath's economic policies. Inevitably, he became a focus for right-wing Conservative critics of Heath. Other former cabinet ministers, apparently feeling bound by ties of personal loyalty to Heath and collective responsibility for the record of the last Conservative government, refused to stand.

Margaret Thatcher came from a small town, Grantham, in the East Midlands, once voted the most boring town in Britain. Her parents had run a small grocer's shop and her father had been a local councillor. Through hard work, earnestness (she had little time for social frills), and brains, she won a place at Oxford in 1943, qualifying first as a research chemist and then as a tax lawyer. Like politics, both fields were and still are male dominated and were unusual careers for a woman to pursue. She married a wealthy businessman, Dennis Thatcher, and his money provided her with the opportunity to pursue a career as a professional politician. She entered Parliament in 1959 at age thirty-four and was appointed "shadow cabinet" spokesman on Education in 1967. On becoming prime minister in 1970, Heath appointed her to the post of Secretary of State for Education and Science, a post which she held until the fall of Heath's government.

When she challenged Heath for the leadership, she had been an MP for only sixteen years, and her previous ministerial experience at the cabinet level was confined to a relatively minor department. Party leaders in Britain usually emerge after a more lengthy and varied apprenticeship. They typically ascend a ministerial hierarchy and prove their political and administrative ability to parliamentary colleagues over the years. In comparison to other postwar Conservative leaders, such as Churchill, Eden, and Macmillan, Thatcher clearly was a newcomer. Not since Baldwin, in 1922, had a Conservative leader had so little prior experience of high office. He, also, was a product of backbench reactions against the party leadership.

In standing for election, Thatcher drew support from diverse quarters: those who felt slighted by Heath, those critical of the U-turns or policy reversals made by his government, a number of right-wingers, and those who simply felt it was time for a change of leader if the party was to win the next election. Attempts were subsequently made to invest Thatcher's election with an ideological significance. Many of her free-market and monetarist instincts were present, but her policies were developed after she became leader (Young, 1984). In the leadership race, the decisive consideration was that she was the only serious candidate to oppose Heath, and it was necessary for MPs to vote for her (though not necessarily for her ideas) if they wanted a change. Heath had the support of many senior figures in the party and most of the national press, and he was heavily backed among Conservative peers and constituency activists. But, crucially, many MPs did not share this sentiment in favor of Heath, and, in the election on 4 February, Thatcher defeated him by 130 votes to 119. Heath had not cultivated the backbenchers—a lesson not to be lost on his successor.

A second ballot was necessary because Thatcher had not reached the required figure of 139 votes, i.e., an overall majority of votes and a lead of 15 percent of those eligible to vote. The second ballot on 11 February proved decisive, and Thatcher easily defeated William Whitelaw and became the first woman leader of a British political party.

The Conservative party had changed in the decades since 1945. Although the front-bench MPs remained predominantly upper-middle-class products of public schools and Oxbridge, Heath and Thatcher represented a more meritocratic strain. Both came from comparatively modest family backgrounds; both won scholarships to grammar schools and Oxford; and both were self-made professional politicians. As Anthony King notes (1974:6), they belonged to the "tough-minded" rather than the "tender-minded" wing of the party, in that they were impatient with the status quo and favored more radical free-market solutions to the economy's problems. But there were important differences. Although he was the first leader chosen by MPs in a contested election, Heath long had been a member of the party leadership, had ascended the ministerial hierarchy, and might well have "emerged" under the old system of informal consultation. He also represented continuity with many of the "One Nation" principles associated with Sir Anthony Eden, Harold Macmillan, and R. A. Butler. Thatcher, however, had overthrown an established leader, had not previously served in any of the major offices of state, was the product of a backbench rebellion against the leadership, and lacked weighty frontbench support on the first ballot. She was very much an intruder, and her victory was a measure of Tory backbench disaffection with her predecessor.

Political Beliefs

A determinant of a leader's political style is his or her political beliefs. Their importance, however, obviously varies with the person. Few doubt that Thatcher has a coherent set of political ideas and that these are related to her behavior. She regards politics as a suitable arena for the expression of these beliefs and often relates them to her early experiences rather than to abstract theory (occasionally invoking early memories of her father, her school days, and even her head mistress). From her secure family background come the values of self-reliance, hard work, thrift, family, and a belief in just rewards and not looking to the "nanny state." These ideas subsequently have been reinforced by her reading of some of the economic writings of Friedman (particularly on income policies and his advocacy of monetary control) and the philosophical works of von Hayek

(Young, 1984). She also has turned for intellectual sustenance to the ideas of Sir Keith Joseph and to think tanks like the Institute of Economic Affairs and the Centre for Policy Studies.

These beliefs come out in her party conference speeches and, more explicitly, in interviews. To a lesser extent they are reflected in the actions of her government. The main elements in her belief system can be stated in terms of several propositions:

1. The limited capacity of government to do lasting good, but its great capacity to do harm
2. The importance of individual responsibility and freedom (she is one of the few Conservative Cabinet ministers to vote regularly for the restoration of the death penalty)
3. The state should be strong enough to perform its "primary" tasks of ensuring adequate defence and law and order
4. People should solve their own problems (or help their families and neighbors solve theirs), rather than turning to the government
5. Increasing public expenditure, without economic growth, involves more taxation and less choice for individuals
6. The free market is the best means of promoting economic growth and free choice and of safeguarding personal liberty
7. More expenditure on one service usually means less on another, unless one resorts to borrowing or inflation. Each service is paid for by "hard-pressed" taxpayers, many of whom may be poorer than the beneficiaries of particular programs
8. Government intervention may be counterproductive in terms of inhibiting society's ability to adapt in a changing world
9. "Correct" programs (in terms of the above) are more useful than expressions of sympathy for the weak, unemployed and sick

Circumstances have helped these ideas to gain some acceptance. By the mid-1970s, rampant inflation, industrial disruption, and the growing influence of trade unions made a number of people in Britain willing to try an alternative approach. Keynesian techniques of economic management did not appear to have an answer to "slumpflation." The slowdown of economic growth and high inflation made it difficult to finance many state programs, particularly in social welfare. Support for the postwar consensus of high public spending, a mixed economy, and income policies, was declining in both major parties. The left gained ground in Labour, particularly after the party's election defeats in 1970 and 1979, and the right gained in the Conservative party with the election defeats in 1974 and Heath's exit. In other Western countries also, economic policies of cash limits, curbing the growth of public expenditure, controlling the money supply, and extending the role of the market gained greater acceptance.

In foreign affairs Thatcher has proved to be something of a "little Englander." In her early years as prime minister, she largely left the negotiations over Rhodesia-Zimbabwe and the E.E.C. to the Foreign Office. Her deep involvement in the Falklands war and determination to retain British sovereignty over the islands has to be set against Britain's negotiated return of Hong Kong to China and refusals to support or condemn the U.S. invasion of Grenada (part of the Commonwealth). Indeed, there is some evidence that only with the Argentine invasion of the Falklands and the loss of British servicemen did the "Fortress Falklands" policy emerge. She has a traditional Tory view of the Soviet Union and communism as evil and expansionist. But she is not a visionary in international affairs and, unlike Macmillan or Heath, does not much enjoy summits and gatherings of heads of states.

Her image as a confrontational politician stems from her conviction that British politics is becoming an important, even a decisive, battle of ideas. Thatcher is one of the few senior politicians who takes pride in stating her political convictions and insists that policies should derive from coherent principles. Without such a starting point, she argues, a leader is at the mercy of events and unlikely to produce successful policies. When taxed in 1978 by the present author about the basis of her political strategy, she replied: "My political beliefs."

The confrontational image also is aided by her forceful style of speaking and assertive personality. At times, her self-confidence and certainty make her overbearing in discussion. More than one skeptical senior colleague has been admonished, "Don't tell me what; tell me how. I know what." It is as if political goals are what she decides, and the role of ministers, civil servants, and advisers is to implement them. Even friends acknowledge that she approaches conversations as an intellectual exchange rather than as an opportunity to empathize; her invitations to colleagues to define their terms and to explain "precisely" what they mean often disconcert the unprepared. Her denunciations of high levels of taxation and public expenditure and of big government and the diminution of individual freedom and choice are passionate and deeply felt. She frequently expresses these beliefs in moralistic attacks on the baneful effects of inflation and governments that debase the economy or borrow rather than balance their income and expenditure.

Her ideal society is one where the market underpins personal choice and freedom; where people spend more of their rising incomes on better services than the state can provide; where the welfare state operates as a safety net; and where more people can turn to private health insurance rather than the National Health Service and to private education rather than the local state comprehensive school. The economic growth necessary for the realization of this vision will come from more incentives, particularly lower taxes, fewer government controls, and the opportunity for people to accumulate capital of their own. The creation of more wealth and the reduced economic and social role of government are the ways to expand individual freedom and opportunities for people to advance. Little in this litany is at odds with previous Conservative manifestoes. What is different is the greater zeal with which Thatcher has articulated these principles.

She dismisses talk of consensus policies, complaining in particular that there can be no compromise with the Labour party as long as it is captive of the left, or has policies that lead to a fully planned society. There is, she believes, a fundamental divide between socialism and freedom, and people must be made aware of it. She also has been determined to attach Labour's assumption of moral superiority and its claims to be the "compassionate party." She has been outspoken in her disapproval of the Conservative skeptics who favor a middle way and of those who, because of what she terms "bourgeois guilt," do not stand up against alleged abuses of power by the trade unions and Labour's militant left wing. These remarks obviously are levelled at political opponents as well as doubtful Conservative colleagues. She regards much talk of consensus as being sloppy, a euphemism for the "easy way" or "middle way" and her task is to challenge and change ideas.[1]

Consider two statements by Mrs. Thatcher. In a speech in the 1979 election she claimed: "The Old Testament prophets did not say 'Brothers I want a consensus.' They said: 'This is my faith. This is what I believe. If you believe it too, then come with me.' " In 1981, in Australia, she replied to Heath's criticism that she was abandoning consensus policies by saying "For me, consensus seems to be the process of abandoning all beliefs, principles, values and policies. So it is something in which no one believes and to which no one objects."

This is a negative perception of consensus politics as one which sees conciliation and agreement as an ultimate goal, at the expense of almost any other principle, however vital. What is remarkable is Thatcher's (a) particular definition of consensus and (b) her disavowal, in contrast to most other British party leaders, of the goal of seeking consensus.

From the outset, some of her senior colleagues were worried by her view of politics as an ideological battleground and by her disavowal of many crossbench attitudes. They feared that she was seen to be, and indeed was, too abrasive and lacking in compassion. She is famous for berating and lecturing ministers, civil servants, TUC delegations, and the House of Commons: "rubbish," or "what mean?" and other rude comments are annotated to civil servants' papers. Phrases such as "TINA" (there is no alternative) in answer to critics of her economic policy, and "We want our money" to her E.E.C. partners over the perennial problem of Britain's budget payments, sum up the spirit of what she feels and argues.

Political Style

Conservative leaders traditionally have accommodated major interests and sought compromises. After 1951, Winston Churchill and his successors protected the welfare state, sought full employment, and conciliated the trade unions. They regarded these policies as necessary to retain working-class electoral support; consensual, moderate, and middle-of-the-road were the watchwords of postwar conservatism. Thatcher, on the other hand, claimed that previous Tory leaders had agreed on the country's problems and what needed to be done—cutting public expenditure and direct taxation, reforming the unions, and restoring the incentives and financial discipline of the free market—but failed to carry through the policies. Moreover, by the mid-1970s, collectivist policies, and the constraints on government they represented, were so deeply entrenched that a virtual counterrevolution was required (Aughey, 1983). She saw herself as providing the political resolution that had been lacking.

An insight into Thatcher's character is conveyed by the kind of people with whom she feels comfortable. In contrast to the immediate postwar generation of Conservative leaders (Churchill, Eden, Butler, and Macmillan), she felt little sense of guilt about the unemployment of the 1930s. But such feelings were important among a number of One Nation Tories in the 1950s. As prime minister in 1955, Sir Anthony Eden regarded the policy of deliberately increasing unemployment to stem inflationary wage claims as "politically not tolerable" (1960:363). Harold Macmillan, his successor, never forgot his experience as an MP in the economically depressed northeast England in the 1930s. As prime minister, he accepted the resignation of his Chancellor of the Exchequer in 1958 rather than agree to modest public expenditure cuts. But in the 1970s, few self-made first generation Conservative politicians had personal memories of the 1930s or were inclined to conciliate the trade unions and to make full employment the main goal of government.

In public and private she is a relentless educator. Indeed, an important task of leadership is, in her view, to win the battle of ideas, and this is done by frequently expressing basic beliefs and principles. Initially, some Cabinet colleagues were embarrassed by what they regarded as her "preaching" and "moralizing," but in the end accepted it as part of the Thatcher style. Unlike Harold Wilson, she does not have the reputation of a "fixer," compromiser, or manager in her Cabinet. Indeed, she once described herself as "the cabinet rebel." Discussions with colleagues and interviewers often are interrupted by rhetorical questions, "Do you see?" or "Have I made that clear?" When taxed about her "bossy" or "headmistressy" role in the 1983 election she replied: "Yes, I do believe certain things very strongly. Yes, I do believe in trying to persuade people that the things I believe in are the things they should follow. . . . I am far too old to change now" (Butler and Kavanagh, 1984:88–89).

She has a passion for being well-briefed for parliamentary questions, press conferences, media interviews, and committees. The outcome has been, until recently at least, a tendency to go into over-detailed explanations of issues in interviews. She is fond of spelling out what she regards as "obvious" relationships between increases in unemployment, wage levels, taxation, inflation, and public spending.

Her own radicalism clearly is tilted against particular institutions and interests. In January 1984, she told a gathering of parliamentary lobby journalists that she wished to be remembered for breaking the consensus and tackling traditionally "immune targets." These included the trade unions, nationalized industries, local government, civil service, universities, and, surprisingly for a Conservative leader, the monopoly professions, like solicitors and opticians (The Times, 19 January 1984). But she also is out of sympathy with the previous Conservative leaders' liking for "deals" with the major interests, conciliating the trade unions, and being a "good European" at almost any cost.

Cabinet Management

The formal duties and responsibilities of the office of a British prime minister are not laid down in a constitution or statute. Although Asquith exaggerated when he said "the office of the Prime Minister is what its holder chooses and is able to make of it," the personality of a prime minister does give a particular character to his/her administration. A prime minister faces certain role demands—chairing the Cabinet, answering parliamentary questions, making appointments, and choosing the time for dissolution of Parliament. Unlike most recent prime ministers, Thatcher sees herself as an activist rather than an arbitrator in Cabinet disputes or speaker for a collective view. Her job is to push ministers "to do what is right": this involves reminding them of the Government's strategy and combating what she regards as the inertial tendencies in departments. Given the government's commitment to restrict public expenditure, spending battles dominated the first three years of her first administration. The Economist (October 4, 1980) noted: "Mrs. Thatcher often seems

more of an external pressure group on her Cabinet than the traditional resolver of its conflicting forces. . . . She hectors, bullies and
bashes ministers mercilessly."

British prime ministers do not have a department to administer.
This opportunity to take a broad view is useful if the incumbent has
the requisite information. The support staff is tiny in comparison
with that of a Cabinet minister or U.S. President—about eighty staff
working in Downing Street of whom the great majority (about 60) are
typists, messengers, clerks, or administrators of the machine. For all
the talk of the prime ministerial government in Britain, one has to
remember the unequal battle he or she faces when confronted by
more than a score of powerful departments. Number 10 Downing
Street, in the words of a former political secretary of Heath, is "A
house, not an office" (Hurd, 1979:32).

The prime minister's private office at present consists of about six
fairly senior civil servants who help with official speeches and parliamentary business, and liaise between the PM and departmental
ministers. In addition, there is a policy unit of eight or nine political
advisers. This body was established by Harold Wilson in 1974 and
has been retained by his successors. Its members are political appointees, and they help with advice on policy and papers from other
departments, liaise with the party and, occasionally, help with
speech writing. They are particularly concerned with looking for the
party political consequences of events and policies. In 1970, Heath
established the Central Policy Review Staff to deal with the long-
term strategy matters and provide briefs for the Cabinet as a whole.
Thatcher abolished the body after the election victory in 1983—an
example of her dislike for so-called professional advice that purports
to be above party politics.

The usual criticisms of the way she works in Downing Street are
that her political staff is too small and inexperienced. Her lack of
confidence in the senior civil service was well known in advance. In
January 1981, worried over failures to control the money supply, she
recruited Professor Alan Walters from the United States to be her
personal economic advisor and provide advice independent of that
of the Bank of England and Treasury. In particular, she felt the need
of somebody who could argue with these two bodies about control of
the money supply. Her disenchantment with the Foreign Office, already evident over Rhodesia and the E.E.C., came to a head during
the Falklands War. She brought in Sir Anthony Parson to advise on
foreign affairs and appointed Roger Jackling to advise on defence.
This clutch of appointments, together with her apparent dominance
over the Cabinet, was widely seen as heralding the introduction of a
prime minister's department. It was more, however, a reflection of
her antiestablishment outlook and her determination to shake up the
civil service hierarchy.

The main argument for a contemporary prime minister having a stronger support system is that he or she has to speak on a wide range of matters for the government at home and abroad. To an increasing degree, a prime minister animates and directs government policy and therefore has to monitor and understand a range of politics. Some Cabinet ministers objected to the expansion of the system of advisers for the prime minister on the grounds that their own right of access to her might be reduced and the collective role of the Cabinet would be weakened. There were also the predictable objections from departments that did not want to have their own policy advice scrutinized by outside experts.

The view that Britain was moving to prime ministerial government was encouraged by Mrs. Thatcher's dominant personality. But there were other factors as well—her ruthless dismissal of Cabinet dissenters in 1981, the abolition of the Civil Service department (which effectively gave her more direct control over senior civil servants), and her close involvement in the promotion of permanent secretaries. She expanded the size of her policy unit, became more interventionist, and increasingly relied on her aides. Shorly after the abolition of the CPRS, Professor George Jones noted: "While she has been strengthening her own personal staff resources, she has weakened those at the disposal of her Cabinet colleagues for the performance of their collective deliberations by abolishing the CPRS. So she has tipped the system a little away from collective to presidential government" (1984:8). But Jones fairly adds that "the tipping is only slight." Although there is a general trend for the private offices of political heads of state to increase in size and influence (Rose and Suleiman, 1981), the British prime minister still appears to be less well endowed with this type of political support than leaders of most other states.

Government decisions in Britain are made in the name of the Cabinet, in contrast to the United States where they are made in the name of the president. The British Cabinet consists of most of the ruling party's political "heavyweights," politicians who have either acknowledged expertise, a political following, or close ties with the prime minister (Rose, 1971). Most of the twenty or so men and women in the Cabinet are well known to one another and have worked together over some years. But most are also rivals for promotion to top cabinet offices and, ultimately, for the prime minister's job.

The Cabinet provides collective leadership. Yet the prime minister is more than *primus inter pares*, and the ability to hire and fire distinguishes him or her from Cabinet colleagues. In this regard, it is interesting to consider Thatcher's appointments in the major departments at three stages, in opposition in 1975, before the 1979 election, and in government since 1979. Two points are noteworthy about the early appointments. First, in making her appointments to the consultative committee or shadow cabinet, Thatcher displayed conciliating traits in retaining many of Heath's appointees. Of the twenty original members it is likely that only two (Sir Keith Joseph and Airey Neave) voted for her on the first ballot for the leadership election in 1975. A shadow cabinet containing senior figures like Lord Carrington, Whitelaw, Prior, Maudling, and Pym—most of whom had already achieved office under Heath and owed little to her—meant that Thatcher was in a minority in a number of policy battles while the party was in opposition. Although her appointments were made with an eye to preserving party unity as well as recognizing ability, Thatcherites—often young and lacking ministerial experience—were not obvious candidates for promotion at the time.

The second noteworthy feature is her initial caution in refusing to reshuffle spokesmen. Most of the "shadows" remained in post for the four years of opposition, and all of the spokesmen were appointed to the Cabinet in 1979, usually to departments they had shadowed in opposition. Thatcher, like Heath before her, clearly regarded opposition as a time of preparation for government.

Continuity also meant, however, that Thatcher was in a minority over some policy areas in the new Cabinet. Some ministers were openly disgruntled with her style of leadership and the Treasury's economic strategy. There was a clear separation between the Cabinet and Thatcher in the minds of many Conservative activists and observers. Many right-wing backbench critics of the government could voice their criticism without including her and liked to present her as a political prisoner of Cabinet "Wets." After a while, Thatcher herself, in coded language and indirect statements (through some of the Number 10 Staff), may have provided encouragement for them. But a prime minister's power of appointment is not limited to the selection of ministers: equally important is the allocation to particular posts. Thatcher was careful on the whole to send her supporters to the important economic ministries. Sir Keith Joseph went to Industry, Sir Geoffrey Howe and John Biffen to the Treasury, John Nott to Trade. Such likely opponents of the economic strategy as Lord Carrington and Sir Ian Gilmour were banished to the Foreign Office and Francis Pym to Defence. She also ensured that she chaired the important Cabinet EA Committee on economic strategy and that it contained a majority of her supporters.

Yet the Cabinet was spectacularly divided by the end of the first two years, notably over the 1981 Budget and reviews to cut public spending programs. During the course of 1981, however, Thatcher dismissed a number of notable Cabinet dissenters. By autumn 1981 all the major economic ministries (Energy, Employment, Trade, and Industry), apart from the Treasury, had new ministers. The reshuffle was a notable display of prime ministerial power and perhaps also of her frustration with the original appointments. In the new government of June 1983, the move to a more homogeneous Cabinet was continued. The prime minister's use of her power of appointment to produce a more politically sympathetic Cabinet had been wielded gradually but effectively. However, the high turnover left Thatcher open to the familiar criticisms of inconsistency and unsettling the ministries (*Economist*, October 22, 1983). In the new government of June 1983, only Lord Hailsham in the Lord Chancellor's Office, the ministers for Wales and Scotland, and Thatcher herself had remained in the same posts since May 1979.

The secrecy of British Cabinet discussions has long been defended on the grounds that it encourages frank discussion between members and upholds collective responsibility. In recent years, leaks about government thinking from ministers in divided Labour governments (1964–70, and 1974–79) became almost routine. The same pattern was evident in Thatcher's first government.

One explanation for this was Thatcher's style. Her propensity to express her views boldly at the outset of a discussion, combined with a sometimes dismissive attitude to colleagues, tended to charge the atmosphere and polarize Cabinet discussions. This contrasted with the approach of some other prime ministers, such as Attlee, Macmillan, Wilson, and Callaghan, who often waited for a policy line to emerge before committing themselves. They also regarded their influence as a finite resource to be husbanded—used on major issues rather than frittered away on minor skirmishes or issues on which they were likely to be in a minority in Cabinet. By contrast, Thatcher leads from the front, has views on most issues, and is quick to voice them.

Another reason for the divisions was that, for much of her first term, some of the economic policies were skeptically regarded by many colleagues. Monetarism was a particularly divisive policy and a number of colleagues argued for a reversal of strategy, as unemployment increased remorselessly and the government's popularity in opinion polls and by-elections slumped. Her public speeches contained thinly-veiled warning messages to colleagues who doubted the strategy. Statements such as "The Lady's not for turning" and "Are we going to go back? Hell, no, we've only just got here" were directed at them. In the first two years of office she had to give way to Cabinet pressure on pay raises for MPs, the scale of public spending cuts in November 1981, gas prices, the Rhodesian settlement, the settlement of the EEC budget, and (while Prior was at Employment) the action against trade union immunities and the closed shop. She also had to bow to objections from colleagues and permit Cabinet discussion of economic strategy in 1982; and, in September 1982, she had to abandon discussion of the paper from the Central Policy Review about the implications of the rising trend of public expenditure and its drastic proposals for curbing welfare spending. It was a remarkable catalogue of rebuffs. Her experience was not one that supported theories of the power of the prime minister.

Her frequent outbursts against the civil service machine may well have reflected a sense of failing to get it working effectively in directions that she wanted. Certainly she was impatient with a number of departments for displaying less than whole-hearted devotion to her policies. Whitehall departments are almost independent fiefdoms. They have their own networks of lobbies, hierarchies of civil servants, attentive public and parliamentary groups, and specialist teams of mass media reporters. As a consequence, prime ministers have to work extremely hard to make government operate in a coherent and consistent way. A prime minister may intervene in the work of some departments, but at the cost of neglecting broad strategy and the work of other departments. Departments must ultimately be left alone to implement policies. But Thatcher interfered in departmental matters to a greater degree than many of her predecessors. She busied herself in the promotion of senior civil servants and regularly badgered departments about progress on particular policies.

In the regular battles to contain public expenditure, she was not on the side of the big spending departments (with the exception of the defense and police budgets) who tried to resist the Treasury. She frequently reminded them that they were all the custodians of a collective strategy to cut the burden of taxation and roll back the frontiers of the state. Yet public spending and taxation as proportions of G.N.P. actually increased after 1979. Why, then, did she eventually come to dominate the Cabinet, bearing in mind that many ministers were not supporters of her economic strategy? An examination of some of the reasons may provide an insight into the sources of a modern prime minister's power.

One tactic she used was to decide matters outside the formal Cabinet, either in committees or in informal groups. She exploited her control of the agenda and powers to appoint members of Cabinet committees or groups and draw up their terms of reference. It is worth looking at three important policy areas to illustrate this feature. First, the purchase of the Trident Missiles program involved a massive commitment of future financial resources and, de facto, decided British defense policy for the rest of the century. It appears that this decision was effectively decided by a small group of ministers, outside Cabinet, in early 1981. Second, the presentation of annual budgets is left to the Chancellor of the Exchequer, though he or she is careful to consult with the prime minister about the strategy and discuss changes beforehand with ministers whose departments are likely to be affected. The final contents of the budget are only revealed to the Cabinet the day before the budget is presented to the House of Commons, when it is too late for any major changes.

Thatcher and Sir Geoffrey Howe did not depart from practice. But two budgets shocked a number of ministers: the 1979 budget included a doubling of the standard rate of VAT, which further contributed to inflation, and the 1981 budget was severely deflationary at a time when over two million were out of work. Ministers' complaints about being "bounced" into accepting last-minute decisions were widely reported in the media. Disgruntled ministers also forced Thatcher to debate economic strategy in Cabinet, but their efforts had little impact on changing it.

Finally, the 1984 decision to ban trade union membership for workers at the intelligence gathering center (Government Communications Headquarters) at Cheltenham was taken outside the Cabinet and Cabinet committees. The decision was initially taken by Thatcher, Howe (Foreign Secretary), and Michael Heseltine (Minister of Defense). A few other ministers were involved at a later stage, yet, according to *The Times* (February 7, 1984): "The first most Cabinet ministers knew was when Sir Geoffrey Howe announced the decision in the Commons on January 25." The report also noted that the traditional practice for Cabinet committee decisions to be reported to the full Cabinet had ceased under Thatcher. Sir Geoffrey, interviewed by the London *Daily Mail* on February 6, 1984 said: "It was discussed, as almost every Government decision is discussed, by the group Ministers most directly involved. . . . There are very few discussions of Government decisions by full Cabinet." Commentators speculated that this secretive pattern of decision-making was prompted by the fear of Cabinet leaks on sensitive matters and/or was an indication of Thatcher's wish to bypass the Cabinet, while using the convention of collective responsibility to gain its acquiescence. Many prime ministers have tried to bypass Cabinets in taking policy initiatives, either because they needed to take decisions quickly or because they considered it the best way to advance a line of policy. However, Thatcher appears to have relied less on her Cabinet than other recent prime ministers.

Another factor in her success has been her appointments. As noted, she gradually acquired a Cabinet that was more to her liking and whose new members owed their preferment to her. Political events also helped. Once the rate of inflation declined during 1981 and 1982 and public spending was under control, the Cabinet proved much easier to handle. In conversations with the author, one member compared the change as "from night to day," and another claimed "there was simply nothing left to argue about." No doubt Thatcher and Howe would claim that it was because their economic strategy was beginning to work. Then, the successful recapture of the Falklands transformed not only her own position but also the government's. The popularity of both soared in the opinion polls, as the electorate rallied behind the government at a time of crisis.

Finally, Thatcher's position was also secure because the Cabinet opposition was internally divided. The so-called Wets were never a coherent group; the term mistakenly unified a diverse set of critics. Prior, Walker, and Sir Ian Gilmour opposed many of Thatcher's and the Chancellor's economic policies, and all three at some time seriously considered resignation over the 1981 budget. However, they differed on the emphasis they accorded income policies, reflation, or tougher measures against the trade unions. Two ministers who were dismissed, Gilmour in 1981 and Pym in 1983, were unlikely to lead backbench revolts. But Walker and Prior, also well-known doubters, were retained (Prior until September 1984), no doubt for fear they might prove troublesome on the backbench. Outside the Cabinet, the rejected Heath became a more isolated political figure and was increasingly seen as a "bad loser."

These are all classic devices of prime ministerial dominance over the Cabinet. The first two (Cabinet membership and deciding the members and agenda of committees) lie within the prime minister's control, while the third (events) and fourth (division among dissenters) worked to her advantage. There was also the undoubted increase in her personal self-confidence and stature as a result of the recapture of the Falklands. She enjoyed the experience of making decisions by a small war committee and her self-confidence vis-a-vis the Cabinet as a whole increased. The surge in personal and party popularity attendant upon the Falklands affair transformed her position, and made her an electoral asset rather than a liability.

There is no doubt that in the post-Falklands period Thatcher has been more dominant in Cabinet. Given the Cabinet's acceptance of her political and economic strategy, she has been more concerned with implementation, and this appears to have given a greater role to her policy unit (permanent secretaries in the civil service and ad-hoc groups of officials), advisers, and ministers.

Parliament

Parliament is the arena in which British political leaders are recruited. Compared to leaders in other countries, prime ministers spend a good deal of time in the legislature. Their lengthy stay in Parliament before gaining office certainly gives them time and opportunity to acquire suitable skills. It is difficult to think of a successful prime minister who has not been able to command the House of Commons. The great parliamentary set pieces like Question Time and major debates are particular tests for the prime minister. At Question Time, the prime minister has an advantage over questioners because he or she is backed by civil servants who provide briefs and try to anticipate supplementary questions. Thatcher takes these sessions seriously and goes to enormous lengths to prepare for them.

In the post-war period, foreign affairs and economic issues have tended to dominate the prime ministers' parliamentary attention. Analysis of their involvement in parliamentary debates shows that in the course of an average year they will participate in six debates and make six statements on policy, usually on the economy, foreign affairs, and government business (Rose, 1981:16–17). Thatcher has followed this pattern. Involvement in these issue areas, together with the need to attend to party management tasks means that she normally sees the Chief Whip, Foreign Secretary, and Chancellor of the Exchequer on political business more frequently than she does other Cabinet colleagues.

Party Management

The prime minister also is a leader of a political party in Parliament. In the British system, leadership of a major political party is the first requirement for being a prime minister. A politician, however eminent or popular, who lacks that base will not reach or survive at the top. A party leader who hopes to reach 10 Downing Street has to devote much time to party management, and policies and appointments have to be made with an eye on the reactions of party factions. Of Conservative leaders in the twentieth century, A. J. Balfour (1912), Austen Chamberlain (1922), Neville Chamberlain (1940), Sir Alec Douglas-Home (1965), and Edward Heath (1975) were eventually forced out of the leadership because of the lack of party support in Parliament.

Party management in the Commons is left to the Whips. Through the exploitation of patronage, appeals to party loyalty, and backbenchers' fears of letting the opposition into office, they try to keep their majority intact. For the prime minister and the Cabinet, carrying Parliament means, effectively, carrying their party's backbenchers. Yet, as Norton (1978) has demonstrated, MPs became increasingly rebellious in the 1970s. Thatcher faced backbench revolts on spending cuts in 1981; was defeated on proposed changes in immigration rules in 1982; and faced revolts over legislation to impose a ceiling on local government rates and reforms in trade union law in 1984.

Thatcher has always realized that her power base lay with backbenchers and has tried to be accessible to them. In opposition, she particularly urged her frontbench spokesmen to be attentive to the party's backbench committees relevant to their subjects. In part, the style acknowledges how she came to the leadership and, in part, is a reaction to previous leaders. Churchill, Eden, Macmillan, and Home had emerged through the "magic circle" and not as a result of election by MPs.

Thatcher is in many ways a right-wing liberal. Like many local constituency Conservative party officers who are drawn from the professions and small business, she has gotten where she is through her own efforts and does not come from one of the traditional Tory interests—business, land, or a political family. Her open dislike of direct taxation, public spending, much of the public sector, and trade unions and her protective attitude to the tax reliefs for home-owners and investors and sympathy for farmers, small business, and the forces of law and order are all favorite themes among Tory party activists. She has also proved willing to allocate political honors to party workers whereas Heath had been particularly niggardly in this regard. Thatcher, however, has not been interested in problems of the party bureaucracy—Central Office and the Research Department. She was so dissatisfied with the "Wet" political tone of the latter body before 1979 that she turned for advice increasingly to the inde-pendent Centre for Policy Studies, and the Research Department has never recovered its former position in resources or influence. For advice she calls on her Policy Unit and for help on speeches she often relies on people who have no formal position in the party or Downing Street.

Public Role and Image

British prime ministers frequently do not enjoy wide popularity. Over a hundred years ago Bagehot drew attention to the prime minis-ter's lack of the visible and dramatic trappings attached to the mon-archy and a "fused" presidency. The monarchy still attracts more positive emotion than the prime minister: while the former is a na-tional symbol, standing above party conflict, the latter is seen in a partisan perspective, a perception that limits the extent of his or her popular appeal (Rose and Kavanagh, 1976). For only five years be-tween 1945 and 1983 has approval for the prime minister exceeded that of his party by more than 10 percent, and Harold Wilson and Harold Macmillan are the only postwar PMs to have retained the support of 50 percent or more of the electorate for two successive years (Table 1). Thatcher's approval rating on Gallup fell to a record low of 28 percent in October 1981. Although the Falklands improved her standing, the approval ratings are still lower than those for leaders in the 1950s and early 1960s.

Political leaders, where they can be set apart from the party, may help to shape a party's image. In Britain, however, they have limited effects on voting behavior and election outcomes. In 1979 Labour decisively lost the election, although Callaghan was more popular than either his party or Thatcher. In 1983 whereas only 15 percent of the electorate thought that Foot was doing a good job as Labour Leader, 28 percent voted Labour. In 1979, MORI surveys found that the Conservatives were preferred over Labour on policies by 40 per-

TABLE 1.

Approval for Leader of the Two Major Parties, 1955–83 Gallup Poll (in percentages)

Parliament	Prime Minister	Opposition Leader	Combined Approval
1955–1959	55	44	99
1959–1964	51	51	102
1964–1966	59	41	100
1966–1970	41	33	74
1970–1974	46	47	83
1974	46	34	80
1974–1979	46	41	87
1979–1983 (April)	39	33	72

Note: All figures are the average (mean) monthly rating.

Source: Adapted from Richard Rose, "Why won't we play follow-my leader?" New Society, 4, November, 1982, and Gallup Political Barometers, Social Surveys (Gallup Poll) Ltd., London.

cent to 35 percent, but actually trailed in terms of the popularity of leaders by 41 to 35 percent. In 1983 the Conservatives had pulled further ahead on policies by 46 to 23 percent and achieved an astonishing reversal on leadership ratings of 55 to 16 percent. The latter figures notwithstanding, however, it may be argued that the traditional influences on voting, namely party loyalty and social class, though weakening, remain sufficiently strong to depress the electoral impact of the personality of the leader (Butler and Stokes, 1974:367–68; Crewe, 1985).

Yet mass media coverage of general elections and parliamentary politics is highly personalized and concentrates on the party leaders. General elections have become more presidential, and the mass media virtually ignore secondary party leaders.[2] For the past quarter-century, the prime minister alone has regularly received more attention in The Times than the three leading ministers together—the Foreign Secretary, Chancellor of the Exchequer, and Leader of the House of Commons (Rose, 1981: 19–21). Television and the popular press are even more likely to accentuate this pattern of reporting. The imbalance in coverage stems from the prime minister's engagement in more newsworthy activities and from the fact that, as leader of the government, he or she is newsworthy. A prime minister has many opportunities to personify the government and act as its spokesperson. In the mass media, on foreign visits, and in Parliament, the prime minister is regarded as the authoritative spokesperson for Cabinet policy. Thatcher was particularly prone, as opposition leader and early in her premiership, to "make policy" in television and other interviews, almost committing her Cabinet in advance, for example, on such issues as industrial relations (1980), the Vietnamese refugees (1980), and the EEC budget (1981).

Surveys indicate that Thatcher is not regarded as a warm or compassionate person. She does score highly on the qualities of being decisive, resolute, and principled, a perception augmented by the Falklands war and comparisons with Michael Foot, the former Labour leader. The Conservative 1983 campaign slogan of "The Resolute Approach" leaned heavily on these aspects of her image. A Harris poll in 1983 suggested that she outscored Foot on the following leadership qualities: "gaining respect for Britain abroad" (61–15 percent), "having good judgement in a crisis" (57–19 percent), and "having a vision of where he/she wants to lead the country" (53–26 percent).

Thatcher has also polarized public opinion more than other party leaders. People either like or dislike her; they are not indifferent. In the 1983 election, many Conservative and Labour politicians reported the doorstep hostility to Thatcher, as well as respect for her.[3] Her perception of herself (courageous, persistent, and sticking to a course no matter how unpopular) is matched by the public perception, according to a Gallup survey on the personality images of various leading British politicians. Table 2 shows the proportion agreeing with those propositions on which Thatcher scored higher than any other politicians.

The image of her as a superwoman also is fuelled by eulogies of the sympathetic tabloid press as well as the "devil theory" of Labour politicians. Consider the two following examples:

> Surging down the runway at 145 miles an hour I can feel Mrs. Thatcher vibrating with crusading passion. . . . She's an astonishing bird . . . Superwoman . . . Mrs. Big, Britain's boss. (Jean Rook, *Daily Express*, May 23, 1983)

> Who is the Mephistopheles behind this shabby Faust? The answer is clear enough—to quote her own backbenchers—the great she-elephant, she who must be obeyed, the Catherine the Great of Finchley, the Prime Minister herself. . . . it is her pig-headed bigotry which has prevented her closest colleagues and Sir Robert Armstrong from offering and accepting a compromise on this matter. (Denis Healey, leading the Labour attack in the House of Commons on the government's handling of the G.C.H.Q. affair, February 27, 1984)

As a public personality Thatcher spares few pains. She has been a determined exponent of the use of the mass media, particularly television, and has been willing to organize her campaign tours to take account of the need for photo sessions, television interviews, and political broadcasts and to dovetail her speeches with the party's

TABLE 2.

Thatcher's Personality Image

Not in touch with people	39%
You can't believe anything she says	33%
Not sincere	30%
Cold and distant	38%
Says what she believes	46%
Presents her ideas clearly	46%
You know where she stands on issues	50%
A strong forceful personality	68%

Source: Gallup Poll, February 1984

overall communications strategy. In contrast, Attlee, Heath, Calla-ghan, and Foot were less willing to find time for, or adapt to, the demands of the mass media or the requirements of public relations. Her campaign managers before 1979 arranged voice training (to make it softer and gentler) and changed her hairstyle. She even spent half-an-hour in a field in Suffolk fondling a cow for the benefit of photographers. David Wood, the Political Editor of The Times in 1979, was moved to comment:

> There has been no leader's election campaign before the war or since that so blatantly exploited modern communications in public rela-tions terms. Words were at a discount. The writing press were the spears in a Shakespearean play who marched on and off looking like an army. To adapt McLuhan, the picture was the message and the message was the picture. Perhaps the public relations men were right: If you are ahead in the opinion polls, show business is the answer and you may be as apolitical, antiverbal, and irrational as you wish. (The Times, 30 April 1979, European Edition)

The same pattern was repeated in 1983, and she made only six major speeches during the election campaign.

How does the role of a Conservative prime minister compare with that of leaders in other western states? The concentration of formal political power in the Cabinet, the Cabinet's ability to use its party majority to push legislation through the House of Commons and the absence of formal checks and balances all appear, on the surface, to make political leadership relatively straight-forward in Britain. An American president has a personal mandate, but the constitutional separation of powers and the weakness of the political parties means that cross-party coalitions must be constructed to get a good share of policy proposals through Congress. The President rarely has assured majority party support, and there is no equivalent of the British Cabinet to share the burdens of office. Compared to a British prime minister, the president has to spend more time on public presentation and pondering how best to assure reelection.

In France, the possibility for conflict implied in the separation of powers between Parliament and president was not tested until 1986, as the latter had previously enjoyed a majority in the National Assembly. The existence of more than one right-wing party since 1958 means that a would-be presidential candidate has either to bargain with another party or establish a clear lead on the first presidential election ballot to insure front-runner status for the political party of the right. In comparison to Britain, French political parties are less institutionalized and to some extent are personal followings of presidential candidates. Like their American counterparts, French presidents are concerned with their public image, but the seven-year term of office makes them less preoccupied with elections because of the greater likelihood of a concurrent majority. Presidents more obviously dominate the Cabinet and have usually left parliamentary and party matters to their prime ministers.

In Germany, which has a parliamentary system, the leader of the Christian Democratic party has to bargain with the leader of the Bavarian Social Christians (CSU), and both Social Democratic and Christian Democratic Chancellors have had to bargain in government coalitions with the Free Democrats about policies and Cabinet appointments. There is some formal separation of power between the Chancellor, Cabinet, and individual ministers, and the latter may not be instructed, even by the Chancellor, on matters in their domain. The party (or parties) in control of the federal government also may be checked by the opposition party if the latter has a majority in the federal council or federal diet. Adenauer (1949–63) was the most autocratic Christian Democratic Leader and Chancellor. In government he was prepared to ignore the Cabinet and rely on his "kitchen cabinet." His CDU successors, however, have been more of a *primus inter pares* (Edinger, 1977). Even more constrained is the leader of the Christian Democratic party in Italy. Although the DC is clearly the dominant party in postwar Italian politics and the normal party of government, DC premiers have to engage in elaborate negotiations with the leaders of factions in their party and form the necessary coalitions with other parties.

The British prime minister is inevitably pushed to play a major public role—head of the government in Parliament, public spokesperson for the government, leader of the nation on visits abroad, and chairman and summarizer of Cabinet discussions. Compared to an American or French president, the tasks of cultivating and presenting the prime minister's personality are probably less demanding, while those of party management and maintaining Cabinet cohesion are more insistent, though perhaps less so than for a German chancellor or an Italian premier (cf. Rose, 1981:49).

Conclusion: Mobilizer Not Reconciler

Thatcher has proved herself a remarkable figure. She was a political outsider and relatively inexperienced when she came to the leadership, toppled an established Tory leader (the first to do so for nearly sixty years), and actually increased her seats majority in 1983. She also has challenged a number of long-established political assumptions. She has helped to change the balance in her party in support of a free market and monetarist approach to economic policy. Among the public there has been a positive response to some so-called Thatcherite ideas, e.g., individual self-reliance, not blaming the government for high unemployment, encouraging the private sector, imposing legal limits on trade union immunities and rights, and a government sticking to its principles, however unpopular (Crewe, 1984). Most British prime ministers and party leaders gradually have lost popularity over time and retired when their reputation was at a low point. In her first term at least, Thatcher defied this trend (largely because of the Falklands) and was more popular in 1983 than when she first became prime minister. Moreover, she has retained her ideological commitment, and the shortcomings as well as the successes of her government record are invoked by her as reasons to press on with the original strategy.

On the other hand she did not always get her own way in Cabinet, particularly early on, and on a number of issues informed observers were able to distinguish her own preferences from those of most of her Cabinet, hardly a sign of successful political management. Regarding public attitudes, surveys show strong support for welfare programs and a willingness to pay more taxes to expand them. Crewe (1985) reports that the electorate did not move to the right between 1979 and 1983. In many respects the 1983 election victory was won by default of Labour, a case of "How to Win a Landslide without Really Trying." Her main objective was to reverse the country's economic decline, but, in terms of her goals of economic growth, unemployment, taxation, public spending and shifting economic activity from the public to private sector, she has failed. Apart from the lowering of inflation, her government has followed the long-term (since 1957) relative economic decline of all governments (Riddell, 1983; Rose, 1984).

Reference was made earlier to the *mobilizing* and *reconciling* styles of leadership. Effective political leaders have to take account of both role demands. It is possible, however, to classify most British political leaders according to the relative importance they attach to these values. In the interwar years, Stanley Baldwin and Ramsay MacDonald, by temperament and political conviction, were reconcilers. They were relatively nonpartisan and pursued policies that would least disturb the social fabric. Gladstone, Lloyd George, and

Chamberlain were classic cases of mobilizers. They were not re-specters of party lines and, the last two in particular, were widely distrusted among parliamentary colleagues. The mobilizing style has a greater appeal when there is dissatisfaction with status quo and a feeling that new policies are required.

There is little doubt that Thatcher belongs to the camp of the mobilizers. She is impatient with the status quo and the traditional style of decision-making by compromising with the major interests. She has repudiated policies associated with previous Conservative leaders and has divided public opinion. She has been highly critical of many established institutions, e.g., the senior civil service, For-eign Office, Bank of England, universities, and local government. She is also something of a populist, expressing sympathy for the idea of referendums and appealing over the heads of interest group leaders to communicate directly with the public. Her views on capi-tal punishment, immigration, and the trade unions resemble those of the right-wing tabloid press. Yet, to a greater extent than other mobi-lizers, she has operated within the established political institutions of Parliament and party.

In Britain, the character of being a mobilizer or a reconciler is not related to being in a particular party or being in opposition or gov-ernment. The movement between the two has often been cyclical, with one style breeding a reaction in favor of the other. A leader may start out as a mobilizer but end as a conciliator. In 1964 Wilson presented himself as a radical figure, but by 1974 he was comparing himself to a family doctor, and hoped, in his words, "to achieve . . . peace and quiet for the country." Heath in 1970 also was a radical leader, and many of his policies were enacted in the face of bitter opposition in and out of Parliament. Yet by October 1974 the once radical Heath was espousing the cause of conciliation and national unity, arguing that the grave problems facing the country and the necessary mobilization of consent required a cross-party coalition.

Thatcher, however, has remained a mobilizer; she clearly regards herself as a Heath plus—providing greater political will and persis-tence. Talk of a policy U-turn or reversal, associated with Heath from 1972 onward, has almost disappeared from the political vocabulary in Britain. Thatcher prides herself on her reputation as an "Iron Lady." But she also is reacting against the political "fixer" style of leadership associated with the Labour Prime Ministers Wilson and Callaghan in the mid-1970s. Philip Williams (1982) has drawn a distinction between Labour party leaders who are path-finders, who look for new solutions or try to lead the party in new directions, and stabilizers, who are concerned above all with preserving party unity. Labour, with its well-entrenched factions, egalitarian values, myths about the sovereignty of the party Conference, and separation of powers between the National Executive, Conference, and Parliamentary party, has required coalition building skills of a high order. Both Wilson and Callaghan were determined to keep the Labour party together; the party was a "broad church" and its different factions had to co-exist. They thought that this required the abandonment of any directive or heroic leadership and the careful balancing of rival right– and left-wing factions in Cabinet. Critics inveighed at the fudging, the soothing formuli, the trimming, and the unheroic style, all to keep the party together.

It is always difficult to assess the political significance of an individual leader. One not satisfactory approach is to imagine different outcomes in the past and ask "What if?" For example, what if Heath had won the February 1974 general election, as he nearly did, and carried on as prime minister and Conservative party leader? What if Whitelaw, the heir apparent, had stood on the first leadership ballot in 1975 and won, as many think he would have? Even to pose such questions reminds us that there was a large element of chance in Thatcher's emergence. It seems reasonable to associate Thatcher's presence with a number of distinctive policies, particularly the government's economic strategy, attempts to contain the public sector, toleration of high unemployment, attacks on trade unions, privatisation, and the vigorous prosecution of the Falklands War. Some Cabinet colleagues had doubts about all these policies, and some are prepared to claim that things would have been different without her. Moreover, she has proved to be a radical figure in her second administration. But circumstances, or "luck," also have been important, particularly the outburst of industrial unrest in 1979, which so damaged the Labour government, and the Argentine invasion of the Falklands in 1982.

To date, however, she has proved to be a mobilizer of a rather immobilist society. Both Lloyd George and Churchill were helped by their style suiting the temper of the times. "Thatcherism" has been more a matter of political style and rhetoric than actual results. The deep-rooted political institutions and social stability in Britain make the task of the political mobilizer difficult. It remains to be seen whether Thatcher translates the style into substantial and lasting achievements outside of Whitehall.

Notes

ACKNOWLEDGMENTS: At times I have drawn on material from interviews with Thatcher in December 1974, August 1978, and July 1983. For comments on an earlier version of this paper, I am grateful to George Jones, Peter Morris, Richard Rose, and members of Thatcher's Staff.

1. She may also suspect that *consensus* is sometimes used as a code-word by critics of her political style.

2. In 1979 the two main party leaders gained over 60 percent of the time devoted to their political parties on BBC and ITV coverage of the election. No other politician reached double figures. In 1983 Thatcher gained over 60 percent of her party's coverage and Foot over 50 percent of his party's coverage. These figures are drawn from David Butler and Dennis Kavanagh, *The British General Election of 1979*, London: Macmillan, 1980:209, and *The British General Election of 1983*, London: Macmillan, 1984:160.

3. A BBC Gallup election poll found that 46 percent thought she would make the best prime minister, and 26 percent the worst, the highest figures for any leader.

References

Aughey, A. (1983) "Mrs. Thatcher's Philosophy." *Parliamentary Affairs* 36:389–98.

Avril, P. (1969) *Politics in France*. London: Penguin.

Brown, A.H. (1968) "Prime Ministerial Power." *Public Law* (Spring and Summer): 28–51; 96–118.

Burch, M. (1983) "Mrs. Thatcher's Approach to Leadership in Government 1979–June 1983." *Parliamentary Affairs* 36:399–416.

Butler, D., and D. Kavanagh (1984) *The British General Election of 1983*. London: Macmillan.

Butler, D., and D. Stokes (1974) *Political Change in Britain*. 2d ed. London: Macmillan.

Crewe, I. (1985) "How to Win a Landslide Without Really Trying: Why the Conservatives Won in 1983." In *Britain at the Polls, 1983*, edited by A. Ranney. Durham, N.C.: American Enterprise Institute and Duke University Press.

Crossman, R. (1963) "Introduction." In *The English Constitution* by W. Bagehot. London: Fontana.

Eden, Sir Anthony (1960) *The Memoirs of Sir Anthony Eden: Full Circle*. Boston: Houghton Mifflin.

Edinger, L. (1977) *Politics in West Germany*. Boston: Little Brown.

Hoffman, S. (1967) "Heroic Leadership: The Case of Modern France." In *Political Leadership in Industrialized Societies*, edited by L. Edinger. New York: Wiley.

Hurd, D. (1979) *An End to Promises*. London: Collins.

Jenkins, P. (1970) *The Battle of Downing Street*. London: Charles Knight.

Jones, G. (1965) "The Prime Minister's Power." *Parliamentary Affairs* 18:167–85.

——— (1984) "The Prime Minister's Office Under Mrs. Thatcher." Unpublished paper, London School of Economics.

Kavanagh, D. (1974) "Crisis, Charisma and British Political Leadership." London: Sage Professional Papers in Political Sociology.

——— (1980) "From Gentlemen to Players." In *Britain: Progress and Decline*, edited by W. Gwynn and R. Rose. London: Macmillan.

King, A. (1974) "The Election that Everyone Lost." In *Britain at the Polls: The Parliamentary Elections of 1974*, edited by H. Penniman. Washington, D.C.: American Enterprise Institute.

Leech, R. (1984) "The Philosophy of Thatcherism—A Radical Departure?" *Politics* 4(I): 9–14.

Mackintosh, J. (1977) *The British Cabinet.* London: Stevens.

Norton, P. (1978) *Conservative Dissidents.* London: Temple Smith.

Putnam, R. (1973) *The Beliefs of Politicians.* New Haven: Yale University Press.

Riddell, P. (1983) *The Thatcher Government.* Oxford: Martin Robertson.

Rose, R. (1971) "The Making of Cabinet Ministers." *British Journal of Political Science* 1:393–414.

———— (1981) "British Government: The Job at the Top." In *Presidents and Prime Ministers,* edited by R. Rose and E. Suleiman. Washington, D.C.: American Enterprise Institute.

Rose, R., and D. Kavanagh (1976) "The Monarchy in Contemporary Political Culture." *Comparative Politics* 8:548–76.

Seymour-Ure, C. (1971) "The Disintegration of the Cabinet and the Neglected Question of Cabinet Reform." *Parliamentary Affairs* 25:196–207.

Thatcher, M. (1977) *Let Our Children Grow Tall.* London: Centre for Policy Studies.

Wapshott, N., and G. Brock (1983) *Margaret Thatcher.* London: Futara, MacDonald.

Williams, P. (1982) "Changing Styles of Labour Leadership." In *The Politics of the Labour Party,* edited by D. Kavanagh. London: Allen and Unwin.

Young, H. (1984) "On First Reading Hayek." *The Guardian,* October 8.

PART THREE
THE UNITED STATES

From Staff Aide to Election: The Recruitment of U.S. Representatives

Susan Webb Hammond

The typical route to election to the United States Congress has been through local or state elective office or party activity. Within Congress, in recent years, major change has occurred: resources and power are more widely distributed, and organizational decentralization has increased. There also has been change in the recruitment of members to Congress, and, in particular, service in the federal executive or on a congressional staff has become a more frequent route to election to the House of Representatives. Explaining why this change has occurred and identifying some possible consequences of the increased recruitment of former staff to the House are the focus of this paper. The study covers the twelve congressional elections held between 1960 and 1982.

For any political office the structure of opportunity shapes recruitment patterns (Schlesinger, 1966), and changes in the supply of and demand for potential eligibles will vary (Seligman, 1961, 1967). Demand is, of course, related to opportunity structure. If staffing has become a more typical route to elective office and, more specifically, to election to the House of Representatives, changes may have occurred in the recruitment pool: the supply of possible recruits, i.e., eligibles, may have increased and/or the qualifications of eligibles may have improved. Changes in demand also may have occurred: the number or type of vacancies may have changed.

This study focuses on staff (especially legislative staff) as a pool of eligibles. Quantitative variations in the supply of eligibles can be examined by analyzing changes in staff numbers. Changes in demand can be operationalized as changes in the number of open seats and changes in marginal wins. If there are more open and/or marginal seats, demand will have increased as there are fewer costs associated with running, less risk of loss, and greater possibility of benefit (winning).

In addition, changes in the nature of the staff job may have occurred.

Staff positions may offer increased opportunity for political apprenticeship, which is an important aspect of preselection activity. Jacob
(1962) concludes that apprenticeship positions offer the opportunity
to play a brokerage role, and apprentices are able to develop needed
skills and a network of contacts. In the United States, apprenticeship
positions often are appointive public office positions (Czudnowski,
1975). Marvick (1976:36–37), assessing recruitment studies, notes
that skill needs may change: "The career perspectives of each generation are molded both by new priorities placed on skills and (new)
knowledge to meet changing functional needs. . . . Typically, even at
early stages in their careers, tomorrow's leaders are being screened for
capacities their elders never had to possess."

Czudnowski (1975) further argues that as politics has become professionalized, increasing skill specialization is required. This might
result in needs for *substantive* skills (e.g., knowledge of a policy
area) or *political* skills (negotiating, bargaining).

Context affects Congress as an institution and the individuals
within it (Cooper and Brady, 1981; Cooper and Mackenzie, 1981;
Hammond, Mulhollan, and Stevens, 1981). As issues with which
politicians must deal become more complicated and as political institutions (legislatures, executive establishments) become more specialized and differentiated, individuals occupying political roles
also must specialize. Professionalization, in the sense of training,
learned skills, and shared values relating to professional roles, occurs. This can affect elected officials as well as legislative staff and
may make staff skills more easily transferable to elective positions.

If staff positions have become a more useful and frequent route to
the House of Representatives, our broad expectations are that there
have been changes in one or more aspects of eligibility: an increase
in numbers of staff; and/or shifts in the opportunity structure (e.g.,
open seats, vulnerable incumbents) so that there are more opportunities for success; and/or changes in the staff job itself so that staffing
positions better serve political apprenticeship needs.

Further expectations regarding aides elected to the House are as
follows:

1. Party differences, as in age of first election or routes to
   election, will be evident.
2. Electoral success will be achieved primarily in open seats.
3. Aides with experience as members of legislators' personal
   staffs (especially those with experience in field representative positions) will predominate.
4. Aides who run for election after recently holding a staff
   position will have held a high-level position.

Expectations 1 and 2 are based on previous recruitment studies:
Schlesinger (1966), for example, found overall party differences in

recruitment to high office. Furthermore, potential candidates, especially politically skilled former staff, can be expected to run for seats if there is some real possibility of winning. With regard to 3 and 4, if the expectations as to apprenticeship positions are accurate, it would follow that certain staff positions offer more opportunity to learn political skills and to build a network of supporters and contacts— staff who win would be likely to have served in these positions.

Data

The research covers the 87th through the 98th Congresses, 1961–1984, a period of major reform in Congress and of alternating party control of the Presidency. Data on senators and representatives chosen in the biennial elections 1960–1982 are drawn from various publications such as the *Biographical Directory of the United States Congress: 1789–1971*, various editions of *The Congressional Directory* and *The Almanac of American Politics, Politics in America 1982 and 1984, American Votes*, and *Congressional Quarterly Weekly*. The data set includes all freshmen senators and representatives elected during this period who held Congressional staff positions or nonlegislative jobs with the federal government at some time in their careers (intern positions are not included).[1] The analysis focuses on members of the House of Representatives with this background who were elected for the first time during this era. "Retread" representatives (those legislators who previously served in the House and who were out of office one or more terms before election to another freshman term) are excluded; staff service is not technically a route to elective office after service in that office.

Similarly, senators are excluded from the analysis. Except in the case of Dick Clark (D–Iowa), who was elected to the Senate in 1972 directly from a staff position as Administrative Assistant to Representative John Culver of Iowa, and Nancy Kassebaum (R–Kansas), elected in 1978, who had served on Senator Pearson's field staff, all freshman senators with staff experience elected between 1960 and 1982 had served in major statewide or national legislative elective office prior to entering the Senate. Many had served in the U.S. House of Representatives, using that, not staff work, as their route to the Senate. Election to the Senate is different than election to the House (e.g., Davidson and Oleszak, 1981; Fenno, 1982), and inclusion of senators would obscure, not illuminate, the analysis.

Eligibles and Opportunities

In recent years, the number of congressional staff has increased substantially.[2] Between 1960 and 1982, the total personal staff of senators and representatives increased from 1418 to 3638; and from

2630 to 7487, respectively (Table 1). During this period, the Senate increased the total allowance per senator for personal staff salaries, and gave senators personal aides to assist them with their committee work if they did not control committee or subcommittee staff. Consequently, virtually all senators added personal staff and appointed special legislative aides to assist them with committee assignments, and the size of the average personal staff rose from fourteen to thirty-seven. In the House, allowances for personal staff salaries were increased, and the limitation on the number of personal staff aides rose from eight in 1960 to eighteen full-time and four part-time or temporary employees in 1982. The size of the average staff increased from six to seventeen.

Committee staff have also increased: in the Senate, standing committee staff increased from 470 in 1960 to 1022 in 1982; in the House, during the same period, standing committee staff increased from 440 to 1843. Since about 1978 committee staff numbers have stabilized or decreased slightly, but the higher staffing levels that are a result of the trends since 1960 continue.

Total growth, however substantial, in the number of congressional staff, is an inadequate indicator of the increase in the pool of potential eligibles for recruitment to the House. Disaggregating staff increases to specific positions will shed further light on the eligible pool. Studies reveal that staff positions that might be expected to serve as sources of House candidates (e.g., committee professionals, legislative assistants, press aides, administrative assistants) have increased in both chambers. These are staff jobs with substantive policy and often, especially in the case of an administrative assistant, political content (Brady, 1981; Fox and Hammond, 1977; Hammond, 1976, 1981; U.S. House, 1977).

As these changes were occurring in Washington, senators and representatives also were establishing permanently staffed offices in their states and districts, thus offering staff a local base. New staff travel allowances covered the expense of travel to the state or district for staff based in Washington, D.C. In 1960, the typical field representative, if a senator or representative appointed one, was a part-time employee who appeared at state or district functions and held occasional office hours. Most constituent communications were handled by the Washington office: newsletters to constituents were not a regular feature of office work.

By 1982, however, all senators and representatives had one or more permanent state or district offices, and a part of every personal staff was state or district based. Often, the field representative was a high-level aide who served as the congressman's alter ego, in some cases rivalling the administrative assistant in responsibility and prestige. Aides had a permanent local base for cultivating the constituency, both for the boss and for themselves.

TABLE 1.

Congressional Staff, 86th–97th Congresses

Staff	86th Congress (1959-1960)	97th Congress (1981-1982)
	Year	
Senate Personal	1418	3638
House Personal	2630	7487
Average Senate Personal	14	37
Average House Personal	6	17
Senate Committee	470	1022
House Committee	440	1843

Source: Davidson and Cook (1984a, 1984b); Fox and Hammond (1977, 1978); Hammond (1973); Ornstein, Mann, Malbin and Bibby (1982).

Somewhat similar changes occurred in the executive branch, which has undergone specialization and increased organizational complexity. Within departments, there has been an increase in the number of special assistants to high-level presidential appointees, and an increase in the layering of top-level positions; there also has been an increase in the number of positions at existing levels (e.g., assistant and deputy secretary) (Kaufman, 1976; Heclo, 1978). Similar changes have occurred in White House staff patterns (Fox and Hammond, 1975; Cronin, 1980; Hess, 1976).

The substance of legislative staff jobs also has changed. Congressional aides are increasingly specialized: several legislative assistants (LA) divide the areas handled by one LA twenty years ago; press duties now are handled by a press secretary and perhaps a press assistant rather than by the administrative assistant. This specialization of functions permits aides to work in detail in all areas of the legislative and representative process. As one study summarized,

> staff exercise control over communications into and within a committee and personal office. They participate in identifying issues and developing legislative positions. They conduct research, gather background data on specific legislative matters, and draft legislation. They prepare testimony, speeches, Floor statements, explanations to constituents, and reports. Increasingly, they coordinate legislative strategy. They brief congressmen on pending legislation. Most important, they are expected to offer their opinions and act as a "sounding board" for Senators and Representatives. (Fox and Hammond, 1977:2)

Indeed, some scholars argue that staff serve as "unelected representatives," and thereby undermine the representative function of elected legislators that is basic to the constitutional system (Malbin, 1981). Legislators themselves point to the role of staff: "This country is basically run by the legislative staffs of the Members of the Senate and the House of Representatives" (Senator Robert Morgan, *Congressional Record*, September 8, 1976, S15432).

For present purposes, the central point is that staff aides have an opportunity to assist senators and representatives in every phase of their work. Staff now participate in virtually all congressional activities except voting. The roles of professional staff on Capitol Hill clearly are very different from the early clerk and secretarial roles.

An important component of Jacob's model of recruitment to elective office candidacy is the brokerage role often occupied by potential eligibles (1962). The current congressional staff job is a typical brokerage position: staff sift information and bargain, negotiate, and compromise; and they are in regular contact with constituents. Even if Washington-based, aides are able to build a network of contacts that later can be translated into support. In some jobs, especially those of administrative assistant, field representative, and press secretary, aides usually come from the state or district. Hired because of local knowledge and perhaps local contacts, staff in these highly visible positions have an opportunity to expand their district base, to build political capital, and, perhaps, to position themselves for election. Recent research shows that aides have other useful political attributes and skills as well. Fox and Hammond (1977:36–37) report that staff aides hold political ideologies quite similar to those of the congressmen for whom they work. Aides rate high on leadership skills and on "total interactions initiated"; they generally like people and get along well with others.

The structure of opportunity also has changed. The number of congressional retirements has increased: from an average of slightly over thirty-two in the 85th–90th Congresses to slightly over forty-six in the 91st–95th Congresses (Cooper and West, 1981:84). Although the number of deaths in office dropped slightly, the total number of open seats expanded considerably due to retirements. Between the 1960–1970 and 1972–1982 elections, the average number of open seats[3] rose by twelve, from forty-one to fifty-three. The importance of open seats is that most incumbents who run for reelection to the House continue to win, and marginal wins by incumbents have declined. Thus, the increase in open seats is important to staff contemplating an election run.

An expanded opportunity structure occasioned by the presence of more open seats, when combined with the changes in the pool of potential aspirants discussed above, should provide the basis for enhanced recruitment of former staff personnel to Congress. To determine if this has occurred, we will now consider data for the 87th–98th Congresses.

Findings

Elections—The 87th–98th Congresses

In the twelve biennial elections between 1960 and 1980, 135 men and women[4] with previous legislative or executive job experience were first elected to the House of Representatives. Of these, 63 percent were Democrats and 37 percent were Republicans. Slightly more than half (51 percent) were under forty years of age at the time of first election. More than two-thirds (69 percent) ran for open seats; only 31 percent challenged and defeated incumbents.[5] Seventy-three of the freshmen (54 percent) won by more than 55 percent of the vote; sixty-two (46 percent) won by smaller margins.

Of the 135 freshmen with staff experience, 45 percent had served only on a congressional staff, and 42 percent had only nonlegislative federal experience. When freshmen with both executive and legislative experience are included, seventy-eight (58 percent) of all freshmen with staff experience had worked on congressional staffs; sixty-four (47 percent) had worked in nonlegislative federal positions.

A more critical test of the hypothesis that staff experience facilitates a congressional career involves an examination of recent staff experience: if staff work helps election to the House of Representatives, one would expect that aides could move directly from a staff position to election. To examine this proposition, staff jobs were coded as recent (held in the four years immediately prior to election to the House) and not recent (held more than four years prior to election).[6] Sixty-three (47 percent) of the newly elected representatives with staff experience had held recent legislative or executive jobs. Slightly more than one-fourth (27 percent) had recently held congressional staff jobs.

How do these data fit into the overall context of these elections? Eight hundred and twenty-five freshmen were elected to the 87th–98th Congresses and, as noted, 135 (16 percent) had staff experience (Table 2). A higher ratio of Democrats to Republicans won seats among those with staff experience than among all representatives: 63 percent of the staff winning were Democrats, and 37 percent were Republicans, in contrast to 57 percent Democratic and 43 percent Republican for all representatives first elected during these years. The ratio of Democrats to Republicans is somewhat higher when only open seats are examined: 66 percent of the open seats were won by Democrats and 34 percent by Republicans. Sixty-eight percent of all of the seats won by freshmen were open seats; a similar proportion, 69 percent, of the seats won by former staffers were open seats. Although the ratio of open seats won by staff to all seats won by staff varied, it never fell below 50 percent (Table 2, columns 3 and 4). In more than half the elections, 70 percent or more of the former staffers

TABLE 2.

Freshmen Elected to House of Representatives, 1960-1982 (Frequencies)

	All Freshmen		Former Staff		
	Elected	Open Seats	Elected	Open Seats	
1960	62	37	7	5	Average 1960-1970
1962	65	51	11	10	
1964	86	44	14	7	Staff Elected: 9
1966	62	32	4	2	Staff Open Seats: 6
1968	39	34	8	6	
1970	56	45	8	5	Average 1972-1982
1972	70	61	12	8	
1974	88	49	14	7	Staff Elected: 14
1976	67	54	13	11	Staff Open Seats: 10
1978	77	58	17	13	
1980	74	38	13	7	
1982	79	57	14	12	
Total	825	560	135	93	
Party Affiliation					
Democrats	58%	57%	63%	66%	
Republican	42	43	37	34	

captured open seats: in several elections, over 85 percent of the victorious former staffers won in such seats.

The total number of staff wins increased in the six most recent Congresses (eighty-three seats in contrast to fifty-two seats in the earlier Congresses), and the average number of staff elected in each Congress increased from nine to fourteen. The total number of open seats won by former staff rose from thirty-five to fifty-eight, with the average number of open seats won each election rising from six to ten (Table 2). The percentage of freshmen seats won by former staff also increases: from 14 percent in the earlier Congresses to 18 percent in the most recent ones (Table 3). As expected, with a shift in the opportunity structure, staff wins increase.

Overall, the effect of these twelve elections has been to increase the proportion of House members who have had staff experience; 15 percent of all 1961–1962 House members were former staffers, and this rose to 19 percent in 1983–1984 (Table 3). (The number of House members with staff experience is dependent on the election of freshmen and also on the retirement and electoral vulnerability of incumbents with staff experience.) As Table 3 reveals, the shift to higher levels of former staff aides among all House members lags that of freshmen; not until the 95th Congress (1977–1978) does the

TABLE 3.

Former Staff Aides Serving in the House of Representatives 87th-98th Congresses (in percent)

	Congress											
	87	88	89	90	91	92	93	94	95	96	97	98
Former Aides Serving in House	15	14	15	14	16	15	14	14	17	18	17	19
Legislative Experience	5	6	6	6	6	5	6	7	8	11	11	12
Recent Legislative Experience	3	4	4	4	4	3	3	3	4	5	6	6
Freshman Former Aides in House	2	3	3	1	2	2	3	3	3	4	3	3
Freshman Former Aides as Percent of All Freshmen	11	17	16	6	21	14	17	16	19	22	18	18

former shift occur. In contrast, for freshmen the shift occurs two Congresses earlier (compare rows 1 and 5).

When the data are disaggregated, interesting recruitment patterns appear. The number of newly elected representatives with only federal executive experience decreased between the 87th–92nd and the 93rd–98th Congresses (see Table 4). In contrast, the number of those with legislative experience only or with both legislative and executive experience rose. The number of freshmen with legislative staff experience more than doubled, and the number with recent legislative experience more than tripled. It appears that in recent years executive staff work experience among representatives has become slightly less common and legislative staff work much more typical. These data may reflect changing patterns of House-constituent relationships and House localism, as well as the difficulties of cultivating the district and establishing a local network of supporters from a nonlegislative federal base.

The change in the mix of legislative and executive experience is more pronounced when only representatives with recent staff experience are considered. As Table 4 reveals, the percentage using legislative staff work as a springboard to House election has more than doubled (from 33 to 69 percent) when the 93rd–98th Congresses are compared to the 87th–92nd ones. Also, over these two periods, the percentage with recent executive experience has been halved, to just under one third, although the actual number using executive work as a springboard is about the same because total numbers have increased substantially.

By party, 45 percent of the Democrats and 38 percent of the Republicans with staff experience have had only executive (or law clerk) experience; 46 percent of the Democrats and 44 percent of the Republicans have had only legislative staffing experience; 9 percent of the Democrats but 18 percent of the Republicans have had both legislative and executive experience. Fifty percent of the Republican former staffers and 55 percent of their Democratic counterparts have had some nonlegislative experience; 54 percent of the Democrats and 62 percent of the Republicans have had legislative staff experience. However, more Democratic former staffers than Republicans have had executive or legislative experience only: in both categories, nearly twice as many Democrats as Republicans have served in staff positions.

As routes to elective office, legislative staffing experience has increased and nonlegislative federal experience has ·decreased. Between 1961 and 1972, more than half of the Democratic and Republican freshmen former staffers had executive experience only; about one third from both parties had been legislative staffers only. In more recent years (1973–1984) those percentages reverse: about one third

TABLE 4.

Number of Freshmen with Various Types of Staff Experience, 87th–98th Congresses

Congress	Executive Only		Legislative Only		Executive and Legislative	
	N	%	N	%	N	%
87–92	31	60	17	33	4	7
93–98	26	31	44	53	13	16
Total	57	42	61	45	17	13
	Recent Staff Experience					
	N	%	N	%	N	%
87–92	15	62	8	33	1	4
93–98	12	31	7	69	0	0

of the Democratic and Republican former staffers had executive experience, and slightly more than one half had only legislative experience. In addition, in both parties the percentage previously holding both executive and legislative staff positions increased: for Democrats from 3 percent to 11 percent; for Republicans, from 14 percent to 18 percent.

The increasing complexity of the political environment, the growing interdependence of issues, and the rise in the number of crosscutting issues has led to increased organizational complexity and to specialization and professionalization of staffing jobs on Capitol Hill and within the federal executive. Subsystems have evolved into issue networks (Heclo, 1978); policy specialists move in and out of government as issue salience changes. Within issue networks there has been an increase in private sector think tanks and interest groups. These changes have increased job opportunities and mobility, as individuals move around a network, in and out of, or between, branches of government. Interbranch mobility appears to have been enhanced in recent years by the fairly regular alteration of parties in control of the presidency and by programs designed to move personnel to government or to a different institution of government on a short-term basis (e.g., the White House Fellows Program, the Commerce-Science Fellows Program). Contrary to expectation, however, the data do not demonstrate increased movement between the branches by aides who later are elected to the House.

The change that does appear is that the increasing professionalization of Capitol Hill staff has made staff work a useful "credentialing" or springboard experience for election. Thirty-five aides with recent congressional staff experience won election to the House and twenty-seven aides with recent executive experience did so. One additional freshman had both recent legislative and executive experience. Although legislative staffing is the preferred route, executive positions also are an accepted means of achieving national elective office.

Age and Education Levels

Since 1960 the average age of members of the House gradually has decreased: from fifty-two years in 1961 (the 87th Congress) to forty-eight years in 1981 (the 97th Congress). In January 1983, at the start of the 98th Congress, the average age of representatives had dropped to forty-six years (Congressional Quarterly *Guide to Congress,* 1982:644; Vogler, 1983:62). We would expect freshman representatives to be somewhat younger than most incumbents: at the start of the 97th Congress (1981) eight freshmen were under thirty.

Over the last twenty-four years *freshman* former aides, as expected, have been younger than the House average: the average age of freshmen elected to the 87th Congress (1961) was forty years; to the 98th Congress (1983) it was forty-two years. The average age of former aides elected as freshmen during the last six Congresses was lower than those elected earlier: thirty-nine years in contrast to forty-three years. The average age of Republican and Democratic former aides newly elected to Congress is similar.

Former aides have high levels of education. Czudnowski reports that among former aides to representatives, senators or federal executives who served in Congress in 1968–1972 and 1976–1980 nearly one-half (43 percent) held doctorates, 17 percent held master's degrees, and 22 percent held at least a bachelor's degree (1983:36). Aides in professional staff positions in Congress are highly trained: in 1972–1974, 35 percent held at least a bachelor's degree, 16 percent held at least a master's degree, 32 percent held law degrees, and 5 percent held either a Ph.D. or M.D. (Fox and Hammond, 1977:175). Although many former aides have legal training, the percentage of Congressmen with such training is even greater. In 1980, for example, 23 percent of all members held bachelor's degrees, 12 percent held master's degrees, 5 percent held Ph.D. or M.D. degrees, but nearly half (46 percent) held law degrees (Czudnowski, 1983:17). More generally, it appears that former aides elected to the House differ from both all House members and other types of former staffers in their formal education. In addition to political skills, former aides also bring a diversification of expertise to the House of Representatives.

Former Congressional Staff

Most former congressional aides running for the House have had experience on personal staffs. Seventy-one of the seventy-eight former legislative aides (89 percent) served on the personal staffs of senators or representatives. Thirteen of the seventy-eight (17 percent) had committee experience. Seven had only committee experience. Of the seventy-eight House freshmen with previous legislative staff experience, 60 percent are Democrats; 40 percent are Republicans; 64 percent were under forty when first elected; 70 percent ran in open seats; and 46 percent won marginally.

Contrary to expectation, most aides come from Washington jobs: 78 percent of all former legislative aides (including those with committee experience) worked on Capitol Hill, not in the state or district. Of aides with recent legislative experience, an even higher percentage (81 percent) worked in Washington. Only seven aides (6 percent) worked in state or district offices. This seems a surprising finding, but confirms the argument that Washington positions, *especially those on personal staffs,* are apprenticeship positions. Also, personal staffs seem to be better incubators for congressional ambitions than do committee staffs. Early in a career, the former jobs can be used for "credentialing," giving the aide both Washington experience and a base of local contacts that may serve to launch a political career. Later, it appears that personal staff positions offer aides an opportunity to keep in touch with district or state concerns, and to build a network of contacts and support critical to an immediate Congressional election bid.

As expected, aides with legislative experience just prior to an election bid held predominantly high-level positions. Twenty-six of the thirty personal staff aides with recent legislative experience (87 percent) held such positions. (Field representatives, administrative assistants, and legislative assistants were considered high-level positions: because of variation in office titles, particularly for field staff, it may be that the number of high-level aides is underreported.) Among aides with legislative experience earlier in a career, only about half (54 percent) had occupied high-level positions.

Between 1960 and 1972 (the 87th–92nd Congresses), only one representative (a Republican) had field experience; all other freshmen who were former legislative staffers had worked in Washington. In contrast, since 1972, a higher proportion of aides elected to Congress have served in field offices. When Democrats and Republicans elected between 1972 and 1982 are compared, a larger percentage of Republicans—25 percent in contrast to 12 percent of the Democrats—have been field aides. Among those representatives with recent staff experience, a similar pattern is evident. In the later Congresses, field aides run for election, and there are differences between the parties.

An examination of total career patterns by party reveals few differences. Twice as many Democrats as Republicans have nonlegislative federal experience only (thirty-eight in contrast to nineteen). About the same number from each party have served in staff positions in both the legislative and executive branches. However, a much higher proportion of the Republicans have served in both branches; a slightly higher proportion of Democrats than Republicans have served in the executive branch only; about the same proportion of each party have worked only for Congress. These patterns in the data do not appear to be a consequence of shifts in the opportunity structure. Employment patterns are similar whether the comparison is between early and later Congresses, periods of Democratic or Republican control of the White House (with an expectation of more opportunity for executive branch employment for staff who are of the same party as the President), or periods that allow time to elapse before staff move following changes in party control of the Presidency.

Freshman legislators with legislative staff experience have longtime ties with their state. Seventy-six percent are elected from the same state as their former bosses; 35 percent represent the same congressional district. Most aides who run in a different state than their former bosses have served on a congressional staff early in their careers and subsequently relocated in a new state, or they have worked for a senator or representative from a different state than their own but subsequently returned to their own state. Taking into account early career shifts in residence, it is striking that 76 percent of the freshman legislators represent the same state as their former bosses. Elective careers, even at the federal level, are strongly local (see Matthews, 1960, 1954).

Some legislative aides are active in state or local party politics while serving on congressional staffs. Some serve in party office or as convention delegates.[7] Most have been active in their bosses' congressional campaigns.[8]

Freshman representatives who use recent legislative staff experience as a springboard to election in the same district often have been chosen as their bosses' heirs apparent. For example, among those elected in recent Congresses, Charles Whiteley (D–NC), elected in 1976, had served as a top aide to Representative Henderson, whom he succeeded. Similarly, Henderson had served on the staff of his predecessor, Graham Barden. Whiteley nurtured district ties by handling federal projects and constituent casework matters for Henderson and by working for Henderson back in North Carolina for a period before his first campaign. As a second example, James Oberstar (D–MN) served as administrative assistant, and also administrator of the House Public Works Committee, for John Blatnik (D–MN), his predecessor and mentor. Blatnik supported Oberstar's 1974 election bid to succeed him. That support was considered crucial to the latter's success in a close primary fight. Finally, staff work occasionally results in heir apparent status although the aide does not have recent staff experience. Ed Jenkins (D–GA) had served as administrative assistant to Philip Landrum (D–GA). After leaving the Hill for a career back in Georgia, he and Landrum were law partners. In 1976, Jenkins was endorsed by Landrum as his successor. Landrum is regarded as having been "able to pass the district along to his former aide" (*Almanac of American Politics*, 1980).

Federal Experience, Nonlegislative

In the 87th–98th Congresses, fifty-seven freshman legislators came to the House with some federal government experience: most worked in the executive branch; a few served as law clerks to federal judges. Thirty-seven representatives (65 percent) had left these jobs more than four years before running for election to the House; that experience is coded as nonrecent. For most of the thirty-seven, the federal work experience was early in a career; members worked as FBI agents, staff attorneys in federal agencies, or professional staff in Washington or field offices. In many cases, these jobs were used for credentialing.

Some freshman representatives use their executive experience as an immediate springboard to election. Rather surprisingly, given the presumed importance of strong local ties for electoral success, more of those with recent experience have served in Washington than in the field: twelve (60 percent) in contrast to eight (40 percent). Most served in high government positions. Of the newly elected representatives who previously had held federal field jobs, some had been U.S. Attorneys or Assistant U.S. Attorneys. Others, like Bob Bergland, had headed federal agency field offices. (Bergland served for five years as Midwest Area Director of the Agricultural Stabilization and Conservation Service.)

It should be more difficult to run for the House from a recent Washington position than from a local base. Some candidates run on their Washington expertise, but go back to the district for a period of time to expand district ties. Tim Wirth (D–CO), after a career spent in Washington as White House Fellow, Special Assistant to the Secretary of HEW, and Assistant Secretary of HEW, returned in 1970 to work in Colorado before his November 1974 election. Richard Cheney's Washington career, which included serving as Chief of Staff to President Ford, became a positive campaign factor when he was able to emphasize he was a Wyoming native who had high national visibility.

In general, both Washington and field-based executive positions serve as a source of recruitment for some few representatives. A Washington position may enhance visibility, but candidates must also develop, and convince constituents of, local ties. Once in office, such representatives draw on the expertise developed in their executive branch work (e.g., Les Aspin [D–WI] who worked as an assistant to Secretary of Defense Robert McNamara). As the data show, in recent years legislative and executive staff experience have become more and less typical, respectively, as routes to House election.

In Office: House Activity

The data permit some analysis of activity of former aides after election to the House. One expectation was that, once in office, representatives with legislative staff experience would seek service on the same committees as those on which their bosses had served. The expectation was, further, that freshman representatives with committee staff experience would serve on that committee. In order to examine these hypotheses, the committee assignments of the freshmen representatives and their bosses were examined. If their committees were the same or in the same subject matter area (e.g., Armed Services Committee and DOD Appropriations Subcommittee), the expectation would be supported. It turns out, however, that only 23 percent of the representatives with legislative staff experience exhibited such committee continuity in their freshman term. As with other indicators, there has been some shift between the 87th–92nd and the 93rd–98th Congresses. During the first period, only 17 percent of those elected served on the same commmittees: in the more recent Congresses, 26 percent did.

What are possible explanations for these findings? First, aides on personal staffs may not have worked on committee legislation for their bosses, but instead worked on legislative matters not relating to their bosses' committee assignments; the freshman may ask for assignment to those other committees. Second, and alternatively, those with legislative staff experience early in their career may have developed other interests and/or expertise by the time they are elected to Congress. Third, assignment to the same committees, when it does occur, may be a consequence of constituency factors rather than representative expertise. Minnesota, Iowa, and Kansas representatives, for example, frequently serve on the Agriculture committee; Virginia representatives often seek assignment on Armed Services; representatives from districts with a strong labor presence often serve on Education and Labor. In such instances, whether freshman representatives already had worked on certain committee matters as staff aides would be of little consequence in determining their committee assignments.

What are the consequences of staff experience for the activities of the individual legislator? A number of former staffers turned legislator occupy party and committee leadership positions in the House: Bob Michel (R–IL) as House Republican Leader; Richard Cheney (R–

WY), chairman of the Republican Policy committee; Thomas Foley (D–WA), Democratic Whip; and Tony Coelho (D–CA), chairman of the Democratic Congressional Campaign committee. Others serve in committee leadership positions: Tim Wirth (D–CO), for example, as chairman of the Telecommunications Subcommittee and Michael Barnes (D–MD) as chairman of the Western Hemisphere Affairs Subcommittee.

Former aides usually are relatively young when first elected. If they choose to do so, they are in a position to serve in Congress for a long period of time and to climb the career ladder to institutional power. With knowledge of congressional norms and procedures acquired prior to election, they also are in a position to move quickly to participate in policy making. It appears that former aides do occupy positions of power and policy making relatively early in their congressional careers. Committed to the House as an institution, and with an apparent goal of power therein, many achieve long careers in that institution. This is especially the case for former aides with recent legislative staff experience.

Former aides appear to have a somewhat higher rate of reelection: 7 percent of all former aides serving in the 87th Congress continued to serve in the 98th Congress. In contrast, 5 percent of all House members in the 87th Congress also served in the 98th. Three of the four former aides who served in both the 87th and 98th Congresses had legislative staff experience. Two of the four had served on a congressional staff just prior to election. Both now serve in high-level positions: Bob Michel (R-Ill.) as Republican Leader and Melvin Price (D-Ill.), until the 99th Congress, as Chairman of the Armed Services Committee.

The 96th Congress freshmen are illustrative of the House careers of former aides (see the study by Loomis in this volume for all House freshmen). The former aides continue to win elections and have moved quickly into influential positions. All former aides were reelected to the 97th Congress; sixteen of the seventeen were reelected to the 98th (one resigned during the 97th). Of the sixteen first elected in 1978 and still serving in 1983–1984, most are active and visible party, committee, or legislative-policy figures. Five (31 percent) serve in party leadership positions. Seven (44 percent) chair or are ranking minority members of subcommittees; in these positions, they have been active legislative leaders. Others, e.g., Dachle (D–SD), have used their committee assignments to become active and respected participants in the legislative process.

Progressive Ambition and the Staff Job

Staff aides who run for elective office are not anonymous bureaucrats. Some staff do make a career on Capitol Hill or in the executive.

In recent years, the rewards of a staff job, at least in Congress, have increased: aides are now often identified by name as playing a major role in legislative policy making. But many aides do expect to move on. Fifty-eight percent of House administrative assistants surveyed in 1977 expected that more than 75 percent of the staff aides in their office would be working off the Hill within ten years (U.S. House, 1977:100).

With appointment to a legislative staff position, aides enter the political arena. For most, it is a first political experience. For a few, who have been party activists at the student level or in political campaigns, it is a further step in politics. In either case, the staff position provides an opportunity to develop or refine professional political skills of negotiation and bargaining. Individuals also develop substantive knowledge within particular policy areas. Black's description of city council members in the San Francisco Bay area could apply to congressional staff: "[they are] involved in the process of professionalization," i.e., the learning of norms and skills necessary to the profession of politician, and "the more ambitious of the councilmen are learning a set of orientations and attitudes that will aid them in the pursuit of future political goals" (1970:878).

Staff jobs are brokerage positions. Aides can build support networks critical to electoral success. They can survey political opportunities. A staff job also may contribute to aides' progressive ambition. Increasingly knowledgeable about state and district issues; developing political skills of negotiation, bargaining, and compromise; and positioned so that available opportunities can be identified, it is natural that ambition may become focused on a run for elective office.

Conclusion

Staffing is an increasingly frequent route to election to the United States House of Representatives, whether used early in a career for credentialing or later as a direct springboard to office. More representatives and a higher proportion of freshman representatives with experience as legislative or executive aides are being elected to the House. The pool of legislative staff has expanded. The nature of the job has changèd so that political skills can be developed. The opportunity structure has expanded and increased the possibility of a successful run.

Federal government staff experience, especially legislative work, is used increasingly as a base for election to the House. Former aides may be very well situated to sell themselves to the electorate. Staff already know both the district and Congress. They have worked on legislative and constituency matters. As issues have become more complicated and interrelated, as subsystems have given way to networks, and as professionalization and specialization occur in a context of job fluidity, it may be that staff experience is more easily exchanged for service as an elected representative than it once was.

Contrary to expectations, few party differences are evident. As opportunities have expanded and skill levels increased, individuals in both parties have responded similarly: entering Congress after national legislative or executive staff experience has become more frequent.

The findings suggest further inquiry. Prestaff political activity might be explored. Are individuals who enter legislative or executive policy-making jobs with previous political activity more likely than their colleagues to seek elective office? How do personal attitudes and motivations, opportunity structures, and recruitment processes interact to induce some individuals to run for Congress and others to enter law firms, corporations, or lobbying groups in the private sector? Research also might focus more closely on activity in Congress, especially on the effect of involving an increasing number of former aides as major actors in the policy process.

A commitment to a professional political career, with skills and ambition for power in the House, appears to be the hallmark of former staffers. Staff aides develop political skills for election and for operating effectively in Congress. As the pool of staffers has increased and the opportunity structure has shifted, staffing has become an increasingly well-travelled route to House election.

Notes

I appreciate the very able research assistance of Jeff Andrade and Scott Rudolf.

1. All nonlegislative federal positions are reported under the executive category. This includes a few representatives who served as law clerks to federal district, appeals, or Supreme Court judges.

2. Sources of data for this section are Fox and Hammond (1976, 1977), Hammond (1973), Ornstein, Mann, Malbin, and Bibby (1982), and Davidson and Cook (1984a, 1984b).

3. All seats, including new or redrawn, with no incumbent running are counted as open.

4. Only two women, one with executive staff experience and one with (district office) legislative staff experience, were elected to the House during this time. This probably reflects the somewhat different career paths of many women candidates, as well as that most professional staff positions on the Hill have, until quite recently, been occupied by men. One woman with legislative staff experience, Nancy Kassebaum (R–KS), was elected to the Senate during this period.

5. Data are for the general election. Primary elections are not included in the data set.

6. Because one individual may have held several executive or congressional jobs, in the analysis *recent* overrides *nonrecent*; i.e., if someone

served as an administrative assistant on a congressional staff immediately prior to election and in the executive branch five to eight years before election, only the legislative position appears in the analysis.

7. Party activity and offices are not systematically reported in biographical data on representatives; hence, the data set analyzed here is not complete.

8. Representatives with experience on a campaign staff (presidential, congressional or gubernatorial) but with no experience on a congressional or other federal staff were not included in the data set.

References

Barone, Michael, Grant Ujifusa, and Douglas Matthews (1972–1984) *Almanac of American Politics*. Various editions. E.P. Dutton; Barone & Co.; National Journal.

Biographical Directory of the U. S. Congress, 1789–1971. Washington, D.C.: Government Printing Office.

Black, Gordon S. (1970) "A Theory of Professionalization in Politics." *American Political Science Review*, 64:865–78.

Brady, David W. (1981) "Personnel Management in the House." In *The House at Work*, edited by Joseph Cooper and G. Calvin Mackenzie. Austin: University of Texas Press.

Congressional Quarterly (1982) *Guide to the Congress*. 3d ed. Washington, D.C.: Congressional Quarterly Press.

Congressional Quarterly (Various 1960-1983) *Weekly*. Washington, D. C.: Congressional Quarterly Press.

Cooper, Joseph, and David W. Brady (1981) "Institutional Content and Leadership Style: The House from Cannon to Rayburn." *American Political Science Review* 75:411-425.

Cooper, Joseph, and G. Calvin Mackenzie, eds. (1981) *The House at Work*. Austin: University of Texas Press.

Cooper, Joseph, and William West (1981) "The Congressional Career in the 1970's." In *Congress Reconsidered*, 2d ed., edited by Lawrence Dodd and Bruce Oppenheimer. Washington, D. C.: Congressional Quarterly Press.

Cronin, Thomas E. (1980) *The State of the Presidency*. 2d ed. Boston: Little, Brown.

Czudnowski, Moshe M. (1975) "Political Recruitment." In *Handbook of Political Science*, vol. 4, edited by Fred I. Greenstein and Nelson W. Polsby. Reading, MA: Addison-Wesley.

——— (1983) "Higher Education and Liberalism among Political Elites." In *Political Elites and Social Change*, edited by Moshe Czudnowski. DeKalb: Northern Illinois University Press.

Davidson, Roger H., and Mary Etta Cook (1984a) "Indicators of House of Representatives Workload and Activity." Washington, D. C.: Congressional Research Service.

——— (1984b) "Indicators of Senate Activity and Workload." Washington, D. C.:Congressional Research Service.

Davidson, Roger H., and Walter Oleszak (1981) *Congress and Its Members*. Washington, D. C.: Congressional Quarterly Press.

Erenhalt, Alan, ed. (1982, 1984) *Politics in America*. Washington, D. C.: Congressional Quarterly Press.

Fenno, Richard F. (1982) *The United States Senate: A Bicameral Perspective.* Washington, D. C.: American Enterprise Institute.

Fox, Harrison W., Jr., and Susan Webb Hammond (1976) "Trends in Legislative Staffing." Paper presented at the 1976 Annual Meeting of the Southern Political Science Association, New Orleans.

——— (1977) *Congressional Staffs: The Invisible Force in American Lawmaking.* New York: The Free Press.

Hammond, Susan Webb (1973) "The Personal Staffs of Members of the U. S. House of Representatives." Unpublished Ph.D. dissertation, The Johns Hopkins University.

——— (1976) "The Operation of Senators' Offices." In *Senators: Office, Ethics and Pressures,* Commission on the Operation of the Senate, United States Senate. Washington, D. C.: Government Printing Office.

——— (1981) "The Management of Legislative Offices." In *The House at Work,* edited by Joseph Cooper and G. Calvin Mackenzie. Austin: University of Texas Press.

Hammond, Susan Webb, Daniel P. Mulhollan, and Arthur G. Stevens, Jr. (1981) "The Institutionalization of Interests in Congress: The Organization of Informal Groups." Paper presented at the 1981 Annual Meeting of the Southwest Political Science Association, Dallas.

Heclo, Hugh (1977) *A Government of Strangers.* Washington, D. C.: The Brookings Institution.

——— (1978) "Issue Networks and the Executive Establishment." In *The New American Political System,* edited by Anthony King. Washington, D. C.: The American Enterprise Institute.

Hess, Stephen (1976) *Organizing the Presidency.* Washington, D. C.: The Brookings Institution.

Jacob, Herbert (1962) "Initial Recruitment of Elected Officials in the U.S.—A Model." *Journal of Politics* 20:703–16.

Kaufman, Herbert (1976) *Are Government Organizations Immortal?* Washington, D. C.: The Brookings Institution.

Malbin, Michael J. (1981) "Delegation, Deliberation, and the New Role of Congressional Staff." In *The New Congress,* edited by Thomas E. Mann and Norman J. Ornstein. Washington, D. C.: The American Enterprise Institute.

Marvick, Dwaine (1976) "Continuities in Recruitment Theory and Research: Toward a New Model." In *Elite Recruitment in Democratic Politics: Comparative Studies Across Nations,* edited by Heinz Eulau and Moshe M. Czudnowski. Beverly Hills: Sage Publications.

Matthews, Donald R. (1954) *The Social Background of Political Decisionmakers.* New York: Random House.

——— (1960) *U. S. Senators and Their World.* New York: Random House (Vintage).

Ornstein, Norman J., Thomas E. Mann, Michael J. Malbin, and John F. Bibby. (1982) *Vital Statistics on Congress.* Washington, D. C.: The American Enterprise Institute.

Scammon, Richard, ed. (1959–1982) *America Votes,* vols. 3–15. University of Pittsburgh Press; Congressional Quarterly Inc.

Schlesinger, Joseph A. (1966) *Ambition and Politics.* Chicago: Rand McNally.

Seligman, Lester G. (1961) "Political Recruitment and Party Structure: A Case Study." *American Political Science Review* 55:77–86.

——— (1967) "Political Parties and the Recruitment of Political Leadership." In *Political Leadership in Industrialized Societies*, edited by Lewis J. Edinger. New York: Wiley.

U. S. Congress (1971) *Biographical Directory of the United States Congress, 1789-1971*. Washington, D. C.: Government Printing Office.

——— (1961–1983) *Congressional Directory* (Various editions). Washington, D. C.: Government Printing Office.

U. S. House of Representatives (1977) *Administrative Reorganization and Legislative Management: Work Management*, vol. 2. Report of the Commission on Administrative Review, 95th Congress, 1st Session. House Document No. 95-232. Washington, D. C.: Government Printing Office.

Vogler, David J. (1983) *The Politics of Congress*. Boston: Allyn & Bacon.

Survival in the U.S. Congress

Robert G. Brookshire and
Dean F. Duncan III

The framers of the Constitution of the United States did not intend that members of Congress make careers out of service in the House or Senate. These intentions have been frustrated. Both the House and the Senate are characterized by low turnover in their memberships, and senators and representatives seek to develop and maintain long careers in these chambers. Career protection through reelection has been described as the primary goal of these legislators (e.g., Fiorina, 1977); indeed, "some have no other interests" (Davidson, 1977:109). It may be unfair to view all members of Congress as single-minded seekers of reelection, but as David Price points out, "the collective portrayal in many respects rings true" (1977:162). Even for those members who do not concentrate solely on career maintenance, this goal is vital. A legislative career must be developed in order to achieve anything else of importance in Congress (Mayhew, 1974).

The development of careerism in Congress has had profound consequences for the legislative branch. Not only is career development a major influence on the behavior of individual senators and representatives, the rise of careerism has shaped the internal organization of the House and Senate (e.g., Dodd and Oppenheimer, 1977a). Careerism, as translated into professionalization, is a major indicator of the institutionalization of a legislative body (Polsby, 1968), and Congress "is probably the most highly 'professionalized' of legislatures, in that it promotes careerism among its members and gives them the salaries, staff and other resources to sustain careers" (Mayhew, 1974:7). Thus, the development and nature of careerism in Congress is an important subject of study, both for its effects on the structure and dynamics of the House and Senate and as an indicator of institutionalization in comparison with other legislatures.

Careerism refers to the practice of making service in the House or the Senate a full-time, permanent occupation. A member seeking a congressional career is distinguished from one who uses Congress as a stepping stone to another office, such as the presidency or a governorship. Likewise, we distinguish House and Senate careerists from those who use membership in one chamber as a springboard to a career in the other. Neither is careerism shown by members who seek to remain in Congress for only a limited number of terms. Defined in this way, careerism is evidence of static, rather than discrete or progressive ambition (Schlesinger, 1966). And, in this study, we concentrate almost exclusively on members' careers in the chambers, as opposed to their careers in their districts (Fenno, 1978).

In the early years, congressional careers were not very popular. Turnover in the House has been described as "enormous" (Polsby, 1968:146), and this was mirrored in the Senate (Douglas Price, 1977). After Reconstruction, however, senators began to develop stable career patterns, and after 1896, representatives followed suit (e.g, Brookshire and Duncan, 1983a, 1983b). Many factors seem to have contributed to these developments. These can be divided broadly into changes in electoral influences on career patterns, institutional changes in Congress, and changes in individuals seeking congressional seats.

The Causes of Increased Careerism

Most students of Congress agree that the realignment of 1896 had a profound effect on career patterns in the House (e.g., Fiorina, Rohde, and Wissel, 1975; Fiorina, 1977; Kernell, 1977). By reducing interparty competition this realignment created safe seats and gave representatives the opportunity to develop lengthy careers. There were many other changes in electoral arrangements in the nineteenth century that also played a part, however. The decline of the practice of rotation in office (Kernell, 1977; Fiorina, 1977), ballot reform and the expansion of voter registration (Price, 1973), reapportionment (Fiorina, Rohde, and Wissel, 1975), and a decline in the number of contested House elections (Douglas Price, 1977) all served to enhance the ability of representatives to win reelection. Electoral influences also played a role in the rise of careerism in the Senate, especially with the spread of the direct primary and the inauguration of the direct election of senators (Price, 1973; Brookshire and Duncan, 1983b). However, the biggest changes in Senate career patterns occurred in the 1880s and predate these electoral developments.

Changes in electoral arrangements and realignments cannot tell the whole story. These factors only affect the ability of congressmen to achieve reelection and do not explain why senators and representatives took advantage of the opportunities provided. There were institutional changes in Congress that made careers more attractive. First was the increase in the importance of the national government

(Polsby, 1968; Fiorina, 1977). After the Civil War firmly established the locus of authority in the federal system, service at the national level was no longer secondary in power and influence to service in states and localities. In addition, the power of both the House and the Senate increased vis-a-vis that of other branches of government over the second half of the nineteenth century. Of three peaks in the power of the House identified by Huntington, two occurred during this period (Huntington, 1973). The 1870s and 1880s also were the apogee of the power of the Senate (Douglas Price, 1977). Ambitious legislators in the late nineteenth century found the Congress a much more attractive place for the exercise of influence.

In the House, party control was more stable, and the Speaker's influence on committee assignments declined. These factors helped the House to retain senior members and spurred institutionalization of the seniority system (Price, 1971). The concomitant decentralization of power increased the influence of individual members (Polsby, 1968). These institutional changes, in combination with the realignment of 1896 and other electoral changes, set up a "feedback loop" (Douglas Price, 1977) in which the desirability of a House career increased, the opportunity to develop such a career increased, and the House responded to these nascent careerists by further increasing the rewards of long tenure.

After the Civil War, the Senate entered a period of "one-party government" during which Republicans established the chamber as the most powerful body at the national level. Its membership grew substantially with the admission of the western states and became dominated by professional politicians who maintained control over state party machines (Diamond, 1976). The influence of state legislatures on senators diminished (Price, 1975) and allowed members to exercise more control over their own actions. Toward the end of the century, the spread of primary elections further weakened senators' dependence on their legislatures. The Senate also developed a tradition of party organization and leadership, first under Conkling and later under Republicans Allison and Aldrich and Democrat Gorman (Diamond, 1976). These factors made it both desirable and possible for senators to develop careers, and the average number of terms served increased dramatically (Diamond, 1976; Brookshire and Duncan, 1983b).

Changes in the type of people who pursued congressional office may well have contributed to the development of careerism in both chambers. Unfortunately, these influences have been investigated previously only for representatives. Witmer has observed that the average age of freshmen in the House has decreased and that the average age of members as a whole has increased. He assigns some of the increase in careerism to representatives entering the House earlier in their lives and living longer (Witmer, 1964). Kernell (1977) disputes this finding, however, and other authors have called for further study of this factor (Fiorina et al., 1975). Bogue et al., concluding a comprehensive study of the backgrounds of representatives from 1789 to 1960, find "little change can be observed in the characteristics and experiences of representatives before entry into House service" (1976:300). Although differences in levels and types of education, increasing variety of pre-House occupations, and changes in the military backgrounds of congressmen were found, these authors do not attribute the much larger changes in the behavior of representatives to these variations. Even though modern congressmen are different from their predecessors, students of Congress have yet to attribute changes in careerism to differences in personal characteristics and backgrounds.

The Consequences of Careerism

There may be some dispute about the etiology of careerism in Congress, but there is no doubt that its development has had profound impact on the institution and the way its members behave. The most obvious result is the seniority system. When members declined to serve long terms, the assignment of committee positions based on length of service was not important. As careerism developed, however, "members with long service wanted their experience recognized and were unwilling to have all committee posts and chairmanships up for grabs every two years" (Douglas Price, 1973:61). The relationship between the growth of careerism and the establishment of the seniority system is symbiotic, since careerists demand seniority rewards for their long tenure, and seniority fosters the development of more careerism among congressmen (e.g., Fiorina, 1977; Schaefer, 1983).

Careerism is both the direct and indirect cause of the decentralization of power in the House and Senate. Legislators interested in maintaining their careers call for more autonomy within their chambers. In order to facilitate reelection, they also demand more influence on their committees (e.g., David Price, 1977). Committee chairmen, rising through seniority, develop bases of power independent of the House and Senate leadership, furthering the dispersal of power (Polsby, Gallaher, and Rundquist, 1969). This decentralization has weakened the institution's "ability to generate authoritative leadership and institutional cohesion" (Dodd, 1977), cheapened the value of its leadership roles (Baldino, 1983), and reduced its legislative role to delay and amendment (Huntington, 1973).

Careerism also has served to make Congress more conservative as a body (Fiorina et al., 1975; Mayhew, 1974). Opportunities for entry are fewer, and rising to power in the ranks takes longer, thus entrenching the old guard (Witmer, 1964). Reduced turnover has insulated members from the impact of public opinion (e.g., Dodd and

Oppenheimer, 1977a), thwarting the intentions of the framers of the Constitution.

Constitutional relationships between the House and Senate and between Congress and the other branches of government have been affected by the growth of congressional careers. It has increased the power of the House within the political system generally (Polsby, 1968; Fiorina et al., 1975) and especially with regard to the Senate and the Executive. Careers in the House now are similar to those in the Senate in length, making the chambers more alike (Witmer, 1964; Dodd and Oppenheimer, 1977b). Longer careers have enabled representatives to develop more expertise, which increases their oversight power (Witmer, 1964). On the other hand, decentralization of power has weakened the role of Congress in the political system (Huntington, 1973). Since the executive branch controls the pork barrel and casework resolution system, which are vital to reelection, congressmen find themselves beholden to the bureaucracy (Fiorina, 1977).

The growth of careerism also has affected the behavior of individual congressmen. Legislators who demand independence and control over their own careers rely less on the party for voting cues (Schaefer, 1983), which weakens party discipline (Fiorina, 1977; Douglas Price, 1977). With reelection of paramount importance, their behavior becomes dominated by activities fostering this goal, such as advertising, credit claiming, and position taking (Mayhew, 1974). Consequently, less time is spent on lawmaking, and more on casework and pork barrel activities. As a result "public policy emerges from the system almost as an afterthought. The shape of policy is a by-product of the way the system operates, rather than a consciously directed effort to deal with social and economic problems" (Fiorina, 1977:73).

The rise of the professional member of Congress is thus one of the major factors influencing the structure of the institution, the constitutional relationships between its chambers and between it and the other branches of government, and the activities of its members. Careerism and stable standing committees have been called the "twin pillars of the modern Congress" (Douglas Price, 1977). The development of careerism through the history of Congress and the identification of factors that influence the ability of members to establish careers are therefore important subjects of study, which this study will address.

Analyzing Survival in Congress

The data on which our analysis is based are from a collection by Carroll McKibbin and the Inter-university Consortium for Political and Social Research entitled "Biographical Characteristics of Members of the United States Congress."[1] These data contain biographical information on the backgrounds and careers of almost every member of Congress from 1789 to 1981.

The analysis proceeds in two stages. We first examine variations in career lengths in the House and Senate in terms of differences in the biographical characteristics of members across the entire history of Congress. This will allow us to identify variables that have influenced survival in Congress and to locate differences between the two chambers. Next, we use a multivariate technique known as *survival analysis* to compare career patterns between the chambers. This allows us to determine factors that contribute to building a lengthy congressional career. We also control for the historical party system in this part of the analysis. As noted, scholars generally agree that congressional careers have changed considerably with major changes in the partisan alignment of the electorate. Following Ladd (1970) and McCormick (1975), we divide the party systems into five eras: 1789 to 1824, 1824 to 1860, 1860 to 1896, 1896 to 1932, and 1932 to the present.

We will examine several different characteristics of members. Age at entry to the House or Senate is clearly a variable that can influence career length (Witmer, 1964). It is also critical to control for the effect of age when investigating the influences of other factors. Region is another variable that has been hypothesized to have some bearing on survival. Southern senators and representatives have a reputation for lengthy service; there may well be important political incentives that could contribute to this tradition (Fiorina, Rohde, and Wissel, 1975). Congressmen who are natives of the states they represent may have electoral advantages that allow them to develop longer careers than their nonnative colleagues. Education is another variable that may influence careerism. Better-educated congressmen may have a wider variety of career choices, lessening their inclination to stay in Congress, or they may perceive the role of the elected official differently than their less well-educated counterparts. Military experience may contribute to careerism by socializing future congressmen to federal service or providing a record of experience voters, state legislators, and party officials appreciate. Having a relative who served in Congress might socialize members to the ethic of career service. It may also contribute to name recognition, which could be important in reelection. Prior experience in government at the local, state, or federal level could have similar effects. Finally, partisan affiliation could well contribute to careerism. Members of the majority party in Congress might find it easier to build careers, and members who belong to a third party will certainly find it more difficult.

Careers in the Senate

Analyses indicate that some of the variables mentioned previously seem to have little effect on Senate career length. Region represented, previous military experience, and having relatives who served in the Senate offer few advantages in building a Senate career. Being a native of the state represented seems to contribute somewhat to a senator's career, but differences are not dramatic. Also, politicians with previous experience in office before entering the Senate do not have a significant advantage over those without prior experience: most senators (88 percent) have held some governmental office before entering the chamber.

A factor that does appear related to the length of a Senate career is whether the senator attended college or university. Senators who did so served an average of 8.4 years—more than one-and-one-third years longer than those without college or university experience. Further, of senators who attended college or university, over 41 percent stayed in office for more than six years, while only 31 percent of their less well-educated colleagues remained in the Senate after six years. At the end of a third term, almost twice as many senators who attended college or university were still in office as those who did not. At least part of this difference, however, may be due to historical trends in levels of education. In the decade from 1870 to 1880, enrollment in institutions of higher education doubled and doubled again by the turn of the century. Since this period of rapid growth in higher education parallels the growth of careerism in the Senate, the tendency of senators with higher education to have longer careers at least partly reflects the expansion of post-secondary education in the population as a whole.

There are many reasons why party affiliation might affect the length of a Senate career. Members of the majority party have access to important leadership posts on committees and within the chamber as a whole. However, members of the minority party might find less competition for assignments on influential committees or for positions in the party leadership. Members of other parties could find their ambitions frustrated as they come up against the entrenched partisan structure of power in the Senate. Empirically, freshman senators in the majority party have careers that last slightly less than eight years on average, while freshmen in the minority or some other party have careers that last slightly longer than eight years. The rate of leaving office is also approximately the same. There are only 149 senators who are classified as not belonging to either the minority party or the majority party as freshmen. These persons tend to have fairly short careers and to leave office at a faster rate than other senators. Less than a third of these other-party freshmen are in office after six years, while nearly 38 percent of majority-party and more than 42 percent of minority-party freshmen remain in office at that time.

Why does membership in the majority party not contribute to the development of a long Senate career? One answer may be that majority party senators face more competition for committee assignments and leadership posts and thereby find it more difficult to engage effectively in credit claiming, advertising, and position taking. Shifts in partisan control of the chamber will be more costly for majority party members—when either the minority party supplants them or the majority is extended, further intraparty competition is created. Another factor not taken into account in our data is that the majority party in the senator's state may not be the same as the one which controls the Senate. Thus, factors outside the chamber may interfere with the senator's career.

Senators first elected as members of the party out of power in the Senate oftentimes may be particularly strong electorally—either they come from states whose legislature or electorate is dominated by the minority party or their personal organization or appeal is strong enough to counter prevailing electoral forces. Once in the Senate, minority party members will find reduced competition for committee assignments and leadership positions within their own party (compared to the majority) and may find it easier to indulge in position taking and advertising. Minority party members also may look toward the possibility of becoming the majority, which may encourage them to extend their careers.

Senators who are not members of either the majority or minority party have shorter than average careers for several reasons. First, since power in the Senate is allocated along partisan lines, these senators can hold little hope of achieving important positions within the chamber. Second, many of these senators were elected during major party realignments, and their parties were quickly absorbed into the major parties, or disappeared when the issues that gave them birth lost salience. Finally, several such senators held office early in the nineteenth century, before careerism developed in the Senate.

The factor that seems to show the clearest relationship to length of a Senate career is the party system under which the senator was elected. Senators elected during the first party system had short careers, the average length being less than one term—5.9 years. There is a gradual increase in average career length during the second party system: by the third party system, average career length increased to about eight-and-a-half years. In addition, there is a substantial change in the rate at which senators remained in office. The number still in office after twelve years during the third party system is more than twice that of senators elected during the second party system. Although there is little difference between the third and fourth party systems in the rate at which senators left office, the average length of career does increase by about six months (from 8.5 years to 9.1 years). In contrast, the proportion of senators remaining in office increases in the fifth party system, while there is not a substantial increase in average career length.

Senators elected during the fifth party system have an average career length of 9.4 years. After six years, more than 46 percent remain in office, while at the end of twelve years, more than one in four is still serving. After eighteen years, nearly 15 percent are still in office. These data underestimate the career length of senators elected during the fifth party system. Of the 413 senators included in this period, 100 (about one-fourth) have their careers arbitrarily ended with the 96th Congress, the last Congress for which information was available. If the actual career length were known for these senators, there would be an increase in the average length of career and the rate at which these senators remain in office.

Careers in the House

There are several differences between the way the various factors discussed affect careers of members of the House as compared to their Senate colleagues. The first noticeable difference involves region. Although region represented had little impact on the length of Senate careers, there is a substantial difference for members of the House. Representatives from the South have careers that last an average of 7.1 years as opposed to 5.8 years for those who do not represent Southern districts. There also is a difference between the House and Senate in the relationship between a congressman being a native of the state represented and average career length. Representatives born in the state in which their district is located not only have longer careers but also tend to maintain their seats at a higher rate than their House colleagues. Again in contrast to the Senate findings, there is a monotonic increase in the length of an average House career with number of levels of prior governmental experience. However, prior governmental experience at any particular level does not seem to contribute to a House career. Likewise, prior military experience and having relatives who served in the House offer no special advantages to a representative.

Similar to the situation for senators, congressmen who attended college have had substantially longer careers (two years on average) than their less well-educated colleagues. Like the Senate case, however, this finding also reflects the spread of higher education in the late nineteenth century—an increase that occurred at the same time as careers were lengthening in the House. Moreover, as Bogue et al. (1976:283) point out, although the increase in levels of education for representatives has been dramatic, "this increase was slower than the improvement of the educational levels of the total population."

The relationship between party membership and length of House career is similar to that found earlier for Senators. Freshman congressmen in the majority party tend to have slightly shorter careers than other representatives (6.0 years compared to 6.2 years), while congressmen in the minority party have careers that average almost a year longer than those of others. After three terms, nearly one-third of minority party congressmen are still in office, while only one-quarter of their nonminority party colleagues remain. At the end of twelve years, 16 percent of the minority party congressmen remain in the House, as compared to 10 percent of the nonminority congressmen.

The same reasons that cause minority party members to have longer careers than their nonminority colleagues in the Senate hold true for representatives, but with even more force. The greater number of members in the House and that representatives must stand for election more frequently make majority party membership less of an asset (and third party membership a hindrance) in building a House career. Competition for committee assignments and leadership positions is much sharper in the House than the Senate, and credit claiming and position taking are more difficult in the larger body. Members of the minority party may face less intraparty competition and may come from safer districts. As in the Senate, third-party representatives tend to be elected during periods of electoral instability and realignment, and their smaller electoral base makes them even more vulnerable than third-party senators.

The most important factor affecting the length of House careers is the party system period in which the congressman was first elected. Members of the House elected during the first period had careers that lasted an average of 4.8 years. Those elected during the second party system had even shorter careers—less than two terms on average. By the third party system, the average length of career had increased to 4.9 years. This increase was partially due to a small group of congressmen who held their seats for a fairly long time. At the end of twelve years, 6.5 percent of the third party system representatives were in office; at the end of eighteen years, 2.4 percent were still there. These percentages are substantially greater than those for earlier party systems, and show a change in the way members of the House viewed their careers. By the third party system, representatives had begun to view service in the House as a career.

There is a marked change in the length of congressional careers between the third and fourth party systems. Those representatives elected during the fourth period have careers that average slightly more than eight years, more than three years longer than those elected during the third period. The change in average length of career is not as stunning, however, as the proportion of congressmen remaining in office more than six years. This more than doubled, increasing to 43 percent. The desire among congressmen to maintain their seats corresponds to the growth of professionalism in the modern House. During the fourth party system, nearly three times as many representatives served six terms or more than in the third system. These findings are consistent with those of other studies (e.g., Fiorina, Rohde, and Wissel, 1975; Price, 1975), which have indicated that the biggest increases in House career lengths occurred with the realignment of 1896.

Average career length continues to increase during the fifth party system, as does the percentage of representatives retaining their seats after six years. The average House career during the fifth party system is only a few days short of nine years. Further, almost half the congressmen retain their seats for longer than twelve years and over one in ten for longer than eighteen years. Also, the 435 congressmen in the 96th Congress (about 23 percent of all fifth party system representatives) have had their terms truncated to the number of years served at the end of that Congress. This underestimates their average career length and lowers estimates of the proportions remaining in office. Nevertheless, the pattern is clear—being elected during the fifth party system is the single most important factor determining whether a congressman will have a long career.

This conclusion may be interesting from a historical perspective, but it tells us nothing about factors governing the dynamics of survival within various sociopolitical periods. Multivariate analysis enables us to examine these factors in detail.

Survival in the House and Senate

This investigation was conducted using the method known as *survival analysis* developed by D. R. Cox (1972). Survival analysis is a multivariate statistical technique in which a set of predictor variables, which can include dichotomous indicator variables designating group memberships, are fit to a dependent variable, which measures the time elapsed to the "failure" of the subjects, according to an exponential decay function. This technique has achieved wide use in biomedical and actuarial research where the dependent variables often measure the time until death or remission of a disease, and the independent variables measure methods of treatment. By using survival analysis on data for members of the House and Senate, we are able to observe what factors are related to a congressman failing to return to his or her seat at the next election.

The Cox technique is similar in application to ordinary least squares regression, but there are substantial differences in interpretation of the coefficients. In survival analysis, coefficients can be converted to a relative risk or hazard ratio. This ratio is calculated as follows:

$$\text{Relative Risk Ratio} = e^{B_j(X_{ij} - M_j)}$$

where e is the base of natural logarithms, B is the survival analysis coefficient of the jth independent variable, X_{ij} is the value of the independent variable for a particular unit of analysis, and M_j is the mean of the independent variable for all units of analysis. If the survival analysis coefficient is positive and the value of X_{ij} for a particular congressman is less than the mean, the relative risk ratio is less than one. This indicates that the odds of a congressman failing to return to Congress are less than 1:1, so absence is less likely than return. Conversely, if the value of X_{ij} is greater than its mean, the relative risk ratio is greater than one, and absence is more likely than return. If the value of X_{ij} is equal to the mean, the relative risk ratio is one (i.e., $e^0 = 1$), and return is as likely as absence.

What this means in the current study is that a congressman who lacks a particular characteristic will have a value of zero for X_{ij}. As such, this value will necessarily be less than the mean, since the mean must fall between zero, the minimum value for the indicator variable, and one, the maximum value for the indicator variable. If the survival analysis coefficient is greater than zero and the value of X_{ij} is zero, the congressman will have a risk ratio of less than one, and is more likely to return to Congress. If the congressman has the characteristic (i.e., X_{ij} equals 1) and the coefficient is greater than zero, the risk ratio is greater than one, indicating that chances of not returning to Congress are greater than 1:1. When the survival analysis coefficient is less than zero, the odds reverse themselves.[2]

Survival analyses for senators and representatives were conducted using several independent variables: age on entry to the chamber, and whether the congressman represented a Southern district, was a native of the state represented, had any college-level education, had served in the military, had relatives who served in the chamber (either concurrently or previously), had prior political experience at any level of government, and was first elected as a member of the minority party. Employing the PHGLM program in SAS (Harrell, 1983), the best-fitting model for each chamber and party period was arrived at using a backward elimination procedure, i.e., variables with statistically insignificant coefficients were removed in successive steps until all remaining coefficients were significant.

Results for senators are shown in Table 1. In all five party periods, age when initially taking office is an important factor. During the fourth and fifth party periods, age at entry is the only significant factor related to whether an individual failed to return to the Senate. During the first party period, the only factor other than age related to the risk of a Senate seat is prior governmental experience. During the second party period, region of the country represented is important. During the third period, the only significant factor other than age is whether the senator is a member of the minority party when first elected.

Since relative risk ratios are calculated with respect to the mean for the independent variables, an analysis of the effect of age is a

TABLE 1.

Survival Analysis Results for Senators

Variable	Mean	Coefficient*
First Party Period		
Age at Entry	40.27	0.03
Any Prior Experience at Local, State, or Federal Level	0.92	−0.61
Second Party Period		
Age at Entry	41.76	0.03
Senator Represents a Non-Southern State	0.65	−0.41
Third Party Period		
Age at Entry	45.65	0.02
Member of the Minority Party at Entry	0.34	−0.33
Fourth Party Period		
Age at Entry	48.87	0.04
Fifth Party Period		
Age at Entry	47.37	0.05

*$p \leq .05$ for all variables, X^2, df = 1.

control, in a sense, for differences in life expectancy, health care, and other age-related factors that differ for the party systems. Although the mean age of senators has increased, the effect of age on senatorial careers also has increased. In the modern era, a person who enters the Senate at age fifty is more likely to return than a fifty-year old in the first party system, with risk ratios of 1.13:1 and 1.30:1, respectively. However, with respect to their colleagues, older senators today face more risk than senators in the past. Freshman senators who were fifteen years older than the average of their colleagues had a relative risk of 1.50:1 to their careers in the late eighteenth and early nineteenth centuries, while after the Civil War, the risk ratio was only 1.37:1. However, modern freshman senators who are that much older than their colleagues are almost twice as likely to fail to return to the Senate as other senators in their class, with a risk ratio of 1.99:1. The increased risk associated with age in the modern era may well be due to senators' increased work load, which puts a premium on youthful vigor, and to the youth-oriented nature of American culture, which values a young appearance.

The relative risk ratios for failing to return to the Senate for the indicator variables in our analysis are given in Table 2. During the first party period, the odds of senators being replaced if they had no prior governmental experience at the local, state, or federal level were 1.75:1, while the odds for senators who had some prior experience were only .95:1. During the second party period, senators who represented non-Southern states had a risk ratio of .87:1. Southern senators, on the other hand, had a risk ratio of 1.31:1. During the

TABLE 2.

Relative Risk Ratios for Senators Broken Down by Party Period

Characteristic	Risk Ratio If Senator Has Characteristic	Risk Ratio If Senator Doesn't Have Characteristic
First Party Period		
Any Prior Experience at the Local, State, or Federal Level	.95	1.75
Second Party Period		
Senator Represents a Non-Southern State	.87	1.31
Third Party Period		
Member of Minority Party when First Elected	.81	1.12

third party system, the most important characteristic besides age was whether senators were members of the minority party when first elected. Those who were not members of the minority party had a 1.12:1 chance of failing to return, while those who were members of the minority party had a risk ratio of only .81:1.

The survival analysis thus uncovers some important qualifications to the bivariate results presented earlier. Prior experience, representing a Southern state, and membership in the minority party are important determinants of Senate survival only during certain historical periods. In the early years of the Senate, state legislators seem to have preferred experienced politicians when choosing senators. This seems especially true when we recall the number of early senators who had served in the Continental Congress and the colonial and state governments. As Price (1975:6) points out, too, "some states used their senatorships as a sinecure for defeated House members," which implies that it would be almost impossible for politicians without prior experience to gain Senate seats in those states. On the other hand, just because senators had previous political experience does not mean they would make a career in the Senate. The odds for these senators retaining their seats are almost even, indicating they were replaced about as often as they stayed.

In the second party system, senators from states outside the South seem to have a better survival rate than their Southern colleagues. This probably is due to an influence of the Civil War, which cut short the careers of almost all Southern senators serving at the end of this party period. This impact is so strong that it obscures the nascent careerism of Southern senators in the 1850s who "dig in their heels and hang on for all they are worth" (Price, 1975:7). The Civil

War nipped this developing careerism in the bud, and it took another generation for it to flower properly.

In the post-Civil War party system, the Democrats controlled the Senate during only two sessions of Congress—the 46th (1879) and the 53rd (1893). The vast majority of those who had a lower career risk in the third party system due to their membership in the minority party were, therefore, Democrats. Of these Democrats, of course, the majority were Southern; so, to at least some extent, the effects of region and party are intertwined. We also may add to this that some of the Republicans who were disadvantaged as a result of their majority party membership were Reconstruction senators from the South and border states. These reasons may account for the increased importance of minority party membership in the third party system.

Table 3 presents survival coefficients for members of the House. There are a number of differences between risk factors for senators and those for representatives: length of a career in the House seems to be affected by both more and different factors. For example, while age is the only important factor for senators during the fourth and fifth party periods, there are three factors in addition to age that are significant for members of the House during the fourth party period, and four factors in addition to age during the fifth period. Finally, age at entry does not appear to be an important factor for representatives during the early years of the Republic.

The benefits to representatives of being young when they are first elected have grown. For example, the odds of not losing a seat have increased about 14 percent from the second party period to the present for a forty-year-old freshman. In contrast to the Senate, however, representatives who enter Congress at age fifty in the modern era are less likely to return than their predecessors: a fifty-year-old freshman today faces a risk ratio of 1.24:1, compared to about 1.08:1 during the third and fourth party systems, and 1.12:1 during the second. This pattern, in which the risk associated with increasing age declines through the nineteenth century but rises during the fifth party system, holds for the age groups into which most representatives fall. Possibly, this pattern is explained by the interaction of increased life expectancy, better health care, and increased rewards for seniority within the House (which would allow older representatives to look forward to extended careers) and increasing work load, which discourages tenure. In the fifth party system, the latter overtakes the former factors.

Cooper and West (1977) found that age did not seem to be a factor in the increased retirement from the House in recent years. They found, rather, that disaffection with House service seemed to cause representatives to retire. Our analysis covers more congressmen than Cooper and West examined, however, and leads us to conclude that

TABLE 3.

Survival Analysis Results for Representatives

Variable	Mean	Coefficient*
First Party Period		
Represents a Non-Southern District	0.73	0.32
Represents a District in State of Birth	0.35	0.17
Second Party Period		
Age at Entry	41.04	0.01
Represents a Non-Southern District	0.77	0.15
Third Party Period		
Age at Entry	44.92	0.02
Represents a Non-Southern District	0.78	0.13
Represents a District in State of Birth	0.47	0.12
College Educated	0.57	−0.10
Member of the Minority Party at Entry	0.37	−0.11
Any Prior Experience at Local, State, or Federal Level	0.81	−0.16
Fourth Party Period		
Age at Entry	45.88	0.02
Represents a Non-Southern District	0.83	0.48
Member of the Minority Party at Entry	0.41	−0.14
Any Prior Experience at Local, State, or Federal Level	0.80	−0.20
Fifth Party Period		
Age at Entry	47.37	0.05
Represents a Non-Southern District	0.80	0.22
Any Military Experience	0.57	−0.15
Member of the Minority Party at Entry	0.41	−0.15
Any Prior Experience at Local, State, or Federal Level	0.85	−0.23

*$p \leq .05$ for all variables, X^2, df = 1.

on the whole, since 1932, age has been a more important determinant in ending careers for all reasons, not just retirement. It may be, too, that disaffection affects older representatives more than it does younger House members.

It is interesting that the risk associated with age is identical in the modern House and Senate. Comparing the coefficients across party periods, however, we find that, in the House, increased age has generally carried about half the risk it has in the Senate, and only in the present day Congress have the two chambers achieved parity. This may be because, despite the dramatic increases in House career lengths under the fourth party system, only since the 1930s has the average career length of representatives approached that of senators.

The risk ratios for the indicator variables for congressmen are shown in Table 4. One factor that is generally important is whether the congressmen represented a non-Southern state. During the first

TABLE 4.

Relative Risk Ratios for Representatives Broken Down by Party Period

Characteristic	Risk Ratio If Member Has Characteristic	Risk Ratio If Member Doesn't Have Characteristic
First Party Period		
Represents a Non-Southern District	1.09	.79
Represents a District in State of Birth	.94	1.12
Second Party Period		
Represents a Non-Southern District	1.03	.89
Third Party Period		
Represents a Non-Southern District	1.03	.90
Represents a District in State of Birth	.94	1.07
College Educated	.95	1.05
Member of Minority Party when First Elected	.93	1.04
Any Prior Experience at Local, State, or Federal Level	.97	1.14
Fourth Party Period		
Represents a Non-Southern District	1.09	.67
Member of the Minority Party when First Elected	.92	1.06
Any Prior Experience at the Local, State, or Federal Level	.96	1.17
Fifth Party Period		
Represents a Non-Southern District	1.05	.84
Any Military Experience	.94	1.09
Member of the Minority Party when First Elected	.92	1.06
Any Prior Experience at the Local, State, or Federal Level	.96	1.28

party period the risk ratio for Southern congressmen was .79:1, while that for their non-Southern colleagues was slightly greater than one. The chances of Southern congressmen losing their seats were marginally higher during the second party system—.89:1. In the third period, which began with the Civil War, the chances of Southern congressmen losing their seats rose to .90:1. Southern congressmen serving in the fourth period have the lowest risk ratio, only .67:1. The chances of Southern congressmen losing their seats have risen again during the modern era to .84:1.

Fiorina, Rohde, and Wissel (1975:35–37), examining regional variations in House turnover, hypothesize that "Southern leaders saw greater potential payoffs for congressional careers than did their Northern counterparts," and that this, combined with fewer available career opportunities for the ambitious, caused politicians in the South to value congressional seats more highly than Northerners did. These authors find that Southern representatives show lower turnover than other congressmen in every party system. Also, throughout the nineteenth century, the payoffs, in terms of per capita federal expenditures, are higher for Southern states than for other regions. The increased value of a Southern congressional seat probably accounts for some of the lower career risk associated with representing a Southern state. This argument would seem to apply with equal, if not greater, force to the Senate, where the South is represented in greater proportion, and over whose members state party leaders historically have had more control. It is somewhat surprising, therefore, that Southern senators do not seem to have a better survival rate than non-Southerners.

Party competition may explain the variation between party systems in the advantage Southerners derive. At the end of the second partisan era and the beginning of the third, representing a Southern state was fatal to a career in the House due to the Civil War, Reconstruction, and the concomitant upheavals in the party system. Higher risk ratios for Southerners in these periods are thus to be expected. After the realignment of 1896 established a highly sectional partisan balance, Southern representatives held seats that were virtually immune from interparty competition. We therefore see a correspondingly lower risk ratio for the fourth party system. In the modern era, increased interparty competition and fractionalization within the Democratic Party may account for the increase in risk compared with the previous period.

Being born in the state represented was an advantage during two of the party periods. During the first period, nonnatives had a hazard ratio of 1.12:1, while those born in the state represented had odds of .94 to 1 of not returning to the House. Following the Civil War, natives also had an advantage over those not born in the state represented. In the early days of the Republic, representatives who were natives of their states apparently were more willing to serve longer terms in the House, and voters were inclined to support them. This finding is consonant with the interstate rivalry that characterized politics in the new nation. Only a little more than a third of House members were natives, however, and the advantage derived from this status was not large. The post-Civil War era also exhibited intense sectional rivalry, first between North and South and then between East and West. Again, representatives who were natives of their states were somewhat more likely to return to the House.

Attending college or university was a benefit for those congressmen elected during the third party period, the time in American history that witnessed a great expansion of higher education. The increased societal value of post-secondary study this expansion indicates seems to carry over to members of the House as well: constituents may have preferred candidates who shared their educational aspirations. It also may be that increased competition for nonpolitical jobs requiring higher education made careers in the House more attractive. Finally, the reform movement, which admired the highly trained expert, began during this era. Candidates with advanced educational credentials thus derived political as well as intellectual profit from their learning.

Two factors became significant determinants of survival in the House after the Civil War and have remained so to the present. It is notable that they become important at the same time that careerism began to develop in the House and that they increase in effect along with professionalism. One of these factors is having prior governmental experience before serving in the House; the other is membership in the minority party as a freshman.

During the third period, congressmen without prior governmental experience had odds of 1.14 to 1 of failing to return to the House at the next session. These odds rose to 1.17 to 1 after 1896, and increased again to 1.28 to 1 after the New Deal realignment. Interestingly, the odds of survival have stayed fairly constant for congressmen with other governmental experience, their risk ratios decreasing from .97:1 to .96:1. This illustrates that since the Civil War the House increasingly has been populated by professional politicians, who have paid their dues in state, local, or federal positions. Those who do not possess these qualifications face greater hazard to their careers, indicating that voters prefer candidates with a record of governmental service. This may be because experienced representatives were able to use their former positions to develop bases of support that make election and reelection easier. Prior experience in government also would provide an advantage in expertise, perhaps enabling these representatives to provide better constituent services and act more effectively within the House.

During the past 100 years, the benefits of being a minority party member have increased; the liabilities of being a majority party member have risen. From the Civil War to the New Deal, most freshman minority members were Democrats, and many of these were Southern. Thus, some of the advantage indexed by minority status in the third and fourth periods reflects reduced interparty competition and the value Southerners placed on a congressional seat. A larger portion of this advantage, especially since 1932, probably is due to decreased competition within the party structure in the House for committee assignments and leadership posts. This argument is bolstered by the observation that the risk ratios for minority members decrease as the institutionalization of the House proceeds.

The final variable that seems to influence survival in the House is military experience, which is only significant in the modern era. Over half of the representatives in this period have served in the military, and they seem to have somewhat longer careers than other congressmen.

Conclusions

The authors of the Constitution intended that career patterns in the House and Senate be different, as an adjunct to the checks and balances of the two chambers. However, one of the consequences of careerism in both chambers may be that representatives can "overcome the built-in advantages of the senatorial six-year term of office" (Witmer, 1964:534). Data on careers seem to bear this out, as the average length of a House career now approximates that in the Senate. Our analysis shows, however, that there are many more differences between careers in the chambers than there are similarities.

The only influence on survival that both chambers share is that of age. Members of the House and Senate who are older than average have been, historically, less likely to continue in office. Today, despite improvements in living conditions, health care, and life expectancy, this tendency is more pronounced than previously. In the modern Senate, this is the only risk factor of importance of those examined. It seems that enhancement in the quality of life, both in the nation generally and in Washington, even when combined with the increased staff and other allowances congressmen receive, cannot counter the effects of increased work load on and disaffection of older members of the House and Senate. It may be, too, that a cultural bias toward youth plays a part in increasing the electoral vulnerability of older congressmen.

In the House, we have identified three other factors that increase risk to representatives' careers, especially since the 1860s when careerism began to develop in that chamber. Prior political experience, not surprisingly, advances career prospects. Prior experience probably increases a member's ability to manipulate the strings of government and makes constituency service efforts more effective. It also may contribute to electability through increased name recognition and the development of important political ties. Voters also may tend to appreciate political experience in candidates. Even though some aspirants for public office "run against Washington," it apparently is still helpful to a career in the House if candidates have held other public offices.

Over the last century, House members from Southern districts have tended to have longer careers than their colleagues from other regions. The lack of two-party competition in many Southern districts undoubtedly contributes to this, but it may well be that politicians in the South value service in the House more highly than do non-Southerners. The Southern advantage is not as great today as it was between 1896 and 1932, however, which suggests that most of the effect is due to the lack of serious Republican challengers for Southern congressional seats.

Another long-standing factor encouraging survival in the House is membership in the minority party when first elected. This effect is important both in the Republican-dominated third and fourth partisan eras, as well as in the Democratic controlled House of the post-New Deal period. Again, this relationship may be largely due to lack of interparty competition, especially in the nineteenth and early twentieth centuries. Some of the importance of party membership, however, may result from decreased competition within the House for committee assignments and party positions. The effect of this latter factor has increased somewhat through the history of Congress, even after the realignment of 1932. The importance of this variable could be a reflection of the increased role party caucuses have played in the organization of the House.

Obviously, there are many other factors that influence survival in Congress. In every election redistricting, scandal, health problems, progressive ambition, coattails from other races, and considerations of family or business affect the careers of individual congressmen. However, studying career patterns in Congress through all its historical periods gives us insight into major trends that have influenced this branch of government and allows us, as Loomis (1982:10) writes, "the opportunity to explore connections between an era's broad political environment and the relevant institutional responses." The behavior of Congress is the sum of the behaviors, over time, of all its members. Only by expanding our focus from the individual to the collectivity can we discern those factors that affect how Congress behaves as an actor in the larger political system.

Notes

1. The data were provided by the ICPSR, which, of course, bears no responsibility for our analyses or interpretations.

2. For those readers who have difficulty interpreting odds ratios, these may be easily converted to probabilities by dividing the risk ratio by itself plus one. A risk ratio of 1.0:1 represents a probability of failure of 0.50 (½), and a ratio of 1.3:1 translates to a 0.565 probability of failure (1.3/2.3). Risk ratios less than 1.0:1 represent a probability of failure less than .50. For example, a risk ratio of .80:1 translates to a probability of .44 (.80/1.80). For more on odds ratios and their interpretation, see Reynolds (1977:20–25).

References

Baldino, Thomas J. (1983) "The House is No Longer a Home: Aspects of Deinstitutionalization in the U.S. House of Representatives 1970–1982." Paper delivered at the Annual Meeting of the Midwest Political Science Association, Chicago, Illinois.

Bogue, Allan G., Jerome M. Clubb, Carroll R. McKibbin, and Santa M. Traugott (1976) "Members of the House of Representatives and the Process of Modernization, 1789–1960." *The Journal of American History* 43:275–302.

Brookshire, Robert G., and Dean F. Duncan III (1983a) "Congressional Career Patterns and Party Systems." *Legislative Studies Quarterly* 8:65–78.

―――― (1983b) "Changes in Senate Careers Over Time." Paper delivered at the Annual Meeting of the Legislative Studies Group, American Political Science Association, Chicago, Illinois.

Cooper, Joseph, and William West (1977) "The Congressional Career in the 1970s." In *Congress Reconsidered,* edited by Lawrence C. Dodd and Bruce I. Oppenheimer. Washington: Congressional Quarterly Press.

Cover, Albert D., and David R. Mayhew (1977) "Congressional Dynamics and the Decline of Competitive Congressional Elections." In *Congress Reconsidered,* edited by Lawrence C. Dodd and Bruce I. Oppenheimer. Washington: Congressional Quarterly Press.

Cox. D. R. (1972) "Regression Models and Life Tables." *Journal of the Royal Statistical Society B,* 34:187–202.

Davidson, Roger H. (1977) "Two Avenues of Change: House and Senate Committee Reorganization." In *Congress Reconsidered,* edited by Lawrence C. Dodd and Bruce I. Oppenheimer. Washington: Congressional Quarterly Press.

Diamond, Robert A. (1976) *The Origins and Development of Congress.* Washington: Congressional Quarterly, Inc.

Dodd, Lawrence C. (1977) "Congress, the Constitution, and the Crisis of Legitimation." In *Congress Reconsidered,* edited by Lawrence C. Dodd and Bruce I. Oppenheimer. Washington: Congressional Quarterly Press.

Dodd, Lawrence C., and Bruce I. Oppenheimer (1977a) "Electoral Upheaval and Congressional Change: A Prologue to the 1980s." In *Congress Reconsidered,* edited by Lawrence C. Dodd and Bruce I. Oppenheimer. Washington: Congressional Quarterly Press.

―――― (1977b) "The House in Transition: Change and Consolidation." In *Congress Reconsidered,* edited by Lawrence C. Dodd and Bruce I. Oppenheimer. Washington: Congressional Quarterly Press.

Fenno, Richard F. (1973) *Congressmen in Committees.* Boston: Little, Brown.

―――― (1978) *Home Style: House Members in the Districts.* Boston: Little, Brown.

Fiorina, Morris P. (1977) *Congress: Keystone of the Washington Establishment.* New Haven: Yale University Press.

Fiorina, Morris P., David W. Rohde, and Peter Wissel (1975) "Historical Change in House Turnover." In *Congress in Change,* edited by Norman J. Ornstein. New York: Praeger.

Goodwin, George, Jr. (1959) "The Seniority System in Congress." *American Political Science Review* 53:412–36.

Hamilton, Alexander (1788) "Federalist No. 61." In *The Federalist Papers*, edited by Clinton Rossiter. New York: New American Library.

Harrell, Frank B. (1983) "The PHGLM Procedure." In *SUGI Supplemental Library User's Guide*, edited by Stephanie P. Joyner. Cary, NC: SAS Institute, Inc.

Harris, Seymour E. (1972) *A Statistical Portrait of Higher Education*. New York: McGraw-Hill.

Huntington, Samuel P. (1973) "Congressional Responses to the Twentieth Century." In *The Congress and America's Future*, edited by David B. Truman. Englewood Cliffs: Prentice-Hall.

Josephy, Alvin M., Jr. (1979) *On the Hill: A History of the American Congress*. New York: Simon and Schuster.

Kernell, Samuel (1977) "Toward Understanding 19th Century Congressional Careers: Ambition, Competition and Rotation." *American Journal of Political Science* 21:669–93.

Ladd, Everett Carll (1970) *American Political Parties: Social Change and Political Response*. New York: Norton.

Loomis, Burdett (1982) "Congressmen and Their Careers: Muddling Toward a Theory." Paper delivered at the Annual Meeting of the American Political Science Association, Denver, Colorado.

Madison, James (1788a) "Federalist No. 51." In *The Federalist Papers*, edited by Clinton Rossiter. New York: New American Library.

——— (1788b) "Federalist No. 52." In *The Federalist Papers*, edited by Clinton Rossiter. New York: New American Library.

——— (1788c) "Federalist No. 53." In *The Federalist Papers*, edited by Clinton Rossiter. New York: New American Library.

Mayhew, David R. (1974) *Congress: The Electoral Connection*. New Haven: Yale University Press.

McCormick, Richard P. (1975) "Political Development and the Second Party System." In *The American Party Systems: Stages of Political Development*, edited by William N. Chambers and Walter Dean Burnham. New York: Oxford University Press.

Ornstein, Norman J., Robert L. Peabody, and David W. Rohde (1977) "The Contemporary Senate: Into the 1980s." In *Congress Reconsidered*, edited by Lawrence C. Dodd and Bruce I. Oppenheimer. Washington: Congressional Quarterly Press.

Polsby, Nelson W. (1968). "The Institutionalization of the U.S. House of Representatives." *American Political Science Review* 62:144–68.

Polsby, Nelson W., Miriam Gallaher, and Barry S. Rundquist (1969) "The Growth of the Seniority System in the U.S. House of Representatives." *American Political Science Review* 63:787–807.

Price, David E. (1977) "Congressional Committees in the Policy Process." In *Congress Reconsidered*, edited by Lawrence C. Dodd and Bruce I. Oppenheimer. Washington: Congressional Quarterly Press.

Price, H. Douglas (1971) "The Congressional Career Then and Now." In *Congressional Behavior*, edited by Nelson W. Polsby. New York: Random House.

——— (1973) "The Electoral Arena." In *The Congress and America's Future*, edited by David B. Truman. Englewood Cliffs: Prentice-Hall.

——— (1975) "Congress and the Evolution of Legislative 'Professionalism.' " In *Congress in Change*, edited by Norman J. Ornstein. New York: Praeger.

———— (1977) "Careers and Committees in the American Congress: The Problem of Structural Change." In *The History of Parliamentary Behavior*, edited by William O. Aydelotte. Princeton: Princeton University Press.

Reynolds, H. T. (1977) *Analysis of Nominal Data*. Sage University Paper series on Quantitative Applications in the Social Sciences, series no. 07–001. Beverly Hills: Sage Publications.

Schaefer, William P. (1983) "The Career Development and Maturation of the Watergate Class." Paper delivered at the Annual Meeting of the American Political Science Association, Chicago, Illinois.

Schlesinger, Joseph A. (1966) *Ambition and Politics: Political Careers in the United States*. Chicago: Rand McNally.

Stokes, Donald E. (1967) "Parties and the Nationalization of Electoral Forces." In *The American Party Systems: Stages of Political Development*, edited by William N. Chambers and Walter D. Burnham. New York: Oxford University Press.

Witmer, Richard (1964) "The Aging of the House." *Political Science Quarterly* 79:526–41.

Taking the Queue:
Careers and Policy in the
U.S. House of Representatives

Burdett Loomis

*A lot of younger members see themselves as the "new model"
member of Congress—the first with style, with tailoring, with
media awareness. They see themselves as qualitatively removed from those who came before. In 1964 we came in
thinking we were building a new model, too.*
Senior House Democrat

The United States Congress, like all legislative bodies, does its business in a rich and rooted context. This context includes both external forces, for example, inflation rates and presidential landslides,
and internal components (e.g., legislative rules and resources) (see
Kozak, 1984). It is within such a context that legislators' careers run
their course. Indeed, the patterns of these careers are important parts
of the legislative environment, and, like most other parts, they
change over time.

This study makes a set of related arguments, linking legislative
careers to the policy-making process. These arguments proceed
thusly: first, the structure of opportunities in the United States
House of Representatives has changed substantially over the past
twenty years; second, one important aspect of congressional careers
is the length of the party's seniority queue confronting a member
(i.e., how many fellow partisans rank ahead of a member at a given
stage in his or her career); third, changes in opportunity structures
and the length of queues have policy implications; and fourth, the
patterns of active legislative participation by more members earlier
in their careers and "inclusive" leadership strategies (which involve
increased numbers of members) may lead to diminished influence
for most legislators.

There is an ultimate irony in the current, open structure of opportunities in the House. Representatives, as always, have produced a
legislative body that apparently serves their individual needs very
well (Mayhew, 1974; Fiorina, 1977). Rates of reelection remain high,
and, after a spate of retirements by mostly older members, voluntary
turnover has returned to its historically low level.

This same open structure also allows most members, even first-
termers, a real chance to affect the legislative process. But such an

opportunity structure encourages more legislative players and en-hanced expectations. The result is a snarled and difficult policy process and a host of disappointed legislators. Disappointment sets in first because the apparent impact on the policy process is just that—apparent. Second, and more profoundly, when something "must be done" in response to a crisis or a strong burst of political sentiment, the House frequently must defer to decisions reached in private, centralized bargaining sessions where nonlegislative par-ticipants are extremely important. Members of Congress often are left with only an up-or-down vote on an immense, complicated package like the 1981 budget or the 1983 social security reforms.

In short, current career patterns in the House encourage some indi-vidual-level successes (e.g., reelection or issue promotion), while severely limiting the legislative power of many members and the body as a whole.

When third-term subcommittee chairmen and junior minority members can set the legislative agenda on key issues, as they fre-quently do in the House, we need to examine how the careers of such activists take shape. Parliamentary parties can and do encourage young talent, but usually through a seasoning process in which ju-nior members slowly gain increased experience. In the United States Congress this also happens as legislators advance through the com-mittee system. This movement is often more haphazard because House members play musical chairs in their subcommittee assign-ments every two years. As one Democratic leader noted, in the House, "everyone's time is so fractionated. The culture of the place limits the application of expertise. In parliamentary systems, mem-bers have multiple opportunities to develop expertise. There's a need for talented, energetic people to obtain expertise."

Junior members increasingly act as independent policy entrepre-neurs (D. Price, 1971; Uslaner, 1978), seeking to develop issues that will win acceptance and advance their careers. Rep. Jack Kemp is a classic example here. Perhaps the key figure in promoting supply-side economics, Kemp noted, in 1984, that "I'm convinced that I'm right [about supply-side economics]. But if, in a year or two, infla-tion and unemployment are at or near 10 percent, then we've failed. If the economy goes over a cliff, we're finished. Forget Jack Kemp. Well, I'm willing to take that chance" (Reeves, 1984:112–14). For Kemp and many of his colleagues in both parties, the blending of personal ambition with policy positions comes naturally. Ambitious politicians need publicity, as do many congressional issue activists, who push favored policies, irrespective of their career goals.

Any legislative body could use a Jack Kemp or two, but what about 200 or more? Decentralization and democratization have affected the ways legislators do business and how their careers develop. Con-gress and its members have changed, perhaps profoundly, in the "post-reform" era of the 1980s. To see where the institution is headed, however, one needs to look backward, at where it has been.

The Twentieth Century House

In and around 1910, sharp changes occurred in the conditions shaping career patterns in the House (Jones, 1968; Polsby, 1968; Swenson, 1982). The strength of elected party leaders was checked, and the pattern that was to be committee government began to take shape. Between 1910 and 1970 an extremely well-articulated structure of opportunities emerged in the House. Its cornerstone was a committee system that emphasized, for most members, a slow march toward a full committee chairmanship. With patience, a safe seat, and good health, almost any member could become a committee chairman simply by surviving; after 1955 such chances were limited to Democrats. Seniority (unbroken tenure on a committee) meant everything. Most opportunities came through the committee system, although a handful of senior members moved into the party leadership stream as well. Committee chairmen and party leaders were old, if not always superannuated, and few rewards went to the impatient (mavericks) or the outspoken (showhorses).

Coupled with the seniority system and the small number of key committee/party positions was a secular trend through the 1950s and 1960s toward dwindling numbers of competitive seats (Mayhew, 1974). This development, along with a well-defined structure of opportunities, produced a House in which career advancement was tortuously slow and eminently predictable. Ironically, this system took individuals in their most productive years and forced them to wait several terms before becoming active participants in the legislative process. Even then, they could not hope to exercise much influence until they sat on a power committee (Rules, Appropriations, or Ways and Means) or chaired a committee or subcommittee. In 1955, to take a representative year, 145 members occupied these slots. In truth, most subcommittee chairmanships carried little authority with them. And at the real pinnacles of power—the top party leadership positions and the full committee chairs—a minimum of two decades of prior House service was a virtual requirement (Bullock and Loomis, 1985).

During the 1970s, the House underwent its greatest changes since the 1910 revolution against Joe Cannon and the strong speaker system. No single dramatic event rivalled the confrontation between Cannon and his foes (although the 1975 ouster of three senior committee chairmen came close), but the cumulative changes may have been equally profound (see Dodd and Oppenheimer, 1981; Mann and Ornstein, 1981). For example, the number of members who held either a committee chair, a subcommittee chair, or a power committee position had swollen to 219 by 1983, and a new power committee (Budget) had been created.

These changes have been detailed at length (Davidson and Oleszek, 1981; Smith and Deering, 1984), and the major thrusts emphasized democratization of the process for choosing committee and subcommittee chairs and decentralization of authority to subcommittees, the floor of the House, and informal caucases. At the same time, many House members retired voluntarily or ran for higher office during the 1970s (Hibbing, 1982; Cooper and West, 1981; Bullock and Loomis, 1985). The ranks of careerist members were reduced substantially, and a new generation of representatives entered the House.

The dispersal of power and the increased turnover during the 1970s have combined to produce a new structure of opportunities— one that incorporates an increased range of congressional career options, patterns, and styles. In turn, these affect the processes, politics, and policies of the House.

The Structure of Opportunities in the Post-Reform House

By midcentury, the structure of opportunities was bottom heavy. Most members held no institutional base of power (Bullock and Loomis, 1985). There were a great many backbenchers who contributed relatively little to a legislative process that was controlled by an overlapping oligarchy of full committee chairmen and top majority party leaders. This pattern has changed sharply, and any number of different data illustrate the point.

Committees

In the 85th Congress (1957–58) there were 98 subcommittees (of standing committees); twenty years later the comparable figure was 137 (Smith and Deering, 1984:275). More importantly, by the late 1970s, no member could chair more than a single subcommittee with legislative responsibilities. The number of units (subcommittees) increased, as did the number of effective participants (subcommittee chairs). In addition, subcommittee chairs generally assumed greater responsibilities, largely due to the "subcommittee bill of rights." Subcommittees now manage a growing amount of legislation (Smith and Deering, 1984:194–97), frequently hire their own staff, and have real pieces of turf to protect.

The role of power committees' membership has also changed. The number of power committee seats has been increased and thus devalued. The Budget committee has taken its place as a prestigious competitor to both Ways and Means and (especially) Appropriations, and Democrats stripped Ways and Means of its committee on committees status. Although members still seek power committee membership, the value of most seats has, objectively speaking, declined.

Parties

In numbers, if not in actual power, the party leadership (especially for Democrats) expanded greatly during the 1970s. During the 92nd Congress (1971–72), only twenty-four Democrats occupied party positions of legislative leadership (speaker, majority leader, whip, and twenty-one deputy or zone whips). Ten years later, the Democratic legislative team comprised at least fifty-seven members (speaker, majority leader, whip, forty-three deputy, at large, and zone whips, plus eleven Rules Committee members) and perhaps as many as 100 (all of the above, plus Budget and Steering and Policy Committee members). In addition, Rep. Tony Coelho (D–CA) revitalized the Democratic campaign committee, establishing himself as an important party leader. Republicans have not increased their leadership numbers as much, but there was nearly a 50 percent rise (from 61 to 90) between 1971 and 1981, if the Budget Committee is given leadership standing (Deering, 1984:19).

The driving force behind the expansion of leadership slots has been the idea of inclusion. In particular, Democrats, with their larger numbers and ideological diversity, have embraced an inclusive strategy as a necessary means to pull together their troops. Inclusion can mean giving more members a stake in the issues at hand or, alternatively, diluting the entire idea of party leadership. As one leader observed, in discussing the Democrats' attempts to accommodate their conservative faction,

> The Speaker said, "We'll appoint two or three more of you to [the Steering and Policy] committee." We did. The irony of it is that we did this in an attempt to accommodate the conservative wing and to bring it into the family, and the next thing we discover was that they're deserting the family as soon as the family is under siege from the landlord. They go and join the landlord. (Sinclair, 1983:75–76)

Expanding the opportunity structure is not a cost-free strategy for the leadership. Consultation takes time and effort, yet given the mix of other opportunities in the House, there seems no reasonable alternative.

Caucuses and Task Forces—"Semistructured" Opportunities

With under a term's service, Rep. Bill Richardson (D–NM) took over the reins of the Congressional Hispanic Caucus at its 1984 annual dinner, which boasted an attendance of over 1000, including Democratic presidential nominee Walter Mondale. In his third term, Rep.

Bob Edgar (D–PA) assumed the leadership of the Northwest-Midwest Coalition/Institute with over twenty staff members. Throughout the 1970s caucuses popped up like weeds, complementing the more orderly rows of committees. Some caucuses have faded, some have moved off the Hill, but the general result has been a significant expansion in leadership opportunities for members with little seniority.

Similarly, the Democrats' use of task forces to rally support on single pieces of legislation has provided new opportunities for junior members. By their second or third term, individuals such as Richard Gephardt (D–MO) and Tim Wirth (D–CO) had led their party colleagues on key pieces of legislation (see Sinclair, 1981, 1983). Like the Budget Committee, where Gephardt and Wirth held seats in the 98th Congress, task forces have afforded both party leaders and the rank-and-file a chance to assess the capabilities of junior members.

In sum, changes in committees, parties, and caucuses have combined to enlarge the structure of opportunities in the House. Members need not be content to act as a backbencher, though some may choose such a role.

The Congressional Queue

Rep. John Young (D–TX) won election to the House in 1956, and served eleven terms. After his third reelection, Young had less tenure than 150 of the 259 House Democrats. After five full terms he followed 102 fellow Democrats; after seven, he still trailed 76 of his party colleagues. In his eleventh and final term, Young had reached number 37 on the Democrats' seniority roster. Sitting on the Rules Committee, he ranked fifth in seniority at the end of a 22 year career.

Rep. Phil Sharp (D–IN) won his House seat in 1974. After three full terms of service he ranked behind only 94 Democrats in seniority. In 1985, with five terms under his belt, he found himself behind 74 party colleagues. Sharp won an important subcommittee chair in the fourth term; in so doing he joined most of his fellow Democrats who were first elected in 1974.

Times changed, of course, between John Young's congressional experience and Phil Sharp's. But Sharp profited from more than just an altered opportunity structure. With high levels of turnover in the 1970s, Sharp (and his class of 1974 colleagues) found themselves waiting for key positions in a relatively short queue (see Figure 1).

The idea of a queue is especially significant in institutions where seniority is important. Although the seniority system of the 1950s/1960s no longer exists, a modified seniority norm continues to operate in Congress. For example, until 1984, every current full committee chair, in both House and Senate, was the majority member with the longest consecutive service on that committee.

The number of members who rank as more senior to any member who has completed:

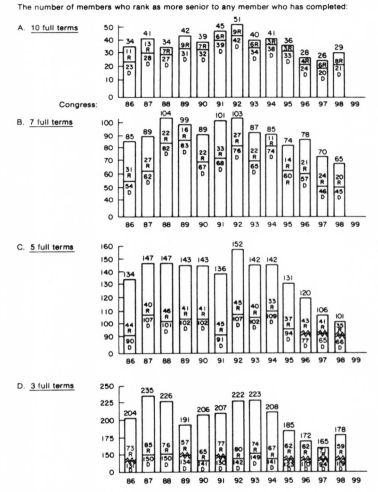

Note: R = Republican   D = Democrat

FIGURE 1. The Queue in the House of Representatives. Overall and by Party

Top party leaders are excepted. Tenure remains a central part of congressional life, both formally and informally. Long-term friend-ships and working arrangements traditionally have played major roles in muting partisan and ideological divisions in Congress (e.g., see Fenno, 1966, on Reps. Cannon and Tabor).

Two clear findings emerge from the data in Figure 1. First, there has been a long-term trend toward a shorter queue for all House members, especially for House Democrats. During the 1970s, many older members (and some others) retired, and many younger members ran for higher office. The current glut of junior House members will thin out some, but it is doubtful that careerism will reach past levels. In the 92nd Congress (1971–72), for example, forty-two Democrats (about one in six) were serving in their eleventh term. Current rewards may be inadequate to tempt most members into ten-plus term careers in the House. Somewhat larger numbers of senior members run for higher office (see Table 1), and the congressional job's demands on time and effort may exhaust the most dedicated and energetic member.

Even more striking than the shortening of the full House and Democratic queues is the consistently truncated Republican queue. Not since 1961–62 has a Congress contained more than ten GOP members with ten-plus consecutive terms. In the mid-1970s, when Democrats held commanding two-to-one majorities in the House, there were only three ten-plus term senior Republicans. And in 1983–84, only 59 (of 167) Republicans had served three or more full terms. Not only does the minority party lack senior leaders, it also is short at the middle management level that is so important in the contemporary House.

To speak of a single House structure of opportunities is clearly misleading. Senior Republicans have virtually no chance to chair a committee, to control the legislative schedule, or to set subcommittee agendas. It is thus no mystery to find the minority members leaving in frustration. Twenty-year veteran Rep. Barber Conable (R–NY), ranking minority member on Ways and Means, probably would not have retired in 1984 had he been that committee's chairman. On the other hand, should lightning strike and a Republican majority emerge, as it has in the Senate, Republican control would produce a set of committee chairs with relatively little experience and even less commitment to ongoing programs.

To summarize, in the 1970s the House's structure of opportunities became increasingly broad and open; simultaneously, the congressional queue was shrinking, especially for majority Democrats. These developments produced rapid advancement for many junior members and established expectations that subsequent generations of representatives would take active legislative roles early in their careers.

Legislatures are not, we continually rediscover, static organizations (see Cooper and Brady, 1981). They change with their members as well as with the forces that help elect them. It thus makes sense to examine the implications for congressional careers that can be drawn from the structure of opportunity and queue changes. Two distinct, but complementary, perspectives can be adopted: (1) a generational, or cohort, approach or (2) a life-cycle point of view. There are good reasons to use these prisms in assessing how legislators'

TABLE 1.

Career Development of Selected House Classes

	1946		1958		1964		1974	
	%	(N)	%	(N)	%	(N)	%	(N)
After 3 terms								
In House	37	(33)	51	(40)	46	(38)	65	(54)
Sought Higher Office	9	(8)	7	(6)	11	(10)	11	(10)
Defeated	48	(43)	32	(25)	34	(28)	22	(20)
Retired/Resigned	4	(4)	6	(5)	6	(5)	2	(2)
Died	2	(2)	4	(3)	2	(2)		——
After 5 Terms								
In House	28	(25)	46	(36)	34	(28)	37	(32)
Sought Higher Office	12	(11)	9	(7)	14	(12)	23	(20)
Defeated	51	(46)	34	(27)	41	(34)	30	(26)
Retired/Resigned	7	(6)	8	(6)	8	(7)	8	(7)
Died	2	(2)	4	(3)	2	(2)	1	(1)
Total Class		(90)		(79)		(83)		(86)

careers develop, largely because both place the legislature within broader contexts. A generational framework encourages linking representatives to common outside forces that shaped their, and their contemporaries', experiences. Life-cycle perspectives build on a different kind of commonality—a (very) rough sequence of stages that most people pass through during the aging process.

In the case of the U.S. Congress, as opportunities change, as the congressional queue lengthens or shortens, generational and life-cycle effects interact with a legislature that reconstructs itself every two years. Each Congress differs from its predecessor. Continuities are great, but every successive Congress contains a changed membership, affected both by elections and the aging process. Although life-cycle changes are significant (Hain, 1974; Loomis, 1984b), attention here will focus on the over-time impact of political cohorts.

Political Generations and the Post-Reform Congress

As Congress biennially reconstitutes itself, the institution takes on a new shape in its mix of partisans, ideologues, professionals, (in)experienced legislators, publicity seekers, and possible candidates for higher office. Ordinarily, the composition of Congress changes slowly; most incumbents win, and overall turnover rarely tops 20 percent in the House (it is less in the Senate, of course, where only a third of the seats are contested in any given election). On occasion, however, an electoral breakthrough allows a new wave of members to flow into the chamber. In the postwar era, the House elections of 1946,

1948, 1958, 1964, and 1974 represent such watershed years. In addition, more modest, sequential gains, such as the Republican advances in 1978 and 1980, may produce similar changes.

The obvious question in the wake of a large turnover is What happens next? On occasion, an immediate answer is forthcoming. The 89th Congress (1965–66) produced a historic array of activist legislation (Sundquist, 1968). The 97th Congress (1981–82) supported President Reagan's large-scale changes in patterns of taxing and spending. But strong, active majorities are the exception, not the rule, in American politics; in most instances, electoral readjustments soon follow the buildup of large majorities. Thus, in 1966, House Republicans gained forty-seven seats, much as the Democrats recovered enough ground in 1948 to regain control of the House. The focus here, however, is not on the electoral swings and the subsequent partisan balance in the Congress. Rather, concern lies with the long-term impact of a political generation upon a legislative body.

Generational Survival

Large cohorts of first-term members are extremely susceptible to a rapid reduction in their ranks. National forces may provide the margin of victory in many competitive seats, but these districts become the most inviting targets for the opposition in ensuing contests. Historically, members have been most vulnerable in their first reelection bid (Peabody, 1976). In 1948, for example, forty-four single-term Republicans lost their seats, and in 1966, twenty-six freshman Democrats went down in defeat.

In 1976, things changed. Of the seventy-five new Democratic members elected in 1974, seventy-four sought reelection to the House and seventy-two won. Although this group benefitted from some good luck and a relatively dispirited Republican congressional effort, much of their 1976 success derived from the rising value of House incumbency. In particular this has led to the "sophomore surge" phenomenon, detailed by Cover (1977); first-term House incumbents have done especially well since 1970, although scholars have not convincingly explained how the incumbency effect works.

Winning the initial reelection campaign is one key to a cohort's long-term survival (see Table 1). For example, the GOP-dominated class of 1946 lost over 60 percent of its members after three terms of service, as did the overwhelmingly Democratic class of 1964. After ten years of service, only about one-fourth of these cohorts remained. Over half of the 1946 group lost a reelection bid, but the 1964 group, reflecting greater electoral safety, experienced a lesser (41 percent) defeat rate. Of the 1974 cohort, less than a fourth lost a reelection bid through the first three terms, and only 30 percent have suffered such a defeat after five terms of service.

Increased rates of survival would be of minor interest if the House had not changed a great deal. The Class of 1958, which proved to be a hardy political group, came into Congress at the time of a constricted opportunity structure and a fairly long queue. In their sixth term of service (1969–70), seventeen of twenty-five of the remaining Democrats first elected in 1958 chaired a subcommittee, and four served on one of the power committees (Rules, Appropriations, Ways and Means). Even though the queue did shorten a bit for incoming members in 1958, there remained ninety-one more senior Democrats after the 1958 freshman had served five full terms in the House.

Compared to the Class of 1974, whose members entered a very different, decentralized Congress, the 1958 group proceeded at a snail's pace. By the start of their *fourth* terms, in 1981–82, all but three (of forty-four) Class of 1974 Democrats had risen to chair subcommittees or held power committee slots (Loomis, 1984a). After five terms, the queue for these Democrats placed them behind seventy-four more senior partisans.

In sum, while the congressional opportunity structure expanded tremendously, the queue of senior members became shorter in the 1970s. As recently elected members acquire seniority, the queue will lengthen once again. Given the large number of party, committee, and caucus slots, however, all but the most junior members will hold some position of modest authority.

Generations and Policy

Looking for systematic policy effects from a political generation is asking for trouble. Even members in large classes, who often bring with them a lot of policy baggage, become institutionally oriented actors if they hope to affect policy directly. At the same time, large cohorts, like the pig consumed by the python, do maintain a certain shape and do produce visible results as they are digested by the legislative serpent. One basic difference among various cohorts is whether they are dominated by majority or minority partisans; majority members must help run the institution, while their minority counterparts have the option of sniping away at will. Let us turn to four recent cohorts to examine how generations have helped shape the policy process.

1958 — Formation of a Liberal Democratic Block

As James Sundquist (1968) clearly describes, the arrival of the large, heavily Democratic Class of 1958 did not change congressional policies in any immediate or profound way. In the House, votes became closer and more partisan, but few results were altered (see Mayhew, 1966). Short-term policy effects, however, do not constitute an adequate criterion for judging the impact of a cohort. The 1958 group, which survived very nicely into the 1970s (see Table 1), provided the votes, resources, and energy for the formation of an identifiable and long-lasting "liberal block" (see Stevens, et al., 1974; Ferber, 1971). The Democratic Study Group was and is a concrete manifestation of this tendency, but the impact goes beyond simply forming one of the original House caucuses. With adequate numbers, the liberal block could help to articulate issues, contribute to reforms (e.g., expansion of the Rules Committee in 1961), and, during the Nixon Administration, hold down many of the crucial middle management positions (e.g., subcommittee chairs) essential for overseeing policies enacted in the mid-1960s.

For the 1958 group, however, many of the old rules, like seniority, still apply. After a quarter-century of service, for example, only one (Illinois' Dan Rostenkowski) of the four surviving Democrats chairs a full committee. At the upper echelons, there remains a long wait for most top slots, even if these positions may be less valuable than they once were.

The Democrats of 1964 — "Cannon Fodder for the Great Society"

Only rarely do first-term members of the U.S. House get a chance to have a real policy impact. Freshmen Democrats in the 89th Congress enjoyed such an opportunity. Collectively, they made the difference on any number of Great Society proposals. This class paid a real political price for its short-term impact (their votes did not afford them much effect on the policies at hand). Of the seventy-one Democrats swept into office in the Johnson landslide of 1964, only forty-one returned in 1966 (see Fishel, 1973). The 1964 cohort has, however, exercised considerable policy leverage over time by rising into positions of full committee power. By their seventh term, five members (from both parties) had risen to full committee chairs or ranking minority member status. In their tenth term, only one (of seven) remaining Democrat had not served as a full committee chair.

Most cohorts' policy impact ultimately derives from the positions of authority their members obtain. Such slots have required sufficient waiting that the cohort loses most ideological or issue-based identity that it might once have had. Few mavericks or, in more recent parlance, "grenade-throwers," stay in the House long enough to wield real power.

1974 — A New Wave

In terms of matching a cohort's size with the number of opportunities available, the heavily Democratic Class of 1974 was destined for success as long as it survived at the polls. Both the opportunity structure and the shrinking majority queue played directly into these members' hands. Indeed, one freshman from 1974 (Steve Neal, D–NC) chaired a subcommittee in his first term, an unprecedented opportunity in the contemporary House. The 1974 generation will continue to be lucky as time passes, in that the Democratic queue will be smaller for this group's members, at all stages of their careers, than for any other post-1945 cohort.

This good fortune, however, would be of little significance if it did not relate to other, long-term changes in the nature of legislators' careers. The Class of 1974 did rise quickly to occupy positions of authority and power, but at least equally important, its members produced a new legislative *style* that has directly affected subsequent cohorts of entering members.

Central to the style polished (if not totally developed) by the Class of 1974 are dual emphases on policy and publicity. Although not all of its members fit the mold of policy activist, many do and have taken on visible roles from the outset of their careers. Thus, in the 1975–78 period, a host of junior members helped set the agenda on a wide variety of issues. Robert Krueger (D–TX) on natural gas deregulation, Toby Moffett (D–CT) on consumer issues, and Henry Hyde (R–IL) on antiabortion legislation are only three examples of such visible policy activists (see Uslaner, 1978). In 1979, third-term members Moffett and Henry Waxman (D–CA) aggressively pursued key policy positions by successfully contesting more senior members' bids for important subcommittee chairs.

The members' new style included elements of both the policy-oriented entrepreneur and the reformist "amateur democrat" (Uslaner, 1978). The reformist streak remains significant, though somewhat muted, within this (and later) cohorts. Watergate played an important, if idiosyncratic, role for the 1974 group, in that reform, vaguely defined, persisted as a key, defining element of the cohort. As for the amateur democrat notion, even after a decade of service, several fifth-term members of the 1974 group agreed that, despite their political skills, they still did not (and would never) think of themselves as professional politicians.

For members of the Class of 1974, the analytically distinct goals of reelection, good policy, internal power, and higher office become inextricably melded together. Publicity often serves as the glue that holds an emerging career together. Junior members can now play to a national audience through such vehicles as expanded morning news shows, hour-long public television evening news, public radio (three-and-a-half hours of news per day), weekend network interview programs, the Cable News Network, and late-night major network coverage of one or two major stories in some depth. Added to that are opportunities afforded by C-SPAN coverage of Congress, which is essentially unedited.

Although the audiences for news/analyses vary greatly, even the smallest (C-SPAN's roughly 200,000) are worth courting. In the past, when legislative backbenchers commanded little public attention, they had no real alternative to seeking rewards within the chamber. The more extensive coverage of Capitol Hill increasingly enables any representative to address a national audience. A clever press aide and an ability to develop a position on an emerging issue may win a member some semblance of external prestige. (Among others, Hyde and George Miller (D–CA), both 1974 entrants, are very skillful at this.) Members thereby can obtain rewards that are controlled by neither the chamber nor the party hierarchy. This is especially true for subcommittee chairs, who dictate much of the pace and content of the legislative process.

1978 and 1980 — What a Difference a Majority Makes

> You should have seen the body language of the old guys when I got to Congress in 1979. They walked onto the floor like they expected the Democrats to start kicking them around—and sure enough. . . .
> Republican Rep. Newt Gingrich (GA) (Reeves, 1984:114)
> God didn't make the school prayer amendment. Some yahoo up here wrote it.
> Republican Sen. David Durenberger (MN) (Ehrenhalt, 1984:1287)

Throughout most of the post-World War II era, Republicans in Congress have not been required to worry about governing. From 1955 to 1981 they were always in the minority. Such long-term minority status reduced career incentives for Republicans and tended to keep their careers relatively short. It also allowed junior members to assert themselves early in their congressional tenure. As the Congress, especially the House, gave its members increasing resources and leeway to carve out their own policy agendas, junior Republicans have taken full advantage of the situation and the perennially short GOP seniority queue to attract attention to themselves and their ideas.

Without a doubt, younger Republicans have succeeded in attracting attention. With its televised proceedings, the House has opened up new career options for publicity-conscious members—particularly those who are not committed to making the legislative process work by employment of the traditional instruments of courtesy and compromise. A relative handful of Republican conservatives has raised issues (and hackles) through their use of sharp partisan and personal attacks that attract considerable media attention.

Although some GOP veterans, such as Kemp (first elected in 1970) and Rep. Trent Lott (MS) (the minority whip, elected in 1972) occasionally join their younger colleagues, the Republicans who first entered the Congress in 1978 and 1980 set much of the House minority's strident policy tone. The major political forces behind the 1978 and 1980 elections were, respectively, California's tax-reduction referendum, Proposition 13, and the successful presidential candidacy of Ronald Reagan. These same forces helped deliver the Senate into Republican hands in 1980 for the first time in twenty-six years. But the requirements of serving as the majority and, with Reagan, the governing party are much different from those of representing a continuing minority.

Many Senate Republicans are conservative by any standard, and senators can far more easily garner media attention than can representatives, but it remains junior GOP House members who have led the activist conservative charge on Capitol Hill. In the 98th Congress, only fifty-nine House Republicans had served more than three full terms. Many key minority positions were held by junior members, and occupancy of such slots encouraged these members to adopt a spokesman role, either formally (e.g., Richard Cheney [WY], head of the Republican Policy Committee, and Tom Loeffler [TX], chief deputy whip) or informally (Newt Gingrich [GA], Vin Weber [MN], and other members of the media-conscious Conservative Opportunity Society). Indeed, several first-term Republicans, such as Texan Steve Bartlett or Florida's Connie Mack, could begin their careers with plans to become highly visible actors on a range of policy questions. For them the queue was virtually nonexistent and the opportunity structure almost completely open.

Discussion

New political generations interact with, sometimes confront, the given context of any legislative body. With relatively weak party discipline and very little screening of candidates, the U.S. House of Representatives may be changed more than most legislatures by its entering cohorts. In the past, however, a political generation could have immediate impact only if it provided key votes to change the political complexion of the body (e.g., 1946 Republican control of the House or the 1964 and 1980 changes in the composition and size of the Democratic majorities). At present, members of even small cohorts can have effects very early in their careers.

Three basic reasons for these changes exist. First, the House structure of opportunities has been greatly enlarged. With more committee and party positions, along with the great growth in nonofficial caucuses, almost any member can obtain a piece of policy turf soon after entering the House. Second, the seniority queues have grown shorter in the House, especially for Democrats. This may be of passing importance if younger Democrats build up great amounts of seniority, but the smaller queues clearly benefit the Democrats who arrived in the mid-1970s. Third, junior members have developed publicity-oriented styles that emphasize activist stances on a variety of issues. Again, the context of legislative politics encourages such styles, and the younger members have moved aggressively in using their ample staff resources and subcommittee/caucus positions to engage the national press. There still may be an apprenticeship period for new members of the House, but it consists of the active learning of the legislative ropes and often includes immediate lessons in publicly affecting the policy agenda.

There remain, however, some important limits on the abilities of cohorts or individual members to affect the legislative process. First, a great majority of House members are veterans. Second, the waiting periods for the top legislative jobs—key committee chairs and the highest party leadership positions—have not decreased in recent years. By the time a political generation reaches these highest rungs of the opportunity ladder, its impact as a cohort has almost completely disappeared. Finally, there is much more of a chance to move up within the minority Republican party than within the majority Democrats. The Democratic Class of 1974 is something of an exception here, but even they have not advanced as quickly as the 1978–80 Republicans. At the same time, a virtually permanent minority status renders an extended House career considerably less promising or rewarding to a GOP member than to a Democrat who is likely to become a subcommittee chair by the third or fourth term.

Implications for Individual Members

We do not know how current members will react to their experiences in a House that is very different from the body of twenty years ago. If Republicans remain in the minority, their patterns of greater turnover and truncated House careers will probably persist. For such members there are no great incentives for staying in the House, although the ability to raise issues and obtain an audience has been enhanced. In addition, Republican leaders have had increasing difficulties in dealing with contentious and ideological junior members. This does little to make the leadership positions attractive to careerist legislators.

For Democrats, it is unclear if early advancement into positions of authority will produce long, legislatively productive House careers or lead to increasing frustrations over time. Some subcommittee chairs have extremely interesting and important policy jurisdictions (e.g., Waxman on health and the environment, Wirth on telecommunications and consumer issues), but many other subcommittee slots, while initially attractive, have little to recommend them as long-term pursuits. Given the extended period required to gain full committee chairs, it remains an open question how many members will want to stay in the House, commanding a bit of turf but having relatively little overall policy impact.

The policy activists in the contemporary House may resolve this problem by running for higher office (especially the Senate) rather than retiring. The 1970 and 1974 cohorts produced a great number of such candidates—willing to take a substantial electoral chance and give up some important policy turf in the House. For example, Rep. Paul Simon (D–IL) surrendered his Education and Labor subcommittee chairmanship on higher education in 1984 to run for the Senate against incumbent Charles Percy.

In sum, despite the ability to exercise real, if limited, power early in their careers and to obtain substantial publicity, House members may be choosing to make their legislative careers shorter and more active. The job itself, with its demands on time and energy, is difficult, and for many members there are few incentives to encourage them to remain the twenty to thirty years essential to qualify as top committee or party leader.

Institutional Implications

The House has become an increasingly individualistic body. This is despite the majority of Democrats having given Tip O'Neill greater formal powers than any Speaker since Joe Cannon (on some occasions O'Neill has negotiated directly with the President, representing the Democratically controlled House). A somewhat more powerful speaker cannot offset the decentralizing tendencies that have dominated the House context since 1970. On most key issues, the decentralization of resources, structure, and authority has allowed large numbers of members to become involved in the policy process.

There is always dissatisfaction over the alleged inability of the Congress to deal with major, politically sensitive issues. In the past, however, it was much easier to single out a particular committee chairman or party leader as responsible for the inaction (e.g., Rules Committee chairman Howard Smith (D–VA) on civil rights issues circa 1960). At present, responsibility is not so easily placed. Many members can get an issue on the agenda, but few command the resources and skill to build consistent majorities. Ironically, this means that the legislative branch must frequently abandon its policy-making role on extremely important issues, as with social security in 1983.

By creating a broad-based structure of opportunities and providing substantial resources for individual members, the House may have limited its institutional capacity to deal with difficult problems, ranging from illegal immigration to acid rain. The visible, often talented policy activists must find ways to build majorities on tough issues. The current career patterns and decentralized system of incentives and authority tend to reinforce the institution's difficulties in confronting complex policy questions. New generations of House members, regardless of their talents and resources or how they reflect significant political forces, may be rendered ineffective by the individualistic and fragmented structure of power that their prede- cessors created and that the new generation perpetuates.

Conclusion

> Why would anyone want to serve in the House today?
> *Former Administrative Assistant*

As citizens, we receive, as Richard Fenno reminds us, the kind of House the members give us. From around 1970 we have received a body that is (1) fragmented; (2) resource-rich, especially in terms of staff and office perquisites; (3) geared to active participation from all members; and (4) increasingly capable of obtaining national news coverage, on an individual member-by-member basis. For new members these elements help create, in turn, a set of expectations that they will rise quickly to positions of eminence and visibility. In a series of 1984 interviews with members initially elected in 1982, one much-repeated theme was the desire to "hit the ground running" in order to influence the process as quickly as possible.

Although such expectations were not, generally speaking, unrea- sonable, these first-term members soon encountered some of the hard realities of congressional life. One key bit of reality, for Demo- crats, is that a long queue of relatively young and junior members stretches out in front of the newcomers. Despite emulating the me- dia-conscious style of those who arrived in the mid-1970s, newly elected representatives will probably not obtain the easy access to key platforms—subcommittee chairs or budget committee slots, for example—their predecessors moved into early in their careers, and often continue to hold.

Junior Republicans confront a more intractable problem—the mi- nority status that has been theirs since 1955. Indeed, much of the rhetoric among the younger GOP representatives emphasizes the need to build a majority in the House, which, among other things, would make the body immensely more attractive for young and tal- ented politicians.

In response to these ongoing realities of congressional career de- velopment, junior members from both parties have adopted strate- gies and tactics that often exacerbate the fragmentation that besets the House. Freshmen Democrats, for example, formed a budget task force in 1983–84 that pressured the leadership to accept lower levels of spending. Also, as noted, some junior Republicans, led by Rep. Newt Gingrich, have formed the activist and publicity-conscious

Conservative Opportunity Society (COS), which effectively uses television coverage of the House to make many of its criticisms. Although both the freshmen Democrats and the junior Republicans see themselves ultimately as forces of unity, the short-term results of their actions often are more fractionalization and, at least with the COS, less civility.

The House, as it currently exists, serves its members well in any number of particularistic ways; the Senate does likewise. Careers develop within this context, members are ordinarily reelected, but policy making, especially on tough issues, frequently becomes bogged down. When this occurs, the Congress as a whole, particularly the rank-and-file members, often are shut out of the decision-making process. Presidents may dominate, as Reagan did on 1981 budget policy, through the use of reconciliation. Interbranch commissions or informal "gangs" may hold closed and sometimes secret meetings that decide crucial issues, like social security (Light, 1985). Most members are then left to make an up or down vote on a legislative package they have had no hand in constructing.

The shape of political careers is only one contributing force here. The range of opportunities, the expectation of participation, the apparently permanent minority status of the Republicans, and the lengthening queue for the Democrats all combine to produce a House of Representatives that continues to act in the best interests of its members at the expense of the collective interest of the institution as a whole.

Note

All uncited quotations are drawn from personal interviews in which members and staff were guaranteed anonymity.

References

Black, Gordon (1972) "A Theory of Political Ambition: Career Choices and the Role of Structural Incentives." *American Political Science Review* 66:144–59.

Bullock, Charles (1972) "House Careerists: Changing Patterns of Longevity and Attrition." *American Political Science Review* 66:1295–1305.

Bullock, Charles, and Burdett Loomis (1985) "The Changing Congressional Career." In *Congress Reconsidered*, 3rd ed., edited by Lawrence Dodd and Bruce Oppenheimer. Washington: Congressional Quarterly Press.

Cooper, Joseph, and David Brady (1981) "Toward a Diachronic Analysis of Congress." *American Political Science Review* 75:988–1007.

Cooper, Joseph, and William West (1981) "Voluntary Retirement, Incumbency, and the Modern House." *Political Science Quarterly* (Summer):279–300.

Cover, Albert D. (1977) "One Good Term Deserves Another: The Advantage of Incumbency in Congressional Elections." *American Journal of Political Science* 71:523–41.

Davidson, Roger, and Walter Oleszek (1981) *Congress and Its Members.* Washington, D.C.: Congressional Quarterly Press.

Deering, Christopher J. (1984) "The New Apprenticeship: Strategies of Effectiveness for New Members of the House." Paper presented at the Annual Meeting of the American Political Science Association.

Dodd, Lawrence, and Bruce Oppenheimer, eds. (1981) "The House in Transition: Change and Consolidation." In *Congress Reconsidered*, 2d ed., edited by Lawrence Dodd and Bruce Oppenheimer. Washington: Congressional Quarterly Press.

Ehrenhalt, Alan (1984) "GOP Moderates: Balance of Senate Power." *Congressional Quarterly Weekly Report*, May 26:1287.

Fenno, Richard F., Jr. (1966) *The Power of the Purse.* Boston: Little Brown.

Ferber, Mark (1971) "The Formation of the Democratic Study Group." In *Congressional Behavior*, edited by Nelson W. Polsby. New York: Random House.

Fiorina, Morris (1977) *Congress: Keystone of the Washington Establishment.* New Haven: Yale University Press.

Fishel, Jeff (1973) *Party and Opposition.* New York: David McKay.

Hain, Paul L. (1974) "Age, Ambitions, and Political Careers: The Middle-Age Crisis." *Western Political Quarterly* 27:265–74.

Hibbing, John (1982) "Voluntary Retirement from the U.S. House: The Costs of Congressional Service." *Legislative Studies Quarterly* 7:57–74.

Jacobson, Gary, and Samuel Kernell (1981) *Strategy and Choice in Congressional Elections.* New Haven: Yale University Press.

Jones, Charles O. (1968) "Joseph G. Cannon and Howard W. Smith: An Essay on the Limits of Leadership in the House of Representatives." *Journal of Politics* 30:617–46.

Kozak, David (1984) *The Contexts of Congressional Decision Behavior.* Lanham, Maryland: University Press of America.

Light, Paul (1985) *Artful Work.* New York: Random House.

Loomis, Burdett A. (1984a) "Congressional Careers and Party Leadership in the Contemporary House of Representatives." *American Journal of Political Science* 28:180–201.

——— (1984b) "On Knife's Edge: Public Officials and The Life Cycle." *PS* 17:536–43.

Mann, Thomas E., and Norman J. Ornstein, eds. (1981) *The New Congress.* Washington: American Enterprise Institute.

Mayhew, David (1966) *Party Loyalty Among Congressmen.* Cambridge: Harvard University Press.

——— (1974) "Congressional Elections: The Case of the Vanishing Marginals." *Polity* 6:295–317.

Peabody, Robert L. (1976) *Leadership in Congress: Stability, Succession and Change.* Boston: Little, Brown.

Polsby, Nelson (1968) "The Institutionalization of the U.S. House of Representatives." *American Political Science Review* 62:144–68.

Price, David E. (1971) "Professionals and 'Entrepreneurs': Staff Orientations and Policy Making on Three Senate Committees." *Journal of Politics* 53 (May):316–36.

Price, H. Douglas (1971) "The Congressional Career: Then and Now." In *Congressional Behavior*, edited by Nelson W. Polsby. New York: Random House.

Reeves, Richard (1984) "The Republicans." *The New York Times Magazine* (September 9).

Schlesinger, Joseph A. (1966) *Ambition and Politics*. Chicago: Rand McNally.

Sinclair, Barbara (1981) "The Speaker's Task Force in the Post-Reform House of Representatives." *American Political Science Review* 75:397–410.

—— (1983) *Majority Leadership in the U.S. House*. Baltimore: The Johns Hopkins University Press.

Smith, Steven S., and Christopher J. Deering (1984) *Committees in Congress*. Washington, D.C.: Congressional Quarterly Press.

Stevens, Arthur G., Jr., Arthur H. Miller, and Thomas E. Mann (1974) "Mobilization of Liberal Strength in the House: 1955–1970: The Democratic Study Group." *American Political Science Review* 68:667–81.

Sundquist, James (1968) *Politics and Policy: The Eisenhower, Kennedy and Johnson Years*. Washington, D.C.: Brookings.

Swenson, Peter (1982) "The Influence of Recruitment on the Structure of Power in the U.S. House, 1870–1940." *Legislative Studies Quarterly* 7:7–36.

Uslaner, Eric (1978) "Procedural Reforms and Policy Incentives in the Contemporary House of Representatives." Paper presented at the Annual Meeting of the Midwest Political Science Association.

PART FOUR
NEW ZEALAND

Selection Versus Election: Choosing Cabinets in New Zealand

Elizabeth M. McLeay

Political leadership is in part the product of structural forces, both those provided by the constraints of institutional arrangements and those imposed by the informal, but no less influential, constraints of beliefs and accepted modes of behavior concerning the processes and outcomes of selection. Just how influential these structural constraints can be is shown in the choice of the New Zealand Cabinet. Because in New Zealand one of the major political parties selects its Cabinet and the other elects, this example of leadership selection shows how the structure of institutions can interact with ideological notions about the nature of power and authority.

The New Zealand Cabinet, acting through the sovereign power of Parliament, effectively holds the supreme position in political decision making. Moreover, the small, centralized, unitary state places the Cabinet in a position unchallenged by other elected authorities in the country. Compared with most other countries, the political structure of New Zealand is simple. Government is unitary; the attempt to establish a degree of regional government was abandoned when the provinces were abolished in 1876. Social forces and geographical distinctions were never sufficiently strong to counteract tendencies towards centralization. So, throughout the country's history, centralization has been opposed not by regionalism but by parochialism (Sutch, 1964). In this way the roots of centralized political strength early established themselves.

New Zealand has had unicameral government since the Legislative Council was abolished by legislative enactment in 1950 (Jackson, 1972; Scott, 1962:9–10). Responsible government has existed since 1856, and ministers must be drawn from Parliament. Until the abolition of the Legislative Council, ministers of the Crown came from the Council as well as from the House of Representatives. Now Cabinets are created entirely from the membership of the House.

From the 1890s until the 1970s the Cabinet grew from about eight members to twenty. Expressed proportionately, in 1890 those in Cabinet (including the premier) were just over one-tenth of the members of the House of Representatives. By 1972 the number reached 23 percent, to drop very slightly with the enlarged House of 1978. There is no constitutional limit to the size of the Cabinet. Because Cabinet is not a legally created body, there is no formal procedure for appointing to Cabinet, and this task is managed by the parliamentary parties.

The New Zealand Cabinet is an essentially amateur executive, set to arbitrate between the skilled worlds of pressure groups and a large, professional public service. The unitary, centralized state has engendered a complex system composed of numerous governmental agencies (Polaschek, 1958; Smith, 1974; Webley, 1978). Ministers usually hold several portfolios that may or may not bear some relation to one another. Despite the fragmentation of administrative roles and the increased size of Cabinets, the Cabinet still includes all ministers, unlike the British case. Coordination is mainly achieved through Cabinet committees (Talboys, 1970). Thus, the role of the Cabinet minister in New Zealand is diverse in its administrative demands. Moreover, the Cabinet is constantly reminded of its political role by the triennial general elections.

From 1978 until 1984 there were ninety-two parliamentary seats, four of them providing special representation for the Maori population (Jackson and Wood, 1965; Ward, 1976; McLeay, 1980).[1] The idiosyncrasy of special representation apart, however, the New Zealand political system is structurally simple insofar as the "opportunity structure" for aspirants to top political office is concerned (Schlesinger, 1966). Elected political positions above the local city, board, or county council level are restricted to the relatively few seats in the House of Representatives. The politically ambitious are channelled to the central level of government.

The New Zealand House demonstrates a very high "degree of congruence in the attitudes and behavior of party members" (Janda, 1983:327). Explanations for party cohesiveness in liberal democracies have been identified as the existence of responsible party government (legislative votes directly affecting the government in power) and, contingently, constituency parties with the ability to deselect MPs who do not follow the party line (Ranney, 1968). Linked with these two factors are characteristics of opportunity structure: party dominance over the recruitment of aspirants providing an increasingly closed preparliamentary apprenticeship that effectively socializes MPs into partisan norms; and the situation where the polity's top executive positions come from the legislature. Activist and leadership socialization (Marvick, 1976:37) reinforce partisanship. Thus, the goals of the ambitious synchronize with the party goals of gaining and achieving power. And these are achieved by party cohesion in the legislature.

None of this is, of course, unique to New Zealand. What this example of leadership selection shows, however, is how the structural constraint of the *size* of a legislature interacts with party beliefs about the nature of authority and constitutional requirements to influence norms of legislative behavior—in particular, those relating to leadership selection.

What is the theoretical rationale for including the size of the institution as an independent variable for explaining legislative and leadership behavior (Kimberly, 1976: 573)? Increased size has been said to lead to greater division of labor, greater differentiation between units, more levels in a hierarchy and, consequently, less need for intraunit coordination but more need for interunit coordination, more formalization of behavior and increased use of planning control systems (Mintzberg, 1979: 234). Insofar as legislative behavior is concerned, larger numbers of members have been found to be correlated with more resources and talent, greater structural complexity, more hierarchical arrangements, greater specialization, more impersonal relations, less individual participation in debate and decision making, more "unwieldy" conduct of business, and more rigid rules of procedure (Hedlund, 1984: 89-90; Eulau, 1972). So, size, besides having fairly obvious practical implications (affecting the size of the pool available for selection, for example), also establishes distinctive normative features.

The difficulty is to ascertain the critical points at which legislatures can be classified as "small," and at what stage an increase in numbers of a legislature can be said to alter its internal functioning. This is particularly difficult since most of the organizational and social psychological literature on "small groups" deals with groups of ten or less (Verba, 1961).

There are two further problems. The first has to do with establishing a causal relationship (Kimberly, 1976: 579). It might be the case that size of a legislative institution is the product of environmental factors (large or small population, societal heterogeneity or homogeneity, regional distinctions or the lack of them), and it is these features, extraneous to the institution itself, that are the principal independent variables in an explanation of legislative behavior. I shall argue that in the New Zealand case, size is at least equally important as these exogenous factors. Second, we need to be sure that we are assessing the significance of the size of the legislature and not the sizes of the legislative parties. The former, of course, restricts the latter. But while a small legislature will inevitably have small parties (comparatively speaking), a large legislature may have a few large parties or, conversely, more than a few small ones. Comparisons between different types of party systems thus would need to proceed cautiously.

When parliaments are sufficiently small, the constraints that exist on individuals in all small communities provide social sanctions that reinforce those provided by the possibility of the reward of Cabinet office. The small number within the institution's parties creates a situation where legislative and partisan norms and values are exaggerated by close ties formed by shared preparliamentary socialization, small entry cohorts, and day-to-day personal contact. The higher the chance of reward in a situation where competition for office is slight, the less likely it is that ministerial hopefuls will risk failure by behaving in a nonconformist manner. Political conformity is given added strength through the nonhierarchical and participatory values that tend to exist within small institutions.

One of the clearest statements about the relationship between organizational size and behavior is Mancur Olson's *The Logic of Collective Action* (1965; see also Barnes, 1968). Olson's work is particularly useful for identifying significant factors in political parties because of his interest in defining links between sanctions and participation in noncommercial organizations of various sizes.

The collective goods relevant to legislative parties are the achievement of electoral victory in the case of a responsible party system, the achievement of certain legislative changes in the case of nonresponsible party systems, or the sharing of power within the governing coalition in the case of multiparty systems. The assumption of rational behavior then leads us to ask the question not, as is usually asked, what makes legislators behave in a dissenting manner, but what makes them pursue the collective goal in question, a goal that can only be achieved by cohesive intraparty behavior. Olson's explanation is, of course, that in large organizations "in which no single individual's contribution makes a perceptible difference to the group as a whole, or the burden or benefit of any single member of the group, it is certain that a collective good will *not* be provided unless there is coercion or some outside inducements that will lead the members of the large group to act in their common interest" (1965:44). We can hypothesize that, in the case of legislatures, coercion could be provided by the threat of the withdrawal of party renomination or the threat of dissolution (the latter applying only in the cases of governing parties). The selective benefits, it could be hypothesized, are the rewards of higher office—committee chairs or ministerial positions. But of course none of these sanctions or rewards provide sufficient incentives to act loyally and therefore achieve the collective goals when parties are large.

Social acceptance and social status, however, must also be regarded as selective incentives, argues Olson (1965:61). But these only operate in groups small enough to allow face-to-face contact. The existence of these social incentives means that collective goals are pursued. It is rational for individuals to seek social acceptance through cooperation and the sharing of the costs of collective goods. It must be remembered, nevertheless, if the assumption of rationality is to be consistently followed, that sanctions must underlie the norms of organizational behavior: "we must insist that rational men do not bow to significant social pressure as a result of any *intrinsic* desire to do so, but as an instrumental means of furthering their individual self-interest" (Laver, 1981:63). Collectively decided and enforced sanctions must be present. In the case of small legislative parties, the high chance of achieving official positions may act as an incentive toward conformity: the chances of not obtaining such a position if an aspirant has a secure legislative seat are slight. Thus, norms of party conformity are reinforced by rewards and punishments.

It is argued here that the New Zealand case shows that relatively small institutional size can be a significant variable in the explanation of legislative behavior and Cabinet selection. Originally, the small size of the House was a consequence of the tiny nineteenth century colonial society. Yet despite population growth, increased social complexity, technological change, and a continued expansion of the role of the state, the New Zealand Parliament has remained comparatively small (has even reduced its size if one considers the abolition of the upper house).

Cabinet Selection and Election

The parliamentary caucus ensures party cohesion through its practice of meeting regularly. Conformity with party policy is ensured in Labour by the pledge made by every candidate to vote on all questions in accordance with the decision of caucus. National does not demand this, but requires that all candidates be loyal to its organization and chosen leader (Jackson, 1978: 165). A former National Prime Minister has written: "Loyalty is the one essential. Unless a parliamentary party, having made a decision in accordance with its policy and principles, can stand together until that decision is carried out, then the standard of government will suffer accordingly" (Muldoon, 1981: 23). This tends to mean that although caucus is "theoretically a democratic device, in practice the senior status and readier access to information of Cabinet members makes it difficult to promote alternative policies effectively" (Jackson, 1978: 161).

In all programmatic parties there is a strong commitment to follow party policy. But in New Zealand, it has been argued, this commitment is exacerbated by the practice of formulating very detailed election platforms, which limit the scope for intraparty disagreement (Mulgan, 1984:57). It is apparent from a set of interviews conducted in 1971 and 1972 that party loyalty is very strongly valued by both parliamentary parties.[2] Several MPs believed that too much stress was placed on loyalty. The behavioral norm of the legislature is conformity; the degree of permissible divergence is interpreted as being that which takes place in caucus. Disagreement is a family affair, best dealt with by the family: "It's no good being different just for the sake of being different. [A person who does this] is not Cabinet material, then, because he is not a balanced person. I think that each one of us must have some measure of humility that will persuade us that our opinion after all may not be right. A member must accept majority rule" (National MP). "The more a chap [sic] differs (and he's got to do this in caucus) the more you suspect him. But once it becomes a party line he's got to stick with it" (Labour MP).

Cohesive legislative behavior has been a feature of the New Zealand Parliament since the establishment of the Labour/National two-party system. Cross-voting is very unusual and speaking out against the party line or deliberately abstaining from a vote is also rare (Kelson, 1972: 106; Kelson, 1964; May, 1972; Jackson, 1978).

Individual ambition is controlled by the values of partisanship, which are directed through conformity and loyalty. Majoritarianism is also a strongly held value in the New Zealand Parliament as shown by the role of caucus and Cabinet elections. But, as often has been observed, majoritarianism also serves to suppress individual dissent.

The Labour Party and the Elective Method

In the years of opposition from 1916 until 1935, the habit of majoritarianism was established in the Parliamentary Labour party. With the growing number of Labour MPs produced by elections in the 1920s some disciplinary controls were needed to maintain party unity. Regulations were invented on such matters as leaving the House, following the majority opinion of caucus, and order of precedence in debates (to be determined by ballot rather than seniority). By the time Labour was elected to government, a firm tradition of following majority opinion in the determination of policy, in the settling of policy disputes, and in the election of parliamentary party officers had been established. Elections were held according to the practice of exhaustive ballot.[3]

Until 1964 the accepted habit was to hold triennial elections of the leader, these being held at the start of the parliamentary session of an election year. In 1964 the three-year cycle was altered so that elections were held "as nearly as practicable to the beginning of December in the year prior to the General Election." This was to give a new leader time to become established before a general election. In accordance with the accepted way of doing things and the view of the Labour party that Cabinet must be responsive to caucus, it was believed that a Labour Cabinet, like the leader, would be elected by the caucus. It was not until 1974, however, that rules that specifically laid down how Cabinet was to be selected were included in the *Caucus Rules*.

Once in power, countervailing forces tend to challenge established habits and beliefs. Party unity and the task of persuading the electorate demand a degree of leadership assertion. When the pull of an attractive, strong and successful leader is added to these tendencies, tension develops between the leadership and the organizational values of democratic control.

At the first meeting of the Labour Caucus after the 1935 general election a motion was moved, and carried unanimously, that the leader, Michael Joseph Savage, be asked to select Cabinet members. This move was due to a combination of gratitude for successful leadership and an appreciation of the problems involved if the many new members were to vote for Cabinet. One of the results of this move against accepted habit, however, was to create doubts about the legitimacy of the leader's new powers, especially when he continued to insist upon his prerogative to appoint. Individual discontents, born of disappointment that could be justified in terms of principle, expanded into group disapproval of Savage personally and meshed into policy disagreements, especially about economic affairs (Brown, 1962; Lee, 1963; Sinclair, 1976; Olssen, 1977; Lee, 1981). The central ambivalence in Labour about the leadership role—always much more problematic than in National—became open discontent in the 1930s. Attempts to reestablish caucus control over Cabinet selection were unsuccessful until after Savage's death in 1940. His successor, Peter Fraser, allowed vacancies to be filled by nomination and election by caucus: after the 1943 and 1946 general elections, each minister had to submit to ballot.

When Labour regained office in 1957 there was no doubt that Cabinet would be elected by caucus. Speaker, Chairman of Committees, ministers, and whips—all were chosen by secret, exhaustive ballot. In 1972, when Labour was returned to power for a second three-year term of office, Cabinet again was elected. Caucus also decided that under-secretaries were to be appointed by the leader. The leader, Norman Kirk, never declared himself in favor of anything other than election. He described the caucus in 1971 to be already thinking about the consequences of possible electoral victory, and "weighing up personality, character and common sense." The lessons of party history had been learned, judging from his comment that traditionally in Labour there had been a "quite strong opposition to the idea that one man has the right to rule over others." In 1971, from the evidence of interviews conducted in 1971 and 1972, there had been caucus discussion over the issue of leadership selection or election and a subcommittee was set up to report on the matter. No changes were made to the principle of caucus election, however, and the matter of what happens in office regarding changes in Cabinet composition was shelved.

In 1974, when the Labour Government was experiencing a number of economic problems and there was concern about its performance, aspects of Cabinet election again were discussed, including the grey areas of midterm vacancies and changes. Kirk proposed that, between elections, whenever a vacancy occurred because of resignation, death, or dismissal, the leader could come to caucus with a name or names to be endorsed or refused by caucus vote. He argued that he could then reallocate and reshuffle more easily. On dismissal, he said that if a minister refused to accept his advice to resign, that minister could go to caucus where he would have the right to appeal—such appeal to be determined by secret ballot. Kirk added that he realized this motion constituted an extension of his powers (Bassett, 1976:153). One month later Kirk died. After the election of his successor, Bill Rowling, caucus decided that there would be a complete reelection of Cabinet. Every member's name was on the ballot paper. In the event, the caucus made as few changes as possible: the election of the one replacement member.

By 1974 most of the major issues about Cabinet appointment in Labour had been resolved and written down either in that year or in 1976 after further discussion and another subcommittee report. In July 1984 the Cabinet again was elected by caucus.

Although two-thirds (sixteen of twenty-three) of the Labour MPs interviewed were in favor of electing Cabinet members, several expressed reservations. One MP stated that the prime minister had the problem of finding "jobs to fit men rather than men to fit jobs." Another mentioned that election inhibited group and regional representation, and one said that election meant it was difficult to remove ministers. Other criticisms were that the method prevents the creation of a shadow Cabinet, that the leader organizes the voting, that the leader may have better judgment than the followers, and that, since the leader is elected and therefore has the confidence of caucus, he or she should be able to select the team. Two MPs said that election encouraged conformity, making outspokenness disadvantageous. Three said that those with the most ability can miss out. Also, there was some anxiety about newly elected MPs: they could be influenced by the newspapers or by lobbying. A member who had entered Parliament in 1957 said: "Had I had the opportunity of voting six months later I would not have voted for two I had voted for. My mind had been poisoned against one man."

The reasons given in favor of the elective method, moreover, tended to be of the negative sort. Ten of the twenty-three members interviewed said something similar to the following: "The Labour method stops crawlers and sycophants. When the PM selects he's only likely to hear what potential Cabinet ministers think is pleasant to his ears—

and you get less independence from the ministers themselves. A person appointed by caucus is more likely to act independently."

Positive reasons were also put forward, however. Seven MPs saw a major advantage in that "the parliamentary party gets what it wants." Also, those elected knew that they had the confidence of their colleagues, and more power is given to caucus against the Leader. Eight members argued in terms of the party's traditional democratic and participatory ideas: "It gives everybody a chance to express an opinion; it allows participation at the base level as opposed to giving a leader mandatory power to pick whom he likes." Four said something like "collective judgment is better than the judgment of one man." Three-quarters of those interviewed, however, judged that the leader has some influence over the election of ministers, particularly in cases involving the choice of opposition spokesmen.

Cabinet Selection in the National Party

The way in which National selects its Cabinets reflects its origins and its readiness to adapt traditional habits and beliefs to the peculiarities of New Zealand political structure. In National, the Leader, elected by caucus, chooses the ministers, but in response to the small, tightly-knit parliamentary party and, perhaps, to New Zealand egalitarianism, National prime ministers consult extensively among their colleagues.

As the domination of the ministry over the House increased with the development of cohesive parties, demands for MPs' participation in the selection of Cabinets began. In both New Zealand and Australia there were movements seeking the replacement of the traditional system with one of electing ministries (Lipson, 1948:129–31; Miller, 1953). By the time the National party was formed in 1936, however, there seems to have been no claim for any form of elective ministry within the non-Labour forces. Undoubtedly, the need to bind together the splinters of the former coalition against the victorious Labour party meant that a strong leader was necessary (Jackson, 1975). A National prime minister, then, chooses the Cabinet and other parliamentary officers, including the shadow Cabinet. At the same time, the claims of those who asked for elective ministries have their reflection in the National caucuses of today, which make claims for participation in policy making. The party has not been unaffected by what has been called the *legitimacy of democracy* (Duverger, 1964:133). National leaders, too, have sought to legitimize their positions within the parliamentary party, not only by being elected themselves, but also by conducting "straw polls" and extensive consultation about who should go into Cabinet.

With individual consultation, the trappings of democratic decision making are present, and various points of view may be voiced and considered. But the leader retains the power of patronage, and overt conflict, particularly dangerous in a small parliamentary party, is avoided. Authority of the prime minister has been maintained by the leader's close contact and consultation with MPs, thus simultaneously strengthening and moderating leadership power. The imagery employed by Nationalists in interviews and in the press has referred to leaders as father figures, team leaders, and managing directors. All are role configurations that imply contact and consultation as well as power and influence—limits as well as latitude. Once elected by caucus the National leader's right to select Cabinet is accepted, but this is diluted and controlled by the demands of the small caucus.

Almost half of the National MPs interviewed commented on straw polls. The informal not the formal aspect of the selection process was criticized within the party. The interviews suggest that about one-quarter of the MPs had reservations about the polls. They were referred to by one member as "the silly nonsense, the charade you go through, putting down the names." None of the dissidents, however, wanted caucus to elect the Cabinet. And, indeed, a majority of MPs felt that polling their opinions was either harmless or an actual help to the prime minister: "There's no harm in a straw poll as an indication of the way caucus was feeling. [But] I'd hate to see it as election by caucus." And, "It gives an indication of how the boys are thinking." There was no concern that popularity might become a factor in Cabinet selection, a perception that is, of course, perfectly consistent with the appreciation of the limited effects straw polls may have on the prime minister's choices.

A factor that did emerge from the interviews was a pronounced emphasis on the importance of loyalty to the leader. With only a few exceptions, National members were reluctant to say that loyalty was overemphasized to the point where it became disadvantageous to be critical of the leadership. Most MPs, while observing the importance of the loyalty factor in securing selection, were either neutral or noncommittal about its effects, or else they praised it.

In contrast to Labour, in National there was complete agreement with the principle of prime ministerial selection of Cabinet ministers. Although agreement on the practice of caucus consultation was not unanimous, the taking of soundings did not appear to have decreased the leader's legitimacy in exercising the sole right to make the choice of minister.

Leaders and Cabinets

Basic to the method of Cabinet selection adopted by a political party is its notion of the role and authority of the prime minister. In turn, this is dependent upon party ideology and tradition. Along with the

National party's image of the Cabinet as a board of directors goes a view of the role of the chairman of the board that is essentially a premodern view: the prime minister needs to form an administration, as had to be done in the nineteenth century New Zealand House of Representatives. This notion envisions the prime minister as the unifying spirit of the party, an image that has gained new vigor in the television age. In return, the leader is granted the authority to appoint and to dismiss. In contrast, the Labour party, the product of twentieth century collectivist ideology, regards the prime minister as the primary representative of the group, not its architect. As such, the prime minister is expected to work with a Cabinet elected by caucus.

In both parties, however, the collective will of the parliamentary party manifests itself in two major ways. Partisan goals and the desire for office produce party loyalty and the sharing of tasks and decision making—especially in the small parliamentary party—thus creating in the parties strong traditions of caucus influence. Sectionality defines differences within the parties, but the sections share beliefs about the fundamental rules of the political, and the economic, game. Political structure makes similar the habits of the two parliamentary parties. Both parties, therefore, always have elected their Leaders. Paradoxically, the leaders that have managed to keep their positions have been the ones who have been able to project personal strength and utilize to the full the adversarial basis of party politics. This personalization of politics can strengthen the leader of either party against the collective team tendency. The participatory and consultative norms, nevertheless, are strong countervailing forces; disobedience to these norms, plus, perhaps, leading one's party to defeat, dangerously expose New Zealand leaders to challenges from rivals, as Robert Muldoon discovered in 1984.

Theoretically, the two methods of Cabinet selection would seem to produce more power for National rather than for Labour prime ministers. This is probably true when the National leader is successful electorally. Success, however, is related to the choice of ministers. Additionally, every patronage decision excludes other potential recipients. "The first opinion that is formed of a ruler's intelligence is based on the quality of the men he has around him. When they are competent and loyal he can always be considered wise, because he has been able to recognize their competence and to keep them loyal. But when they are otherwise, the prince is always open to adverse criticism; because his first mistake has been in the choice of his ministers" (Machiavelli, 1967:124). Labour prime ministers, provided they follow the rules, do not have this burden to bear. In practice, though, the different methods of Cabinet selection have little impact upon the positions of prime ministers in the two parties. In both, ministers are subject to the constraints of generational loyalties and the intimacy of small parliamentary parties in a small House of Representatives.

The Cabinet Ministers

Luck plays its part for those who aspire to top political leadership—a party whose fortunes are rising is obviously a better choice than one on the decline. But an aspirant cannot foresee the future. In addition, the parties' sectional bases discriminate between the safeness and marginality of seats and consequential parliamentary apprenticeship serving. Once safely in Parliament, however, the chances of promotion—for those who have filled the apprenticeship requirements of a minimum of three years of useful but orthodox political behavior— are high. Table 1 demonstrates this point by showing the pool of MPs available with at least three years parliamentary experience for the six Cabinets formed after six changes of government. National in 1949 had the biggest choice with 22 eligible MPs left over after Cabinet was selected while National in 1975 had the smallest choice with only ten MPs not included. The virtue of a slow build up of seats culminating in eventual victory shows its benefit for Cabinet selection here.[4] These data also show how, once the other official positions of whips, speaker, chairman of committees, and under-secretaries are removed, the backbenchers within the governing party are reduced to a bare majority. Once again, conformity to group behavior and loyalty to caucus decisions are reinforced, and indeed partly explained, by the small size of the Parliament. Given the narrowness of choice indicated by Table 1, it is not surprising that Cabinets reflect fairly faithfully the parliamentary parties from which they have been drawn.

Maori and Women Ministers

Five Maoris were ministers between 1935 and 1984, although the two in the First Labour Government did not hold portfolios. There were only three women ministers. There were no women in the National Cabinets between 1960 and 1984. There seemed to be some notion that, like Maoris, women ministers were performing a representative function. Unlike Maoris, however, they were there to look after the portfolios they were directly concerned with as representatives of their gender (health, women and children, child welfare).

These two aspects (race and gender) are important in what they show about certain representative functions of Cabinets. Representatives of entire classifications of the population serve both symbolic and messenger functions in that their importance lies first in simply being in Cabinet and second in that they are seen as interpreting and conveying the wishes of the societal groups from which they come.

TABLE 1.

Availability for Selection to Cabinet in Labour and National Parties

	Labour 1935	National 1949	Labour 1957	National 1960	Labour 1972	National 1975
Total number in parliamentary party	55	46	41	46	55	55
Number of MPs ineligible for cabinet selection because new entrants	28	8	7	10	16	25
Number of MPs eligible for cabinet selection having minimum 3 years experience	27	38	34	36	39	30
Size of cabinet	13	16	16	16	20	20
Number of eligible MPs remaining after cabinet is selected	14	22	18	20	19	10
Number of MPs in other parliamentary offices*	5	4	4	6	7	7
Total number of non-office-holding MPs in parliamentary party	37	26	21	24	28	28
Total number of officeholders in parliamentary party	18	20	20	22	27	27

* Speaker, Deputy-Speaker, whips and under-secretaries

Here the parties have differed—Labour has been notably more responsive to the demands of this sort of representation than has
National.[5] The other representative functions of New Zealand Cabinets have to do with geographical areas and sectionalism.

Age, Occupation, and Education

When the ages of ministers at first entry into Cabinet were analyzed, the overall pattern reflected a trend towards younger politicians. Party fortunes also are relevant—the age of Cabinets being
affected by the size of the pool of experienced, senior MPs that has
been established. As a general rule, age trends in Cabinet reflect
trends in age at entry to Parliaments, providing seats move from
one party to another in small and not large numbers. The time-gap
produced by parliamentary apprenticeship requirements readily
can be filled by younger MPs going into Cabinet only if they are not
subject to losing their seats. Both parties have produced similarly
aged cabinets—each is susceptible to identical social pressures and
structural constraints.

In a political system that appoints its top executive from outside
the legislature, the relationship between what a person has done in
terms of occupations and party service and that person's appointment is close. Skills are seen as relevant and transferable. In a system
such as New Zealand, executive training is amateur rather than professional when judged in terms of vocational training. Ceteris pari-
bus, it is political skill that determines selection to Cabinet. What
might be desirable and what is realistically available and structurally determined, as usual, interact.

In Labour, 23 percent of ministers have been blue-collar workers
and 16 percent have been trade union officials, both proportionately
more than the total number of Labour MPs in these categories. However, the proportion of blue-collar ministers dropped from just under
one-third in the first Labour government to about one-fifth in the
third. A similar trend occurred for trade union officials. Farmers have
formed a high proportion of National administrations, contributing
34 percent, slightly under-representing their numbers in Parliament.
Labour Cabinets contained 9 percent farmers, although almost all of
these persons served between 1935 and 1949. Professionals formed 33
percent of National and 23 percent of Labour Cabinets, the proportions remaining roughly the same in the former but increasing to
about half in the last Labour government. National Cabinets have had
their representative share of the business category; but in Labour
Cabinets, those in small business have been under-represented.[6] On
the other hand, rather more than the due proportion of party officials
have become ministers.

Regarding educational qualifications, the differences between

House and Cabinet are slight, as they are also between parliamentary party and Cabinet. Generally, National Cabinets have had more formal education but, over time, all Cabinets have contained more highly educated ministers.

Preparliamentary Experience

The parties present a mirror image in which Cabinets reflect MPs' party experience. Second, as one would expect, fewer National than Labour ministers (62 percent v. 77 percent) have been party officials. Third, far more Labour members and especially ministers have had experience at the top levels of their party than have their National counterparts.

Generally, New Zealand ministers, like other MPs, are highly party politicized. Their partisan backgrounds certainly must contribute to the general norms of loyalty to the party and conformity in the House. At Cabinet level the solid political training received by ministers undoubtedly encourages collective solidarity.

Concerning other adult political socialization experiences, majorities of Labour (52 percent) and National ministers (55 percent) were known to have been involved in at least one interest group. The ministers are hardly distinguishable from the House in interest group activity. There were few discernible trends through time in interest group involvement, except for a noticeable increase in involvement among National ministers from the first to the second National governments and a marked decline in the number of Labour ministers who had been involved with blue-collar unions.

Previous involvement in interest group activities has a two-fold effect on Cabinet members. Interest groups effectively have direct representation in Cabinet. From that point of view the business and farming communities have been well placed in National administrations—enjoying an extension of the link that exists at the individual level between MPs and members of these organizations, the largest of which have full-time lobbyists in Wellington. The second part of the effect of ministers' involvement with pressure groups has to do with political training. Not only have those who have played parts in such organizations learned about a particular economic field, but they have also learned (even before they get to Parliament and Cabinet) about the complex relationship between groups and state in New Zealand's mixed economy.

The extent of local government activity experienced by the New Zealand ministers (55 percent for Labour, 50 percent for National) shows patterns similar to those for the House as a whole. A convergence between the parties is observable. In both, a sufficient number of ministers have the knowledge gained about local affairs to contribute at the Cabinet table, although a possible side effect of this might be to exacerbate parochialism and the importance of geographical representation.

As a final observation, one of the most striking characteristics in the data is the similarity of the profiles of ministers and MPs. In no sense has the New Zealand Cabinet been an elite within an elite. The constraints of the small size of the House have prevented this from occurring.

Parliamentary Apprenticeship Requirements

National ministers had more prior parliamentary experience in terms of the official positions held (as whips, Speaker, chairman of committees, under-secretaries) than had Labour ministers. Overall, twenty-seven out of fifty-six Labour ministers had held some such position, compared with forty-seven out of fifty-nine National ministers. It is not party that explains the difference, however, rather the opportunity or lack thereof. When a party is in office for some years and spends quite short periods out of power, the opportunity structure within the institution is extended. The consequences of a party's electoral fortunes rather than its notions about leadership training determine ministers' experience.

No MP ever has been promoted to Cabinet before spending three years in Parliament. This norm of legislative behavior almost has the status of a parliamentary convention. Although Table 2 shows the biggest single bulge in the Labour distribution as the four-to-six-years category, note the number (compared with National) who entered after thirteen years in Parliament. Probably this reflects, once again, Labour's long years out of power.

The role of Cabinet minister in a responsible party system is primarily a parliamentary one. The years spent in Parliament prior to promotion and the tasks undertaken in those years may prepare MPs for Cabinet. Some learn how to become effective parliamentary and caucus politicians; some manage adequately; and some never learn the skills: it is probably the latter who, despite their accumulation of service and seniority, never go into Cabinet. "Certain folk impress you by the way in which they can get their case together, present it. They emerge. No one can forecast this in advance. But after all you can see their potential. It sometimes takes a long time" (Labour MP).

Geographical and Sectional Representation

Federalism forces parties "to give institutional recognition to the reality of scattered centers of power within their own organizations" (Jupp, 1968:38). Cabinets in the federal governments of Australia, Canada, and the United States of America appease regional demands and recognize structural reality by spreading the allocation of offices.

TABLE 2.

Number of Years in Parliament Before First Entry into
Cabinet by Party

Number of Years	Labour	National	Total
1–3	15%	13%	14%
4–6	21	38	30
7–9	15	25	21
10–12	15	14	14
13–15	15	6	10
16–18	15	3	8
19 plus	4	3	3
(N)	(53)	(72)	(125)

*Excludes Labour ministers (3) and National ministers (1) appointed from the Legislative Council

Although this process is not constitutionally specified it is a response to and is legitimized by the federal basis of the constitution.

Demands for geographical recognition in Cabinet are voiced noisily within the small state of New Zealand, especially in the press. These demands are recognized by the structures of the parties, especially National. But the actual allocation of Cabinet posts in a way that produces wide geographical representation has ambiguous legitimacy for the parliamentarians. Many felt, on being interviewed about geography's claim, that the quality of a minister ought to be more important than areal representation. National MPs believed, however, that the achievement of geographical balance was important in Cabinet selection. Only one of thirty-six with whom this was discussed deemed geography to be unimportant. Frequently, examples were given of ministers who had been helped by the area they represented. It was pointed out by a senior minister that, "Sometimes it may mean that someone marginally superior is left out rather than someone marginally inferior." The prime ministers and deputies interviewed agreed that it was a factor considered in selection, although one commented, "It is an extraordinary thing that the law of averages works here. If you had two people of equal capacity then geography would be another factor you'd take into account." It also was observed that the regional structure of the National Party contributed to the need to have a geographical spread in Cabinet. When asked whether geographical representation ought to be important, a majority (eleven of eighteen) agreed.

Labour members were not asked the general questions about whether the achievement of a geographical balance had been important, since those who had experienced the process of Cabinet election were asked more specific questions about what had actually happened. A few examples of geography playing its part were given from the first two Labour Governments and those interviewed about the Third Labour Government recognized that geography had been a factor in every ballot after the first. Twelve Labour MPs thought that it should be a factor considered when voting for Cabinet, while nine did not, demonstrating a disagreement about the issue similar to that in National.

Both parties have spread their ministers fairly evenly through the areas.[7] Differences, when Cabinet representation was compared with the representation of parties in the House, were slight. Despite the commonsense belief that it is easier for one who selects to obtain geographical balance than the many who elect, Labour Cabinets were only slightly less balanced than National's. The exhaustive ballot employed by Labour makes this sort of area recognition possible.

Sectional representation also has been demanded. It was believed that urban and rural areas should be directly and fairly balanced. Often this is simply expressed in a demand for farmer representation. In this way the sectional divisions of New Zealand society and economy project themselves into top political leadership. Sectionalism, like geography, is important in shaping Cabinets, but it is more subject to the nature of the electoral bases of the two parties.

In the small society of the New Zealand legislature, representativeness plays a part not only in terms of legitimizing and recognizing the demands of groups and regions in the larger society but also in terms of simplifying choice. To be rejected because one represents the wrong area or is yet another farmer is not as personally hurtful as rejection on the grounds of competence since the former can be interpreted as furthering the general good of the party. Thus, bonds of loyalty, created by years of party service, are cemented by nonpersonalized criteria for promotion.

Intraparliamentary party politics in New Zealand are not the politics of ongoing, ideological groups involving the intricacies of balancing opinions in the process of Cabinet composition. (Although this is not to say that sporadic periods of dissent have not occurred, for they certainly have.) Articulating and representing distinctive viewpoints is not the task of the makers of New Zealand Cabinets, except for the generalized goal of representing sectional societal divisions.

Seniority

If an aspirant has managed to be elected to a reasonably safe seat then the chances of obtaining a Cabinet post—if that aspirant has chosen the right party—are high. Seniority is, indeed, the single most accurate predictor of the choice of ministers for the New Zealand Cabinet.[8] Given the norm of party loyalty and the constraint of small numbers, it is not surprising that seniority counts more than anything else, for reward for loyal service is unarguable. Interviews showed that the legitimacy of promotion through seniority was generally accepted by the MPs: "you know what a seniority system does. It almost guarantees that eventually you'll get Cabinet rank, although there are the odd ones who get side-tracked and feel bitter. But they all know that the argument for seniority could be used in their favour" (National backbencher). Seniority, even more than representativeness, makes it easy for selectors to justify their choices in the small confines of the New Zealand parliamentary party.

Cabinet Regeneration

Throughout the whole period under consideration only one minister was forced to leave Cabinet in a publicly forced resignation. In 1982 the minister of Works and Development, D. F. Quigley, disagreed with the government's interventionist strategy for economic growth. The Prime Minister, Muldoon, publicly forced him to resign, saying that the alternative was a public apology.[9] Furthermore, there have been very few cases of former ministers not being reappointed after a general election.[10]

The process of Cabinet regeneration has been achieved by voluntary retirement, death, or defeat, a process speeded up by triennial general elections, with mixed results for the caliber of Cabinets, since new blood is usually competing against administrative continuity. The pattern of New Zealand parliamentary politics has worked against the occurrence of public dismissal. Small size, as usual, has fostered loyalty and conformity, while the tradition of the influential caucus has limited the power and therefore the flexibility of the prime minister. The authority handed to the prime minister by caucus is strictly limited by the obligation to consult and, more importantly, to protect. And protection of those chosen becomes not only a matter of loyalty to colleagues but also a matter of protecting one's authority by not admitting that mistakes were made in selection. When caucus elects, however, the situation is rather more complex.

In the National party, apart from the accidents of death and defeat, ministers have tended to retire from Parliament and leave Cabinet at the same time.[11] As an under-secretary observed, "You have certain people who want to retire for age or health or other reasons who feel it is time to pull out. They do it of their own free will. It is recognized in the party that it is good for the party, good for the government, that this happens." Of course, it is probable that pressure may have been brought to bear on such ministers by the prime minister who can indicate that patronage may be withdrawn if the minister returns to Parliament.

Nature and party norms of career behavior together have produced a distinctive pattern of ministerial turnover, with several consequences. First, it removes the possibility that those who have retired from Cabinet will stay in Parliament and give authoritative support to the ministry from the backbenches. Second, and conversely, it removes from the backbenches the possibility of an experienced nucleus of opposition to the leadership, this being especially likely if a minister has been dismissed or forced to resign on a matter of principle. Third, it has perpetuated the belief that ministers will not be sacked, and that, however incompetent, they will at least be able to serve out the parliamentary term. A Cabinet can carry on loyally protecting an ineffective rump provided the period for which they do so is finite. Obvious errors of judgment have been dealt with through exchanges of portfolios.

In party government, and if the prime minister so wishes, ministers can be protected by wrapping them in the cloak of Cabinet responsibility and relying on their colleagues' partisanship to support the action. Because credit and blame for performance tend to be interpreted collectively, then errors of principle, particularly in a society where the press is not inquisitive or critical, can be disguised and reinterpreted.

The uncertainty as to who among the Labour caucus has the authority to remove ministers from their posts, if that is deemed necessary, was demonstrated by the responses of Labour MPs questioned about this aspect of the Cabinet election process. The constraint of smallness is added to the complexity of relationships within the party between prime minister and caucus and caucus and Cabinet. Within caucus the prime minister's authority is circumscribed by the belief in the limitations on the leader's powers. And in the two cases where the leader was given the opportunity of having a minister removed by caucus, both times the prime minister in question did not encourage such an outcome.[12] Although ministers have not been sacked, there were two apparently voluntary resignations in the first Labour government. Fewer Labour than National ministers have left Cabinet by leaving Parliament, but Labour ministers, similar to their National counterparts, have not resigned on issues of ministerial responsibility.

It would appear that if a prime minister chooses the ministers then they can more easily be removed than if a caucus elects. The structural constraints arising from the small parties in the small legislature, however, blur the effect of party differences in the method of choice. But with the power to appoint, the National leader can threaten to withdraw patronage if a minister returns to Parliament against advice.

Conclusion

Selected entirely from the small number of MPs of one party in a single chamber house, New Zealand's top political leadership, the

Cabinet, naturally mirrors its source. There has been some distortion in this representativeness, however, toward those who come from party strongholds, i.e., safe seats, a distortion exaggerated in times of rapid and extensive electoral movement and governmental change. Whether a Cabinet is the result of a change in the party in office or whether it is the Cabinet of a party that has been in power for some years, it will nevertheless represent a relatively wide range of occupational backgrounds and geographical areas. In part this occurs because there is so little flexibility of choice; but, in part, also, it is because representativeness is a valued characteristic of Cabinet selection.

In New Zealand the norm of being loyal is reinforced, probably by the values of the society as a whole, but certainly by strong bonds that develop between the politicians in the small parliamentary parties of the New Zealand House. Caucus involvement in policy making, employing backbench as well as frontbench talents, commits participants to the values of the group. Conformity with the decisions of the majority and a belief in the value of loyalty to the party become inextricably intertwined. In this way the shape of the political structure—the small size of the House—works with cultural and party variables to influence the political process. The two-party system is doubly entrenched by pronounced partisanship. This is so despite or, perhaps, because of, the absence of a fundamental ideological cleavage between the two major parties.

The norms of conformity and loyalty affect and are affected by the process of Cabinet selection. Ability and individuality must be directed toward furthering the goals of the party. This is the case even though the risks of incurring party or prime ministerial blame for being divergent and, as a consequence, missing out on a place in Cabinet would seem to be lessened by the very high chance that an MP possesses of becoming a minister. The constraint of small size creates familylike, inhibiting bonds around the politicians. Disagreements threaten schisms and so drastically reduce the likelihood that groups inside caucus will emerge and have to be recognized in the construction of Cabinet.

The primary criterion for selection to Cabinet is parliamentary experience, although representativeness also plays its part. Where people know each other well, where it is essential that they work together, and where those who are unsuccessful in gaining promotion are small in number and therefore conspicuous in their failure, the criterion of parliamentary seniority is perhaps the least controversial basis on which to choose and reject.

Despite the shared institutional norms of loyalty, seniority, and caucus participation, there have been important differences between the parties, illustrated in the ways in which they have chosen their Cabinets. Their notions differ in regard to the rights of the collective body of the parliamentary party and the limits of the authority of the leader of the party. Nevertheless, it is difficult to see differences in the composition of the two sets of Cabinets that are contingent upon the different selection methods rather than upon ideological views about the representative roles of Cabinets. Moreover, Labour, which has employed both methods, did not choose Cabinets that were discernibly different through one method or the other. The constraints surrounding the behavior of individuals in the Labour caucus are probably almost as powerful as those surrounding the National MPs who feel that they must show loyalty to the selector. Where caucus elects there is undoubtedly some pressure not to antagonize colleagues. The impetus towards conformity exists in both parties despite the different Cabinet selection procedures.

Although the National leader may have a little more flexibility by being able to test people for Cabinet office in other official positions or by being able to fit ministers with portfolios in the most appropriate manner, the constraint of the available choice for Cabinet limits the extent of these party differences. The multiplicity of portfolios to be filled, the paucity of really able people available, and the constraint of seniority all severely restrict prime ministerial flexibility. When the prime minister chooses, it seems possible to hasten Cabinet regeneration by quietly influencing ministers to retire. But neither process has produced a system of open dismissal. There has been no tradition of ministerial responsibility in New Zealand, a regrettable consequence not only of the Cabinet's control over Parliament through cohesive and loyal party majorities, but also of the overriding emphasis upon Cabinet solidarity.

In Labour the prime minister's patronage is circumscribed by the procedure of caucus election of Cabinet. Attempting to increase the leader's powers has been shown to be dangerous both to his authority and to the party. The tradition of democratic control is strong: when the rules that symbolize and implement this tradition are challenged or bent, splits have developed in the party and the position of the leader questioned. When the rules have been unclear, as they have been for most of the period under examination, the issue of Cabinet election, which is involved with party ideology as well as individual ambition, has become divisive.

National, too, has a caucus participatory tradition. However, it is one with a more limited notion of democratic control, which allows the Leader to appoint the Cabinet. Despite the consultation that has occurred, it is in the end the prime minister who chooses and who assumes responsibility for that choice. This power produces deference to the leader. But the use of the power creates enemies. Thus, National leaders, too, must respect institutional and party norms and values in order to protect their position and retain a cohesive parliamentary party.

The cabinet selection behavior of New Zealand political parties, therefore, provides an excellent illustration of the way in which political processes and structures interact and the importance of groups having clearly defined and obeyed rules where individual ambitions are affected. Moreover, this behavior shows how a model of government, the Westminster system, has been reinterpreted to suit specific social and political characteristics.

The small size of the New Zealand legislature has been a constant explanatory factor in this discussion of leadership recruitment. Close personal bonds are formed, and norms of loyalty and conformity are generally obeyed. The sanctions are, ultimately, the rewards of office holding. The high chance of gaining office in small political parties, it is suggested, underpins these norms and values (strong anyway in legislatures from which the executive is chosen). The collective good of becoming the governing party is achieved through partisan loyalty, and that is reinforced by the goal of achieving office for the individual. Of course, this assumes that the politically rational parliamentarian is ambitious for higher office, an assumption confirmed by the interviews undertaken for this research (McLeay, 1978). A few, but only a very few, New Zealand parliamentarians did not conform in the period covered by this analysis. Their careers invariably suffered, thus providing examples of how nonconformist behavior is treated in a small political organization. This last generalization includes party leaders, too, because prime ministers and leaders of the opposition have been faced with threats to their own positions, through extraordinary intraparty dissent, when individuals have felt that their Leaders have not obeyed party norms. When governing majorities have been large, there has been a tendency for the norms of party cohesion to be lessened, thus bearing out the assertion that party size is related to patterns of legislative and selection behavior.

The New Zealand case, too, exemplifies the tension that always exists in cabinet systems between demands for expertise and demands for representativeness. New Zealand ministers are politically trained, not experts in the areas they administer. Neither have they been an elite in terms of social background or educational qualifications, although recent Cabinets have been significantly better educated. It might be argued that if the members of the New Zealand Parliament were better qualified, then government would be more effective (Ovenden, 1975; and the response by Mulgan, 1977). This, however, would not necessarily be the case. It is certainly desirable that New Zealand ministers be of better quality than they are. It is by no means certain, however, that the professionally qualified, highly educated and administratively trained minister is better able to solve problems involved in the allocation of resources and the ordering of political and economic priorities than is the socially representative and politically trained minister. There is nothing inherently wrong with the nonexpert minister provided that there is an efficient, honest and well-qualified public service and a variety of types of advice available. The representative, nonexpert, Cabinet can be justified in that it can articulate the many beliefs and viewpoints characteristic of a pluralist society.

Cabinet government, in itself, even in a nonelite legislature, is not what is wrong. Representativeness, as John Stuart Mill recognized, is one of the major functions of a legislature. The actual representation of groups and sections in a legislature can provide potential channels of access to those in power. These representative functions are especially important for weaker groups in society. The legislature which is broadly representative of social divisions, together with the ready availability of legislators to the public, are important features of the New Zealand political system. They establish strong linkages between those in power and those who put them there. A larger Parliament might enable both these characteristics to be perpetuated, while providing a larger pool of MPs on which to draw for Cabinet. The small number of representatives in the New Zealand Parliament has constrained public debate and argument and allowed too little choice in the recruitment of ministers for the New Zealand Cabinet.

Notes

ACKNOWLEDGMENTS: This paper was written while I was on leave at the University of Exeter. I am grateful for the facilities granted to me as Honorary Research Fellow in the Department of Politics, Exeter, and for the leave allowed me by the City of London Polytechnic. I also wish to thank Professor Robert Chapman who granted me access to his files on New Zealand electoral information.

1. There have been many criticisms of the Maori seats from those who argue that the seats are a form of apartheid. It has also been argued that since Maoris constitute about one-tenth of the total population they are actually underrepresented and ought to have more seats.

2. A series of in-depth interviews with MPs and ministers of both parties was conducted by the author. There was a two-fold purpose: to gain information about the process of promotion to Cabinet and to uncover the attitudes of MPs concerning the norms and values of New Zealand legislative behavior generally (McLeay, 1978) and Cabinet selection in particular. The bulk of the interviews were carried out in 1971 and 1972, at the time of the second National government and then immediately after the 1972 general election when the Labour party was elected. For various reasons (the need, for example, to find out about past selections in Labour, the fact that Labour had been in opposition for so long, and because, as the interviews became known in parliamentary circles opportunities for interview were offered) a strictly selected sample was not obtained. Some respon-

dents were interviewed several times. Not all MPs were interviewed about the same topics. Altogether eighty-seven MPs (forty-one Labour and forty-six National) plus thirty-one ministers were interviewed (eight Labour and twenty-three National). The sample included interviews with MPs from every prime ministership in the period. One incumbent prime minister, two deputy prime ministers (both of whom subsequently became prime ministers), and two leaders of the opposition (also future prime ministers) were interviewed.

3. The 1964 version of the *Caucus Rules* stipulates that caucus elections be held by an "exhaustive ballot" that requires that no one can be elected until a clear majority of the vote has been obtained. See Rule 18, *Caucus Rules*, 1964.

4. Although Labour's July 1984 Cabinet could not be included in the statistical analysis, it ought to be noted that the circumstances in which this Cabinet was recruited tend to support the generalization. The party gradually accumulated new MPs after its sweeping defeat in 1975. In 1984 Labour won fifty-six seats (compared with National's thirty-seven and Social Credit's two). After the Cabinet was selected there were nineteen MPs remaining who had at least three years' parliamentary experience.

5. The Labour government elected in July 1984 has continued the tradition; two women and two Maoris were elected to Cabinet. Leader David Lange evidently told caucus that two women, at least two Maoris, and a spread of ages ought to be included (*New Zealand Herald*, 1984: 3).

6. In 1971, 12 percent of the population were farmers, 38 percent were manual laborers, and 41 percent were engaged in white-collar occupations. See Dunstall (1981:406–12).

7. Because the Labour party only recently has begun to develop a regional structure (Gustafson, 1978), the boundaries used in the analysis were those employed by the National party in demarcating its divisional areas—Auckland, Waikato, Wellington, Canterbury-Westland, and Otago-Southland. The Maori seats were not so categorized.

8. At the same time, there has been a recent tendency in both parties to appoint second-term MPs to Cabinet.

9. This case shows how dismissal can rebound upon the leader. Here, a respected minister, with support in caucus, was lost to the government, and Robert Muldoon's own position in caucus and the country was weakened.

10. After the 1978 general election, one minister was not reappointed by Muldoon. Two MPs who had been ministers in the 1972–1975 Labour government failed to be elected in the July 1984 choice, an interesting departure from tradition. (Four were reelected.)

11. When Keith Holyoake was succeeded by John Marshall in early 1972 as leader and prime minister (although Holyoake stayed in cabinet), five ministers announced that, as they planned to retire from Parliament at the end of the year, they would retire from Cabinet immediately.

12. After the 1946 election one minister failed to be reelected to Cabinet but was saved by Prime Minister Peter Fraser, who extended the size of his Cabinet. In 1974, when Wallace Rowling succeeded Norman Kirk as leader, a minister was only narrowly reelected. This failure of caucus to make any changes might have been an over-reaction to their new leader's plea that not too many changes should be made (Bassett, 1976: 168).

References

Barnes, Samuel H. (1968) "Party Democracy and the Logic of Collective Action." In *Approaches to the Study of Party Organization*, edited by William J. Crotty. Boston: Allyn and Bacon, Inc.

Bassett, Michael (1976) *The Third Labour Government*. Palmerston North: The Dunmore Press.

Brown, Bruce (1962) *The Rise of New Zealand Labour. A History of the New Zealand Labour Party from 1916 to 1940*. Wellington: Price Milburn.

Caucus Rules (1964) Rule 18.

Dunstall, Graeme (1981) "The Social Pattern." In *The Oxford History of New Zealand*, edited by W. H. Oliver with B. R. Williams. Oxford and Wellington: The Claredon Press and Oxford University Press.

Duverger, Maurice (1964) *Political Parties*. London: Methuen.

Eulau, Heinz (1972) "Decisional Structures in Small Legislative Bodies." In *Comparative Legislative Behavior: Frontiers of Research*, edited by Sammuel C. Patterson and John C. Wahlke. New York: Wiley.

Gustafson, Barry S. (1978) "Towards Centralization or Decentralization?: The Regional Organization of the New Zealand Labour Party." In *Politics in New Zealand: A Reader*, edited by Stephen Levine. Sydney: George Allen and Unwin.

Hedlund, Ronald D. (1984) "Organizational Attributes of Legislatures: Structure, Rules, Norms, Resources." *Legislative Studies Quarterly* 9:51–121.

Jackson, Keith (1975) "Political Leadership and Succession in the New Zealand National Party." *Political Science* 27:1–25.

——— (1978) "Caucus: the Anti-Parliament System?" *Parliamentarian* 59:159–64.

Jackson, W. K. (1972) *The New Zealand Legislative Council*. Dunedin: University of Otago Press.

Jackson, W. K., and G. A. Wood (1965) "The New Zealand Parliament and Maori Representation." *Historical Studies* 11:383–96.

Janda, Kenneth (1983) "Cross-National Measures of Party Organizations and Organizational Theory." *European Journal of Political Research* 11:310–32.

Jupp, J. (1968) *Australian Party Politics*. Melbourne: Melbourne University Press.

Kelson, R. N. (1964) *The Private Members of Parliament and the Formation of Public Policy*. Toronto: University of Toronto Press.

——— (1972) "Voting in the New Zealand House of Representatives 1947–54." In *Readings in New Zealand Government*, edited by L. Cleveland and A. D. Robinson. Wellington: A. H. and A. W. Reed.

Kimberly, John R. (1976) "Organizational Size and the Structural Perceptive: A Review, Critique and Proposal." *Administrative Science Quarterly* 21:571–97.

Laver, Michael (1981) *The Politics of Private Desires*. Harmondsworth: Penguin.

Lee, John A. (1963) *Simple on a Soap-box*. Auckland: Collins Brothers.

——— (1981) *The John A. Lee Diaries: 1936–40*. Christchurch: Whitcoulls Publishers.

Lipson, Leslie (1948) *The Politics of Equality*. Chicago: University of Chicago Press.

Machiavelli, Niccolo (1967) *The Prince*, translated by George Bell. London: Penguin Books.

McLeay, E. M. (1978) "Parliamentary Careers in a Two-Party System: Cabinet Selection in New Zealand." Unpublished Ph.D. thesis, University of Auckland.

———— (1980) "Political Argument about Representation: The Case of the Maori Seats." *Political Studies* 28:43–62.

Marvick, Dwaine (1976) "Continuities in Recruitment Theory and Research." In *Elite Recruitment in Democratic Polities. Comparative Studies Across Nations*, edited by Heinz Eulau and Moshe M. Czudnowski. New York: Sage Publications.

May, Therese (1972) "Parliamentary Discipline in New Zealand, 1953–63." In *Readings in New Zealand Government*, edited by L. Cleveland and A. D. Robinson. Wellington: A. H. and A. W. Reed.

Miller, J. B. D. (1953) "David Syme and Elective Ministries." *Historical Studies* 6:1–15.

Mintzberg, Henry (1979) *The Structure of Organizations*. Englewood Cliffs, N.J: Prentice-Hall.

Muldoon, R. D. (1981) *My Way*. Wellington: A. H. and A. W. Reed.

Mulgan, Alan (1984) *Democracy and Power in New Zealand. A Study of New Zealand Politics*. Auckland: Oxford University Press.

Mulgan, R. C. (1977) "The Need for More Graduate MPs: A Sceptical Note." *Political Science* 29:66–71.

New Zealand Herald (1984) 18 July, p. 3.

O'Farrell, P. J. (1964) *Harry Holland, Militant Socialist*. Canberra: Australian National University Press.

Olson, Mancur (1965) *The Logic of Collective Action: Public Goods and the Theory of Groups*. Cambridge, Mass.: Harvard University Press.

Olssen, Eric (1977) *John A. Lee*. Dunedin: University of Otago Press.

Ovenden, Keith (1975) "On the Absence of Political Ideas." In *Labour in Power—Promise and Performance*, edited by Ray Goldstein with Rod Alley. Wellington: Price Milburn for New Zealand University Press.

Polaschek, R. J. (1958) *Government Administration in New Zealand*. Wellington: New Zealand Institute of Public Administration and Oxford University Press.

Ranney, A. (1968) "Candidate Selection and Party Cohesion." In *Approaches to the Study of Party Organization*, edited by William J. Crotty. Boston: Allyn and Bacon, Inc.

Schlesinger, J. A. (1966) *Ambition and Politics: Political Careers in the United States*. Chicago: Rand McNally.

Scott, K. J. (1962) *The New Zealand Constitution*. Oxford: Oxford University Press.

Sinclair, Keith (1976) *Walter Nash*. Auckland: Auckland University Press.

Smith, Thomas D. (1974) *The New Zealand Bureaucrat*. Wellington: Cheshire.

Sutch, W. B. (1964) *Local Government in New Zealand: A History of Defeat*. Wellington: Department of Industries and Commerce.

Talboys, B. E. (1970) "The Cabinet Committee System." *New Zealand Journal of Public Administration* 33:1–7.

Verba, Sidney (1961) *Small Groups and Political Behavior.* Princeton, N. J.: Princeton University Press.

Ward, A. D. (1976) *A Show of Justice: Racial "Amalgamation" in New Zealand.* Canberra: Australian National University Press.

Webley, Irene A. (1978) "State Intervention in the Economy: The Use of Public Corporations in New Zealand." In *Politics in New Zealand: A Reader,* edited by Stephen Levine. Sydney: George Allen and Unwin.

Wilson, J. O. (1982) "Party Research Units in the New Zealand Parliament." *Parliamentarian* 63:86–91.

PART FIVE
IMPACT OF THE
BRITISH TRADITION

Political Leadership
in the Commonwealth:
The British Legacy

Jean Blondel

Below the level of the United Nations, the Commonwealth is the only organization that spans all the continents. Yet the Commonwealth is, in many respects, less of an organization than the United Nations: its structure is loose and its decision-making process is not formalized and does not lead to binding arrangements. At best, there are a number of "understandings" that give the Commonwealth the character of a club whose members stay together because, presumably, they find some benefits in doing so. Britain has clearly lost any superior position in this club: there is no way in which she could impose a policy line even if she was tempted to do so.

The Commonwealth thus has an institutional framework so vague that it is nonexistent; moreover, the broad cultural background, as well as the socioeconomic characteristics of the forty-seven countries that belong to it, are vastly different.[1] Four of them constitute the Old Commonwealth (Britain, Canada, Australia, and New Zealand), the Republic of Ireland having voluntarily left in 1949, and South Africa having, in effect, been made to leave in 1961. Two other countries, Cyprus and Malta, can be said to belong, in a broad sense, to the "white" Commonwealth, although they were colonies and became independent in the 1960s. The other forty-one members are divided fairly evenly among Central American or Caribbean countries (eleven states), black African countries (fifteen states), and Asian and Pacific countries (fifteen states). All races are represented and all major religions are practiced. There are rich and poor states; there are very large and populous countries, as well as tiny ones. Perhaps the one widespread characteristic—which may politically be of some importance—is that the Commonwealth is composed of twenty-five island countries, while, among the more than a hundred other polities in the world, only sixteen are islands. There are, of course, also large continental countries (India, Canada, Australia), as well as states with borders and coasts, but there are relatively few land-locked members of the Commonwealth, all of them being in black Africa.

Despite their diversity and weak legal bonds, Commonwealth countries are tied together in many ways. To begin with, although many of the new Commonwealth countries have adopted national languages, English is an important vehicle of communication. This makes it possible for the flow of information between Commonwealth countries to be substantial and for diffusion to take place on a large scale.[2] Ideas, suggestions, proposals, and policies are generally well-known from one country to another: if they are not, there are established channels through which one can easily find out what is being proposed or has been adopted in other Commonwealth countries. In many aspects of social life there is a certain commonality of approach that constitutes a context allowing for similarities in political life to occur.

Admittedly, variations in the extent of diffusion also are substantial, as there are clearly differences in the extent to which member countries wish to follow procedures that have been adopted in others in the group. It may not be surprising to find that British influence has been vast in the Old Commonwealth, since it is largely populated by persons of British stock. But in the New Commonwealth, very long periods of colonization in most of the Caribbean countries contrast with a relatively short British rule in many parts of black Africa, especially in the interior. In Uganda and Tanzania, for instance, the British were in control for less than half a century, Germany having been the colonial power until 1914; in some other countries, colonization by the United Kingdom did not last more than a hundred years and often much less.

Common Characteristics of Commonwealth Political Systems

This complex mixture of similarities and differences in the overall approach to political and social life within the Commonwealth clearly constitutes an important element, accounting for a substantial degree of commonality of specific political structures and patterns of political behavior. Specifically, Commonwealth countries are appreciably more likely than others, especially other Third World countries, to operate under what might be termed an *effective party system*. Admittedly, there is a marked split among Commonwealth countries—some are ruled by a single party: others have a pluralistic system. But, in each of these two categories, Commonwealth countries form a special group. On the one hand, they are more likely than any other set of pluralistic countries to have two (or near two) party systems—a point that is often related, of course, to the "first-past-the-post" electoral system, which rarely exists outside the Commonwealth. On the other hand, the Commonwealth is the group in which one finds the most lively and, at least in relative terms, liberal single-party systems. This means that Commonwealth countries are more likely than others, and in particular more likely than other Third World countries, to have an effective party system. There is a greater probability that the political system will have extensive roots in the population and, consequently, will remain stable—a point to which we shall return. This also means that the recruitment of political leaders will tend to occur through parties and not, as is often the case elsewhere, through the army or the civil service. But there is more: in many Commonwealth countries, both those of the prime ministerial variety and many of those with strong presidential systems, Parliament plays a significant part, if not in the decision-making process, at least in the determination of the context or arena within which politics takes place. Thus political leadership emerges through Parliament and is connected to Parliament to a much greater extent than is the case elsewhere.

Commonwealth countries not only are characterized by a stronger party structure than most other countries, but also display interesting common characteristics with respect to governmental arrangements. It may not be that British influence alone is responsible for the existence of these common characteristics, but it is interesting that, by and large, the constitutional structure and behavioral patterns prevailing in the Commonwealth are markedly different from those of other Third World countries. If we concentrate on the thirty-seven countries that are both relatively large and were independent before the end of the 1970s, we notice that, with only four exceptions, they fall into two categories.[3] One is composed of competitive, pluralistic parliamentary systems. (Most interestingly, the Commonwealth includes effectively all the competitive prime ministerial systems in the Third World.) This group includes India, Malaysia, Jamaica, Barbados, and Mauritius. Sri Lanka was for generations a prime ministerial system, but it has become semipresidential—dualist—since the late 1970s. In Latin America, Asia, and Africa one does not find examples of competitive prime ministerial systems outside the Commonwealth.

The other category is that of strong presidential systems, of a "charismatic" type, based on a single party. Kenya, Tanzania, Zambia, Sierra Leone, and Malawi are the main examples of this type of political system. There are, admittedly, examples of analogous systems elsewhere, e.g., the Ivory Coast and Cameroon, with Senegal and Mexico being semicompetitive rather than one party. But the Commonwealth probably includes the majority of strong presidential single-party systems in the contemporary world, while it constitutes only a quarter of the world's polities. These strong presidential systems often have become, in recent years, organized on the basis of a "dual leadership" structure, with a prime minister appointed by the president to assist with administrative duties. This has been the case in Tanzania, Zambia, and Sierra Leone.[4]

There are very few examples in the Commonwealth of two types of leadership arrangements common elsewhere—the liberal presidential model and military rule. While "liberal presidentialism" has been common in Latin America, the only liberal presidential system that has existed in the Commonwealth was that in Nigeria, between 1979 and 1983. Military regimes have been confined to five countries: Ghana, Nigeria, Uganda, Bangla Desh, and, for one year, Sierra Leone. Also, although about half the countries of the world have had at least one period of military rule since the Second World War or since independence (including four of the eight countries which left the Commonwealth—Burma, Pakistan, Sudan, and Somalia), only a handful of the countries that remain in the Commonwealth have ever been ruled by the military.

Given these many similarities in the broad political and governmental framework of Commonwealth countries, it is clearly interesting to examine common characteristics among the leaders and ministers. After exploring the background of Commonwealth political leaders, one can go farther and see whether the general environment in which politics takes place and the background and recruitment of the leaders contribute to a form of government shaped differently from elsewhere. We shall examine the duration in office of ministers as well as some characteristics of the composition of Cabinets using data on heads of governments and ministers in the thirty-seven countries that (a) were independent before the end of the 1970s; (b) have a population of over 50,000 inhabitants over the period between independence or 1945 and the end of the 1970s; (c) have a population of over 50,000 inhabitants over the period between independence or 1945 and the end of 1980.[5] Although a number of background characteristics were available only for a proportion of these ministers, this proportion is sufficient to permit generalizations for the whole group as well as for a number of subgroups. Finally, we shall tentatively examine to what extent these broad governmental characteristics can be said to lead to a certain degree of commonality in the overall character and performance of the political systems.

Political Background of Commonwealth Political Leaders

In the Commonwealth, by and large, political leadership tends to emerge through party and Parliament.[6] This is naturally the case in the Old Commonwealth where nonparty ministers are almost never found, except in times of war, and where it is a convention or a rule that members of the Cabinet shall be members of the legislature. This is also usually the case in the New Commonwealth; there, too, ministers and prime ministers tend to be chosen among parliamentarians, and such persons are elected after having followed a career in one of the political parties.

There are, admittedly, some exceptions. First, new countries may not have had a preindependence legislature, or this legislature may have had only a very short existence; this was the case for some of the black African states in particular. As a result, ministers may be chosen from among members of the ruling party because of a preindependence party career, rather than because of a parliamentary-cum-party career. But, after a few years, it tends to become the norm for ministers to be drawn from among the members of Parliament (and, indeed, to lose their positions if they are not reelected to Parliament). This is the case even in some of the one-party systems, such as Tanzania or Kenya.

Naturally enough, what applies to ordinary ministers also applies to heads of governments. By the mid-1980s, only a minority of the original charismatic leaders were still in power, though Singapore, Guyana, Gambia, Lesotho, Malawi, Tanzania, and Zambia were still led by their founders. Many of the original leaders had not had a "normal" parliamentary career. A number of them had been selected by the British authorities to run their country because they had won an election in the preindependence period. But, in many countries, second-generation heads of governments have emerged after a career in the party, in Parliament, and, except if their party had never been in office before, as in Barbados, in government as well.

This general rule tends to apply even to those countries, principally black African, where a form of "strong" presidentialism replaced the prime ministerial or parliamentary system inherited from Britain. President Moi of Kenya, for instance, was a parliamentarian for a long period before becoming vice president and being subsequently elected president at the death of Kenyatta. It is possible that, in the future, nonparliamentarians will be directly elected to the presidency in some of the more presidential states, such as Tanzania or Zambia, but the absence of any succession by the mid-1980s makes it impossible to provide evidence for such a claim. It seems unlikely that this will be the case, however, as many of these strong presidential systems have become dualist in character: the prime minister, who is probably expected, in many cases, to become President, is usually a parliamentarian. Although Presidents are no longer members of the legislature, their previous career is thus likely to have followed a parliamentary pattern. They may be more or less distant from Parliament, but they at least have been associated with Parliament in the past.

Thus, the only genuine exceptions to the pattern of party-cum-parliamentary careers being prerequisites to political leadership in the Commonwealth are provided by the few cases in which civilian rule has been abolished and replaced by military government. In such cases, as in military regimes outside the Commonwealth, heads of government and cabinet ministers tend to be drawn, not from among Parliament or a party (which are usually abolished or suspended), but from the armed forces and civil service. Indeed, in Ghana and Nigeria, as in many other military regimes, these two origins have been reflected in the establishment of two parallel governments. The military council is composed primarily of members of the armed forces, while the regular government is drawn, to a substantial extent, from the civil service.

Ghana, Nigeria, Uganda, and Bangla Desh are, however, the only Commonwealth countries where such an exceptional model has obtained: elsewhere, the parliamentary-cum-party career prevails. This makes the Commonwealth political leadership intrinsically different from most of the Third World where it is very common, even in nonmilitary regimes, for military men and civil servants to achieve ministerial office directly. Although few Commonwealth parliaments can be said to be powerful in the decision-making sense, they are significant because, as in Britain, they are the main avenue to political leadership.

Social Background of Commonwealth Political Leaders

The party and parliamentary origins of leaders are unlikely to have any profound effect on the proportions of men and women among political leaders: as in almost every other country in the world, men form the overwhelming majority. Only three women, Thatcher, Gandhi, and Bandaranaike, have been head of a Commonwealth government since the end of World War II. This is manifestly a tiny proportion of the total, although it is fractionally higher than the proportion of women heads of government in the world as a whole (there were ten altogether in 154 countries between 1945 and 1981). The proportion of women ministers is also very small (as small in the Commonwealth as elsewhere); nor has there been any significant increase since the 1970s, despite the general pressure for greater involvement of women in public affairs. Altogether, forty-eight women have been ministers or prime ministers in the thirty-seven countries being examined here out of slightly less than 3,000 ministers (about 1.5 percent). Probably accidentally, the largest proportion of women ministers (about 5 percent) is in the Caribbean countries of the Commonwealth. In the four Old Commonwealth countries, there were eighteen women cabinet ministers (out of 670—under 3 percent). In black Africa and in South and South-East Asia, women formed about 1 percent of the total (12 out of 1,063 ministers and 6 out of 664 respectively), and there was also a woman minister in each of Malta and Cyprus. As elsewhere in the world women have not made a breakthrough among Common-wealth political leaders.

The age at which Commonwealth leaders come to office is not markedly different either from the age at which men and women become members of governments in the rest of the world. One finds about the same differences in the average age of incoming ministers between Old Commonwealth leaders and New Commonwealth leaders as between Western and Third World leaders. About half of Old Commonwealth ministers are appointed to their first cabinet post at fifty or older, while three-quarters of the New Common-wealth leaders come to office before they are fifty. There is some evidence that Commonwealth leaders are very marginally older, but it is not universal: 49 percent of the Old Commonwealth ministers are appointed to the cabinet before they are fifty, against 52 percent in other Western countries. Of the Commonwealth ministers from black Africa, 81 percent have been appointed to the government before they reached fifty as against 86 percent for the rest of the area. But, in South Asia, the age of incoming ministers is almost identical among Commonwealth and non-Commonwealth countries (exactly 75 percent reach office before they are fifty). In the Caribbean, the pattern is reversed with Commonwealth ministers achieving office appreciably earlier than their colleagues in Latin America (77 per-cent become ministers before they are fifty as compared to 61 per-cent for the area as a whole). This overall proportion, however, is largely the result of the older average age of incoming ministers in a small number of large countries in South America (Argentina, Brazil, Chile, and Peru), and there is little difference between the average age of ministers in Central America and in the Commonwealth coun-tries of the Caribbean.

There are substantial differences between Commonwealth and non-Commonwealth leaders with respect to occupational back-ground. For example, while in South and South-East Asia as a whole, 20 percent of the ministers are drawn from the military, only 7 percent of the Commonwealth ministers have the same origin (nearly half of these being found in Bangla Desh); while a quarter of the ministers are drawn from the military in black Africa as a whole, under a fifth of the Commonwealth political leaders of that area had a similar background, and these were found almost exclusively in Ghana, Nigeria, Uganda, and Sierra Leone.

There are some further distinctions, however. In every part of the Commonwealth, lawyers are better represented than in neighboring non-Commonwealth countries. Also, although the differences are very small in black Africa and in South Asia, business and manage-ment are generally better represented, especially in the Old Common-wealth and in the Caribbean. Finally, while the number of manual workers is very small everywhere except in Communist countries,

TABLE 1.

Occupational Background of Political Leaders (percentages)

	Army	Law	Civil Service	Engineers	Business Management	Teaching	Workers	Totals Overall	Totals In Sample
West									
Old Commonwealth	4	27	8	1	18	12	5	670	450
Cyprus & Malta	3	27	15	—	15	15	—	83	33
Western countries	7	20	15	3	13	17	4	3234	1945
Black Africa									
Commonwealth	19	15	12	3	7	21	3	1063	506
All	26	12	13	5	7	18	1	3806	1392
S. & SE. Asia									
Commonwealth	7	21	6	18	11	11	—	664	325
All	20	20	8	13	9	9	—	3002	1391
Latin America									
Commonwealth	1	29	4	8	17	14	4	226	93
All	36	19	2	14	5	8	0.2	4303	2033

*The results given here do not cover some occupations that are generally poorly represented.

there is fractionally higher representation of this group in several Commonwealth countries. This is also true for farmers.

There is, then, some tendency for the producers and the traditional professions to have a larger voice in the Commonwealth cabinets; there is, conversely, some tendency for the administrators or the planners to provide a somewhat smaller proportion of political leaders. The trend is not very marked, admittedly, but, in the New Commonwealth, given the smaller proportion of military men everywhere, one might have expected a larger proportion of civil servants and specialists if the civilian occupations had all benefited to the same extent. Civil servants are proportionately slightly less numerous in black Africa and in South Asia, while engineers and other specialists are somewhat less numerous in black Africa and in the Caribbean. With respect to engineers, only in South Asia does one find a reversal of this trend; this is indeed especially the case in India, and to a lesser extent in Sri Lanka and in Malaysia. With this one exception, one can say that technical and public service backgrounds play an apparently smaller part in leading to a ministerial career in the Commonwealth than elsewhere.

Commonwealth ministers thus have some common characteristics which tend to distinguish them from ministers in the rest of the world. The differences are not very large, but they tilt the cabinets to some extent, not merely in the direction of career politicians, but also toward the professions and business and away from the public service. The balance is shifted a little in the direction of the representation of outside groups, and of outside middle-class groups in particular. By being somewhat more political in origin, the Commonwealth political leaders are correspondingly a little more different than elsewhere from the public service officials who are responsible to them.

Commonwealth Political Leaders: Office Tenure

The duration of ministers in office is, both on average and in a large majority of cases, appreciably longer in the Commonwealth than in the rest of the non-Communist world. This state of affairs has to be seen in the context of relatively high turnover of ministers in most countries and of a very high turnover in some. Only in Communist countries and in the remaining traditional monarchies does the average tenure of ministers emerge as distinctly high (over six years), while in some parts of the world, especially in Latin America, it is distinctly low (between two and three years). With an average duration of four-and-a-half years, Commonwealth ministers stay in office almost a year and a half more than other leaders in the Third World and even half a year longer than Western European leaders. Indeed, the duration of ministers is above the world average in no less than

Area of Commonwealth

	Old Commonwealth & Mediterranean	Africa South of Sahara	South Asia & Pacific	Central America
10				
9			Tonga 9.2	
8			Singapore 8.7	
7				Trinidad 7.6
		Botswana 7.2	Maldive Rep. 7.1 Malaysia 7.1	
6	Malta 6.6	Kenya 6.9 Lesotho 6.8 Swailand 6.6		Bahamas 6.2
5	N. Zeland 5.5 Australia 5.5	Gambia 5.4	Sri Lanka 5.2	Barbados 5.6
4	Canada 4.8 U.K. 4.6 Cyprus 4.2	Mauritius 4.9 Tanzania 4.7 Zambia 4.7 Sierra Leone 4.2	Fiji 4.5 India 4.3	Jamaica 4.9 Guyana 4.3
3		Zimbabwe 3.6 Malawi 3.4 Nigeria 3.0	W. Samoa 3.8	Grenada 3.2
2		Ghana 2.6 Uganda 2.5 Seychelles 2.4	Bangla Desh 2.3 Papua N.G. 2.2	

FIGURE 1. Ministerial Duration in Commonwealth Countries from 1945 or Independence to End of 1980, in years

twenty-eight of the thirty-seven Commonwealth countries analyzed here.

The tenure of Commonwealth ministers is not merely above average for the whole world, it is also above average in each region, although there are variations in the extent of the difference. The gap is largest in the Americas, where the average for Latin American states is slightly over two years and that of the six Commonwealth countries is over five years. Only two Latin American states, Paraguay and Mexico, have had an average duration of ministers and heads of governments longer than any one of the six Caribbean Commonwealth countries. The difference is a little less marked in South and South-East Asia (4.6 years instead of 3.1 years on average), yet eight of the Commonwealth states of the area (all except Bangla Desh and Papua New Guinea) had a duration of ministers longer than the world average. The difference is only one year between Old Commonwealth countries and other Western states, and it is smallest in black Africa, in part because black African ministers have achieved the longest duration in office throughout the Third World (over 3.6 years and slightly more than the world average). Commonwealth political leaders is that area do, nonetheless, last a few months longer than their colleagues in other countries of the region.

Institutional and Behavioral Patterns in the Tenure of Commonwealth Political Leaders

Although the average tenure of Commonwealth political leaders is not long in an absolute sense, it is substantially longer than that for leaders of most other countries. This is not a fortuitous circumstance, nor is it the result of special situations in a variety of Commonwealth countries. There is such a pervasive trend that an explanation of a general character has to be found in the political structure and behavior of Commonwealth countries.

An examination of the tenure of heads of governments and ministers in these political systems strongly suggests that the political system itself has a marked effect on tenure. On the whole, ministers and heads of governments remain in office for long periods in Communist states, as they do in the few remaining traditional monarchies. On the other hand, office tenure is short in liberal presidential systems and military regimes, irrespective of whether these last or not; the short tenure of ministers is only to a limited extent the consequence of the collapse of the regime. The duration of political leaders is intermediate between these two extremes in prime ministerial systems and in strong presidential regimes.

The analysis of these differences is described in detail elsewhere (see Blondel, 1985: chs. 5, 6). Broadly speaking, there are several possibly relevant institutional and behavioral factors. For instance, institutional factors account for the short duration of ministers in liberal presidential systems in two ways: presidents often are elected for a relatively short period (five or six years maximum), and presidential regimes are highly personalized—therefore it is very rare for new presidents to wish to reappoint to office men and women who have served under a previous president. As there are no presidential systems of the liberal variety among Commonwealth states, there are no political leaders in the group whose duration in office has been shortened for this reason.

In prime ministerial or parliamentary systems, the rule of the head of the government is normally less personalized. In general, it is the party that is elected to power, and ministers, together with the prime minister, constitute the leadership of the party. Since there is a team, it is often not easy, or even possible, for a prime minister to exercise much discretion in the choice of ministers. Consequently, it is not unusual for ministers to remain in office when the prime minister retires and his or her successor, who is likely to have been one of the ministers, takes office. Moreover, unlike liberal presidential systems, prime ministerial systems do not fix a term to the tenure for the head of the government. Taken together, these factors contribute to the greater duration of ministers in prime ministerial systems as compared to liberal presidential regimes.

In addition, when parties alternate in office, ministerial careers will be shorter than if the same party is continuously returned. This is in large part why Sweden achieved a very high rate of ministerial longevity between 1945 and 1976: this is also how Singapore and Malaysia, near-single party systems, have had ministers who have enjoyed lengthy careers. Office tenure is shorter when the party system is complex and there are shifting coalitions. Coalitions form and reform and heads of governments often change frequently in the interims between elections.

In the Commonwealth, since the prime ministerial systems tend to be of the two-party or two-party-plus variety, one of the parties usually has an absolute majority in Parliament. Consequently, the average duration of ministers tends to be greater among Commonwealth prime ministerial systems than in the majority of others. This is why ministers in the Old Commonwealth last a full year longer than ministers in Western European countries.

The tenure of ministers also is relatively long in strong presidential systems. This is because, in such systems, the combination of a charismatic president and a single party militates against volatile ministerial careers. The head of state often has sufficient authority to stay in office for substantial periods. Relatedly, founders of states are among the heads of governments who have the highest probability of staying in office for periods of ten years or more, and many of the charismatic presidents, in the Commonwealth and elsewhere, have been founders of states. These men are not encumbered—and they see to it that they are not encumbered—by any constitutional rule whereby they cannot stand for election more than two terms. Their original prestige is so high that, in most cases, it takes a very long time for their legitimacy to be eroded. Of course, some of them (significantly more outside the Commonwealth than within it) are toppled by military coups. This is probably where the existence of a relatively strong single-party structure plays a part: where the party is weak and lacks roots in the nation, leaders are more isolated and may be more easily overthrown.

These heads of states (and to a lesser extent their successors) have enough authority that they find it unnecessary to change their ministers frequently. To do so would amount to breaking the team that has come to power after independence. There is limited fear that ministers will become dangerous potential opponents (though this has happened in a number of cases). In many countries, then, strong charismatic presidents have kept their ministers in office for a number of years. Only after a considerable time has elapsed does the need to rejuvenate the team become pressing. Yet it is relatively rare for these changes to be numerous or rapid. Wholesale or frequent ministerial change tends to happen only when the head of state begins to see his authority wane. This is probably the reason why President Banda of Malawi, who originally had a stable cabinet, came to change his ministers frequently in the 1970s. But this development contrasts with the much longer tenure of ministers in other presidential polities of the Commonwealth. Thus, in Tanzania, Zambia, and Kenya, the duration of ministers is well above the average for the region and for the world.

Political leaders in Commonwealth prime ministerial and presidential regimes are thereby likely to remain in office longer than leaders in other prime ministerial or strong presidential polities. At the same time, there have been too few military regimes in the Commonwealth to reduce the average markedly. It may seem *prima facie* surprising that the duration of ministers in military regimes should be short. The authors of coups come to office in order to clean up and stabilize government: they also seem to possess the power to rule unfettered by the institutions and constraints that prevail in many civilian political systems. Yet, in practice, their power is rather limited. In many cases, military leaders neither have the legitimacy nor the experience to rule the country they take over. They find it difficult, in particular, to select competent ministers to run government departments. Consequently, even apart from the fact that many military regimes are replaced after only a few years, ministers often are changed and, as in liberal presidential systems, they are rarely reappointed afterwards. This is the main reason why, on the whole, ministerial duration in military regimes tends to be shorter than average. One also can understand why Latin American countries tend to have the most transient ministers of all since they oscillate between military and liberal presidential governments.

The Commonwealth countries that have had military regimes are indeed among those that have also had the lowest average duration of ministers: four of the six Commonwealth countries in which the average duration of ministers has been under three years have had military rule for long periods. (The other two are the Seychelles, which has been politically unstable, and Papua New Guinea, which, similar to the Seychelles, had been independent for only a few years by the beginning of the 1980s.) Furthermore, in the three African Commonwealth countries characterized by long periods of military rule, i.e., Ghana, Nigeria, and Uganda, the duration of ministers was substantially above average before the first military takeover. This confirms the general effect of military rule on ministerial duration. (In Bangla Desh, instability has been such that it is not meaningful to calculate the duration of ministers under civilian rule, although it was a little longer in the early years after independence.)

Tenure of Commonwealth Ministers and the British Legacy

Ministers' tenure is longer in the Commonwealth than elsewhere in the West and the Third World. This state of affairs is clearly no accident. It must be related in very large part to the impact of the British legacy in both the Old and New Commonwealth. First, Britain clearly invented the prime ministerial system and especially the prime ministerial system based on streamlined party arrangements. A rather similar system may have developed independently in Scandinavia, but its extension to the continent of Europe, the only area outside the Commonwealth where it took roots, came as a result of British influence. Outside the Commonwealth and Western Europe, this type of system scarcely exists in the world. It seems, therefore, most unlikely that countries now in the Commonwealth, especially Third World countries, would have adopted such a system of government had it not been for British influence. Thus, Britain helped to create a political context favorable to the longer tenure of ministers.

The impact of the British legacy also can be found in the existence of relatively strong party systems, whether of the competitive or single variety. This, in turn, has given the political process greater cohesion than in most countries elsewhere in the Third World. Parties in these systems channel at least some demands; they attempt to smooth up the process of implementation; and they are important elements in the recruitment of political leaders. In the New Commonwealth, this is true, not only in India, Malaysia, Sri Lanka, Jamaica, and Mauritius, but also in Tanzania and Zambia. In the decolonization period, Britain placed a premium on the establishment of parties; she did so more often and more straightforwardly than France, Belgium, or Holland. As a result, the governmental structure and its underpinnings in society were strengthened; this, in turn, contributed to a reduction in the potential for military coups. It surely is no accident that military takeovers are rarer in the Commonwealth than in the rest of the world. Also, these relatively strong parties—both in competitive and in single-party systems—have contributed to the emergence of teams of political leaders who have been accustomed, more than in other new countries, to live and operate together. Governments thus have been structured on a more collective, or at least more oligarchical, manner than they are in the rest of the Third World, where one-man rule often predominates. We must now examine the characteristics of these governmental structures to see to what extent they differ in the Commonwealth from the rest of the Third World.

Political Leadership in the Commonwealth: More Teams and Less One-Man Rule

The study of governmental decision-making processes in the contemporary world is still in its infancy. We know little about the ways in which cabinets operate, except for a small number of Western countries and, even in these cases, comparisons have been few and rather unsystematic.[7] Although there is much discussion as to whether cabinets make collective decisions or are dominated by a president or prime minister, we are unable to give a precise account of the real situation in the vast majority of countries.

One is forced to rely to a very large extent on somewhat imprecise and peripheral indices that can throw only limited light on the nature of the decision-making processes in Cabinets and, therefore, on the style of leadership.[8] One indicator is the presence of a dual system of leadership (a development that has taken place in many countries) or a dual system of government (as exists in Communist countries and in some military regimes). But clues also emerge from the examination of the movements of ministers and of the posts they occupy—for instance, discovering whether a large number of ministers are appointed to posts that correspond to their prior training. This is the case in the Soviet Union, and it seems fair to conclude that ministers are more likely to be technical or managerial than political in that country. For instance, too, governments are more likely to be collective if they are composed of ministers who move from post to post. If this happens, several political leaders are likely to know the affairs of a number of sectors of government; while, if they remain in the same post, their knowledge, and possibly their interests, are likely to be confined to one field only.

One must exercise some caution in drawing conclusions, admittedly, since one of the apparently most collective governments, the Swiss federal council, is composed of ministers who almost never move from one post to another. But, in this case, the size of the cabinet (seven ministers instead of an average of twenty) and the length of tenure (very high in Switzerland) are probably essential elements. This is why an important aspect of the analysis also must be the duration of ministers in office, especially if, among the ministers, a substantial proportion remains in government for long periods.

Amateurs in Commonwealth Governments

Commonwealth Cabinets, on the whole, tend to be composed of ministers who are less technical and more political. They have the characteristics of amateur bodies rather than those of specialist organizations. For the purpose of an analysis of cabinets, *amateur* ministers are those whose occupational backgrounds have not prepared them in any particular way for the governmental posts they occupy.[9] Overall, across the world, specialists are a minority, albeit a substantial one. Communist ministers are more specialized than others: somewhat over half of them occupy political leadership positions corresponding to their previous training. But specialists also constitute a third of the Atlantic and black African ministers and two-fifths or more of those elsewhere.[10]

In the Commonwealth, specialists are a smaller minority, except in South Asia (Table 2). In the Old Commonwealth, the percentage of specialists ranges from 15 to 23 percent—appreciably below the 30 percent average for Western countries. In black African countries nine of eleven where the percentage of specialists is lowest (21 percent or less) belong to the Commonwealth. As for Caribbean countries, two of them, Jamaica and Barbados, are among the three Latin American countries that have the lowest percentage of specialists, while the others, Guyana and Trinidad, have an appreciably higher proportion of specialist ministers (42 percent), but one which is lower than that of the majority of countries in the region (47 percent).

Only in South Asia does one find several Commonwealth countries with high or very high proportions of specialists in ministerial posts (66 percent in Singapore, 58 percent in Western Samoa, 55 percent in India), and only in that region do Commonwealth countries rank among states with the highest proportion of specialists. This is consistent with and is probably related to the presence of a substantial proportion of engineers and of other graduate technicians among South Asian Commonwealth ministers. In these countries, in one respect at least, political leadership has the technical character which it has in many Third World and other countries.[11]

In other Commonwealth countries, on the contrary, there is a tradition whereby ministers are appointed because they have prior careers in the party, and at least in part, because they are brokers or representatives rather than because they are deemed especially competent to supervise the affairs of a government department. In this respect, Commonwealth ministers contrast particularly sharply with those in the Communist world, especially in the Soviet Union. Other countries, both Western and Third World, are somewhere between these two extremes. In South Asia, in contrast, it seems to have been possible to marry the traditions of parliamentary and

TABLE 2.

Specialists in Commonwealth Cabinets (percentages)

Old Commonwealth		Black Africa		South and Southeast Asia	
United Kingdom	15	Lesotho	6	Malaysia	24
New Zealand	21	Malawi	14	Maldive Republic	40
Australia	22	Sierra Leone	17	Sri Lanka	48
Canada	23	Botswana	18	All S. & SE. Asia	48
		Ghana	19		
All Western		Swaziland	20	India	55
Countries	30	Zambia	20	W. Samoa	58
Malta	31	Zimbabwe	20	Singapore	66
Cyprus	54	Nigeria	21	Latin America	
		Kenya	23		
		Mauritius	25	Jamaica	15
		Tanzania	30	Barbados	26
		All Black Africa	31	Guyana	42
				Trinidad	42
		Gambia	40	All Latin America	47
		Uganda	40		

* 30 countries independent prior to 1970

cabinet government with a large degree of concern for the technical competence of ministers. Elsewhere, the (often unconscious) choice appears to have been to give a premium to political ministers. Recruiting such persons must have some impact on government decision-making processes and must lead to some extent to a more collective executive.

Internal Movements Within the Cabinet

A tendency toward a more collective government is reinforced by Commonwealth ministers being more likely than others to move from post to post. Across the world, this type of movement is relatively rare. Even in Western countries, where it is most frequent, two-thirds of the ministers never occupy more than one position. Elsewhere, the proportion of government members who never direct more than one department is as high as three-quarters.

Differences between Commonwealth countries and others should not be exaggerated, however, as, even in the Commonwealth, a majority of ministers never occupy more than one departmental post. But the proportions of "mobile" political leaders are nonetheless appreciably larger than elsewhere. Among the thirty Commonwealth countries independent before 1970, one finds only five in which the percentage of mobile ministers is low or very low, while in twenty-five the proportion is above average (Table 3). (For the more recently

TABLE 3.

Mobile Ministers in Commonwealth Cabinets (percentages)

Old Commonwealth		Black Africa		South and Southeast Asia	
Canada	47	Botswana	70	Malaysia	62
United Kingdom	46	Kenya	61	Maldive Republic	57
Australia	45	Zambia	57	India	41
New Zealand	40	Lesotho	53	Singapore	36
		Sierra Leone	49	Sri Lanka	35
All Western		Gambia	42		
Countries	33	Ghana	40	All S. & SE. Asia	24
Malta	42			West Samoa	17
Cyprus	18	All Black Africa	33	Latin America	
		Tanzania	32		
		Swaziland	32		
		Zimbabwe	32	Barbados	54
		Malawi	31	Trinidad	49
		Nigeria	25	Jamaica	36
		Uganda	24	Guyana	31
		Mauritius	17	All Latin American	14

World average: 25

*Mobile is defined as having held at least two different successive posts in the Cabinet. Data are for 30 countries independent prior to 1970.

established countries, the probability of internal movement within the cabinet is naturally lower.) In nine of this latter group mobile ministers constitute between two-fifths and one-half of the total; in a further seven, half or over half the ministers have held at least two posts. Mobile ministers are thus not only to be found in the Old Commonwealth; rather they are numerous in every part of the New Commonwealth.

Commonwealth ministers not only are more mobile, but also are appreciably more likely than other ministers to have what might be called a ubiquitous career, being appointed to several departments in succession. Overall, the truly mobile ministers—those who are appointed to at least four different posts in succession— constitute only 3 percent of all the ministers. There are eighteen countries, however, where these ubiquitous ministers form between 5 and 10 percent of the total number of cabinet office-holders and seven of these belong to the Commonwealth. There are a further nineteen countries where these ministers formed over 10 percent of the total number of political leaders and eleven of these belonged to the Commonwealth. Overall, half the countries that have very mobile ministers are Commonwealth countries, while the Commonwealth includes under a quarter of the countries of the world.

The Long-Standing Ministers in the Commonwealth

Political leadership in the Commonwealth is thus composed proportionately more of amateurs and of persons who occupy more than
one post in the government in succession. Such ministers, it would
seem, are more likely than others to be involved in the affairs of the
whole government. This impression is further reinforced by the finding that many Commonwealth office holders remain in cabinet for
longer periods than in most other parts of the world. Overall, about 7
percent of the members of contemporary governments hold office for
a decade or more. The proportion is much higher in the Commonwealth, though it is higher still in Communist states.

This is true both in the Old and in the New Commonwealth. For
instance five of the six black African countries in which over 20
percent of the ministers lasted ten years in office or more are members of the Commonwealth and three of the four South and Southeast
Asian countries where long-standing ministers form 20 percent of
the total also belong to the Commonwealth. Similarly, four Caribbean Commonwealth countries are among the six Latin American
countries in which the proportion of long-standing ministers is
above 10 percent. Overall, in only 24 of 138 countries in existence
before 1970 did 20 percent of the ministers remain in office ten years
or more: a third of these were Communist states; but nine of the
remaining sixteen were Commonwealth countries. In contrast, one
finds only two Commonwealth countries (significantly Ghana and
Nigeria) among the fifty-five states in which the proportion of long-
standing ministers is below 5 percent and another five among
twenty-five countries in which the proportion of long-standing ministers is between 5 and 10 percent.

Single and Collective Leadership in Commonwealth Cabinets

Since ministers of Commonwealth governments often are able to
participate in the affairs of a number of departments in succession,
and since a substantial proportion remain in office for long periods,
they are, to a degree, able to participate actively in the decision-making process of the whole Cabinet. Yet, in Commonwealth governments, presidents and prime ministers are often powerful, equally
long-standing, and indeed endowed with charismatic authority.
This is true not only in new states, but also in countries of the Old
Commonwealth: Menzies and Trudeau are only two examples of
prime ministers whose influence on the Cabinet and the political
system was comparable to that which some Third-World presidents
and prime ministers had on their countries.

Thus, the relatively larger role (at least some) cabinet members
may be in a position to exercise because of their knowledge of the

affairs of a number of departments has to be balanced against the widespread influence heads of governments may achieve. There exists an equilibrium, which shifts from time to time and varies appreciably from country to country, that seems characteristic of Commonwealth Cabinets. There is probably less dominance by one man than in many other political systems, although, conversely, there are probably no instances where Cabinets are as collective as they are (occasionally) in a number of Western European countries in which coalitions are the rule.

By and large, Commonwealth governments have been able to maintain this equilibrium because of the role of parties and, to a lesser extent, the legislature in the recruitment process and in the establishment of conventions of political life. Parties and Parliaments circumscribe the group from which ministers can, on the whole, be chosen, with the former operating in this fashion even in some of the more charismatic presidential systems of the Commonwealth. As a result, members of the group from which ministers are drawn know each other rather well and become accustomed to working together, sometimes even before they are appointed to the cabinet. It is, therefore, difficult for the head of government to confine members of the group to a specific field. There are, of course, major differences, but they seem rather less marked than among other countries. While, from a British point of view, it often may seem that the power of the prime minister is immense and that collective decision making has wholly disappeared, the reality is that, on balance and by comparison with many countries of the contemporary world, Great Britain and other Commonwealth states have been able to maintain a greater amount of influence for ordinary cabinet ministers while continuing to extol the power and prestige of presidents and prime ministers.

The Performance of Commonwealth Governments

The study of governmental performance has to progress substantially before it becomes possible to assess accurately the influence of political factors on policy outcomes. Despite several path-breaking studies, such as those of Wilensky (1975) and Jackman (1975), as well as the work of Gurr (1972) on political violence, the part played by governmental institutions remains obscure. This is due, to some extent, to the use of data related to an earlier period (the 1960s and before, in most cases). It also is the result of the limited amount of data available on strictly political indicators and, in particular, governmental structures. Obviously, the large number of monographs devoted to individual countries are of little help in this respect, especially if one wishes to compare Commonwealth with non-Commonwealth countries.

Conclusions on the performance of Commonwealth countries are, therefore, inevitably tentative at this point. However, a number of remarks can be made relating both to the general impact of the governmental setting and to some aspects of public policy. First, it is possible to compare the stability of Commonwealth and non-Commonwealth countries. Granted that regime stability can provide only a very general indicator of the overall effectiveness of political systems, it is nonetheless the case that, negatively at least, very unstable regimes can be expected to be ineffective and to be held in low public esteem. Second, it is possible to compare the extent to which Commonwealth and non-Commonwealth countries resemble each other from the point of view of the relative openness of procedures and the degree of pluralism in political life. Third, in some respects at least, it is possible to obtain a general impression of the extent to which Commonwealth countries achieve different results from those of other countries and imitate each other in some of their policies.

The Stability of Commonwealth Political Systems

As observed, leadership in the New Commonwealth is more durable, probably more collective, and on the whole more political than that of Third-World countries in general. It is also noticeable that Commonwealth political systems proved to be more stable than those of the rest of the world. Not only do ministers and heads of governments remain in office for longer periods, but the process of government is smoother and more regular. Specifically, there have been markedly fewer coups in New Commonwealth countries than elsewhere in the Third World.

There are only three major exceptions to this general rule—Ghana, Nigeria, and Uganda. In a fourth country, Bangla Desh, the circumstances in which independence occurred were so difficult that it is unrealistic to expect the stabilizing formulas characteristic of most Commonwealth countries. But Ghana, Nigeria, and Uganda (as well as, to a more limited extent, Sierra Leone) are manifest exceptions to the general stability of the group. Attempts at explanation of instability of Third World political systems are notoriously unsatisfactory. In his *Politics in Africa,* Austin (1984:19) warns against premature conclusions and suggests "half a dozen" possible explanations: "interference from outside, either supportive or hostile; the effect (harmful or beneficial) of the route to independence; the character of the nationalist movement; the sociopolitical and military makeup of the former colonial state; the lack of material resources and the political skill of the leaders. It is a formidable list."

Specific explanations can, of course, be given which may seem to account, ex post facto, for the three military regimes in Ghana, the two military regimes in Nigeria, and the military rule of Amin in Uganda.

It is clear, for instance, that the lack of national unity has played, and continues to play, a major part in the problems of Uganda and Nigeria. To a lesser extent, there have been similar problems in Ghana and, indeed, in Sierra Leone. But as Austin notes: "there are exceptions: Ghana is hardly a difficult country to govern. . . . Zambia is divided ethnically to a greater degree than Ghana, yet Kaunda has been in office since independence" (Austin, 1984:21). One can add other explanations, ranging from the purely political point (Nkrumah's regime was much too oppressive) to economic considerations (e.g., that a fall in the price of cocoa seems to precede military coups in Ghana) (Selassie, 1974:242–54).

As a matter of fact, the stability of the other black African Commonwealth countries may be somewhat exaggerated. Although only three of them had really successful military coups, the majority of the others have experienced attempted coups and/or strong disturbances. A military regime lasted one year in Sierra Leone; the 1981 coup in Gambia should perhaps be rated as having been successful since it was crushed only because of the intervention of Senegalese troops. There also have been attempts at coups in Kenya, Tanzania, and Zambia. In Lesotho, the conflict between king and prime minister has taken acute proportions and, in the Seychelles, a civilian coup replaced the legally elected government. Thus, although the proportion of black African Commonwealth governments that remained in office is larger than that of other black African governments, the potential for instability in the black African countries of the Commonwealth appears substantial.

Yet, even if all these states were to undergo successful military coups, it still would remain the case that Commonwealth countries are in general more stable than other Third-World nations. Not only the mainly island Commonwealth states of the Caribbean and the Pacific, but the continental countries of South Asia have, in the main, had stable governments and, indeed, stable pluralistic ones, to a much greater extent than other countries of these regions.

Pluralism in the Commonwealth

The British legacy has not merely brought about political stability, it also has often led to the maintenance of a greater degree of competitiveness and even of tolerance than is common in comparable countries outside the Commonwealth. This obviously is true of the political systems in which there are two or more significant parties. There are proportionately more countries of this type in the Commonwealth than in the rest of the Third World, including Latin America, and it must be remembered that the latter typically oscillate between pluralistic regimes and authoritarian rule. About half (sixteen out of thirty-two) of the Third-World Commonwealth countries that have been independent for a decade or more continuously have had pluralistic political systems. But even some of the single-party systems display pluralistic characteristics, for instance, when there is some competition within the party, or when there is questioning of at least some governmental activities in the legislature (Barkan and Okumu, 1979). Given the limited data presently at the disposal of political scientists and the crude instruments by which pluralism can be measured in modern societies, it is difficult to be precise about the extent and range of competition in Commonwealth polities. But, with few exceptions, political leadership in the Commonwealth seems somewhat more open, tolerant, and responsive than that in other countries.

Public Policy

Greater political stability and greater pluralism are two elements in the performance of political systems; but they may be viewed, by some at least, as less important than aspects of performance relating to social and economic outcomes. In this regard, it may be argued that, far from promoting greater social and economic development, regime stability and pluralism might result in lower efficiency and greater delays in adopting and implementing reforms. Analysis of relationships between political characteristics and policy performance is still too primitive for firm conclusions to be drawn, but it can be said that, in the Third World, stability and pluralism are not highly correlated with greater economic and social development.[12]

Indeed, it could be argued that one characteristic of political leadership in the Commonwealth is likely to lead to reduced efficiency, i.e. (with the remarkable exception of the South Asian countries) this leadership is, in the main, more specifically political and less managerial and technical than elsewhere in the Third World. The point has been made in relation to Britain herself: the relative economic decline she suffered in the 1960s and 1970s has been attributed in part to the fact that her political leadership was composed of persons who were more political and less technically competent than that of some of her neighbors.[13]

Whether this judgment about the influence of Britain's political leadership on its governmental performance is correct is still unclear. It is, therefore, even more difficult to assess whether a political leadership of the same type has or has not been relatively detrimental to the economic development of the countries of the Commonwealth. It does not appear to be the case, however, that these countries have been appreciably less successful economically than other comparable systems. An index based on the ranking of the large majority (twenty-eight) of the Commonwealth countries independent before the 1970s shows that the evolution of GNP per capita varied broadly in the same manner in both Commonwealth and non-

Commonwealth cases: the average rank of these twenty-eight Commonwealth countries dropped from 72.2 to 81.8 between 1973 and 1979, but the 1979 data include nine more countries than in 1973 (141 instead of 132).[14] Indeed, if the fourteen Commonwealth countries from black Africa for which there are data are compared to fifteen ex-French territories of the area, the drop in ranking is almost exactly the same. Over this period, these Commonwealth countries had not done better or worse than the rest of the world. Nor does it appear that India or Sri Lanka has been markedly more successful because their political leadership has included a sizable proportion of technicians and engineers. It is manifestly not the case that Commonwealth countries have been unable to achieve success.

An analysis of the relationship between political characteristics and socioeconomic performance clearly requires a gradual and patient examination of the interplay of a multiplicity of factors. One of these is peculiarly relevant to the Commonwealth, namely the part played by diffusion and imitation among particular groups of countries. As noted at the outset, the diffusion of information is substantial among Commonwealth countries, though its precise extent has not yet been measured.[15] What is known is that in a number of instances, Commonwealth countries have adopted a policy already implemented elsewhere or have rejected a policy another country had found unsuccessful. Most of the cases which have been monitored are relatively technical and could not have affected the socioeconomic development of the country concerned more than marginally; but there is evidence that the process of diffusion also extended to more important policies. There is also evidence that, in some respects at least, Commonwealth countries appear to have some special patterns of expenditure. In particular, they seem to spend somewhat more on health than might be expected on the basis of per capita GNP, and they perhaps also spend a little more on education. There is, therefore, a prima facie case for believing that, to some extent, Commonwealth countries constitute more than just a political category, but are a social and economic category as well, and that the experience of some members of the group has a bearing on the policies adopted by others.

Political life, and indeed perhaps socioeconomic life, in the Commonwealth has a number of common characteristics. In the field of leadership, it is clear that, in contrast to other countries, there are characteristics that make Commonwealth leadership more specifically political. It also is clear that the Commonwealth owes this characteristic to Britain. In both the Old and the New Commonwealth, Britain has laid conditions and exercised influence such that a political class has emerged that is on the whole more open than elsewhere and that plays the game of politics according to rules, which are rather more regular than those adopted by many other countries. There were great hopes, in the late 1940s, when India and Pakistan became independent: Pakistan left the Commonwealth, perhaps in part because the modes of behavior of its leaders did not accord with some of the general rules of the members of the "club"; but India remained a witness to Britain having given independence to what was and continues to be the largest relatively stable and broadly liberal system the world has ever known.

Notes

1. The Commonwealth comprises (as of 1983) (a) seventeen countries that recognize the Queen as Head of State in their country: *Old Commonwealth*—Australia, Canada, New Zealand, and the United Kingdom; *Central America*—Antigua and Barbuda, Bahamas, Barbados, Belize, Grenada, Jamaica, Saint Lucia, Saint Vincent, and the Grenadines; *black Africa*—Mauritius; *South Asia and Pacific*—Fiji, Papua New Guinea, Solomon Island, and Tuvalu; (b) thirty countries that recognize the Queen as Head of the Commonwealth: *Mediterranean*—The Republics of Cyprus and Malta; *Central America*—The Republics of Dominica Guyana and Trinidad and Tobago; *black Africa*—The Republics of Botswana, Gambia, Ghana, Kenya, Malawi, Nigeria, Seychelles, Sierra Leone, Uganda, Tanzania, Zambia, Zimbabwe, and the kingdoms of Lesotho and Swaziland; *South Asia and Pacific*—The Republics of Bangla Desh, India, Kiribati, Maldive, Nauru, Singapore, Sri Lanka, Vanuatu, the Federation of Malaysia, the Kingdom of Tonga, and the Independent State of Western Samoa. Eight states left the Commonwealth: Burma, Cameroon (South), Ireland, Pakistan, Somalia, South Africa, Sudan, and South Yemen.

2. See, in particular, Leichter (1983). The bibliography at the end of this article gives further examples of diffusion. On political structures, see Laing (1962–63).

3. The following ten countries are not included in the analysis because they are either too small (below 50,000 in population) or too recently independent (since 1980): Antigua and Barbuda, Belize, Dominica, Saint Lucia, Saint Vincent in the Caribbean and, in the Pacific, Kiribati, Nauru, Solomon Islands, Tuvalu and Vanuatu.

4. As noted, Sri Lanka also has adopted a dualist form of government within the context of a pluralist party system.

5. The present paper is based on data collected for a world-wide study of heads of governments and ministers. The collection was based on a substantial variety of source books. Social background data cover approximately half the ministers, while duration and positions in the Cabinet are very nearly complete. The first part of the analysis has been published in Blondel (1980). For the analysis of ministers see Blondel (1985). The findings analyzed especially for this paper are not viewed as a substitute for case-studies of countries or individual leaders. Rather the aim is to give a general picture of leadership characteristics, one which perforce cannot emerge from studies of particular leaders or individual countries.

6. See, Spengler (1966) and Braibanti (1966). The latter author points

out that a more "managerial" or "etatistic" tradition was introduced in administration (in part under American influence).

7. See Blondel (1982). There are no truly comparative studies of Cabinets. See, however, Rose and Suleiman (1980) in relation to a number of Western countries.

8. An obviously more direct form of analysis would result from interviews of ministers, but these are rare, even on a single-country basis. For Britain, see Headey (1974).

9. The definition of a *specialist* is, therefore, rather lax, since it includes all those who have had any training in the field corresponding to the department they are heading.

10. Some ministers cannot be specialists since they head departments which are general in character, i.e., ministers of the Interior. They have been excluded from this analysis.

11. See note 6.

12. The literature on this subject has grown, though it is still rather inconclusive. For an examination of the state of the discipline, see in particular Remmer (1978), which covers the literature on this subject in general. See also Grindle (1980).

13. For a strong presentation of the case against British amateurs, see Kellner and Crowther-Hunt (1980).

14. This was compiled from Sivard (1976:24–29; 1980:30–35).

15. See note 2.

References

Austin, D. (1984) *Politics in Africa,* 2d ed. Hanover, N.H.: University Press of New England.

Barkan, J.D., and J.J. Okumu (1979) *Politics and Public Policy in Kenya and Tanzia.* New York: Praeger.

Blondel, J. (1980) *World Leaders.* Beverly Hills: Sage Publications.

——— (1982) *Organization of Governments.* Beverly Hills: Sage Publications.

——— (1985) *Government Ministers in the Contemporary World.* Beverly Hills: Sage Publications.

Braibanti, R.J. (1966) "Elite Cadres in the Bureaucracies of India, Pakistan, Ceylon and Malaya Since Independence." In *A Decade in the Commonwealth, 1955–1964,* edited by W.B. Hamilton et al. Durham, N.C.: Duke University Press.

Grindle, M.S., ed. (1980) *Politics and Policy Implementation in the Third World.* Princeton: Princeton University Press.

Gurr, T.R. (1972) *Why Men Rebel.* Princeton, N.J.: Princeton University Press.

Headey, B. (1974) *British Cabinet Ministers.* London: Allen and Unwin.

Jackman, R.W. (1975) *Politics and Social Inequality.* London: Wiley.

Kellner, P., and L. Crowther-Hunt (1980) *The Civil Servants.* London: MacDonald.

Laing, L.H. (1962–63) "The Diffusion of Political Ideas and Structures in the Commonwealth." *Parliamentary Affairs* 16:46–54.

Leichter, H.M. (1983) "The Patterns and Origins of Policy Diffusion: The Age of the Commonwealth." *Comparative Politics* 15:223–33.

Remmer, K.L. (1978) "Evaluating the Policy Impact of Military Regimes in Latin America." *Latin American Research Review* 13:39–54.

Rose, R., and E. Suleiman, eds. (1980) *Presidents and Prime Ministers*. Washington, D.C.: American Enterprise Institute.

Selassie, B.H. (1974) *The Executive in African Governments*. London: Heinemann.

Sivard, R.L. (1976, 1982) *World Military and Social Expenditures*. Leesburg, VA: World Priorities.

Spengler, J.J. (1966) "The International Diffusion of Economic Ideas Within the Commonwealth." In *A Decade in the Commonwealth, 1955–1964*, edited by W.B. Hamilton et al. Durham, N.C.: Duke University Press.

Wilensky, H. (1975) *The Welfare State and Equality*. Berkeley: University of California Press.